Before and After the Economic Crisis

Before and After the Economic Crisis

What Implications for the 'European Social Model'?

Edited by

Marie-Ange Moreau

Professor, Institut d'Études du Travail de Lyon (IETL), University Lyon 2, France and member of Inter-University Research Centre on Globalization and Work (CRIMT), Montréal, Canada

With assistance from

Iryna Ulasiuk

European University Institute (EUI), Florence, Italy

Edward Elgar

Cheltenham, UK • Northampton, MA, USA

Published by
Edward Elgar Publishing Limited
The Lypiatts
15 Lansdown Road
Cheltenham
Glos GL50 2JA
UK

Edward Elgar Publishing, Inc.
William Pratt House
9 Dewey Court
Northampton
Massachusetts 01060
USA

A catalogue record for this book
is available from the British Library

Library of Congress Control Number: 2011926841

MIX
Paper from
responsible sources
FSC   FSC® C018575
www.fsc.org

ISBN 978 1 84980 992 4

Typeset by Servis Filmsetting Ltd, Stockport, Cheshire
Printed and bound by MPG Books Group, UK

Contents

Section 1   From Equality to Dignity at Work and Social Citizenship

Section 2   Trade Union Action and Workers' Participation

**PART III   THE CHANGING LEGAL FRAMEWORK OF THE
             EUROPEAN SOCIAL MODEL**

Contributors

Nikitas Aliprantis is Professor of Law at the Democritus University of Thrace. He is also a member of the European Committee of Social Rights. He is the author of numerous publications, including *Les droits sociaux dans les instruments européens et internationaux: Défis à l'échelle mondiale* (2009).

Catherine Barnard is Professor of European Union Law and Employment Law and Co-Director of the Centre for European Legal Studies at the University of Cambridge, and Fellow of Trinity College Cambridge. She is the author of *EC Employment Law* (2006) and *The Substantive Law of the EU. The Four Freedoms* (2010).

Mark Bell is Professor of Law at the University of Leicester. He conducts research in the areas of national and European anti-discrimination law and labour law. He is the author of *Racism and Equality in the European Union* (2008) and *Anti-discrimination Law and the European Union* (2002). From 2004 to 2010, he was a member of the European Commission's Network of Legal Experts in the Non-Discrimination Field. He is also a member of the Executive Committee of the Society of Legal Scholars. His current research focuses on EU law and precarious work, such as part-time, fixed-term and agency work.

Simon Deakin is Professor of Law at the University of Cambridge, specialising in labour law, private law, company law, law and economics and EU law. He is a programme director in the Cambridge Centre for Business Research, and an associate Faculty member of the Judge Business School. His books include *Tort Law* (with Basil Markesinis and Angus Johnston), *Labour Law* (with Gillian S. Morris) and *The Law of the Labour Market: Industrialization, Employment, and Legal Evolution* (with Frank Wilkinson). He is a member of the editorial boards of the British Journal of Industrial Relations, the Industrial Law Journal (UK) and the Cambridge Journal of Economics.

Filip Dorssemont is Professor of Labour Law at the Université Catholique de Louvain. He was an academic assistant at Antwerp University (1993–2002) and Lecturer at Antwerp University (2002–2004) and Utrecht University (2002–2008). He was Guest Professor at the Université Robert Schumann de Strasbourg (2001); Cassino University (2002) and Universita Statale di Milano (2008–2010) teaching Community Labour Law.

Anna-Maria Konsta is an Adjunct Professor in European Politics and Law at the American College of Thessaloniki, a Lecturer at the Hellenic National Center of Public Administration and a Thessaloniki Bar Association lawyer. She has been a research fellow at the Boalt Hall School of Law at the University of California at Berkeley, and she has worked both for the European Commission in Brussels and the Council of Europe in Strasbourg. She is the author of the book *Working Time Law in Japan and the European Union: A Comparative Approach in the Context of Legal Culture*, and she has published in the field of European and Comparative Social Law. Her current research project deals with gender and migration in the EU.

Haris Kountouros completed his PhD in the field of European labour law at King's College London (University of London) where he also worked as a Visiting Lecturer in European Law from 1999 to 2004. He has also taught Legal Theory at London Metropolitan University and has given a number of lectures on themes related to European employment law and social policy in other universities as well as conferences. His published work concentrates on EU law, labour law, equality and non-discrimination. He currently works at the European Parliament's Legislative Dialogue Unit in the Directorate for Relations with National Parliaments.

Sylvaine Laulom is Professor of labour law, community social law, comparative law and British labour law at Université Jean Monnet in Saint-Etienne. She is a member of Université de Saint-Etienne's critical law research centre (*Centre de recherches critiques sur le droit*) and has collaborated on a number of European Commission reports, including *Studies on the Implementation of Labour Law Directives in the Enlarged European Union, Transnational Collective Bargaining: Past, Present and Future* and *Impact et perspectives des normes socials européennes.*

Antonio Lo Faro is Professor of Labour Law at the University of Catania and Director of the PhD programme in 'Theory and Praxis of Social Regulation in the EU'. His research activity is mainly devoted to the study of comparative and EU labour law. Within this perspective, specific attention has been given to issues related to occupational health and safety, European collective bargaining, the judicial dialogue between the ECJ and national jurisdictions, immigration law, part-time, transnational mobility of workers and fundamental social rights. His publications include *Funzioni e finzioni della contrattazione collettiva comunitaria. La contrattazione collettiva come risorsa dell'ordinamento giuridico comunitario* (1999) and *Regulating Social Europe. Myths and Reality of European Collective Bargaining in the EC legal system* (2000). He is a Member of the editorial board of *European Journal of Social Law*.

Piera Loi is Professor of Labour Law at the University of Cagliari. She has also taught at the University of Rey Juan Carlos in Madrid and has collaborated with the Universities of Riga and Skopje.

Jonas Malmberg is Professor of Private Law, particularly Labour Law, at the Faculty of Law, Uppsala University. He is founding fellow of Uppsala Center for Labor Studies and member of the Regulating Labour and Markets Programme (ReMarkLab), Stockholm University. He has published many books and articles on Nordic and European labour law, including *Effective Enforcement of EC Labour Law* (2003) and *Stability and Change in Nordic Labour Law* (2002). He is an expert advisor to the Swedish government and the European Commission.

Claire Marzo is Lecturer of Public Law at the University of Paris Est. She previously held a British academy post-doctoral fellowship in the London School of Economics and Political Science. She also participated in several research projects, including a European project sponsored by the European Commission on the management of restructuring. Her research interests include European citizenship, European social law, social rights, European Union law, legal theory, integration of citizens and non-citizens in Europe and minority and migration in Europe.

Marie-Ange Moreau is Professor of Social Law at the EUI and, from 2011, Professor at the Institut d'Études du Travail de Lyon (IETL) at the University Lyon 2. She is also a member of Inter-University Research Centre on Globalization and Work (CRIMT) in Montréal and of the Centre for International and Community Studies and Research at Université d'Aix-Marseille III. Between 2005 and 2008, she was the scientific coordinator of the European research project AgirE. She has written a number of works including *Normes sociales, droit du travail et mondialisation* (2006).

Ulrich Mückenberger is Professor Emeritus of labour law, European law and globalisation at the University of Hamburg; at present, he is a Fellow of the Centre of European Law and Politics at the University of Bremen. He has conducted research during terms as a Visiting Professor at the University of Illinois in Chicago, the University of Antalya in Turkey, the East China Normal University in Shanghai, the EUI and the Universities of Nantes, Bremen and Bari.

Jean Jacques Paris has been a researcher at the EUI in Florence and administrator at the Directorate-General for Employment, Social Affairs and Equal Opportunities of the European Commission. He is currently consultant at Alpha Group (France) working mainly with representatives of the employees, in a European dimension.

Bernard Ryan is Professor in Law at the University of Kent, where he teaches and researches British, EU and international migration law. He recently co-edited the collection *Extraterritorial Immigration Control: Legal Challenges* (2010).

Alain Supiot is Professor at the University of Nantes, Director of the Institute of Advanced Studies of Nantes and Member of the Institut Universitaire de France. He authored numerous books focusing on labour law and social security law (among others, *Critique du droit du travail*) and participated in various collective works (among others *Le travail en perspective, Servir l'intérêt general* and *Beyond Employment. Changes in Work and the Future of Labour Law in Europe.*

Daniel Vaughan-Whitehead has worked with the International Labour Office Team for Central and Eastern Europe based in Budapest and for the European Commission (Directorate General for Employment and Social Affairs). He is also President of the International Association for the Economics of Workers' Participation (IAFEP). He has published various books and articles on transition economies of Central and Eastern European countries, and industrial relations and social dumping in both EU and EU accession countries. His most recent book is *EU Enlargement versus Social Europe? The Uncertain Future of the European Social Model.*

Christophe Vigneau obtained his PhD from the European University Institute in Florence. He is now Senior lecturer at the University of Paris I Panthéon Sorbonne. He teaches labour law, European labour law and comparative labour law.

Lisa Waddington is Professor of Law at the University of Maastricht. In 2000, she received an ASPASIA award from the NWO (Netherlands Organisation for Scientific Research) for the enhancement of the number of women in higher academic positions. She is co-editor of the *European Yearbook of Disability Law* and *Cases, Materials and Text on National, Supranational and International Non-Discrimination Law* (2007). She is the disability coordinator of the European Commission Network of Legal Experts in the Non-Discrimination Field and has published widely on European disability law and European non-discrimination law.

Preface

This book is the follow-up of a conference held on 23 and 24 October 2009 at the European University Institute (EUI) in Florence. The conference aimed to commemorate two of our former colleagues who died in August and October 2008: Brian Bercusson, Professor at King's College (London) and Yota Kravaritou, Professor at the University of Thessaloniki (Greece). Both were professors at the EUI. Both were strong supporters of European social construction and workers' rights in Europe.

They had an intellectual influence throughout their professional life: Brian Bercusson mainly in Britain and Yota Kravaritou in Greece. This explains why in places as different as London, Brussels and Thessaloniki, their colleagues wish to dedicate their conferences or collected volumes to them.

In Florence we wanted to gather those who were students and/or friends, those who were, during the research training, under the influence of their ideas and commitments, mainly at the European University Institute. Our intention here was to honour not only their role in European intellectual thought, but also their role as professors.

This book shows that thanks to the energy propelled by the development of Social Europe, here in Florence, within and around the European University Institute, there has emerged an intellectual thought which now shines bright in the academic world.

We thank all those who participated in the conference and contributed to this volume. Without them the tribute to Brian Bercusson and Yota Kravaritou could not have been paid.

We also thank the President of the EUI, Yves Meny, as well as the Department of Law and the Academy of European Law whose immense support made the publication of this book possible.

We all wish to pay tribute to these two colleagues of ours.

1. Introduction

Marie-Ange Moreau

Discussion about the future of the European Social Model (ESM) needs to be precise with this so-debated notion. If presented as 'European social models', the plural refers to the diversity and the differences of the national social models in Europe and the movement of classification of these models, through limited convergence or common denominators. It has been possible following Espin-Andersen to identify three different models[1] for welfare policies, but the building of 'families' or 'models' of industrial relations systems and labour law systems is highly debatable, especially with 27 member states, because of the original combination in each system between industrial relations, market forces, state intervention and collective bargaining (Hyman, 2009).

The book considers that the ESM is the result of the process created by EU law and EU policies: the reference here to the ESM is not just a political discourse for the future (Jepsen and Serrano, 2006) nor the common denominator of these national models. Then, even the definition giving by Hyman of the four main characteristics of the 'European social model', through industrial relations, market forces, state intervention and collective bargaining is useful to compare the European main tendencies with American or Japanese ones: it is elaborate from a substantial comparative and simplified analysis of the national systems, without a focalization on the process created by the EU Law and the substantial content of EU Law through the Europeanization process.

The European social model is the result of a social and legal construction at the community level. This, as we all know, has been a gradual and fragmented process, marked by institutional advances from Maastricht to Lisbon (Rodière, 2009; Goetshy, 2009). The European social model is based, according to Brian Bercusson, on the 'institutional architecture', which gives social actors an impetus to real action (Bercusson, 2009a).[2] It

---

[1] Nordic, Continental, Anglo-Saxon (Espin-Andersen, 1990) and we now need to add Mediterranean (Meda, 2009).

[2] The concept of a 'European social model' is attributed different meanings

1

is the result of a complex interplay articulated by the treaties, harmonization processes which have led to the introduction of the *acquis communautaire* with respect to social rights, European social dialogue and national interactions, open method of coordination (OMC) and, finally, the current construction of fundamental social rights in the European Union.[3]

Since the beginning of the millennium, the Lisbon Strategy has become a central axis. The successive enlargements of the Union show that a new era is emerging in the European Union, an era in which the unstable equilibrium which had allowed the original normative construction concerning social rights is being challenged. The Lisbon Strategy has opened the road for the 'new governance approach' (Ashiagbor, 2005; Kilpatrick, 2006), increasing the EU learning process and some areas of convergence in the field of employment measures, but without changing the deep diversity of the national models in labour law (Sciarra, 2005), nor the differences of the employment measures and policies in different institutional contexts (Auer and Gazier, 2006; Meda, 2009).

The European Union is being subjected to tensions between the economic interests of member states, compounded by the 'varieties of capitalism' which they represent (Hall and Soskice, 2001; Blackett and Levesque, 2010); added to this are the structural asymmetries of powers between the employer and the employees which have increased considerably due to the international functioning of enterprises (Moreau, 2010).

The European social model, as a result of this complex institutional architecture after the Lisbon Treaty, is therefore subject to new developments in view of strong internal tensions between member states, between social and institutional actors and between various normative methods which characterize it.

Undoubtedly, a new turn was taken when the *Viking* and *Laval* rulings were released in 2007. This has caused a large number of countries in the European Union to seek ways to identify not only the trends that affect the social construction of the Union but also the prerequisites for the preservation in the future of the European social model, a model whose function has traditionally been the protection of workers and, more generally, the most vulnerable persons.

---

perfectly analysed by Jepsen and Serrano (2006). Three aspects of it are commonly retained: the first takes account of the national models of social protection in Europe (in general, reference is made to the models proposed by Espin-Andersen); the second is similar to that adopted here, focused on the *acquis communautaire* and the EU legal order; the third places the European project within a political discourse.

[3]   The Charter of Fundamental Rights was incorporated into the Treaty of Lisbon (see Damjanovic and De Witte 2009).

The research here is based on the belief that the social construction of the European Union structured by the treaties presents a real force which, in the past, enabled the demarcation of the European Union from all other forms of regional integration (Blackett and Levesque, 2010).

This institutional architecture has however been under threat since 2007. Even the most active of its adherents, and/or the most optimistic about the European building, such as Brian Bercusson and Yota Kravaritou, are now strongly concerned or even desperate about the current transformations affecting this architecture.

It is therefore essential to try to identify the underlying trends that have emerged since the early 2000s – before and after the financial and economic crisis. The EU social construction is the result of an evolutionary process marked by the mobilization of institutions and norms by the actors, whether trade unions, workers and citizens, or institutions and judges. In particular, the Commission and the Court of Justice are central actors and their choices since 2007 and during the crisis show the abandonment in social matters of the founding postulates of the Treaty of Rome.

In 2009 when the economic and financial crisis was in full swing until the end of 2010, economic experts were divided between the optimists, often close to governments, who analysed the situation as 'the end of crisis' and the pessimists who stated that if measures were taken to allow the financing of the banking and financial sectors, there is no evidence that this crisis has actually passed. From the social point of view, all the European indicators show a strong deterioration in the terms of employment: not only have unemployment rates remained high but working conditions have dramatically worsened (9.1 per cent unemployment in 2009, Eurostat, 2010).

The situation of crisis proves to be a strong indicator of the capabilities and choices of the Member States of the European Union in legal responses to issues of the deterioration of working and employment conditions and the rise in the social inequalities in the European Union, in general. It highlights the profound ambiguity of the European Union which consists in proposing the construction of a 'social market economy' which embraces both the economic and social objectives of the Treaty.

The authors of this book have sought to analyse the evolution of the European social model within the framework of this new turn: the responses to the economic crisis have declined at the national level, which shows that the emphasis since the beginning of the millennium has been placed on the Lisbon Strategy which foresees an articulation of national policies within the complex procedural framework of articles 154–155 of the TFEU. The decline in the national choices is explained by the diversity of the systems of professional relations in Europe, the fragmentation of the EU instruments and the lack of consensus in terms of social policies in Europe.

Profound political and ideological tendencies which one can see in Europe nowadays lead to the development of fractures which are seriously undermining the EU social objectives. They raise a multitude of issues, both political and legal.

THE NATIONAL LEVEL AS A LEVEL OF REGULATION IN TIMES OF CRISIS: AN OPTION OF THE EUROPEAN SOCIAL MODEL

The crisis has brought to the fore the role of the nation-state. The latter has become an important generator of policies to fight the effects of the economic crisis. The crisis has also evidenced that national policies in the field of employment and working conditions are driven by choices from the national law rather than EU law.

The Return of National Social Policies

In many Member States, the State is directly involved in the 'package of labour market crisis measures', either through national social policies or tripartite pacts (Glassner and Keune, 2010). The nation state regains its position as a central economic actor. It plays an active role in order not to leave the regulation to market forces. Clearly, the financial crisis followed by the multiplication of state policies is proof of the complete failure of the theories based on the ability of social regulation by the market.

Social dialogue and, more broadly, collective bargaining have been mobilized in search of responses to the social effects of the crisis. The framework of collective bargaining remains highly diversified in Europe. The same can be said of the context in which this bargaining has taken place because of the broad variety of anti-crisis public policy measures, particularly in financial, banking and tax sectors.

The first studies show that these responses are very diverse both in their content and orientation and that they are strongly determined by the nature of the industrial relations system of the Member State (Glassner and Keune, 2010). Thus, tripartite pacts have been concluded or negotiated in Austria, Belgium, Netherlands, Italy, Slovenia, Slovakia, Poland, France, Hungary, Ireland, Lithuania, Estonia, Romania and Luxembourg (Glassner and Keune, 2010). This long list of countries indicates both the centrality of social partners in Europe and the choice of governments to rely on social dialogue to facilitate the adoption of measures to respond effectively to the social effects of the crisis. This place of social partners is considered an important indicator of the European social model, even though the conditions of their action vary greatly depending on the national model of industrial relations (Bercusson, 2009a).

Many measures have been short-term measures, and they rely primarily on the broadening of the role of the mechanisms already in place (for example, partial unemployment allowances (*chômage partiel*) in France or extraordinary wages guarantee funds (*cassa integrazione straordinaria*) in Italy). From the first responses to the crisis, it became apparent that Member States which managed to mobilize social institutions were able to limit the social impact of the crisis, at least in the short term (Glassner and Galgoczi, 2009).

Collective agreements as a response to the crisis also take different forms. They include negotiations on restructuring, on wage bargaining, on working time, on flexible working conditions and training. Furthermore, they can be concluded at different levels, including at the company level, the sectoral level and the inter-sectoral level. It appears, however, that here as well, if the specificity of the industrial relations system strongly affects these negotiations both with regard to their content and impact, a strong trend towards decentralization of collective bargaining is confirmed (Glassner and Keune, 2010). This trend is evident even in countries like France and Germany, traditionally very different from countries like Ireland or Britain, and it is combined with structural transformations of decisions of enterprises and their shareholders (Mestre, 2009).

When the coverage rates of collective agreements are too low (Poland, Bulgaria, Great Britain, Hungary), state or unilateral measures by the employer have to be adopted.

Other forms of the adjustment to the crisis appear. The quality of work has been greatly affected by the intensity and increased workloads which become obvious when we take into consideration increased psychosocial risks. Permanent jobs have been replaced by temporary jobs in countries like France, Italy, Bulgaria and the Baltic countries (see Vaughan-Whitehead's chapter). There have been greater wage differences in some countries (France, Bulgaria, UK), while other countries have imposed wage freezes. Some countries, like Poland or Portugal, however, have raised the minimum wage to protect vulnerable workers (see Vaughan-Whitehead's chapter). The adjustments in the internal organization of enterprises, such as work-sharing in Germany, also showed that providing a margin of flexibility may be useful in order to maintain the enterprise. The crisis finally shows the limits of flexicurity. Training programs have often been reduced (especially in Estonia) and groups of workers already experiencing difficulties finding work have been put into a situation of even greater vulnerability whenever the institutional system lacked solid and proven foundations.

It therefore appeared that within this diversity of responses, significant synergies had been used to meet the urgent needs of employers and employees, through different modes of interaction between governments and social partners. Pacts, negotiations and state measures are all various forms of responses to the crisis in the social field deployed within nation-states. We do not talk here, as we did in the early 2000s, about negotiations on deregulation or flexibilization, adaptation to global economic changes, but we talk here about how to survive (Zagelmeyer, 2010).

The conclusion which one can draw from this broad spectrum of responses is two-fold. First, it shows that the state has remained an important actor; and, second, that there exists certain resistance to the crisis nourished by the mobilization of social institutions.

However, these conclusions do not question the plausibility of the analysis concerning the decentralization of the state (Mückenberger, 2010) or the transformation of its function (Chevallier, 2008). They show that the state is capable of remobilization under the pressure from social and economic actors. The institutional response leads to the strengthening of the labour market mechanisms structured by strong social institutions. Social regulation at the national level, on the other hand, even if it does not question the existence of the European social model, and is in line with the principle of subsidiarity, shows the weakness of community responses.

The Reasons for the Absence of Specific EU Social Policies

In 2009 the only tangible response to the economic crisis was changing and softening the conditions of access to the European Globalization Adjustment Fund and integrating the issue of enterprise restructuring in many policy areas (Moreau et al., 2009). But the Commission guidance on best practices for restructuring is more like the deafening silence of the EU social policies in response to the crisis.

The social regulation of the crisis is, thus, purely national. Although it relies on the logic of the principle of subsidiarity and the Union's desire to limit the harmonization process by its narrow competencies in social matters, the lack of European anti-crisis policy stems from several other substantive reasons. It is the result of present-day reliance on liberalism, described by Alain Supiot as ultra-liberalism (Supiot, 2010).

In terms of the Community method, it is consistent with the OMC, which refers the choice of labour market regulation to the sphere of competence of the Member States (De la Rosa, 2007) and shows the inability of the OMC to coordinate anti-crisis measures.

The result of the coordination of the national plans by the Commission in 2010 has not shown visible results at this stage, but it is possible to think that the learning process helped to push Member States into mobilizing their national forces to limit unemployment, and that mimetism has played a role in the choices made by the Member States and/or the social partners in the choice of policies during the crisis. Surprisingly, the new 2020 strategy seems to ignore the impact of the crisis to impose economic objectives.

In January 2011,[4] in the reports published by the Commission, it appears that the reactions of the Member States have been oriented towards minimizing the social consequences, at least in the short term. Despite those policies, the unemployment rate is extremely high – 9.6 per cent – with an important increase of poverty in the EU. Some lessons about the need to avoid temporary contracts and to promote long-term policies for qualification of workers show the huge failure of the European Commission discourse, before the crisis, on the flexibility of the labour market.[5]

It shows the preference of European social partners for national actors who have bargained for a European collective agreement, adopted 25 March 2010, on orientations for an inclusive labour market: this agreement is a general framework for the national social partners, showing clearly that the function of the European social dialogue could only be a source of guidelines, not the creation of an anti-crisis program for a European labour market which does not exist.

These evolutions further demonstrate the preference of European social partners for national actions.

Finally, it also illustrates that the Commission in its social policy plays the role of coordinator of good practices desired by European employers and is not an efficient actor in a period of crisis: the choices made in the field of corporate restructurings, through the elaboration of a 'toolkit' of instruments given to employers and other actors, is a significant example of its role during the crisis.

The absence of specific EU policy is more generally explained by the withdrawal of the European community in the midst of the crisis when even the mighty competition law proved incapable of acting as a real force, leaving state aid regulations unimplemented under the guise of flexibility.

The extraordinary paradox is, as pointed out by Alain Supiot below, that the absolute failure of the regulation by market forces advocated

---

4   Draft joint report on employment, COM (2011)11 final annex 3.
5   On the flexicurity policy of the EU Commission, see Hos (2011).

by the European Commission does not lead the latter to recognize these failures.

Still, it is not so much the return of the nation-state as an actor in the anti-crisis regulation that raises concerns about the future of the European social model. The specificity of the European social model actually lies in its dual dimension, national and European, and the interplay it allows between the Member States, the Commission and the social partners. The anxiety is caused by the 'seismic shifts' which undermine the foundations of the European social model.

THE EUROPEAN SOCIAL MODEL ROCKED BY 'SEISMIC SHIFTS' FROM BELOW

In order to reflect on the future of the European social model, it would seem appropriate to give some thought to the 'seismic shifts' which undermine it.

Undoubtedly, the blow delivered by the *Laval, Viking* and some other judgements is like a systemic shock which traces its origins to the structural evolution of the European Union, the inadequate evaluation of the impact of the enlargements of 2004 and 2007 and, finally, the casting away of the historical foundations of positive integration.

The European Social Model in the Turmoil of Globalization

Generally, the place of the European Union in the framework of the globalized economy has justified its repositioning.[6] Economic theories anchored on Washington consensus have taken root in Europe, particularly in the directions taken by the Barroso Commission (Supiot, 2010). The proliferation of multinational enterprises since the beginning of the millennium, their globe-wide scale of operation and the transformations caused by the development of emerging markets have led to revolutions in the social field: not only the international organization of the means of production caused profound changes in labour rights, but it has also diverted the methods of protection of workers which are largely national (Moreau, 2006).

The asymmetries of power have been greatly enhanced by the interna-

---

[6] See, for example the Commission Work Programme IP/07/1578 'Making Globalisation an Opportunity', available at http://europa.eu/rapid/pressReleases Action.do?reference=IP/07/1578 (accessed December 2010).

tionalization of enterprises. This is despite EU efforts to take into account the internationalization of enterprises in the field of workers' representation (Moreau, 2010; see also Laulom's chapter, this volume). The community social construction was articulated by national social models and European harmonization unable to perceive the intrinsic transformation of labour relations linked to their transnational character.

Despite the adoption in the European Union of the original transnational norms concerning workers' representation in multinational enterprises established in Europe, the implications related to the transnational nature of working relations have clearly found their reflection in legal norms only recently, following the conflicts connected with the adoption of the services directive (2006) and *Laval* and *Viking* judgements (2007–2008).

The argument that the European Union was and could be a social space of transnational regulation without responding to a different logic emanating from national laws (Moreau and Trudeau, 2000; Moreau, 2006; Alberg et al., 2008) is relatively new. It justifies the necessity of transforming the articulation of norms and their structural evolution.

To simply mention the 'deterritorialization' of social norms (De Burca, 2005; see Barnard and Deakin's chapter, this volume) appears insufficient because the underlying model of reference still leaves out national territorial law. Yet, normative transformations require a more considerable change, the acknowledgement of the existence of the original transnational space.

The economic crisis has demonstrated that the financialization of the economy entailed interdependence between national economies and that national divisions were shattered by the transnational overlaps between transnational economic actors and transnational strategies in place.

Paradoxically, the economic crisis has caused the isolation of nation-states although the crisis clearly demonstrates the strength of interdependencies and the need for global and transnational policies. To this day the European Union has not drawn any conclusions in the social field, either theoretical or political.

The Underestimation of the Impact of the EU Enlargements of 2004 and 2007

By 2007 it became clear that the EU wanted to keep some form of regional economic integration which combines the social and economic dimensions. Although from the very beginning one could observe a certain 'constitutional asymmetry' (Scharpf, 2002) between policies promoting economic freedoms and policies promoting social construction, the choice of integration which, in respect for the diversity of national social models, is based on the rights harmonized in favour of workers, was a mark of 'social regionalism' (Blakett and Levesque, 2010).

Moreover, the capacity of social partners to participate in the development of European law under articles 138 and 139 (154–155 TFEU) showed that the Union could justify its choice of the social model by the theory of Reflexive Law (Deakin, 2008). It also proved that the participation of European social partners in tripartite institutions of the Union and in the legislative process was seen as important from the very beginning (Bercusson, 2009a).

In the political context in which the enlargements were decided upon (which was not subject to a democratic process) Member States of the Union greatly minimized the impact of the two recent enlargements on the social dimension. The requirement for new member states to incorporate the *acquis communautaire* and not the institutional framework seemed to provide strong guarantees, supported by past examples of successful social integration of Spain and Portugal.

There have been difficulties in the adoption of directives and a charter of fundamental rights since the times of the accession of Great Britain into the Union. Caused by the confrontation of strong economic interests, these difficulties have been in place since 1990, the year of the first true discussions on the directive on posting of workers in the framework of the provision of services, adopted later in 1996.

The institutional aspect has therefore been understood and has brought about the OMC and an approach based on governance rather than on the rights of workers. This has represented a certain shift the consequences of which we are now beginning to face (Hos, 2011).

We can thus conclude that both the impact of political orientations with regard to the market economy and the deregulation and the actual weakness of the social rights of some new EU Member States have been largely underestimated.

Similarly, worker mobility, the subject of numerous controversies and the object of the adoption of transitional measures restricting the exercise of this freedom for a maximum of seven years, has been poorly evaluated, especially in countries like Great Britain and Ireland. Transport facilities and organizational mobility, the hostile policies of some countries geographically closely situated to the new Member States, coupled with the needs of labour markets based around social competition have all contributed to this phenomenon.

In the same way, so far it has not been easy to evaluate the impact of inappropriate modes of worker participation in the new Member States on the evolution of the European social dialogue (Hos, 2008).

Finally, the enlargements have increased the social differences in Europe and have not led to the adoption of adequate policies of social cohesion which would allow the differences between the regions to be limited, as was the case in Germany with the eastern *Länder* after the fall of the Berlin Wall.

In the context of the policy of normative competition practised by the European Union from the outset, the gap between the standards of living or survival of workers in the EU has serious consequences in terms of increasing inequality. The economic crisis has accentuated these inequalities based on the immediate exclusion of precarious jobs from the labour market. The most vulnerable populations in Europe (who were so even before the crisis: those with the lowest wages, those who are least qualified and engaged in most precarious jobs) signal the existence of a dual labour market, which excludes young and senior people, women, ethnic minorities and migrant workers (Eyraud and Vaughan-Whitehead, 2007). Although EU law has the will to enforce equal treatment and to fight against discrimination, migration law is still not included in discrimination law. What is more, the anti-discrimination standards are limited by an interpretation of the comparability of different situations and possible economic justifications given by the employer.

The enlargements of the EU have therefore laid the ground for a change of attitude to the issue of social Europe. The most recent ruling of the European Court of Justice (ECJ), namely *Commission v. Germany* 15 July 2010,[7] shows that the values that were at the heart of positive integration belong to the past.

The Abandonment of the Original Foundations of Positive European Integration in the Field of Labour Relations

This abandonment is well described by much of the doctrine and in this book by Catherine Barnard and Simon Deakin (Chapter 16). The Spaak Report accepted national differences but required their coordination at the EU level. The compromises reached under the influence of Jacques Delors entailed a manner of articulation limited by EU competencies and a large role was foreseen for the principle of subsidiarity (Schmidt, 2009). The use of EU social construction to limit social protections conferred by the national labour laws was excluded (Moizard, 2000).

Until 2007, it was unimaginable that the EU mechanisms aimed at

---

[7]   *Commission v. Germany*, case C-271/08.

providing more effective protection of workers' rights would be reviewed by the Court in favour of economic freedoms (Valdés Dal-Ré, 2009). Since 2007 the Court has used the principle of proportionality in a restrictive sense which shows that fundamental social rights, even though they are recognized as a general principle of EU law, must be weighed against the judicial assessment (Hos, 2010). The Court which has traditionally been appreciated for its creative function allowing the building of a Praetorian Europe, has chosen to change the already unequal balance between the social and economic rights to accelerate the expansion of the internal market.

Social issues have become issues of the internal market. The social dimension, which in the origins of the Treaty was centred on the protection of workers, is now dissolved in a new societal understanding of the citizen as a consumer (Micklitz, 2009). Trade unions are treated like ordinary organizations, unless they are directly confronted with economic freedoms. The Court rejects the idea that collective agreements could benefit from a regime which excludes them from the public procurement law by negating that solidarity may have an efficient role to play in Europe.[8]

The Court therefore rejects the non-economic values which actually brought about the whole process of positive integration. Work has become a 'commodity'. The dissolution of social issues in the market laws and the internal market laws has led to queries about the need for creating a special chamber on labour rights (Bercusson, 2009a). But it seems that the cause of changes is not a misunderstanding of the labour laws of Member States but rather a denial by the Court of the specificity of work relations in view of their commodification.

The philosophical opposition between the principles of the ILO (Supiot, 2010) and the directions taken by the Court of Justice is obvious. The role of the Court of Justice raises concerns in terms of democratic legitimacy and the Court's own role in the EU legal order.

The judge here is an actor in the social regulation of globalization. It is important, however, to stress that the Court of Justice does

---

[8] In *Gisela Rosenbladt v. Oellerking Gebäudereinigungsges mbH*, C-45/09, 12 October 2010, the Court accepted the recognition of collective agreements as legitimate instruments to decide the orientation of national social policies in favour of privileged groups, subject to the scrutiny of the Court on the discrimination on age. The recognition does not modify the orientation of the Court when there is a conflict between collective agreements and economic freedoms. The case is an illustration of the choice made by member states of the legal instruments they choose for national policies.

not follow in its choices the logic adopted in 2008 by the ECHR or by other constitutional courts around the world (Moreau et al., 2010). The legal field has, thus, become a field in which judicial strategies have increasingly been used to advance liberalism in its current form, including in cases of protections against abuses by multinational enterprises.

And although these judicial forces have not always taken the ultra-liberal form, one cannot but be deeply concerned about the direction the Court of Justice is taking.

THE FUTURE CHALLENGES

This book takes an activist position. In this it resembles Brian Bercusson and Yota Kravaritou whose ideas and actions were marked by high-level activism. This book is pro-active because it tends to highlight not only the major issues to be tackled in the future but it also proposes legal responses which could be an option for the European Union.

All the authors have sought to assess the long-term ramifications of the *Laval* and *Viking* judgements (and others). It becomes clear that the evolution of the Court is not only a timely turnaround. The values of the Union are at stake, to say nothing of European solidarity, which was already fragile (Barnard, 2006).

After the *Commission v. Germany* judgement, which followed the outcry from the world of work and the labour doctrine against the Court's favouring of economic freedoms and its denial of the need for solidarity as a value in Europe, one must be profoundly European or even utopian to expect changes favouring the protection of workers. Nonetheless, in the opinion of the majority of the authors of this book several avenues of hope are emerging.

The first comes from the opportunities which the EU accession to the European Convention on Human Rights presents. Even if there are still technical issues to be finalized, Article 6 para.2 of the Treaty envisages that consistency between the jurisprudence of the two courts shall be assured. The turnaround made by the ECHR in 2008 concerning Article 11 means that the Court will effectively enforce fundamental collective rights, whether the right to strike or the right to collective bargaining (Robin-Olivier, 2009; Moreau, 2006). It also envisages a shift in focus that could enable the Court of Justice to transform the use of the principle of proportionality.

The second is connected with the integration of the Charter in the Treaty of Lisbon. The Advocates-General in the recent cases *Santos*

Palhoha[9] and *Commission v. Germany*[10] based their argumentation on the need to strengthen human rights. The fundamental rights of workers must constitute a minimum protection which justifies the articulation of workers' rights at the European and transnational levels. There is therefore a double challenge: to strengthen human rights is not enough. We must also ensure their impact in the context of labour relations in Member States and at the transnational level.[11]

Finally, the European Union should align itself with the ILO, which represents the real objective of social justice in the Union (Novitz, 2007; Supiot, 2010).

The ideas in this book are directed towards the long-term perspective. Crucial questions for the future of the European construction will be raised here: the human dimension of the European integration in the context of changing economic relations in the times of a crisis, the democratic legitimacy of the social construction and Praetorian construction, the place of workers and trades unions in the EU from the perspective of a multi-level governance and a system of complex industrial relations, which are multi-level too.

The reflection of the above issues in legal terms is also in the focus of the discussion. Attention has been drawn to the means which should be put in place to reduce inequalities, to strengthen fundamental social rights in the field of European and transnational collective action, to provide a proper place to equal treatment and guarantee a future to the European social dialogue, to rethink the governance and the Lisbon strategy in order to enable the emergence of the quality of work against the winds and tides of the search for productivity and expansion in Europe.

This approach, which is intended to be constructive and activist, is based first and foremost on the analysis of the fears that hang over the sustainability of the European social model.

Jonas Malmberg analyses the shock caused by the judgements of the Court on the Swedish system and the tensions between national law and EU law. He focuses on the issue of the articulation of actors at the national and European levels in a multi-level governance system. He questions the

---

[9] *Commission v. Germany*, case C-271/08. In reaction to this 'post-*Laval*' debate, the Commission in January 2011 proposed guidelines to implement the directive on public procurement (2004) and to help the introduction of social clauses.

[10] C-515/08, conclusions of the Advocate-General M. Villalon.

[11] Scharpf (2009) explains from a political perspective that it is impossible to attempt to reconcile the three main systems existing in Europe through liberal market economies, social market economies and the emerging European market economy.

choice made by the Court in favour of integration, notwithstanding the fact that this choice is clearly hostile to one country – Sweden – which was not conducive to the free provision of services. The legislative changes in both Sweden and Denmark show a willingness to accept a reasonable adjustment of national legislation to the EU requirements.

Daniel Vaughan-Whitehead shows that the rising inequality in Europe since the 1990s has been continuous and structural. The causes and symptoms of this inequality are well manifested in wage policies, the inequitable distribution of growth benefits, inequality in average revenues between the Member States, the transformation of the labour market into a dual two-gear market, new worker poverty, and so on. The crisis has increased unemployment and has had a particularly negative impact on a large number of workers in precarious jobs and the most vulnerable workers, especially in Spain, Germany, Hungary and France.

The panorama of the rising inequality in Europe, aggravated by the economic crisis reveals a more than alarming situation: the development of a minimum wage to protect the most vulnerable workers was already in place in 21 out of 27 Member States. This could not be ignored by the European Union. The development of social dialogue is yet another necessary measure when trying to fight against inequality, together with the development of training programs.

Haris Kontouros recalls that the objectives of the Lisbon Strategy, as established in 2000, required compromises to be reached to combine economic development and social objectives, particularly the preservation of the quality of work through the development of 'strong labour standards'. The social partners were to be their guarantors. The failure of the Lisbon Strategy lies essentially in the absence of positive synergies expected in the field of employment and the lack of sufficient coordination with social partners in many countries. More worrying still is the *Europe 2020* program. It incorporates the same techniques, notwithstanding their proved ineffectiveness, and states economic objectives to be achieved, from a purely neoliberal position, without bothering to secure at least some democratic legitimacy. The social dimension, the preservation of the rights of workers, is completely absent. And of course the preservation of the European social model is ignored. If the Union has the ability to overcome the economic crisis, another strategy must be adopted to preserve the quality of employment.

Antonio Lo Faro discusses the 'de-fundamentalisation of collective labour rights in European Social Law', taking up step-by-step the debate stirred by the 'Nordic cases' and questions the solidity of the principle of equal treatment in EU social law. He shows the need for an approach in relative and not absolute terms. He demonstrates the paradox in proclaiming in the European Union the principle of equality and non-discrimination based on nationality while rejecting the principle of equal treatment when it comes to access to the labour market. He also argues that the rights which are recognized as fundamental rights no longer seem to be fundamental at all and regrets that the European social policy is 'left to judges and the markets'.

Finally, Nikitas Aliprantis presents a vivid indictment against the Court of Justice and its excessive expansionism endangering the very foundations of the EU social construction. He proposes that the Constitutional Courts of Member States of the European Union should make efforts to block the dismantling of fundamental social rights by the Court of Justice. He demonstrates the need at the institutional level to control the Court of Justice to maintain consistency between the logic behind fundamental social rights at the national level and the EU legal order.

The second part of the book seeks to assess the place of fundamental rights in the European social model by raising the themes of equality, dignity and citizenship, and finally workers' participation.

Lisa Waddington demonstrates the limits of the European construction in terms of equality and the fight against gender discrimination in the field of career development in Europe. She notes that apart from the general principle, discrimination in career-building is mostly left to national legislation. However, the jurisprudence of the Court since the *Coleman* judgement allows comparisons to be built. Positive actions can also be compatible with Community law.

Anna-Maria Konsta develops the concept of 'plastic citizenship'. The concept based on transsubjectivation proposed by Foucault is used to explain the new requirements posed by gender issues in Europe. The proliferation of 'multiple discrimination', particularly related to working times and the position of migrant workers, calls for a new theoretical approach which would take these vulnerable groups into consideration. The policy of formal equality, the use of soft law and the fragmentation of the jurisprudence of the European Court of Justice limit the equality of rights of certain vulnerable groups. Citizenship must evolve and not be limited to obtaining political rights; it should be oriented towards the search for social rights.

Piera Loi ponders on the principle of reasonableness in the jurisprudence of the Court of Justice and in particular on the difficult issue of discrimination based on age. She shows how the principle is reconciled with the proportionality principle and stresses the huge autonomy left to the judges in the Member States to assess differences in the treatment which result in privileging or discriminating certain categories of people.

The principle of non-discrimination is also analysed by Mark Bell in the context of fixed-term contracts. He shows that behind a broad consensus of acceptance of the principle of equality within the Member States, it is still difficult to apply this principle in non-standard contracts which follow a logic different from that developed in other areas, particularly in the area of gender equality. Mark Bell discusses in detail the jurisprudence of the Court, the difficulties of comparison and analysis of justifications based on 'objective grounds' which may be invoked by the employer. He concludes that the Fixed-Term Work Directive is different from other directives on matters of equality because it entails changes in behaviour in the employment field rather than equality itself.

Bernard Ryan analyses the development of English law with regard to mobility of migrant workers in light of the conflicts which occurred in Great Britain in 2009: the requirement of representation, collective protection, the right to effectively invoke the discrimination law. Bernard Ryan depicts the interplay between the issues of employment law and those governed by migration law.

Claire Marzo examines the evolution of European citizenship and the development of European social citizenship, as proposed by the doctrine. She shows the capacity of the expansion of European citizenship in light of the jurisprudence of the Court which allows the use of legal foundations of citizenship in areas that fall under a broad conception of the social field: education, social security, services of general interest, non-discrimination. Confronted with the Charter of Fundamental Rights, the concept of citizenship reveals a strong ambivalence from the point of view of fundamental rights of third country nationals. As a result, the Court, following the doctrine, requires residency as a condition for granting rights on the ground of citizenship. Another strong ambiguity is revealed in the use of nationality or residence as a criterion for the recognition of rights. This dual approach is explained by both theoretical and historical reasons. But it also shows that a conceptual shift could be possible by bringing together the two concepts that have developed, namely social citizenship and European citizenship.

Sylvaine Laulom reflects on possible synergies in the field of workers' representation. She shows the strength of the framework gradually developed in the field since 1975, with a particular reference to the right to information and workers' consultation and their transnational representations. She also identifies the limits of the European framework which should or could have been strengthened and draws attention to its peculiarities in times of economic crisis. The massive and transnational restructuring, however, necessitates that the European Union should strengthen the protection of workers.

Jean Jacques Paris ponders on the new developments of European social action after the *Laval* and *Viking* cases and proposes two new directions: the first is connected with the international framework agreement and the development of transnational collective bargaining; the second is linked to the possibility for the social partners to bargain after the agreement on stress and harassment, on the socio-psychological risks, to improve the conditions of working in Europe.

Finally, Christophe Vigneau looks closely at the future of European social dialogue. He outlines a broad spectrum of different forms which social dialogue, a key element of the European social model, can take. He then shows that the conditions are lacking the effective development of social dialogue, particularly in times of crisis. The opposition of Business Europe, relayed by the Commission, does not allow negotiation 'in the shadow of the law'. The possibility of collective action at the European level is also missing, together with a clear legitimacy of representatives in the context of transnational negotiations.

Part III explores the capacities of the evolution of the European social model.

Filip Dorssemont shows the need for the European Union to stand out from the current jurisprudence of the Court with regard to the right to take collective action. He analyses in detail the changes that may occur as a result of the accession of the European Union to the European Convention on Human Rights: from despair to hope. The analysis of the jurisprudence of the ECHR allowed the building of a constitutional bridge to a real recognition in Europe of the right to take collective action. It seems necessary that the EU shall not be at odds with the rights envisaged by the ILO.

Catherine Barnard and Simon Deakin assess the state of social Europe after the ravages of the recent judgements of the Court of Justice. They explain in a historical perspective that the compromises respected by the jurisprudence until 2007 were rejected by the Court. The analysis of the judgements in light of the choices made in the USA shows that the choices the ECJ made with respect to decisions concerning labour and social law issues of the Court could have been avoided. The authors analyse the function of the deregulation practised by the Court and its effect on national law. They conclude that evolution can take different directions, including preventing a 'race to the bottom' by social dialogue and, at the transnational level, by the impact of the jurisprudence of the ECtHR and the Treaty of Rome. The authors adhere to the conclusions of the Advocates General who called for the effective implementation of the Charter and therefore of fundamental social rights.

Ulrich Mückenberger shows that the ideas which were originally expressed in the first Manifesto in 1996 and in the second in 2001 (in the drafting of which Brian Bercusson took part) belong to a past in which the values of European construction were respected. This was before the enlargements and 'the remarketisation of the EU and the anti-social change in the ECJ jurisprudence'. He shows the erosion of the founding pact of the European Union and the reasons (accession of former communist countries, neoliberal approach, the Court's shifting to 'a free market fundamentalism' and the need to rethink European issues from a cosmopolitan perspective). He advocates the necessary 'democratization beyond the state', the social character as an essential element of Europe, the need to build a European polity construed from the humane and on the basis of cosmopolitan solidarity. The author also demonstrates the need to rethink the value of collective voices, the democratic foundations of the EU while taking into account the profound changes of the legal orders and the European society.

Alain Supiot agreed to write the conclusion for this book. His magisterial and radical conclusion is worthy of his friendship with Brian Bercusson and Yota Kravaritou and their readiness to engage in a lively intellectual debate.

'Europe's Awakening' is a strong manifesto which goes a long way in exposing the misdeeds of ultra-liberalism, the birth since the recent enlargement of what Alain Supiot aptly calls 'a communist market economy'. First, the author denounces the radical nature of the jurisprudence of the Court, the relative conception of the principle of equality, which in its essence is absolute. He then expresses regrets that through its judgements the Court has lost all the legitimacy which had been acquired over time. It is also in the field of democratic legitimacy that the evolution is unacceptable to the author. He shows the risk of a policy that rejects social democracy and political implications of social injustice. Alain Supiot explores the possible changes: the need to control the Court of Justice by national constitutional courts, as it did in its decision of 30 June in the German Constitutional Court, the impact of the jurisprudence of the ECtHR, the strong position of the ILO in limiting the ideological excesses of the European Union. Finally he calls for the development of institutional counterweights and regrets that the crisis did not present an opportunity to awaken Europe.

This book thus strives to show the doctrinal resistance to a shift to a European Union which will build a Community that is not founded on social justice and social democracy.

REFERENCES

Alberg, K., B. Bercusson, N. Bruun, H. Kountouros, C. Vigneau and L. Zappalà (eds) (2008), *Transnational Labour Law: A Case Study of Temporary Agency Work*, Brussels: Peter Lang.

Ashiagbor, D. (2005), *The European Employment Strategy*, Oxford: Oxford University Press.

Auer, P. and B. Gazier (2006), *L'introuvable sécurité de l'emploi*, Paris: Flammarion.

Barnard, C. (2006), *EC Employment Law*, Oxford: Oxford University Press.

Bercusson, B. (2007), 'The Trade Union Movement and the European Union: Judgment Day', *European Law Journal*, **13** (3), 279–308.

Bercusson, B. (2009a), *European Labour Law*, 2nd edn, Cambridge: Cambridge University Press.

Bercusson, B. (2009b), 'The Institutional Architecture of the European Social Model', in *Labour Law and Social Europe, Selected Writings of Brian Bercusson*, Paris: ETUI.

Blackett, A. and C. Levesque (eds) (2011), *Social Regionalism in the Global Economy*, London: Routledge, pp. 1–17.

Chevallier, J. (2008), *L'Etat post-moderne*, 3rd edn, Paris: LGDJ.

Damjanovic, D. and B. De Witte (2009), 'Welfare Integration through EU Law: The Overall Picture in the Light of the Lisbon Treaty', in U. Neergaard, R. Nielsen and L.M. Roseberry (eds), *Integrating Welfare Functions into EU Law*, Copenhagen: Djof Publishing, pp. 53–96.

Deakin, S. (2008), 'Regulatory Competition after Laval', *Cambridge Yearbook of European Legal Studies*, **10**, 581–609.

De Burca, G. (ed.) (2005), *EU Law and the Welfare State*, Oxford: Oxford University Press.

De la Rosa, S. (2007), *La méthode ouverte de coordination dans le système juridique communautaire*, Brussels: Bruylant.

Espin-Andersen, G. (1990), *The Three Worlds of Welfare Capitalism*, Cambridge, MA: Princeton University Press.

Eyraud, F. and Vaughan-Whitehead, D. (2007), *The Evolving World of Work in the Enlarged EU. Progress and Vulnerability*, Geneva: ILO.

Ghellab, Y. (2009), 'Recovering from the Crisis through the Social Dialogue', Industrial and Employment Relations Department, Brief No.1, Geneva, ILO, available at www.ilo.org/dialogue (accessed December 2010).

Glassner, V. and B. Galgoczi (2009), 'Plant-Level Responses to the Economic Crisis in Europe', Working Paper, Paris, ETUI WP.

Glassner, V. and M. Keune (2010), 'Negotiating the Crisis? Collective Bargaining in Europe during the Economic Downturn', Industrial and Employment Department, Working Paper No.10, Geneva, ILO, available at www.ilo.org/dialogue/WP (accessed December 2010).

Goetshy, J. (2009), 'Construction de l'Europe sociale et droits sociaux', in J. Rideau (ed.), *Les droits fondamentaux de l'union européenne, dans le sillage de la constitution européenne*, Bruxelles: Bruylant, pp. 175–195.

Hall, P.A. and D.W. Soskice (2001), *The Varieties of Capitalism*, Oxford: Oxford University Press.

Hos, N. (2008), 'The Impact of European Law on Regulating Labour Law Dimension of Corporate Restructuring in Central and Eastern Europe', in

M.A. Moreau and M.E. Blas López (eds), *Restructuring in the New EU Member States*, Brussels: PIE, Peter Lang, pp. 103–134.

Hos, N. (2010), 'The Principle of Proportionality in Viking and Laval: An Appropriate Standard of Judicial Review', *European Labour Law Journal*, **2**, 236–253.

Hos, N. (2011), 'Governance and Minimum Harmonisation in the Field of European Labour Law and Social Policy', PhD thesis, European University Institute.

Jepsen, M. and P. Serrano (2006), *Unwrapping the European Social Model*, Bristol: Policy Press.

Kilpatrick, C. (2006), 'New EU Employment Governance and Constitutionalism', in G. De Burca and J. Scott (eds), *Law and governance in the EU and US*, Oxford: Hart Publishing, pp. 56–74.

Mazuyer, E. (2007), 'Les instruments juridiques du dialogue social européen: état des lieux et tentatives de clarification', *Droit social*, pp. 407–442.

Meda, D. (2009), 'Flexicurité: quel équilibre entre flexibilité et sécurité?', *Droit social*, pp. 763–770.

Mestre, B. (2009), *Corporate Governance and Collective Bargaining. A Comparative Analysis in France, UK, Germany, Portugal*, Paris: ETUI.

Micklitz, H. (2009), 'Judicial Activism of the European Court of Justice and the Development of the European Social Model in Anti-Discrimination and Consumer Law', in U. Neergaard, R. Nielsen and L.M. Roseberry (eds), *Integrating Welfare Functions into EU Law*, Copenhagen: Djof Publishing, pp. 25–62.

Moizard, N. (2000), *Droit du travail communautaire et protection sociale renforcée*, Presses Universitaires d'Aix-Marseille.

Moreau, M.A. (2006), *Normes sociales, droit du travail et mondialisation*, Paris: Dalloz.

Moreau, M.A. (2010), 'Les restructurations et les groupes multinationaux', *Droit social*, **11**, 1052–1059.

Moreau, M.A. and G. Trudeau (2000), 'Les normes de droit du travail confrontées à l'évolution de l'économie: de nouveaux enjeux pour l'espace régional', *Journal de droit international*, p. 915.

Moreau, M.A., H. Muirwatt and P. Rodière (2010), *Justice et mondialisation: du rôle du juge aux règlements alternatifs en droit du travail*, Collection Thèmes et commentaires, Dalloz (forthcoming).

Moreau, M.A., P. Pochet and S. Negrelli (2009), *Building Anticipation for Restructuring in Europe*, Brussels: Peter Lang.

Novitz, T. (2007), 'The European Union and International Labour Standards: The Dynamics of Dialogue between the EU and the ILO', in P. Alston (ed.), *Labour Rights as Human Rights*, Oxford: Oxford University Press, pp. 214–241.

Pochet, P. and C. Degryse (2006), *The European Sectoral Social Dialogue*, Brussels: PIE Peter Lang.

Robin-Olivier, S. (2009), 'Normative Interactions and the Development of Labour Law: A European Perspective', *Cambridge Yearbook of European Legal Studies 2008–2009*, **11**, 135–154.

Rodière, P. (2009), *Traité de droit social de l'Union européenne*, Paris: LGDJ.

Scharpf, F. (2002), 'The European Social Model: Coping with the Challenge of Diversity', *Journal of Common Market Studies*, **40**, 645.

Scharpf, F.W. (2009), 'The Double Asymmetry of European Integration, or:

Why the EU cannot be a Social Market Economy', Working Paper 09/12, Max-Planck-Institut für Gesellschaftsforschung.

Schmidt, M. (2009), *Autonomie collective des partenaires sociaux et principe de subsidiarité dans l'ordre juridique communautaire*, Presses Universitaires d'Aix-Marseille.

Sciarra, S. (2005), *The Evolution of Labour Law in Europe (1992–2003)*, General Report, European Commission, Brussels.

Supiot, A. (2010), *L'esprit de Philadelphie. La Justice Sociale face au marché total*, Paris: Seuil.

Valdés Dal-Ré, F. (2009), 'Social Europe: Debates and Blows?', in Edoardo Ales, Teun Jaspers, Pascale Lorber, Corinne Sachs-Durand, Ulrike Wendeling-schroder (eds), *Fundamental Social Rights in Europe: Challenges and Opportunities*, Belgium: Intersentia, pp. xi–xx.

Vaughan-Whitehead, D. (2003), *EU Enlargement versus Social Europe? The Uncertain Future of Social Europe*, Cheltenham, UK and Northampton, MA, USA: Edward Elgar.

Zagelmeyer, S. (2010), 'Company-level Bargaining in Times of Crisis: The Case of Germany', Industrial and Employment Relations Department, Working Paper No. 9, Geneva, ILO, available at www.ilo.org/dialogue (accessed December 2010).

PART I

Threats to the European social model

2. Posting post-*Laval*: Nordic responses

Jonas Malmberg[*]

INTRODUCTION[1]

One of Brian Bercusson's theses was that national labour law and EU labour law should not be regarded as two separate legal systems. Instead he stressed the symbiosis between national labour law systems and EU labour law. He also emphasized a sociological approach to EU labour law: an approach which looks beyond the vertical interaction between Member States and EU institutions. The roles of different actors, processes and outcomes at both European and national level are all of equal importance for understanding how labour law is shaped.[2]

The story of the Posting of Workers Directive,[3] the *Laval* case,[4] the *Rüffert* case,[5] the *Commission vs. Luxembourg*[6] case and the *Viking* case[7] (jointly referred to as the Laval-quartet) and their aftermath lends itself perfectly to such a multi-level governance approach.

The aim of this chapter is to discuss the legal responses in the case law

---

[*] The project is financed by the Swedish Council for Working Life and Social Research and the FORMULA-project, University of Oslo. For a longer version, see J. Malmberg (2010) 'Posting Post Laval – International and National Responses', Working Paper 5, Uppsala Center for Labour Studies, available at http://ucls.nek.uu.se/publications/Working_papers+2010/ (accessed April 2011).

[1] This chapter is partly based on a lecture given together with Professor Niklas Bruun at the Brian Bercusson Memorial Conference, at King's College, London, 30 May 2009. This chapter was finalized in May 2010.

[2] Bercusson (2009).

[3] Directive 96/71/EC concerning the posting of workers in the framework of the provision of services.

[4] C-341/05 *Laval un Partneri* [2007] ECR I-11767.

[5] C-346/06 *Rüffert* [2008] ECR I-1989.

[6] C-319/06 *Commission vs Luxembourg* [2008] ECR I-4323.

[7] C-438/05 *The International Transport Workers' Federation and The Finnish Seamen's Union* [2007] ECR I-10779.

of the Court of Justice of the European Union (ECJ), with particular focus on Denmark and Sweden.

THE SITUATION PRIOR TO THE LAVAL-QUARTET

Before the Posting of Workers Directive

The main question addressed by the Posting of Workers Directive is which employment conditions shall apply to workers temporarily posted from one Member State to another. Even before the adoption of the Directive in 1996, it was clear, according to case law, that the Member State could, if they so decided, extend their national labour laws to posted workers.[8] Extending national labour law to posted workers could be considered a restriction of the free movement of services (Article 56 TFEU, ex 49 EC), which could be justified in accordance with the so-called Gebhard-formula:[9] a restriction on the free movement of services can be accepted only if justified by overriding reasons of public interest and if proportional (that is, the measure is suitable for securing the attainment of the objective pursued and does not go beyond what is necessary in order to attain it).

The Posting of Workers Directive

The main amendment achieved through the Posting of Workers Directive, compared with the previous case law concerning Article 56 TFEU, was that the Directive prescribed that host countries are not merely permitted, but have an obligation to ensure that posted workers have 'a nucleus of mandatory rules for minimum protection' in the host country. This so-called '*hard nucleus*' is defined as rules (a) laid down by statutes or – for the building sector – by collective agreements that have been declared generally applicable and (b) concerning certain specified terms and conditions (health and safety, maximum working hours, minimum wage etc.).

A crucial question concerning the Posting of Workers Directive has been whether the Directive should be interpreted as merely obliging the Member States to protect the posted workers, or does the Directive also limit the ability of a Member State to extend other parts of national labour law to the posted workers? That is, did the Posting of Workers Directive only provide *a floor* of protection that the host states must extend to posted workers? Or did it also establish *a ceiling* of employment conditions

---

[8] See, *inter alia*, C-113/89 *Rush Portuguesa* [1990] ECR I-1417.
[9] See, *inter alia*, C-55/94, *Gebhard* [1995] ECR I-4165.

that host states are allowed to extend to posted workers? Another way of formulating the same question is to ask whether the Posting of Workers Directive is mainly to be understood as a minimum labour law directive (aimed at protecting the host state labour and/or the posted workers) or a free movement of services directive, facilitating cross-border service providers, by limiting the regulatory powers of the host state in relation to posted workers?

Such questions will arise when interpreting the different aspects of the Directive, as illustrated by the following two examples. Article 3(7) of the Directive provides that the obligation to protect the hard nucleus of the host state does not prevent application of terms and conditions of employment that are more favourable to workers. Does this mean that the host state may extend conditions which provide more favourable terms? Or does it only mean that the posted workers may rely on employment conditions in their state of origin if these are more favourable than the terms which apply in the host state? To turn to the second example: the host state may extend to posted workers employment conditions on matters other than the hard nucleus, in the case of public policy provisions (Article 3(10)). How is the concept of public policy provisions to be interpreted? Is it mainly to be defined by the Member State? Should it be considered to have more or less the same meaning as 'overriding reasons of public interest' in the Gebhard-formula (above)? Or should the concept be given a more narrow understanding?

The answers to questions like these are largely dependent upon how the rationale of the Directive is conceived. In this respect the Directive was drafted in a rather ambiguous way, indicating both elements of enhancing the free movement of services and the protection of the posted workers and the protection of the host state labour market. Good legal arguments could be – and have been – put forward for interpreting the Directive both as more of a maximum free movement directive than a minimum labour law directive, as well as the other way around. The question of how the Directive should be conceived is now largely settled through the Laval-quartet, where the ECJ ended up quite close to the 'maximum free movement directive' end of the continuum.

From a perspective of political democracy it is, however, worth pointing out that the institutional debate leading to the Directive clearly indicates that the Directive was thought – at least by many – as being more about establishing a minimum labour law directive, rather than exhaustively coordinating measures that the host state was allowed to adopt in relation to posted workers.

Nevertheless, the Posting of Workers Directive was adopted with reference to EU competence in the field of free movement of services (now

Articles 53 and 62 TFEU). The reason for the choice of the legal base was, at the time, to circumvent the lack of competence for the EU (including the UK) in the social field. By using the competence for the free movement of services the Directive could be adopted through qualified majority voting, instead of demanding unanimous agreement in the Council. The latter alternative was not available since the UK and Portugal were opposing the Directive.

This was, of course, a kind of misuse of the legal base and at the time the Directive was adopted, the choice of legal base was criticized. The argument was that the aim of the Posting of Workers Directive did not include making the free movement of services easier. Rather the Directive was a labour law directive, which would have required unanimity. The question was whether the legality of the Directive would be challenged by the UK in the ECJ.[10]

The Services Directive
The question of the floor or ceiling character of the Posting of Workers Directive re-emerged with the drafting of the Services Directive.[11] According to the Commission's first draft for the Services Directive (the *Bolkestein* proposal) the country of origin principle should have been applied, except for matters covered by the Posting of Workers Directive.[12] The Posting of Workers Directive would then have set the limit for the Member State's competence in relation to posted workers. The proposal was criticized in this respect, *inter alia*, and that part of the proposal was withdrawn in the democratic process leading to the final Directive. The final Service Directive could rather be said to reflect the view that the free movement of services should not affect relations between the social partners, including the right to negotiate and conclude collective agreements, and the right to strike and to take other industrial actions (cf. Art. 1(7)).[13] The European legislator demonstrated in this way that it did not intend the Posting of Workers Directive to be a maximum 'free-movement of service directive' but rather a 'minimum labour law directive'.

---

[10]   For a discussion of these arguments see, Biagi (1996), Biagi (1997) and Davies (1997).
[11]   Directive 2006/123/EC on services in the internal market, O.J. 2006, L 376/36.
[12]   Proposal COM(2004)2 final, Article 17.5.
[13]   See further Barnard (2008).

THE LAVAL-QUARTET

The Laval-quartet has in many respects clarified the interpretation of the Posting of Workers Directive and Articles 49 and 56 TFEU.[14]

First, the Court of Justice interprets the Posting of Workers Directive as an almost exhaustive coordination of the national measures for protecting workers in posting situations. The Court's interpretation thus comes rather close to an understanding of the Posting of Workers Directive as a ceiling: that is, an almost comprehensive description of the competence of the Member State in relation to posted workers.

Through this interpretation the ECJ actually defines the notion of unfair competition. It is not a situation of unacceptable social dumping so long as the hard nucleus of the host state is applied. Other differences in labour standards between the host state and the state of origin are not regarded as unfair competition, according to this interpretation of the Directive. A consequence is that the idea of equal treatment of domestic and foreign-service providers, as regards wages and employment conditions, has been rejected in favour of *a principle of minimum protection*. The aim of establishing such a narrow definition of unfair competition is obviously to promote free movement of services.

The understanding of the notion of unfair competition as a principle of minimum protection is highly controversial. On the one hand, many would argue that different treatment of domestic and posted workers would seriously undermine the possibility of maintaining good working and living conditions in the host states, at least in some sectors and for some categories of workers. Further, it could be argued that considerable differences in conditions between different groups of workers performing similar jobs are a possible cause of social unrest. On the other hand, others would argue that the principle of minimum protection promotes economic integration of the new Member States, by making it possible to utilize the comparative advantage of lower wage costs. It could also be argued that the risk of negative effects on the host state labour markets is exaggerated and the differences in wages will be reduced over time, as a consequence of economic integration.

Second, the ECJ has in several ways clarified the relationship between collective actions and the free movement of services and the right to establishment. According to the ECJ, collective actions initiated by a trade union against a private undertaking in order to induce that undertaking

---

[14]　The literature is enormous. See, *inter alia*, http://www.etui.org/Headline-issues/Viking-Laval-Rueffert-Luxembourg (accessed May 2010).

to enter into a collective agreement are not in principle excluded from Articles 49 and 56 TFEU. Further, collective actions may – at least in cross-border situations like the ones in *Laval* and *Viking* – be considered as a restriction on the freedom of services and the right to establishment. The restrictions may be justified according to the Gebhard-formula. The *Viking* and *Laval* cases concerned various types of collective actions, and the judgements imply that the protection of the right to different kinds of collective actions is not uniform but depends on the nature and aim of the action in question.

The ECJ recognized the right to take collective action, including the right to strike, as a fundamental right which forms an integral part of the general principles of EU law, the observance of which the Court ensures. The Court does not give more substantial guidance about what the fundamental character of the right to collective action means. The Court seems anxious to stress that there are restrictions to the exercise of that right, both at national and EU level. It follows from *Laval* that the free movement of services may impose far-reaching restrictions on the right to collective action, at least if the actions taken by a trade union do not aim directly at regulating the employment conditions of its own members.

NORDIC RESPONSES

Introduction

The interpretation of the Posting of Workers Directive as a maximum free movement directive must have appeared rather surprising for the European legislator, by limiting the Member States' competence in pursuing social aims at national level in an unforeseen manner. The obvious response in such a situation – at least in a national context – would be for the legislator to change the law. If a national parliament at the first instance did not succeed in explaining its intentions for the courts, it would most certainly try to formulate itself more clearly a second time.

In October 2008 the Commission arranged a Forum on Workers' rights and economic freedoms (8 October 2008). At the Forum the Commission and the governments of Germany, France, Denmark, Luxembourg and Sweden confirmed the view that the interpretation of the Posting of Workers Directive made by the ECJ was unforeseen and would cause problems at national level. On the other hand, they seemed reluctant to open the Posting of Workers Directive for revision.

This point of view might be based on what is considered politically possible. It is doubtful whether there is sufficient support amongst the Member States for amending the Posting of Workers Directive in the direction of a minimum labour law directive. Such an amendment would require a qualified majority in the Council. Even if there was, in 1996 with an EU-15, a qualified majority for a 'minimum labour law'-version of the Posting of Workers Directive, this is probably not the case today in the EU-27.

Instead of arguing for a revision of the Posting of Workers Directive, the Commission claimed that it is for the national authorities of the countries concerned, together with the social partners, to assess what needs to be done. However, how this would be achieved was never clearly spelled out. This possibly indicates that the Commission will not, in its capacity as guardian of the Treaty, insist on a strict interpretation of the case law concerning the Posting of Workers Directive, but rather allow the Member States some margin of appreciation when adjusting their different industrial relation regimes to the new case law.

The interpretation of the Posting of Workers Directive as a maximum free movement of services directive will potentially have extensive consequences, especially for Member States such as Denmark and Sweden whose industrial relations regimes are based on the *autonomous collective bargaining model*. In this model, it is on the whole the exclusive responsibility of trade unions to safeguard rather high average levels of wages and flexible employment conditions for all different categories of employees. The unions safeguard the levels of wages by trying to force – ultimately by (threat of) collective action – employers who do not belong to any employers' organization (and thus not as members bound by collective agreement) to conclude 'accessory agreements', i.e. collective agreements in which the employer undertakes to apply the collective agreement covering the branch of activity in question.

In both Denmark and Sweden, immediately after Laval and Viking, it was considered necessary to review the legislation in order to comply with the new case law, while still preserving the autonomous collective bargaining model.

Denmark

In Denmark a tripartite commission was established in spring 2008. The Laval Commission delivered its proposal in June 2008. The proposal was adopted by the Danish Parliament in December and the amendments entered into force on 1 January 2009.

The amendments make it clear that Danish trade unions may use collective actions against foreign service providers in order to conclude collective agreements which regulate pay (but not other employment conditions) for posted workers. The option of resorting to collective action is limited in four ways.

1. The wages should be equal to the wage that Danish employers are obliged to pay for performing similar work.
2. The pay shall be regulated by a collective agreement which is (a) agreed upon by the most representative social partners in Denmark and (b) applied throughout the Danish territory.
3. The foreign service provider shall be informed about the provisions of the collective agreements.
4. The claims in the agreements should be sufficiently clear, containing reference to the salary which must be paid.

Denmark has to some extent actively utilized the possibility of interpreting uncertainties in the *acquis communautaire* in order not to interfere with the Danish labour market model.

First, Denmark has in an innovative manner re-interpreted article 3(8) of the Directive. According to this provision, a Member State which does not have a system for declaring collective agreements universally applicable may refer to 'collective agreements which have been concluded by the most representative employers' and labour organisations at national level and which are applied throughout national territory'. It seems obvious that the drafters of the Directive had a model in mind whereby the Member State, through a decision, identifies a specific collective agreement which shall apply to the posted workers. Instead, the Danish act informs the foreign service provider that he might meet a demand for concluding certain kinds of collective agreement concerning pay.

This interpretation seems to be in line with a view taken by the ECJ that the purpose of the Directive is not to harmonize systems for establishing terms and conditions of employment in the Member States. Rather the Member States are free to choose a system which is not expressly mentioned among those provided for in the Directive (*Laval* para 68).

Second, the Danish interpretation of the concept of minimum pay seems rather extensive. As already mentioned, the right to take collective action may – according to the new Danish law – be exercised only in order to conclude collective agreements regarding pay. The concept of minimum rates of pay may, according to the Directive, be defined by the national law and/ or practice of the host state (Article 3(1)). Denmark has made use of the possibility of defining nationally what constitutes pay. It should, according to *travaux préparatoires* be possible to 'convert' cost that a Danish employer has according to the collective agreement (for instance, regarding holidays and leave) into a fixed sum in cash. It is argued that otherwise there would be no equality between the pay for the posted worker and what a Danish employer has to pay according to the collective agreement.

We could note here some features of the Danish legislative process. The process was extremely fast, the report of the Danish Commission was very short (only 21 pages) and the findings of the Commission were fully supported by both the trade unions and employers' organizations. Further it was not challenged by the government or the parliament.

There seems to be a basic consensus amongst the Danish social parties for preserving their traditional autonomy. As the Danish social partners often state proudly, they are able to 'crack the nuts themselves'. The external pressure put on the Danish industrial relations system by the Laval-quartet seems to have united the social partners as well as the government in finding a practical solution which would not interfere with the functioning of the Danish labour market model.

Sweden

The situation in Sweden was quite different. The *Laval* case was partly financed by the Confederation of Swedish Enterprise, the private employers' organization. This seems to indicate that at least some employers were interested in exploring the possibility of using EU law as a vehicle to change national labour law or the balance between social partners.

In Sweden the Laval-judgement has given rise to two different processes. The first was a legislative process of amending the Swedish law on collective actions in relation to foreign service providers. The second process was the judicial process between Laval and the trade unions in the Labour Court.

Lex Laval
The process of amending the statutes was more controversial in Sweden than in Denmark. Also, in Sweden a Laval Committee was set up. The terms of reference for the Committee were to find a solution where, on the one hand, the Swedish labour market model – and especially the autonomous collective agreements model – was preserved and, on the other hand, EU law was fully respected. The Committee delivered its report in December 2008. The amendments (*Lex Laval*) were finally adopted in March 2010.[15]

The amendments to the Swedish Posted Workers Act make it clear that

---

[15]   See further Bruun and Malmberg (2011).

a trade union may take collective action with the aim of regulating the employment conditions of posted workers, subject to three conditions.

First, the employment conditions which the trade union demands must correspond to the conditions contained in nationwide collective agreement that is generally applied in the relevant sector. This provision is based on the same kind of interpretation of Article 3(8) as was made in Denmark.

Second, the demand may only concern minimum pay or other conditions in the hard nucleus (according to the Directive). In contrast to Denmark the conditions do not only relate to pay but cover also other conditions falling within the scope of the hard nucleus. The Danish idea of 'converting', for instance, holiday costs into pay, was not taken up in Sweden.

Third, collective action is not allowed if the posted workers already enjoy at least the same conditions in the state of origin. This provision is linked to an 'evidential requirement'. A collective action may not be taken if the employer proves that the posted workers have conditions of employment which are essentially at least as favourable as the minimum conditions in the collective agreement.

The Report of the Swedish Laval Committee differs in many ways from its Danish counterpart. The Danish report aimed to find a compromise which the national social partners could accept. In such a report there is no need or interest for a close investigation of possible problems in relation to EU law. The idea seems to be to reach a national compromise which will not be challenged by the social partners, the Danish Courts or the European Commission. If Danish Courts do not make any reference to a preliminary ruling or the Commission does not initiate a proceeding for failure to fulfil an obligation according to the Treaty, then the Danish solution will not be brought before the ECJ. This, of course, if not the question – like in the *Viking* case – will be put before a court in another Member State, less inclined to accept the Danish social and political compromise.

In Sweden it was clear early on that no such consensus would be reached. On the contrary, it was obvious that national interest groups may challenge any solution put forward, arguing that it is not in line with the *acquis communautaire*. Thus, the Swedish report contains a very thorough legal analysis of more than 400 pages. If the Danish report seems anxious not to uncover any hidden obstacles for the compromise, the intention of the Swedish report seems to be to leave no stone unturned in finding a solution that could not be legally questioned.

Although the Danish solution seems bolder in relation to *acquis communautaire*, the Swedish solution is, paradoxically, more controversial at home.

The *Laval* case in the Swedish Labour Court

The Swedish Labour Court delivered its final judgement on 2 December 2009. Since the ECJ in its preliminary ruling had found that the collective actions were unlawful according to EU law, the only question left for the Swedish Labour Court was whether the trade unions were obliged to pay punitive and/or economic damages to Laval due to the unlawful collective actions. Laval claimed damages for economic losses of around 140,000 Euro and punitive damages (that is damages for non-economic losses) of almost the same amount.

In short, the Labour Court considered it to be established that there is a general legal principle within EU law that damages may be awarded between private parties upon violation of a treaty provision. One prerequisite for such horizontal liability is, according to the Labour Court, that the specific EU rule that has been violated has horizontal direct effect. Further, the breach of that rule must be sufficiently serious and there must be a direct causal link between the breach and the loss or damage sustained by the individuals. Since Laval had not proved that it had suffered economic loss to the amount claimed, the economic damages were denied. Laval was awarded punitive damages of around 50,000 Euro. Three out of seven judges were of a dissenting opinion.

CONCLUDING REMARKS

The Posting of Workers Directive and the Laval-quartet mainly deal with the question of what wages and working conditions are to be applied to posted workers. Should the employment relationship of the posted workers be governed by the laws of the host state or the state of origin? Or should the employment conditions partly be regulated by both of the national laws? This chapter has tried to illustrate how the answer to this question is shaped through processes at both international and national levels involving several actors. I will, in the following, consider four different aspects of the multi-level governance.

1. The story of the Posting of Workers Directive and the Laval-quartet highlights the relatively weak position of the political legislative institutions in comparison with the Court of Justice in the processes of European integration. By establishing a principle of minimum protection rather than a principle of equal treatment, the ECJ has considerably limited the Members States' competence of pursuing the social aims at national level. It was far from clear that the Posting of Workers Directive should be interpreted in that way. The Directive

was indeed drafted in a rather ambiguous way and in retrospect the potential for negative integration was clearly underestimated when the Posting of Workers Directive was drafted and adopted.[16] In this way the Laval-quartet could be described as an accident waiting to happen.[17]

When adopting the Posting of Workers Directive the political institutions were not able to clearly address the extent to which EU law should limit the Member States' ability to regulate the wages and employment conditions for posted workers. Nor have these institutions been able to adjust the new balance between EU economic freedoms and national social policy established through the Laval-quartet. This failure of the political institutions is a function of the high consensus requirements of European legislation and the ever-present conflicts of interest among extremely heterogeneous Member States.[18] The adoption of a 'minimum labour law' version of the Posting of Workers Directive covering EU-15 would in 1996 – prior to the Amsterdam Treaty – have required unanimity. This was not possible. Instead the Directive was adopted with a qualified majority and on the legal basis of the free movement of services (now articles 53 and 62 TFEU). Even in order to gather a qualified majority, the basic functions of the Directive had to be blurred and some fundamental ambiguities were inserted in the Directive. In this way the political institutions gave the Court of Justice a rather wide margin of judicial discretion. Nevertheless, taking into account the institutional debate leading to both the Posting of Workers Directive and the Services Directive, the ECJ in the Laval-quartet indicates a lack of loyalty in relation to democratic processes at European level.

2. Further, the Laval-quartet illustrates how integration through the case law of the ECJ is shaped by the actual cases put before the Court and thus underlines the importance of the litigation strategies adopted by different interest groups. In my view at least, the *Laval* judgement could best be understood as a strong reaction from the Court against a Member State and a national industrial relations system which had not shown any sign of reconciling their social policy with the free movement of services. The Swedish Lex Britannia was openly discriminatory against foreign service providers and the autonomous collective

---

[16] Evju (2011).
[17] John Monks, see http://www.etuc.org/IMG/pdf_Brian_Bercusson_memorial_2009 0529.pdf (accessed April 2011).
[18] Scharpf (2010).

bargaining model, as it was applied in practice in the *Laval* dispute, largely lacked transparency in relation to foreign service providers. The national system applied in Sweden, as it must have appeared to the Court, was in this way openly hostile against foreign service providers and went beyond what was necessary even to provide equal treatment between foreign and domestic service providers. Nevertheless, the system was fully supported by the Swedish Government and the trade unions, without any indication of a will to adjust the national industrial relations system in order to facilitate cross-border services while respecting high social protection. This seems to have provoked the ECJ to make use of the judicial discretion left to it by the European political institutions in order to make clear that this attitude by a Member State was not acceptable. In doing this, the ECJ went too far in restricting the Member State's regulatory ability. This, once again, illustrates the maxim that hard cases make bad law.

3. This story also stresses that the actual effect of the doctrines of the ECJ depends on the reception at national level. If the doctrines of the ECJ are not fully accepted at national level, the judgements of the Courts will not be effective. The resistance against the doctrines of the ECJ will typically be silent and not fully visible. As pointed out by Ruth Nielsen, the Member States and the national courts will usually try to create a symbiosis between national and EU law by reinterpreting EU law in the light of national law, or vice versa.[19]

   The amendments of the Danish and Swedish Posting of Workers Acts clearly represent an attempt to reconcile the free movement of services with the national industrial relations systems. The interpretation of Article 3(8) of the Posting of Workers Directive made in the amendments of the Danish and Swedish statutes on posting of workers provides a reasonable adjustment of their national industrial relations system to the Posting of Workers Directive. The autonomous collective agreement model could essentially still apply, although on a level of minimum protection and not on an equal treatment basis. Further, both in Denmark and Sweden, considerable weight was put on improving transparency in relation to foreign-service providers.

4. The story of the Posting of Workers Directive and the Laval-quartet opens up the question of how the ECJ will eventually respond to the reactions to its own case law. As pointed out in the Monti Report (Monti, 2010), the Laval-quartet has implications for the support of the integration project. The judgements have revived the divide

---

[19]   Nielsen (2010) 245.

between advocates of greater market integration and those who feel that the call for economic freedoms and for breaking up regulatory barriers is code for dismantling social rights protected at national level. 'The revival of this divide has the potential to alienate from the Single Market and the EU a segment of public opinion, workers' movements and trade unions, which has over time been a key supporter of economic integration.'[20]

This puts considerable pressure on the ECJ to reconsider its position on the balance between the economic freedoms and national industrial relations. It has been argued that the Lisbon Treaty, which entered into force on 1 December 2009, provides a new legal context for another balance between the internal market and national social regulation.[21] The Lisbon Treaty explicitly states that the Union shall work for social market economy (Article 3(3) TEU). Further, the European Charter of Fundamental Rights has been made legally binding at Treaty level. With this background General Advocate Villón has recently argued that working conditions which constitute overriding requirements of public interest shall, after the entering into force of the Lisbon Treaty, no longer be interpreted restrictively.[22]

It remains to be seen if this line of argument will be accepted by the Court.

REFERENCES

Barnard, C. (2008), 'Employment Rights, Free Movement under the EC Treaty and the Services Directive', in M. Rönnmar (ed.), *EU Industrial Relations v. National Industrial Relations: Comparative and Interdisciplinary Perspectives*, Alphen aan den Rijn: Kluwer Law International.

Barnard, C. (2009), '"British Jobs for British Workers": The Lindsey Oil Refinery Dispute and the Future of Local Labour Clauses in an Integrated EU Market', *Industrial Law Journal*, **38** (3), 245–277.

Bercusson, B. (2009), *European Labour Law*, Cambridge: Cambridge University Press.

Biagi, M. (1996), 'Fortune Smiles on the Italian EU Presidency: Talking Half-Seriously about the Posted Workers and Parental Leave Directives', *The International Journal of Comparative Labour Law and Industrial Relations*, **12**, 97–109.

---

[20]   Monti (2010) 68.

[21]   See for instance Monti (2010).

[22]   C-515/08 *Santos Palhota*, opinion of General Advocate Pedro Cruz Villón. 2010-05-05.

Biagi, M. (1997), 'The "Posted Workers" EU Directive: From Social Dumping to Social Protectionism', in R. Blanpain (ed.), *Labour Law and Industrial Relations in the European Union*, Bulletin of Comparative Labour Relations, **32**, The Hague: Kluwer, pp. 173–180.

Bruun, N. and J. Malmberg (2011), '*Lex Laval*: Collective Actions and Posted Work in Sweden', in Roger Blanpain and Frank Hendrickx (eds), *Labour Law Between Change and Tradition, Liber Amicorum Antoine Jacobs*, Alphen aan den Rijn: Kluwer, pp. 21–33.

Bücker, A. and W. Warneck (eds.) (2010), *Viking – Laval – Rüffert: Consequences and Policy Perspectives*, Brussels: ETUI.

Davies, P. (1997), 'Posted Workers: Single Market or Protection of National Labour Law Systems', *Common Market Law Review*, **34**, 571–602.

Evju, S. (2011), 'Revisiting the Posted Workers Directive: Conflict of Laws and Laws in Contrast', in C. Barnard and O. Odudu (eds), *Cambridge Yearbook of European Legal Studies 2009–2010*, Oxford: Hart Publishing, pp. 151–182.

Monti, M. (2010), *A New Strategy for the Single Market at the Service of Europe's Economy and Society: Report to the President of the European Commission José Manuel Barroso*, available at http://ec.europa.eu/internal_market/strategy/docs/monti_report_final_10_05_2010_en.pdf (accessed May 2010).

Nielsen, R. (2010), 'Scandinavian Legal Realism and EU Law', in Ulla B. Neergaard, Ruth Nielsen and Lynn M. Roseberry (eds), *The Role of Courts in Developing a European Social Model: Theoretical and Methodological Perspectives*, 1st edn, Copenhagen: DJØF.

Scharpf, Fritz W. (2010), *Community and Autonomy Institutions, Policies and Legitimacy in Multilevel Europe*, Frankfurt am Main: Campus-Verl.

3. Inequalities before and after the crisis: what lessons for Social Europe?

Daniel Vaughan-Whitehead

INTRODUCTION

While growing inequalities have been a major policy concern over the past decade (ILO, 2008), the current crisis – the most serious since 1929 – may have exacerbated the problems. Clearly, different categories of workers have different degrees of vulnerability to the consequences of the crisis, both direct – restructuring, lay-offs and falling wages – and indirect – deteriorating working conditions, less access to social dialogue and so on. The issue of inequalities is also relevant for economic recovery. Many economists have emphasized that the crisis may be partly due to the unequal redistribution of growth; this would mean that the issue of inequalities should definitely be addressed in order to allow European and non-European economies to move towards recovery and, even more importantly, sustainable growth.

In this chapter, we address the issue of inequalities before the crisis, before giving the first results of research into inequalities during the crisis. We conclude with some policy recommendations that would make it easier to address work inequalities in the European policy context.

TRENDS IN INEQUALITIES BEFORE THE CRISIS

When we look at the period since the mid-1990s we can see that the European area has generally been characterized by growing inequalities, with at least five major trends particularly catching the eye.

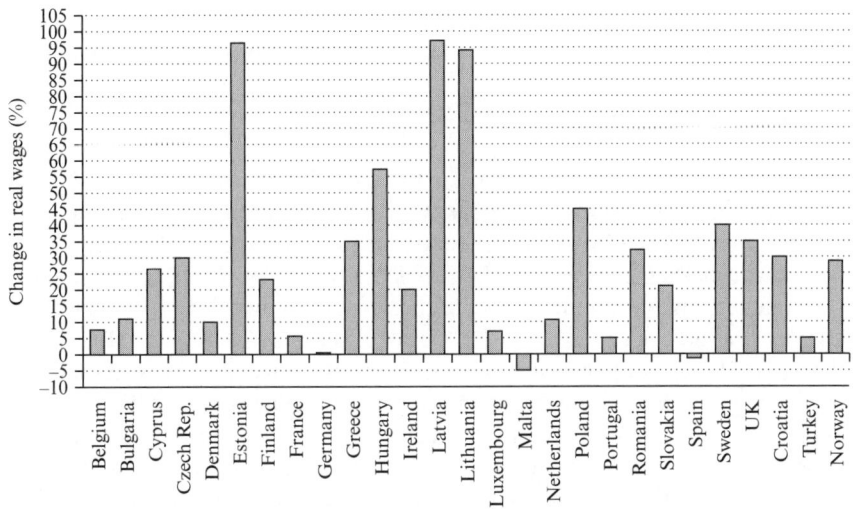

Note: 1996 is taken as index except for Czech Republic (2002), Norway and the UK (1998).

Source: Eurostat; Vaughan-Whitehead (2010).

Figure 3.1   Growth of real wages in European countries, 1996–2006

Wage Moderation Dominating European Countries

The first is to be found on the wage front and the evolution of wage levels over time. Real wages, which measure the evolution of nominal wages, taking into account the development of inflation, allows us to track the evolution of purchasing power over time. Not only have real wages experienced very limited growth, on average (a bit more than 5 per cent over 10 years), but they have also followed different trends between different European countries. As shown in Figure 3.1, real wage growth was highest in the 10 new EU member states from Central and Eastern Europe – much higher than the EU-15 average – which helped them to compensate the sharp deterioration of real wages they had experienced alongside economic output contraction in their transition years in the first half of the 1990s. For the sake of comparison, a similar rapid increase in real wages was observed in Russia and the CIS countries.

At the same time, this means that former EU-15 member countries – which obviously benefit from higher wage levels – have generally known some wage moderation over the same period. This is illustrated by the slow progression or sometimes even decline in countries such as Spain, Austria, Germany and Portugal. Wage moderation has therefore been prevalent.

Unequal Distribution of Economic Growth

The second trend concerns the distribution of growth. The wage share is an indicator that allows us to measure the distribution of growth between labour and capital. Global wage trends around the world have shown that, before the crisis (for the period from 1995 to 2007), a falling wage share was a general phenomenon, reflecting a growth in average wages generally lagging behind the growth in GDP per capita (ILO, 2008). The ILO found that each 1 per cent increase in annual GDP per capita was associated, on average, with a 0.75 per cent increase in average wages. This so-called 'wage elasticity' of 0.75 was interpreted as an indication that increases in productivity had failed to translate fully into higher wages (ILO, 2008).

European countries also share a similar feature: their wage share has generally gone down continuously over the past decade – dominated by high economic growth – as illustrated by the fall in the wage share in GDP in the EU-27 from 59.6 per cent to 57.1 per cent in 1995–2007. The wage share declined in 21 countries and increased in only six (see Figure 3.2). What is more, the declines have been much more substantial than the increases. The fall has been most significant in countries such as Bulgaria (over 15 per cent), Poland, Austria and Slovenia (by more than 10 per cent), but also in Spain, Ireland, Estonia, Hungary and Germany (with more than a 5 per cent decline). The wage share stabilized and sometimes slightly increased in a few countries, such as Romania, Lithuania, Czech Republic, Sweden and Denmark, while it stabilized in the UK.

Such a wage share decline in most countries shows that in European countries generally real wage growth has remained behind productivity growth, which can be explained by the wage moderation process described earlier. It is important to note that those countries that have experienced a progression of their wage share are also those that have benefited from real wage growth – for instance, a few Central and Eastern European countries – something that would confirm that a policy of real wage growth can help to counter the wage share decline.

Growth in Wage and Income Inequalities

Another trend common to most European countries is the increase in wage disparity that we mainly captured by measuring the evolution of the last wage decile over the first wage decile, but also by monitoring the wage gap by sectors, by gender and by different categories of workers.

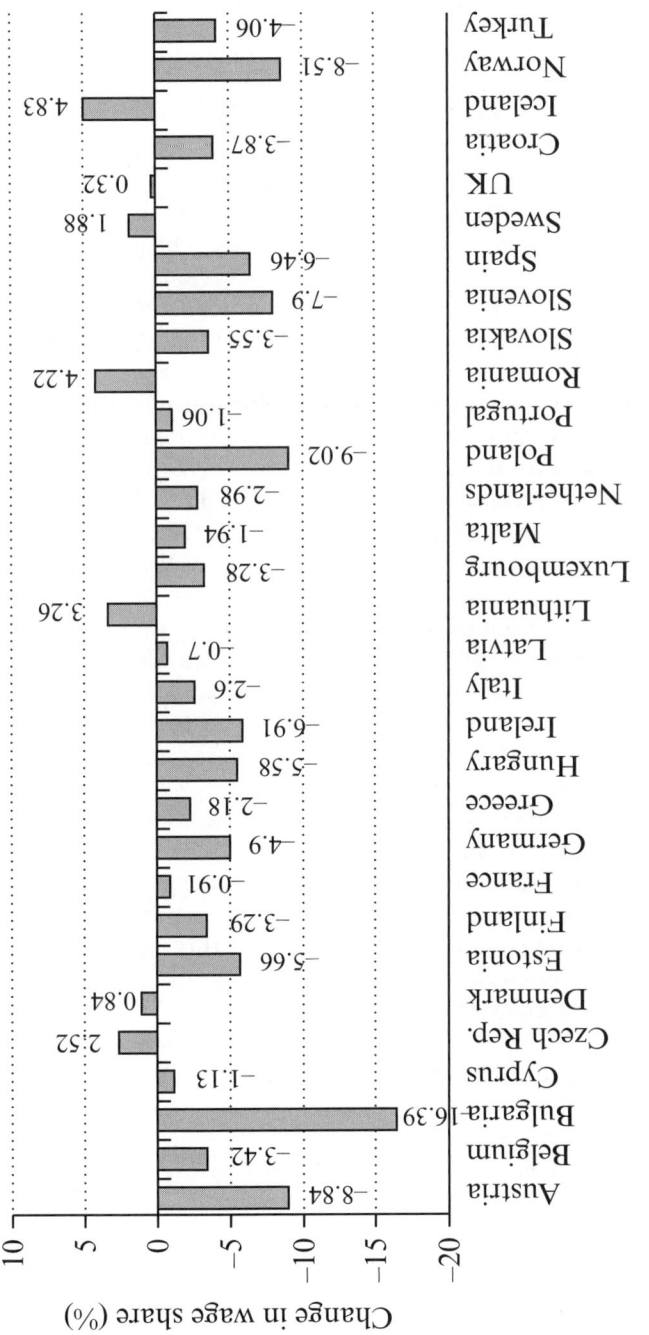

Source: Ameco; Vaughan-Whitehead (2010).

Figure 3.2   Changes in wage share, European countries, 1996–2007

Such growth of wage disparity has been particularly rapid in transition countries which enjoyed relatively low wage differentiation in the Communist regime. The increase of differentiation was particularly striking in Central and Eastern Europe, where all countries have somehow faced increased wage differentiation – particularly high in countries such as Estonia and Hungary. At the same time, the gap between low- and high-wage earners has also increased in several former EU-15 markets in the past 10 years. This can be explained partly by the changing structure of the labour market towards jobs requiring higher qualifications and the presence of skill premia. But this is often not enough and the explanation is also to be found in wage-fixing problems both at the top and the bottom of the wage scale.

As examples, in Austria (Guger and Marterbauer, 2007; Rechnungshof, 2007) but also in Germany the relative gap between the last and first wage deciles has increased from 3.2 in 1996 to 3.7 in 2005, an increase which is particularly striking in eastern Germany – from 2.40 to 3.20 – mainly due to the rising wages of high-wage earners. In western Germany, by contrast, wage inequality is more driven by a fall in wages in the low-wage sector relative to the median.

In most European countries this issue has led to public debates and government intervention, first of all at the top, with a view to returning to more decent executive pay levels – by limiting wages and bonuses distributed to managers – while trying, at the bottom, to limit the growth in the number of low paid workers (notably through the minimum wage). So policy action can make a difference here to reduce wage differentials and improve income distribution, as we shall further explore below.

The increase in the regional income gap has also become a topical issue, especially in large countries, such as Poland. The gender pay gap, a major political goal voiced around Europe remains a concern, and progress remain slow – in some countries, movement on this is actually negative (ILO, 2008). Migrant workers also continue to be discriminated against on European labour markets.

The Increased Duality of European Labour Markets

Changes and reforms in the labour market have also influenced work inequalities. In particular, the growth of atypical forms of contract – such as fixed-term, temporary agency, part-time, on-call and self-employment – has clearly contributed to a polarization of the labour market.

While these new contracts may offer new employment possibilities, they have also been found to put vulnerable groups of workers – women, young people, older workers, migrants and ethnic minorities – who have more recourse to these forms of contract into a disadvantageous position with regard to wages. According to research on the 27 EU member states, while these new types of contract can serve as a stepping stone into the labour market they are often associated with prolonged employment in low-quality and low-paid jobs (Eyraud and Vaughan-Whitehead, 2007).

We should add that the same types of vulnerable workers are often confronted by another source of inequality, namely conditions at their workplace. There is also a trend towards more difficult working conditions, longer working hours, stress at work and atypical forms of contract that particularly affect certain groups of workers, such as women, younger or older workers, and migrant workers.

Low Pay and Working Poor Becoming Established Phenomena

Low pay, which represents the proportion of workers with wages below two-thirds of the median wage, has emerged over the past 15 years in most European countries. Since the second half of the 1990s, low pay has increased in a majority of countries – more than two-thirds of countries for which data are available. The increase was particularly rapid in Germany (8 per cent increase), Luxembourg (6 per cent) and Poland (5 per cent).

As a result, the average proportion of low paid workers has become fairly high in the EU-27 and in several countries since it affects more than 10 per cent of employed persons. The percentage is particularly high in Hungary, Luxembourg, Poland and the UK, where it affects more than 20 per cent of employees (see Figure 3.3). It also applies to more than 20 per cent of full-time employees in Ireland and more than 15 per cent in the Czech Republic. Although to a lesser extent, the phenomenon also affects Scandinavian countries, including Denmark (12 per cent of full-time employees), Finland (8 per cent) and Sweden (6 per cent).

Low wage employment is often concentrated in key sectors such as the retail trade, hotels and restaurants, transport, social services (including household activities) and some areas of manufacturing, such as food processing and textiles.

Low pay is a concern because, even though not all low paid workers are poor, low pay tends to increase the risk of poverty. And while it can represent a first stepping stone towards better paid employment, especially among young workers, it can also turn into a trap from which workers find it difficult to extract themselves due to lack of opportunities for skill or career development. Low pay tends to be concentrated in certain groups of workers, with low levels of education; they also tend to be young, are disproportionately female and are more likely to be members of a disadvantaged ethnic minority, racial or immigrant group. According to the

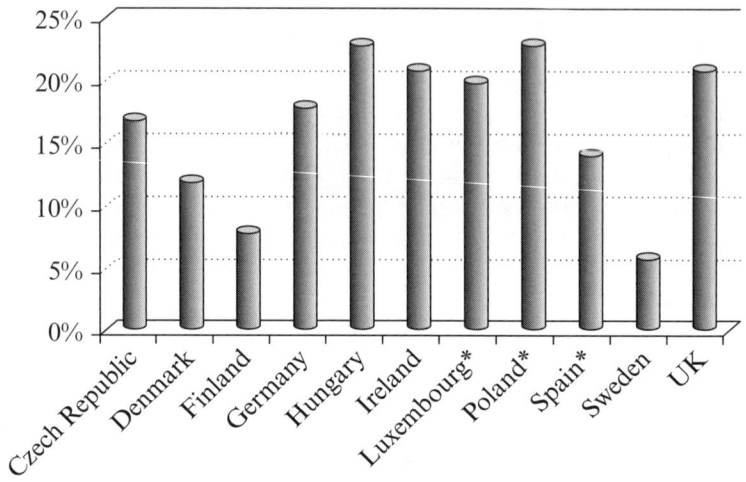

Note: * as a percentage of all employees (generally higher than for full-time employees due to the high proportion of low-paid workers among part-time workers).

Source: ILO, 2010.

Figure 3.3   Low wage employment, EU countries, 2009 (as a percentage of full-time employment)

OECD (2006), in Europe the risk of low pay for the young is more than twice as high as the risk for prime-age workers, with the proportion of young people on low pay ranging from about one in five young workers in Portugal to two-thirds in the Netherlands. Similarly, in most countries, the risk of low wage employment is higher among women than men, as shown by the data in Finland, Belgium and Spain, where women represent more than 65 per cent of low wage employment (ILO, 2010).

It should be noted that low wage work can be problematic not just because of the low level of wages, but also because of the instability of earnings. In EU countries, the possibility of losing one's job is sometimes two or three times higher among low wage workers than higher wage workers (EC, 2005). Not surprisingly, variations in earnings are relatively high among low wage workers. Further, low paid workers are often found in the new forms of atypical contracts earlier described, as shown by the increase in low-paid workers in Germany following the extensive introduction of 'mini-jobs', a sort of low-paid, part-time work arrangement. Permanent and formal jobs are thus associated with lower incidences of low wages, meaning that job insecurity, far from being compensated through higher wages, actually tends to go hand in hand with low pay (ILO, 2010).

Moreover, there is not much evidence showing that low wage jobs would only be a transitory situation. Evidence in European countries shows that 12-month transitions out of low wage and into more highly paid jobs are only experienced by one in three workers. Around half of low wage workers are still in a low wage job the following year and close to one in five moves into a type of labour market status with no pay, such as inactivity or unemployment (EU, 2005; Mason and Salverda, 2009).

DIFFERENCES REFLECTED WITHIN THE CRISIS

Although it is too early to know what the full effects of the crisis on inequalities have been, there are already signs that show that they have been exacerbated. Substantial and detailed evidence on this will be provided in a forthcoming publication (Vaughan-Whitehead, 2011).

As recently indicated by the World Bank the global financial crisis is rapidly becoming an unemployment crisis (World Bank, 2009). And in fact, the first source of inequality unleashed by the crisis was due to the differentiated impact of *employment adjustments* among workers. Employment adjustments to the crisis have differed not only between countries, but also between different categories of workers.

The high percentage of temporary workers in countries such as Germany and Spain, and also Hungary, has led to employment adjustments without these being accompanied by a significant increase in unemployment rates. This also means, however, that temporary workers were the first category to be affected by the crisis, for example in Spain, where they account for 95 per cent of employment adjustments. Short-term work contracts in France have also served as a sort of buffer during the crisis, with 53 per cent of job losses affecting interim agency workers, with not only low-skilled and young workers, but also older workers being severely hit. Self-employed and family workers have also been particularly hard hit in Bulgaria, where the employment loss was also higher among temporary workers (minus 10 per cent) compared to workers on a permanent contract (minus 3 per cent). Employment of those on part-time contracts has also been reduced twice as often as among those on full-time contracts. The duality of labour markets observed before the crisis has thus been directly reflected in employment adjustments within the crisis.

Discriminatory practices have also been on the rise, as shown in Spain, where differentiated employment practices have multiplied on the basic of ethnic origin (reflected in relatively higher growth in unemployment), or in Estonia where job losses have been much higher for non-nationals.

According to the OECD, 'the young, the old and migrants are hit hardest' (OECD, 2009). Younger groups have been severely affected everywhere – often because they are overrepresented among temporary workers – together with those with only basic or no qualifications, as in Spain and the UK – where long-term unemployment has increased significantly among young people (16–17 and 19–24 years of age). In Spain, workers aged 20–29 have absorbed 75 per cent of the employment decrease. In the Netherlands, even young workers (below 25) in full-time jobs with permanent contracts have been hit hard, accounting for almost half of the total decline in employment. Low skilled youth employment fell by more than 25 per cent between 2008 (second quarter) and 2010. Regional differences also seem to have increased, with a greater impact being felt in, for instance, the south than the north of Italy, leading to a sharp fall in living standards and purchasing power in 2008–2009, and a general increase in wage and income inequalities.

Certain sectors have suffered more than others, such as manufacturing and construction, which are dominated by men, and also – in the case of construction – migrant workers. This partly explains why men have so far been hardest hit by the crisis. Italy is an exception, with female – especially young (under 25) – workers so far being most affected by employment adjustments in the crisis.

The crisis has also hurt categories of employees not particularly affected in earlier recessions, such as those in middle-income jobs or in the public sector, or employees from the financial sector. Business failures have also multiplied, leading to a new source of vulnerability and exclusion.

There is also some evidence that the quality of work has significantly declined during the crisis. Intensity at work has often increased, together with the harassment and bullying of regular employees – as witnessed in Spain – while social dialogue and workers' rights became harder to implement. There has also been a reallocation of work from large firms to smaller firms with lower quality jobs, as reported in France in the care sector and in other countries in manufacturing. The rate of undeclared work may also have increased in the current crisis. In most EU countries, quality of work has declined not only for those who remain in work, but also from the perspective of those who have lost their job in the crisis and have had to – or will have to – take another job but of lower quality. The replacement of permanent jobs by temporary jobs (to promote future external flexibility), as currently observed in Bulgaria, France, Italy and the Baltic states, may also have a long-term impact on employment quality.

Adjustments have also been severe on the wage front, with real wage declines almost everywhere, and even significant nominal wage cuts, as in Estonia, Latvia and Lithuania, where 50 per cent of employees have experienced wage reductions. Hungary has experienced massive nominal wage freezes which led to a rapid erosion of real wages in 2009. In general, real wage growth has fallen radically in Central and Eastern Europe, from 6.7 per cent in 2007 to 4.6 per cent in 2008 and –0.2 in 2009 (ILO, 2010). In Germany, real wages fell for three years in a row, including in 2009 when even nominal wages fell for the first time in the history of the Federal Republic (Federal Statistical Office, 2010). In the UK, wage moderation has clearly been one way of coping with the crisis, since 41 per cent of employees in 2009 experienced a wage freeze and 5 per cent even suffered from nominal wage cuts (Grimshaw, 2011).

During the crisis, wage disparity (measured by the highest over the lowest wage decile) has increased in Italy, but also in the Baltic states and other countries, while in Spain the proportion of workers on low incomes has increased – despite massive employment adjustment among the low skilled – together with increasing pressure from employers to renegotiate collective agreements.

The government policy of freezing the minimum wage in Estonia and Lithuania has also contributed to this. Similarly, in the UK, France and also Bulgaria, wage disparity seems to have increased due to the fact that the minimum wage has not been raised during the crisis. This is in contrast to countries such as Poland or Portugal where the minimum wage has been raised to protect the most vulnerable workers (Vaughan-Whitehead, 2010). Non-payment of wages has also been observed, for example in Bulgaria, notably in railways. Violations of labour law – for instance, with regard to the proper payment of working hours and overtime – have been reported in France and other countries.

Alongside wage moderation, enterprises have also adapted through shorter *working hours*. Government intervention seems to have been decisive in Germany, with an average reduction of working time of 3.5 per cent or 50 hours per employee (2008–2009), but also in Sweden and France to promote work sharing and avoid lay-offs in the crisis. In the UK, 20 per cent of interviewed companies also reported shorting working hours because of the crisis. Enterprise data in Hungary also show a reduction of working hours, in both the public and the private sectors. We must report, however, that such avoidance of job losses through working time reduction has affected mainly the core labour force, in other words, permanent employees. In Estonia, working time reduction has occurred mainly for a middle aged, trade unionized labour force.

Trends in social dialogue have also had some impact on inequalities during the crisis. In several countries, sectors covered by collective bargaining seem to have benefited from the negotiation of alternatives to employment cuts. In contrast, where social dialogue was weaker – as in several Central and Eastern European countries – there seems to have been no alternative to immediate employment adjustments, and wage cuts have been immediate and more severe. Labour disputes have increased – for instance, in 2009 their number doubled in Estonia – mainly because of claims for unpaid wages, bonuses and paid holidays, as well as the unlawful termination of employment contracts and abuses with regard to some work contracts. The increasing number of social conflicts are often due to low-paid workers' stronger demands for a more equitable distribution of the costs of the crisis and of the benefits of the recovery, confirming earlier findings that social conflicts tend to grow when inequalities are perceived as too high (ILO, 2008).

The impact of the crisis on other labour issues has also contributed to an increase in inequalities. The reduction in training programmes in the crisis, as witnessed in Estonia and Spain but also other countries, seems to have put unskilled workers in an even more vulnerable position. Short-term effects should also be distinguished from longer-term effects. While women so far may have suffered less from employment adjustments, this may be changing – with, for instance, current job cuts in the public sector and services. Moreover, it does not mean that women may not have suffered more from other types of pressure, for instance on the wage front, or from a deterioration of other working conditions and work and family arrangements that have been radically curtailed by the crisis.

Cuts in training expenditure but also work and family services within the crisis may have weakened even further the potential for employees to shift toward better quality and better paid jobs, an effect that will be visible only much further down the road. It might therefore be expected that, beyond the most obvious increases in inequalities in the crisis, other sources of inequality will become more evident in the years to come. This explains why it will be important to continue monitoring different sources of inequalities.

POLICY LESSONS FOR SOCIAL EUROPE: THE NEED TO LEARN FROM THE CRISIS

What policy conclusions can be drawn from the trends described so far? First, overall, we can conclude that the situation on the social front is alarming. All the figures coming out of a period of relative economic growth have shown a redistribution problem between labour and capital with, in particular, a deterioration of the situation at the lower end of the wage scale, characterized by a growing number of low-paid workers. This is likely to have contributed to generate the economic crisis, due to a lack of wage progression and the growing importance of credit and financial markets to compensate the decline in workers' purchasing power. A group of 30 high-level economists, coordinated by Jean-Paul Fitoussi and Joseph Stiglitz (2010), have concluded that there is a direct link between the long-term decline in the wage share, the increase in wage inequality and the global economic crisis. The crisis probably has its roots in the decline in aggregate demand that preceded the crisis and which was due to unequal income distribution. The increase in inequality in the years before the crisis depressed aggregate demand by transferring money from low-income households – which have a high propensity to spend – to households with higher incomes, which tend to spend less and save more. In particular, people needed to compensate for wage moderation through increased borrowing, so that growth was maintained at the price of increased indebtedness, which ultimately led to the growth and collapse of the financial bubble. A similar argument is made by Onaran (2009) and others, who contend that the decline in the wage share before the crisis underlies the development of the US 'debt-led consumption model' which ultimately proved to be unsustainable.

European statistics are also telling. In 2007, before the economic crisis, 79 million citizens of the European Union were estimated to be 'at risk of poverty', and 32 million were 'materially deprived'.[1] While people in employment are less exposed to the risks of poverty than unemployed persons, 'in-work' poverty certainly affects no fewer than 17.5 million workers.[2]

We have seen that we can expect such decreasing trends to get even worse as the crisis proceeds, as shown by the evidence provided earlier in this chapter, with a further increase in wage disparity and low pay. We also know that wages will need more time to recover after the crisis. It is thus important to try to respond here to basic questions such as: is this desirable at a policy level? Will not a further deterioration in workers' purchasing power slow down the progress of the real economy – which

---

[1]   Eurostat, Statistics in Focus (46/2009).

[2]   The figure of 17.5 million is estimated on the basis of two separate Eurostat reports which document that 8 per cent of the employed population in the EU-27 had an income below the poverty line in 2007 (Eurostat, Statistics in Focus, 46/2009) and that total employment in 2007 was 218,451,000 (Eurostat, Statistics in Focus, 27/2008).

recently has received so much attention in the crisis – by affecting consumption and production and thus economic recovery? Furthermore, is the unequal redistribution of growth sustainable in the long run, or could it not lead to future economic crises?

Finally, what could be done at the EU level not only to strengthen the European Social Model but also to reconsider our European model of economic development?

We would like here to highlight a number of policy considerations and elements in the world of work that we believe deserve particular attention.

First, it is important to better protect the most vulnerable workers. In this regard, one instrument that many governments have been using to avoid low pay is the minimum wage. In fact, a renewed interest may be noted in the statutory minimum wage that exists now in 21 out of 27 EU countries. Over the past 10 years or so, the UK (1999), Ireland (2000) and Austria (2009) have all introduced a national minimum wage. In the UK, this was done in light of the increase in child poverty as well as part of an attempt to implement policies to attract more adults into the labour force by 'making work pay'. Discussions also took place in 2009 on the possible introduction of a statutory minimum wage system in Germany, Sweden and Italy, where minimum wages are traditionally fixed through collective bargaining. This renewed interest in the minimum wage at national level, which the ILO has recently documented (Vaughan-Whitehead, 2010; ILO, 2010), can also be explained by the increasing movements of labour, capital and trade in the enlarged EU, that creates new situations of wage competition, as illustrated by the *Laval* case and other cases brought before the European Court of Justice. These pressures will continue to increase. The statistics indicate a general revisiting of the minimum wage issue, with a general increase in minimum wage levels in real terms, and a rapid increase in the ratio of the minimum wage to the average wage. It is also significant that while several EU countries decided to freeze the minimum wage during the crisis, a number of other EU countries, such as Poland, Portugal and Belgium, decided to use the minimum wage as a protective tool for vulnerable workers within the crisis. This is creating new opportunities to promote common principles on minimum wages at EU level (Schulten, 2008; Vaughan-Whitehead, 2010). The EU as a whole may decide to do more on the minimum wage issue, through for instance a series of common guidelines on the minimum wage in order to attract the attention of EU members to the important role that the minimum wage could play in addressing the low pay and working poor phenomena. At the same time, the minimum wage is not enough to reduce working poverty and should be complemented by other elements of social protection policies to alleviate financial difficulties for the families of low-paid workers.

In this respect, the real policy challenge is to develop a coherent system in which both welfare institutions and labour market measures are articulated such that a minimum level of income is secured for poor households.

Other policy instruments also need to be further promoted to bring about better income distribution.

One obvious policy element to be further developed in this regard is social dialogue. Wages have obviously been found to be influenced by collective bargaining and the presence of trade unions. Global wage trends have shown that the connection between wages and productivity is better in countries where collective bargaining covers more employees (ILO, 2009). In particular, a 1 per cent increase in annual GDP per capita translated into average wage growth of 0.87 per cent in countries with superior collective bargaining coverage, compared to wage growth of only 0.65 per cent in countries with weak coverage. Collective bargaining not only strengthens the link between wages and productivity, but it also helps to reduce inequality. Global findings have also showed that high-coverage countries have significantly less wage inequality than low-coverage countries, both overall and in the lower half of the wage distribution (ILO, 2009). By reducing inequality, collective bargaining can also contribute to reducing the risk of low pay. A review of evidence for 20 OECD countries shows, for example, that there is a strong negative correlation between the incidence of low wage employment and several variables that measure the regulatory strength of wage-setting institutions (Lucifora et al, 2005). This was confirmed by recent ILO findings that estimated that in countries with a union density of less than 15 per cent, the incidence of low pay is on average close to 25 per cent. This low pay incidence is reduced by 3 percentage points for the countries with a medium level of union density (between 15 and 50 per cent) and is almost halved to 12.3 per cent in countries with high coverage (higher than 50 per cent) (ILO, 2010).

Collective bargaining also seems to have played a key role within the crisis, notably by giving rise to some tradeoffs and adjustment mechanisms at enterprise level to avoid massive layoffs.

In several countries, sectors covered by collective bargaining seem to have benefited from the negotiation of alternatives to employment cuts. In Germany, for instance, with the help of state subsidies – which encouraged work sharing arrangements – employers kept their long-term commitments to core workers with the trade unions and works councils which, in return, made concessions in terms of pay and working conditions (Bosch, 2011). In contrast, where social dialogue was weaker – as in several Central and Eastern European countries – there seems to have been no alternative to immediate employment adjustments, and wage cuts have been immediate and more severe. Experience from Hungary shows that, between May 2008 and May 2009, firms covered by collective agreements destroyed fewer jobs than did their otherwise similar counterparts (by 2–4 per cent) (Köllő, 2011). However, because of the small fraction of workers covered by collective bargaining, the typical adjustment in private sector enterprises was to keep hours and nominal wages constant, while reducing employment levels.

Paradoxically, even if social dialogue may have played a useful role in the crisis, the coverage of social dialogue (in terms of the proportion of workers covered by collective agreements or unionized) may have been further reduced within the economic crisis (EC, 2011). This means that social dialogue should be further encouraged at all levels – enterprise, sectoral and national – to allow a better relationship between wages and productivity. The European social dialogue at EU level should also be further strengthened, especially in periods of crisis, precisely to encourage better coordination and interaction of national responses.

Better wage outcomes and, in particular, a better link between wages and productivity will also not be possible without more innovative pay systems. While the pre-crisis period has shown that wages were not following economic performance in periods of growth, wages have also somehow lacked internal flexibility within the crisis (ILO, 2010). At the same time, wages are expected to lag behind economic recovery. More in-built flexibility – provided, for instance, by profit-sharing schemes – could contribute to fewer employment adjustments in periods of economic downturn, while ensuring that the same wages immediately increase in periods of economic improvement. The initial work done by the European Commission and the European Parliament to encourage forms of workers' participation in company results (EC 1991, 1997, 2002, 2006) should thus now be seen in light of the crisis and enjoy more sustained promotion among EU member states.

At the same time, more coordination is needed at EU level to limit wage moderation. Paradoxically, while the crisis has shown the limits of an economic model based on wage moderation, one policy response for 2010–2011 provided by most EU countries on an individual basis seems to be a general reduction of wage costs – with a fall in wages and benefits – notably in the public sector.

More generally, a coordinated answer would be needed on wage issues, although they remain a government prerogative. Nevertheless, is it possible to continue to make progress on Social Europe without touching on wage issues? Will it be possible to keep wages an area of national competence if we want to further strengthen Social Europe and avoid a deterioration of the trends described in this chapter (unequal redistribution of growth, low pay, increased employment and income vulnerability)?

Not only national but also European responses are needed to address the unequal redistribution of growth.

Finally, the crisis has also shown that tools of internal adjustment or flexibility have been successfully implemented in a number of EU countries, such as work sharing in Germany, France and other countries, in contrast to the external flexibility – often in countries with more freedom to hire and fire and dramatic growth in the proportion of atypical forms of contract – which dominated policy reforms in the 1990s and 2000s. The outcomes of the crisis with regard to quality of jobs and working conditions also need to be better documented. Lessons from the crisis would now seem to justify reopening the debate on labour market reforms and their place within the global economic model.

CONCLUSIONS

The crisis has provided us with more knowledge concerning the sustainability of our economic and social models. First, with regard to the reasons for the crisis, a number of economists have concluded that there is a direct link between the long-term decline in the wage share, the increase in wage inequality and the global economic crisis. In fact, the period before the crisis was characterized by alarming trends, such as wage moderation, the continuous fall in the wage share, increasing wage and income disparity and the development of dual labour markets, in parallel with the proliferation of low-paid workers. This has reduced the capacity of the real economy and increased reliance on growth based on debt and the development of the financial sector. This economic model, however, has proved to be unsustainable.

In future, countries may find it in their interest to base their economic growth on stronger household consumption, and on household consumption that is anchored in earned income rather than on increasing debt. Appropriate wage polices should thus be designed to avoid wage deflation and social dumping and more coordination is needed at EU level in this area. Similarly, tax systems made more progressive in a coordinated way could help to reverse the adverse trend in income distribution.

Second, the crisis has led to a number of policy lessons that are relevant for the European Social Model. Inequalities trends are expected to get worse with the crisis, as shown by the first pieces of evidence provided in this chapter. Not only do wage disparity and the number of low paid seem to be increasing, but wages are expected to lag behind economic recovery. We have here presented some possible directions, in terms of wages, social protection and the economic model more generally which we believe should be discussed and progressively considered for our European policy agenda. They range from minimum wages and collective bargaining to in-work benefits and other income support policies. At the same time, skilled workers seem to have better resisted the crisis, in terms of both employment and wages. This calls for the strengthening of European policies on education, training and social inclusion in general, within a general redesign of the welfare system, aimed at redistribution and human capital formation. Labour market reforms should also be revisited in light of the crisis.

The crisis is thus giving us the opportunity to put inequalities at the core of the EU policy agenda. It should lead us finally to address the increase in inequalities in a comprehensive way, through the use of a range of complementary policy instruments at EU and national level, a course of action which is likely to be effective not only in strengthening social cohesion – particularly needed after the economic crisis – but also in ensuring more sustainable economic development in the European Union.

REFERENCES

Bosch, G. (2011), 'Inequalities in the World of Work: The Effect of the Crisis – The Case of Germany', in D. Vaughan-Whitehead (ed.), *Work Inequalities in the Crisis – Evidence from Europe*, Cheltenham, UK and Northampton, MA, USA: Edward Elgar (forthcoming).

EC (European Commission) (1991), *PEPPER I Report* (edited by M. Uvalic) 'Promotion of Employee Participation in Profits and Enterprise Results in the Member States of the European Community', *Social Europe Supplement*, **3** (91), Luxembourg.

EC (European Commission) (1997), PEPPER II Report, 'Promotion of Employee Participation in Profits and Enterprise Results in the Member States of the European Community', *COM (96) 697 Final*, Brussels, 8 January.

EC (European Commission) (2002), Communication on PEPPER schemes, Brussels, EC.

EC (European Commission) (2005), 'Employment in Europe 2005', Brussels, EC.

EC (European Commission) (2006), PEPPER III Report (edited by J. Lowitzsch) 'Promotion of Employee Participation in Profits and Enterprise Results in the New Member and Candidate Countries of the European Union', Inter-University Centre Split/Berlin, Institute for Eastern European Studies, Free University of Berlin.

EC (European Commission) (2011), 'EC Industrial Relations Report 2010', Brussels, EC (forthcoming).

Eyraud, F. and D. Vaughan-Whitehead (2007), *The Evolving World of Work in the Enlarged EU – Progress and Vulnerability*, Geneva: ILO.

Federal Statistical Office of Germany (2010), Press release No. 074/2010-03-03.

Fitoussi, J.-P. and J. Stiglitz (2009), 'The Ways Out of the Crisis and the Building of a More Cohesive World', Observatoire Français des Conjonctures

Economiques, Document de Travail No. 2009-17, Paris: OFCE.

Grimshaw, D. and A. Rafferty (2011), 'Recession and Inequalities: The UK', in D. Vaughan-Whitehead (ed.), *Work Inequalities in the Crisis – Evidence from Europe*, Cheltenham, UK and Northampton, MA, USA: Edward Elgar (forthcoming).

Guger, A. and M. Marterbauer (2007), 'Langfristige Tendenzen der Einkommens – Verteilung in Osterreich – ein Update', WIFo (Austrian Institute of Economic Research) Working Papers 307, Vienna.

ILO (International Labour Office) (2008), World of Work Report 2008, 'Income Inequalities in the Age of Financial Globalization', Geneva: ILO.

ILO (International Labour Office) (2009), Global Wage Report 2008–2009, 'Minimum Wages and Collective Bargaining: Towards Policy Coherence', Geneva: ILO.

ILO (International Labour Office) (2010), Global Wage Report 2010–2011, 'Wage Policies in Times of Crisis and Recovery', December, Geneva: ILO.

Köllő, J. (2011), 'Inequalities and the Crisis in Hungary', in D. Vaughan-Whitehead (ed.), *Work Inequalities in the Crisis – Evidence from Europe*, Cheltenham, UK and Northampton, MA, USA: Edward Elgar (forthcoming).

Lucifora, C., A. McKnight and W. Salverda (2005), 'Low-wage Employment in Europe: A Review of the Evidence', *Socio-Economic Review*, **3** (2), 259–292.

Mason, G. and W. Salverda (2009), 'Low Pay, Living Standards and Employment', in J. Gautié and J. Schmitt (eds), *Low-wage Employment in the United States and Europe*, New York: Russell Sage.

OECD (2006), *Education at a Glance 2009: OECD Indicators*, Paris: OECD.

OECD (2009), 'Tackling the Financial and Economic Crisis', 16 February, OECD Documents, Paris.

Onaran, Ö. (2009), 'From the Crisis of Distribution to the Distribution of the Costs of the Crisis: What Can We Learn from Previous Crises about the Effects of the Financial Crisis on Labour Share?', Political Economy Research Institute Working Paper No. 195, Amherst, MA, University of Massachusetts.

Rechnungshof (2007), Bericht gem. Art 1–8, Bezugebegrenzungsgesetz BGBI. I no. 64/1997.

Schulten, T. (2008), 'Towards a European Minimum Wage Policy? Fair Wages and Social Europe', *European Journal of Industrial Relations*, **14** (4), 421–439.

Vaughan-Whitehead, D. (2010), *The Minimum Wage Revisited in the Enlarged EU*, Cheltenham, UK and Northampton, MA, USA: Edward Elgar.

Vaughan-Whitehead, D. (2011), *Work Inequalities in the Crisis – Evidence from Europe*, Cheltenham, UK and Northampton, MA, USA: Edward Elgar (forthcoming).

World Bank (2009), 'Financial Crisis – Economic Crisis Hitting Poor Hard', in *Topics in Development*, 12 February, World Bank, Washington, DC.

4. 'Quality in work' after the Lisbon Strategy: is there a future?

Haris Kountouros*

The failure of the Lisbon Strategy to achieve the objectives it set a decade ago, coupled with the continuing socio-economic crisis engulfing Europe, raises a serious question as to the future of the European social model. A significant element of this model relates to 'quality in work', a multi-dimensional concept which formed one of the specific objectives of the strategy. What lessons can we draw from the failure of the Lisbon Strategy and what can be the prospects for quality in work after Lisbon? Amidst the crisis, is there any scope for regulatory instruments aiming at better jobs and, if so, on what principles should these be based? Relatedly, does Lisbon have anything still to offer in this respect?

QUALITY IN WORK WITHIN THE LISBON MODEL

In March 2000 the European Council's summit in Lisbon set out political directions for the development of a comprehensive framework of policies and measures involving a range of domestic and supranational actors in a strategy which would aim to make the Union by 2010 the 'most competitive and dynamic knowledge-based economy in the world, capable of sustainable economic growth with more and better jobs and greater social cohesion'.[1] The specific objectives of the three main polices involved – economic, employment and social – were to be promoted on the basis of a triadic model underpinned by 'quality'.[2] The strategy was to be deployed using legislation, the open method of coordination, dialogue between the various stakeholders, the Union funds, and research and analysis.

'Quality in work' formed both a particular objective of the strategy and

---

* The views and opinions expressed in this chapter are strictly personal and do not bind or express the views or positions of the European Parliament.
[1] Lisbon European Council (2000, para. 5).
[2] COM(2000) 379 final, para. 3.1.

also a means to promote its other specific objectives, namely economic growth, competitiveness, the promotion of full employment and greater social cohesion. Within the policy framework the concept was defined indirectly by reference to ten dimensions, encompassing a series of job and labour market characteristics.[3] These ranged from the so-called intrinsic job quality to lifelong learning and career development, health and safety at work, social dialogue and worker involvement, equal opportunities and the balance between flexibility and security. Each of those dimensions included specific policy objectives, while to enable measurement of progress a series of indicators gradually developed.[4] In light of this, a direct definition of the term, in the context of the strategy, may be phrased as follows: '"Quality in work" is the concept which embraces a series of job and labour market related characteristics in an effort to improve those characteristics and, by so doing, contribute to the attainment of the other economic, employment and social objectives of the Lisbon strategy.'

The Lisbon Strategy was certainly the result of political consensus and, regard given to the realities of the European political panorama, could never be said to challenge the economic structure of the Union – a fact that to some represents a crucial inherent weakness. Yet, the key principles which underlay the strategy arguably differentiated it from previous attempts to address socio-economic and employment issues. In so doing they defined a distinctive model which offered a prospect for a clear step forward.

The first key principle regarded the development of its main policies in a manner which could lead to synergies and positive externalities.[5] Declaring its belief in the ability to achieve this, the strategy implicitly rejected *a priori* the notion that the promotion of one particular objective necessarily entails a trade-off with other objectives (though the possibility of such is, quite rightly, never ruled out). The emphasis on positive synergies opens new perspectives on the formation of regulation and acts as a break to exaggerated assumptions about trade-offs when these are not supported by evidence. Discussing the relation between labour standards, employment growth and efficiency, the Nobel laureate Amartya Sen suggests that 'the need for trade-offs [between labour standards and employment or efficiency] is often exaggerated and is typically based on very rudimentary reasoning'.[6] A similar argument is made by Fourage

---

[3]   COM(2001) 313 final.

[4]   However, note that the comprehensiveness of those indicators and their respective values were not devoid of often valid criticism.

[5]   COM(2000) 379 final; COM(2001) 313 final.

[6]   Sen (2000, 121).

who examines the costs stemming from the absence of social policies. He states: 'from a theoretical as well as empirical point of view, [the] trade-off [between efficiency and equity] emanates from a short-sighted understanding of economic mechanisms'.[7] Indeed a considerable body of research shows that lasting competitiveness and stable economic growth can go hand-in-hand with employment gains, better jobs and greater social cohesion.[8] It is not coincidental that Member States with well-developed social policies and standards fare much better in terms of competitiveness and employment participation compared to states with less well developed social policies.[9] In the latest issue of the Global Competitiveness Report, Sweden, Denmark and Finland – all countries with traditionally relatively strong social welfare systems – are the most competitive of all EU Member States and feature in the top six positions of the league of the most competitive nations internationally.[10]

The second defining characteristic of the strategy was the explicit recognition of the positive effect of strong labour standards on growth, competitiveness and employment.[11] This represented a significant departure from the tenets of the economic theory which dominated EU policy and legal reasoning from the Treaty of Rome onwards and which considered that labour and social standards flow from economic development but do not generally contribute to it.[12] In contrast, the Lisbon Strategy proceeded expressly on the premise that 'the European social model, with its developed systems of social protection, must underpin the transformation to the knowledge economy'.[13] Hence, the modernisation and improvement of the European social model, a task which implies the defence of rights at work and commitment to raising labour standards,[14] formed – at least in rhetoric – a basic prerequisite for the successful implementation of the strategy.[15] Social policies and high labour standards were stated to provide both 'an input and a framework' to good economic performance and job creation.[16] As emphasised by the Nice European Council, 'quality in

---

[7]   Fourage (2003, 3).
[8]   See, for instance, the analyses carried out by the yearly 'Employment in Europe' and Joint Employment Reports, published by the Commission.
[9]   Ficher et al. (2010, 12).
[10]   World Economic Forum (2009).
[11]   COM(2000) 379 final; COM(2001) 313 final.
[12]   Hepple (1987, 77).
[13]   Lisbon European Council (2000) para. 31.
[14]   Nice European Council (2000), Annex I, para. 26; COM(2001) 313 final, p. 3.
[15]   Lisbon European Council (2000) paras 5 and 31.
[16]   COM(2001) 313 final, p. 5.

work, quality of industrial relations and quality of social policy as a whole are essential factors if the European Union is to achieve the goals it has set itself regarding competitiveness and full employment'.[17] At the same time it was acknowledged that the social and economic cost of ineffective labour standards and poor social policies is high.[18]

The recognition of the value of labour standards is particularly welcome as it enables a virtuous path towards economic development. Labour standards 'both permit and require firms [and governments] to pursue a high-wage, high-productivity strategy, based on continuous improvements in labour quality'.[19] Empirical research confirms this argument showing that better jobs are translated into more productive jobs which are inherently more flexible, have greater degrees of retention and preservation of know-how and present fewer incidents of industrial conflicts, of absence from sickness or disruptions to the productive process.[20] The opposite is also true: 'those employed in jobs of relatively low quality, which do not offer training and career development opportunities or job security, are at much higher risk of becoming unemployed or withdrawing from the labour force.'[21] The current economic crisis proves this in ample terms. What is more, before the crisis in some countries outflows of disaffected workers reached up to a quarter of those in low quality jobs diminishing the prospects for full employment.[22]

The third key aspect of the Lisbon Strategy concerns its call for partnership and cooperation at all levels in order to enhance its governance and improve its implementation. In the employment field this aspect relates primarily to the relationship between management and labour and their representatives, as well as between these two sides and government through the various forms of social dialogue that can be developed. The value of partnership and cooperation, not least as an effective means of promoting adaptability and change, is well demonstrated. Just to take a couple of examples from a voluminous body of literature on the issue, the Gyllenhammer report on industrial change concludes that 'the quality of

---

[17]   Nice European Council (2000), Annex I, para. 26.
[18]   SEC(2005) 385, p. 7; Fourage (2003).
[19]   Deakin (1996, 86). See also Deakin and Wilkinson (1994, 307–309). See further Sengenberger (1990) who makes a similar point, noting that the role of labour standards, particularly within the context of global restructuring, is to 'ensure that competition is not primarily based on squeezing labour but rather on promoting the productive capacity of the workforce, thereby improving chances for competing through better products, processes and market opportunities', at p. 8.
[20]   SEC(2005) 385 pp. 7–8.
[21]   European Commission (2002, 79).
[22]   European Commission (2001, 11).

social relationships and of dialogue within companies and transparency in social practices, human resource policies and negotiations, are prerequisites for successfully adjusting to change'.[23] The same findings are reached by Ozaki who reports on the findings of an ILO study on the introduction of flexibility and partnership in the workplace, where it is stated that 'the introduction of flexibility can be smoothly implemented only if workers are associated with the process and their views are duly taken into account in selecting the forms of flexibility to be introduced and determining the ways in which they should be introduced'.[24]

Social dialogue concerns the implementation/governance of the strategy and also forms one of the specific dimensions of 'quality in work'. It also provides a negotiating forum and a means by which any trade-offs which might arise in the process of developing standards may be resolved. In this regard Sen suggests that instances where trade-offs are inevitable can best be tackled by taking 'an inclusive approach, which balances competing concerns, than by simply giving full priority to just one group over another'.[25] The same point is made by Kravaritou in her book *Για την Κοινωνική Ευρώπη και το Δίκαιό της* [On Social Europe and its Law], where she provides a most important critique of the existing legal norms on the organisation of the working time. She argues that when tackling disputes which may arise from the flexibilisation of working time, solutions should be sought within the discursive and communicative routes which suppose that the participating parties are ready to acknowledge the position and demands of the opposing sides in a rational and comprehensive manner, taking into account the interests of third parties – something which is rare in the logic of the employer side, but also concerns the attitude of the trade union side.[26] This thesis fits perfectly with the strategy's approach as this originally developed, relying as it did on a balanced promotion of the Lisbon goal as a whole within conditions of improved governance and cooperation.

A SERIES OF FAILURES

The defining principles of the Lisbon model arguably made a strong case for a reconfiguration of the EU and domestic frameworks relating to the design, application and interpretation of regulatory instruments. In the

---

[23] High Level Group on Economic and Social Implications of Industrial Change (1998, 11).
[24] Ozaki (1999, 148).
[25] Sen (2000, 121).
[26] Kravaritou (2002, 93).

employment field in particular the Lisbon Strategy invited a new cognitive approach to the employment relationship and to associated concepts, such as partnership and cooperation, as well as to the formation of standards. More than that, its key principles ruled out practices founded on managerial ideology and liberal economic orthodoxy. A reconfiguration in line with the strategy's principles was necessary both as a matter of adhering to them and in order to flesh out its main objectives and accomplish the strategic goal. A decade later however it is painfully obvious that this reconfiguration has not taken place and that the fundamental principles and requirements of the strategy have not been respected. This has had the double effect of stalling progress and leaving the Union unprepared to deal with the worsening economic environment and the deepening of the crisis. A crisis which, incidentally, can no longer be adequately referred to solely as an economic and financial one. It is reflective of the weak position of the European economy and labour market that within just a few months all gains made during a period of almost 20 years in the economy and in employment were completely wiped out. GDP fell by more than 4 per cent, industrial production dropped back to the levels of the 1990s and 23 million people are now unemployed, that is one in ten workers is currently without a job.[27] Depressingly, 83 million people, representing 16 per cent of the total EU population, live in poverty.

To begin with, policies and measures have not developed in line with the objective to build positive synergies. Instead, measures in the field of economic policy, in particular those in relation to the internal market, continue to be drafted without adequate regard for their consequences on social standards and employment. The Bolkenstein Directive reveals this in ample terms and there are certainly more examples.[28] At the same time, little or nothing was done to tackle issues such as tax evasion and tax havens, stock-market speculation or the lack of fiscal coordination and transparency in the markets. The mistaken belief in the self-corrective mechanism of the market has left havoc in the economy and the victims are as always the least well-off. The current crisis is not, as the Commission propagates, an externally born phenomenon. Rather, it is partly the result of policies pursued by the Member States and by the Union itself.

Furthermore, regulatory measures have not been geared sufficiently towards an improvement of existing standards. In some cases, for instance,

---

[27]   COM(2010) 2020, p. 5.
[28]   COM(2004) 2 final. After being substantially amended by the European Parliament the proposal was adopted as Directive 2006/123/EC on services in the internal market (OJ [2006] L 376/36). See Bercusson and Bruun (2008).

the proposed amendments to the Working Time Directive, a deterioration of existing standards is observed since health and safety standards are sacrificed in the name of flexibility.[29] Moreover, in the European Employment Strategy and more generally the Union's employment policy the heavy emphasis on the flexibilisation of contractual arrangements and self-employment has led to an exponential rise of precarious forms of work and the exclusion of millions of people from the protective scope of labour law. In a similar manner, regarding part-time jobs as a panacea has proved wrong since part-time employment often leads to poverty traps, exclusion from labour and social security legislation, can impede career progress and can in practice lead to more rather than fewer hours since workers, mainly women, may be forced to work on a series of short-time jobs to make ends meet.[30]

As for partnership and cooperation, in the employment field in particular this has remained an unfulfilled objective. In many Member States social partners were not sufficiently or at all involved in the adoption and implementation of national action plans for employment.[31] In terms of legislation, none of the 27 Member States made use of the opportunity created by the EU Information and Consultation Directive to improve their domestic legislation on worker representation, especially by means of strengthening representation in small and medium-sized companies (which, as is well known, is the flagship of the Union's policy on entrepreneurship).[32] More generally, the intensification of competition has added more pressures to the structures of employment relations with many examples of unwillingness to engage in constructive dialogue. At European level, despite the welcome increase of the number of sectoral dialogues, the input of intersectoral social partners can at best be judged as modest. The existing regulatory framework is not conducive to fostering greater involvement since the European social partners continue to be formally excluded from the formation of the main instrument of employment policy at EU level, namely the European Employment Strategy.

Regrettably, the Court of Justice also appears to fail to understand the principles upon which the regulatory instruments of the Union must be interpreted. A series of judgements first in the area of posting of workers and more recently spreading to other areas of economic activity have destabilised collective systems of bargaining lessening the scope for

---

[29] COM(2005) 246 final.
[30] See EFILWC (2003, 92); Fagan (2003, 48); European Parliament, A5-0026/2004, point 21.
[31] COM(2001) 438 final, p. 10.
[32] ETUI (2009, 66).

balanced outcomes and compromises, and have imposed a distinction between social rights and economic freedoms subjugating the former to the latter.[33] Bercusson's famous phrase 'bargaining under the shadow of law'[34] appears to allow for a second, more sinister interpretation where the law turns against what traditionally – in the field of labour law – has been its main purpose: to acknowledge the inherent inequality in the labour relationship and therewith seek to protect the weaker party from exploitation.[35] The Court's recent jurisprudence is more akin to the legal environment of the 19th and early 20th centuries and risks leading to social dumping.

In short, the current state of affairs depicts a systemic failure on behalf of Member States and Union institutions to reconfigure national and European laws, policies and practices with the fundamental tenets of the model upon which the Lisbon Strategy was based and the objectives it has sought to promote. In fairness, it should be clarified that notable differences exist between Member States and that some positive examples can be identified. In general, Member States which invested more in training, education and R&D, which offered conditions fostering social dialogue and worker involvement and which did not neglect the need for security when seeking to adapt their labour markets have fared much better. These countries include Sweden, Denmark and Finland. These states have also been more able to withstand the impact of the crisis. Where, on the other hand, the emphasis has been solely or mainly on growth and competitiveness, results were uneven – that is, growth was not followed by social cohesion or improvement of quality in work – and temporary, since any gains made over the last decade were wiped out once the economic situation worsened. Greece and Latvia are two examples of the latter set of countries.[36]

'EUROPE 2020' – A WRONG RESPONSE

What makes the evolution of the Lisbon Strategy all the more disappointing is the repeated failures of the Union organs to reflect on the

---

[33] Case C-438/05, *Viking* [2007] ECR I-10779; Case C-341/05, *Laval* [2007] ECR I-11767; Case C-346/06, *Rüffert* [2008] ECR I-1989; Case C-319/06, *Commission v Luxembourg* [2008] ECR I-4323; Case C-271/08, *Commission v Germany*, judgment 15 July 2010, nyr. See, *inter alia*, Davies (2008); Barnard (2009); Kilpatrick (2009).

[34] Bercusson (1992; 1994).

[35] Kahn-Freund (1972, 18).

[36] See Atkins (2010); MacCarthy (2010); see also Seferiades (2003).

causes of the lack of progress and to refocus their efforts on the basis of the Lisbon model. Instead, in the light of a series of disappointing results, Commission and Council embarked on repeated reviews of the strategy and its instruments including the European Employment Strategy, 'simplifying', 'clarifying', 'streamlining' policies, measures, objectives and targets. These reviews diluted the strategy's substance and reoriented it away from the triptych 'employment-economy-social policy'.[37] The latest instalment in this mistaken route is the recently adopted post-Lisbon, 'Europe 2020' strategy which focuses exclusively on growth and employment creation, neglecting completely both the qualitative aspects of work and the aim of social inclusion.[38]

The 'New European Strategy for Jobs and Growth' is composed of the following five headline targets:[39]

1. a rise of the employment rate to 75 per cent of the working population aged 20–64 years old;
2. a rise in the level of combined public and private investment in research and development to 3 per cent of GDP;
3. reducing greenhouse gas emissions by 20 per cent compared to 1990 levels, increasing the share of renewables and energy efficiency;
4. improving education levels, aiming at a reduction of school drop-out rates and raising to 40 per cent the proportion of 30–34-year-olds having completed tertiary education; and
5. promoting social inclusion, aiming to lift at least 20 million people out of the risk of poverty and exclusion.

There is no space here for a thorough analysis of the new strategy, but a number of points may be highlighted. In particular we need to highlight three key flaws. The first one concerns its conceptual basis. Drafted before the review of the Lisbon Strategy was completed, the new strategy lacks in reflection, forecloses argumentation and presupposes the solutions. All this is done on the basis of a logic moulded upon the neoliberal economic orthodoxy which dominated policy reasoning pre-Lisbon, though certainly in hindsight this orthodoxy seems to have never been abandoned in practice in breach of the Lisbon model's fundamental requirements. Yet the symbolism and the practical repercussions of the formalisation of this are both clear and disconcerting. It is evident of the reaction to

---

[37] See COM(2005) 24; COM(2008) 412 final.
[38] European Council (2010).
[39] *Ibid.*, Annex I.

the flawed starting premises of the new strategy that the vast majority of the responses to the public consultation organised by the Commission were deeply critical of it.[40] Amongst the critics has been the Chair of the European Parliament's Employment Committee, Pervenche Berès, who has remarked that the plans for the new strategy 'ignore the weaknesses of the Lisbon Strategy and will not build a sustainable Europe' and has criticised the Commission for its 'complete lack of understanding of the causes that have led to the current crisis: i.e. social inequalities, growing divergences within the EU and global imbalances'.[41] In a Resolution passed on 20 May 2010, Parliament 'regrets that this strategy has been proposed before the completion of the review of the current Lisbon strategy'.[42]

A second flaw of the strategy relates to its lack of sufficient involvement of the social partners and of the European Parliament, a fact which diminishes its democratic legitimacy. More specifically, the new strategy continues to exclude the European social partners from the European Employment Strategy and only cursorily involves social partners at national level. Similarly, Parliament is regarded by both the strategy and the integrated employment guidelines as a body to be merely informed or consulted.

Finally, the substance of the strategy and its policy prescriptions are themselves flawed. There is no real prospect of better governance, including economic governance, or of promoting greater regional cohesion and income convergence. This is compounded by a total absence of any tangible proposals in the fields pertaining to quality in work. For instance, neither the new integrated economic and employment guidelines nor the Commission's Communication on the new strategy[43] tackle issues such as the need to address in-work poverty, to foster real worker involvement and democratisation of the workplace, to ensure universal social insurance and the safety of pensions as well as to protect workers from old and new risks to their health and safety, to offer protection from unfair dismissal and to offer an adequate standard of living for those who are unemployed or unable to work. The focus is now exclusively on raising the employment rate, presumably at any cost. But this completely ignores the fact that the scope for reinforced job creation 'depends crucially on both translating quality improvements into practice and strengthening the links between

---

[40]   http://ec.europa.eu/dgs/secretariat_general/eu2020/contrib_orga_en.htm (accessed 7 May 2010).
[41]   http://www.epha.org/a/3758 (accessed 7 May 2010).
[42]   European Parliament, A-7/019/2010, point 16.
[43]   COM(2010) 2020.

the quantitative and qualitative aspects of employment creation'.[44] It is scandalous that in the conclusions of the European Council's summit in June 2010 (that is, the document which formally adopted the new strategy) there is not a single mention of the terms (and consequently the subjects of) 'quality in work', labour standards or European social model. In short, the new strategy fails to tackle the weaknesses of its predecessor and presents a visible regression in matters relating to quality in work. It remains an instrument which is superimposed, fragmented and short-sighted, lacking in vision and solutions.

AN ALTERNATIVE WAY FORWARD

The European Union today is very different from the Union that set the Lisbon Strategy a decade ago. The socio-economic context is obviously a more negative one. The expansion of the Union to 27 Member States has also been accompanied by greater regional and social disparities. Achieving consensus in the Council of Ministers is certainly more difficult today, while one cannot ignore the current balance of political powers across Member States and in the European Parliament. In light of this, it is tempting to assume, as the new 'EU-2020' strategy seems to do, that expectations have to be reduced; that we should be content with a basic level of EU standards in some key aspects and focus on an exit strategy from the crisis. But this is a temptation that we should firmly resist. No strategy can succeed if a two – or three – tier Europe exists and no real prospect for lasting solutions can be built without an improvement of labour and social standards.

The Union has the capacity to overcome the crisis and to create the conditions for sustainable economic growth and rising standards for all its peoples. The existence of an economic bloc in which almost 500 million people live, work and trade goods and services beckons a huge potential for economic and social prosperity. Likewise, the collective power of (the enlarged) Union's workforce constitutes potentially a major force to be reckoned with in the struggle for better working and living conditions. Yet this is a time for serious reflection. The current situation demonstrates in no uncertain terms the failure of liberal economic ideology and its policy prescriptions. This should compel an approach to regulation which in practice sets qualitative improvements to employment at the centre of a path to lasting growth and competitiveness. Yet, if the Lisbon Strategy

---

[44]   European Commission (2002, 106–107).

presented, at least in theoretical terms and despite its flaws, a case for such an approach, the 'EU-2020' agenda does not even achieve that.

Aware of the difficulties, it remains necessary to persist in demanding a better quality of work. By way of a non-exhaustive list the following guidelines can be highlighted. First, there must be a reorientation of policy towards stable, permanent forms of employment, as well as a general reduction of working hours and greater autonomy in working time organisation. Additionally, there must be a strengthening of legislation protecting workers from unfair dismissal with EU-wide rules to that effect.

It is also necessary to work towards the establishment of a minimum guaranteed level of income across the Union. This does not have to mean a uniform minimum wage; there are other ways to achieve this.[45] Furthermore, respect for the labour norms in the country of work must be ensured and the principle of non-regression should be made a standard clause in all EU laws in the fields of employment and social policy.

Training should be made compulsory at least in larger enterprises, while all workers should be offered opportunities for training through participation in lifelong learning programmes. Moreover, employee involvement must be promoted in practice. Companies which do not inform and consult workers' representatives in good time should be excluded from public tendering procedures, or government and Union grants. Importantly, the fundamental collective rights of workers, must be protected and social dialogue should be promoted in the workplace and the formation of national and EU policy and legislation.

Continuing to ignore the need for such an approach risks engulfing the European economy in a state of perpetual crisis, driving people further away from the idea of Europe. Action towards this direction offers the best prospect for a strategy able to take on effectively the challenge for a society which is based on a modern competitive economy, full employment with an adaptable and well-educated workforce, solidarity and respect for people's needs and aspirations.

REFERENCES

Atkins, R. (2010), 'Europe Hopes Bright Spell Will Last', *Financial Times*, 31 August.
Barnard, C. (2009), 'The UK and Posted Workers: The Effect of Commission v. Luxembourg on the Territorial Application of British Labour Law', *Industrial Law Journal*, **38**, 122.

---

[45] Kountouros (2006); Ryan (1997).

Bercusson, B. (1992), 'Maastricht: A Fundamental Change in European Labour Law', *Industrial Relations Journal*, **23** (3), 177–190.

Bercusson, B. (1994), 'The Dynamic of European Labour Law after Maastricht', *Industrial Law Journal*, **23** (1), 1–31.

Bercusson, B. and N. Bruun (2008), 'Free Movement of Services, Transnational Temporary Agency Work and the *Acquis Communautaire*', in K. Ahlberg, B. Bercusson, N. Bruun, H. Kountouros, C. Vigneau and L. Zappalà (eds), *Transnational Labour Regulation. A Case Study of Temporary Agency Work*, Brussels: Peter Lang, pp. 263–318.

Davies, P. (2008), 'Case Note on Rüffert', *Industrial Law Journal*, **37**, 384.

Deakin, S. (1996), 'Labour Law as Market Regulation: The Economic Foundations of European Social Policy', in P. Davies, A. Lyon-Caen, S. Sciarra and S. Simitis (eds), *European Community Labour Law: Principles and Perspectives. Liber Amicorum Lord Wedderburn of Charlton*, Oxford: Clarendon Press, pp. 63–93.

Deakin, S. and F. Wilkinson (1994), 'Rights vs Efficiency? The Economic Case for Transnational Labour Standards', *Industrial Law Journal*, **23** (4), 289–310.

EC (European Commission) (2001), 'Employment in Europe 2001. Recent Trends and Prospects', Luxembourg: OOPEC.

EC (European Commission) (2002), 'Employment in Europe 2002. Recent Trends and Prospects', Luxembourg: OOPEC.

ETUI (European Trade Union Institute) (2009), *Benchmarking Working Europe 2009*, Brussels: ETUI.

European Council (2010), Presidency Conclusions of the Meeting in Brussels, 17 June.

European Foundation for the Improvement of Living and Working Conditions (2003), *A New Organisation of Time over Working Life*, Luxembourg: EFILWC, OOPEC.

European Parliament (2004), 'Resolution on the Organisation of Working Time', (Amendment of Directive 93/104/EC), PE 324.356/DEF, A5-0026/2004).

European Parliament (2010), 'Resolution on the Contribution of the Cohesion policy to the Achievement of Lisbon and the EU 2020 objectives', A7-0129/2010.

Fagan, C. (2003), 'Working Time Preferences and Work-life Balance in the EU: Some Policy Considerations for Enhancing the Quality of Life', A Study for the European Foundation of Living and Working Conditions, Dublin: EFILWC.

Ficher, S., S. Gran, B. Hacker, A.P. Jakobi, S. Petzold, T. Pusch and P. Steinberg (2010), *'Europe 2020' – Proposals for the Post-Lisbon Strategy*, Madrid: Friedrich Ebert Stiftung.

Fourage, D. (2003), 'Costs of Non-Social Policy: Towards an Economic Framework of Quality Social Policies – and the Costs of Not Having Them', Brussels: Report for DG Employment and Social Affairs of the European Commission.

Hepple, B. (1987), 'The Crisis in EEC Labour Law', *Industrial Law Journal*, **16** (1), 77–87.

High Level Group on Economic and Social Implications of Industrial Change (1998), *Managing Change. Final Report*, Brussels: European Commission.

Kahn-Freund, O. (1972), *Labour and the Law*, London: Stevens and Sons.

Kilpatrick, C. (2009), 'The ECJ and Labour Law: A 2008 Retrospective', *Industrial Law Journal*, **38**, 180.

Kountouros, H. (2006), *Quality in Work in a Globalised Economic Environment*, Doctoral thesis deposited in the Library of the University of London.

Kravaritou, Y. (2002), *Για την κοινωνική Ευρώπη και το δίκαιο της* (Εκδόσεις Σάκκουλα, Αθήνα-Θεσσαλονίκη).

MacCarthy, C. (2010), 'Sweden Raises Growth Forecast', *Financial Times*, 5 July.

Ozaki, M. (ed.) (1999), *Negotiating Flexibility. The Role of the Social Partners and the State*, Geneva: ILO.

Ryan, B. (1997), 'Pay, Trade Union Rights and European Community Law', *International Journal of Comparative Labour Law and Industrial Relations,* **13** (4), 305–325.

SEC (2005), 'The Costs of Non-Lisbon. A Survey of Literature on the Economic Impact of Lisbon-Type Reforms', *European Economy*, Brussels: Report for DG for Economic and Financial Affairs.

Seferiades, S. (2003), 'The European Employment Strategy Against a Greek Benchmark: A Critique', *European Journal of Industrial Relations*, **9** (2), 189–203.

Sen, A. (2000), 'Work and Rights', *International Labour Review*, **139** (2), 119–128.

Sengenberger, W. (1990), *The Role of Labour Standards in Industrial Restructuring: Participation, Protection and Promotion*, DP/19/1990 (rev.91), Geneva: ILO.

World Economic Forum (2009), 'Global Competitiveness Report', Geneva.

5. Transnationalism and labour law: the 'British jobs' protests of 2009

Bernard Ryan

In his writing, Brian Bercusson often questioned the disciplinary foundations of labour law. This was evident for example in the introduction to the 1987 textbook on British labour law which he co-authored with Roger Benedictus:

> Currently, British labour law starts from the assumption that the legal concepts and institutional forms which govern the organisation of work and workers are the subject-matter of labour law. The alternative starting-point . . . proposed here is that the subject-matter of labour law is work and workers . . .[1]

A similar outlook lay at the heart of his subsequent focus on European Union labour law. The preface to the first edition to *European Labour Law*, published in 1996, argued that labour law could no longer be conceptualised solely in national terms:

> The aim of this book is to build on the vision of European labour law passed on by comparativists. Their perspective of different national labour law systems focused on comparison, mutual influences, transplantation, and so on. But national, not a transnational, European labour law was the centre of their attention. The argument of the book is that European labour law now has come into its own, as a complex distillation of national labour laws into something original and distinct – and genuinely European in character.[2]

This chapter aims to draw upon the insights that labour law analysis may fruitfully start from labour market developments, and that national labour laws are influenced by transnational forces. It will do so by an examination of the two main labour law questions at issue in a series of protests in Britain in 2009 concerning the employment of foreign workers: the extension of collective agreements to employers not party to

---

[1]   Benedictus and Bercusson (1987, 1–2).
[2]   Bercusson (1996, vii).

them, and discrimination on grounds of nationality in hiring decisions. The chapter will show how the presence of workers from other member states, and the response of British resident workers to it, raised difficult questions for both British and EU law. Its underlying argument is that the events of 2009 are an illustration of the tension between the transnational process of migrant employment and nationally-oriented labour law regimes.

THE PROTESTS OF 2009

British industrial relations saw a new development in 2009: protests against the employment of workers from other EU member states on engineering construction projects. That question first came to national attention with an unofficial labour dispute at the Lindsey oil refinery in Lincolnshire in January 2009, in protest at the posting of Italian and Portuguese workers by an Italian sub-contractor.[3] The Lindsey dispute led to a series of sympathetic unofficial stoppages in the power industry in subsequent days.[4] What gave significance to the initial dispute was that some of the participants called for 'British jobs for British workers'.[5] The initial Lindsey dispute was itself settled by a promise by the main contractor to make 102 new posts available, with the expectation that these would primarily be made available to locally resident, British workers.[6]

Other controversies over the non-hiring of local or British workers soon followed. In February 2009, there were protests at two construction projects run by the French company, Alstom, over the non-hiring of local workers by two Spanish contractors at Staythorpe power station in Nottinghamshire, and by two Polish contractors at the Isle of Grain power station in Kent.[7] In the case of the Isle of Grain dispute, it would also later be alleged that the Polish contractors were paying their workers less than

---

[3] 'Strikers angry at foreign workers', *The Times*, 29 January 2009.

[4] 'Dawn of New Age of Unrest: Strikes at 19 Sites over "British Jobs for British Workers"', *The Times*, 31 January 2009.

[5] The phrase 'British jobs for British workers' is generally seen as a far-right slogan in Britain. Something close to it had also been used by the then prime minister Gordon Brown in a speech to the Trades Union Congress on 10 September 2007, when he set out the goal of 'full employment . . . with a British job on offer for every British worker': 'Union Blues', *The Times*, 11 September 2007.

[6] See the summary, based on interviews and media reports, in Barnard (2009).

[7] 'Up to 1000 Expected at Fresh Protests over Foreign Workers', *The Guardian*, 11 February 2009.

collectively agreed rates.[8] While these protests appear not to have altered those contractors' policies, it was significant that Alstom felt obliged to issue a statement to the effect that two-thirds of the total hours on these projects were to be worked by British nationals.[9]

Two further sets of disputes then occurred in South Wales. In May 2009, unofficial industrial action took place at a natural gas terminal in Milford Haven, in response to the hiring of 40 Polish workers, which was said to be in breach of a prior agreement to hire local workers.[10] That industrial action led to the withdrawal of the Polish workers, and their planned replacement by 'UK workers'.[11] Then, in August–September 2009 there were protests at the Uskmouth power station over the limited use of local labour.[12] On that occasion, the response of the main contractors was a policy of active recruitment in the local area.[13]

THE EXTENSION OF COLLECTIVE AGREEMENTS

A central element of the 2009 protests was the belief that workers posted from other EU member states were in receipt of wages and conditions inferior to those provided for in the relevant collective agreements. From the outset, the fact that the Lindsey dispute concerned posted workers led some to suggest that it revealed the weakness of EU rules on that question.[14] More specifically, the 2009 protests were treated as evidence of the flaws in three widely-criticised decisions of the Court of Justice – *Laval*, *Rüffert* and *Commission* v. *Luxembourg* – which had been delivered between December 2007 and June 2008. [15] These judgments had limited

---

[8] 'Strikes Could be on the Cards in Engineering Construction Sector', *Labour Research*, April 2009.

[9] 'Alston Defends British Staff Numbers', *Daily Telegraph*, 25 February 2009.

[10] 'Wildcat Strikes over Foreign Workers', *The Independent*, 20 May 2009.

[11] 'Deal Reached to End Wildcat Strike: Unions Promised Energy Plant Jobs for Local Labour', *Western Mail*, 21 May 2009.

[12] 'Local Jobs Protest at Newport Power Station', *South Wales Argus*, 7 September 2009.

[13] 'Uskmouth Power Plant to Hold Newport Jobs Fair', *South Wales Argus*, 17 September 2009.

[14] See for example the article by Labour MP Jon Cruddas, 'Freedom of Movement for Workers has Gone Mad in the Race to Cut Wages', *Sunday Mirror*, 1 February 2009, and the comments attributed to Health Secretary Alan Johnson in 'Ministers to Look at "Distorted" EU Employment Law', *The Guardian*, 2 February 2009.

[15] Case C-341/05, *Laval*, [2007] ECR I-11767, Case C-346/06, *Rüffert* [2008] ECR I -1989 and Case C-319/06, *Commission v. Luxembourg* [2008] ECR I-4323.

the possibilities for legal regulation (all three cases) and industrial action (*Laval* only) to extend terms and conditions to posted workers.[16]

Legal regulation to extend collective agreements may be considered first. On this point, it appears that it was not EU law, but British law, which was deficient.[17] The 1996 Posted Workers Directive permits member states to extend the core terms of collective agreements to posted workers.[18] In order to guarantee non-discrimination, however, the Directive set out the pre-condition that the member state in question had a domestic mechanism for extending collective agreements to non-parties. Britain has in the past had legal mechanisms for the extension of collective agreements.[19] These reached their most developed form in Schedule 11 of the Employment Protection Act 1975, with the establishment of a statutory procedure for the enforcement of collective agreements, or of the general level of terms and conditions, against all employers in a given industry and geographical area.[20] The repeal of Schedule 11 by Employment Act 1980 was among the first acts of deregulation by post-1979 Conservative Governments. Related reforms saw the withdrawal in 1982 of the 'fair wages resolution', which required government departments to oblige contractors to respect collectively agreed standards, and the enactment of the Local Government Act 1988, which prohibited local authorities and related bodies from imposing similar obligations upon their contractors. Crucially, none of these steps was reversed in the period of Labour government after 1997, and the law on collective agreements was left unaltered when the Posted Workers Directive came into force in December 1999.

Industrial action taken against posting employers is subject to limits

---

[16] See the newspaper article by Jon Cruddas (above) and Kilpatrick (2009).

[17] For a similar assessment, see Zahn (2010).

[18] Directive 96/71 concerning the posting of workers in the framework of the provision of services, OJ 1997 L 18/1, Articles 3(1) and 3(8). The subjects listed in Article 3(1) are: (a) 'maximum work periods and minimum rest periods'; (b) minimum paid annual holidays; (c) minimum rates of pay; (d) 'the hiring-out of workers'; (e) health, safety and hygiene at work; (f) protective measures for pregnant women, women who have recently given birth and children and young people; and, (g) equality of treatment. In the case of construction activity, there is an obligation to extend collective agreements to posted workers, provided there is a system for declaring collective agreements universally applicable in the given geographical area and profession/ industry.

[19] The starting-point was the Conditions of Employment and National Arbitration Order 1940 (SR&O 1940 No. 1305), Art 5. It was succeeded on this point by the Industrial Disputes Order 1951 (SI 1951 No. 1376) and by the Terms and Conditions of Employment Act 1959, s 8.

[20] Brian Bercusson discussed this provision in his (1978) *Fair Wages Resolutions*, Chapter 20.

deriving from Article 56 TFEU on the cross-border provision of services, as interpreted in *Laval*. The relevant aspects of the *Laval* decision involved two distinct findings: that trade union action was covered by the Treaty rules (horizontal direct effect), and that the industrial action in question was unjustified.

The industrial action at Lindsey was not necessarily at odds with either of these points in the *Laval* ruling, however. Consider first the horizontal effect of the obligations in Article 56 TFEU. In *Laval*, the Court of Justice argued that the application of Article 56 TFEU was

> required in the case of rules which are not public in nature but which are designed to regulate, collectively, the provision of services. The abolition, as between Member States, of obstacles to the freedom to provide services would be compromised if the abolition of State barriers could be neutralised by obstacles resulting from the exercise of their legal autonomy by associations or organisations not governed by public law . . .[21]

While the full implications of this passage are not without uncertainty, it appears to at least require 'the exercise of legal autonomy by associations or organisations' in order for Article 56 TFEU to limit industrial action.[22] If so, unofficial action taken outside of union structures is not covered by the Treaty rules on the free movement of services. Or – to put the point differently – a further extension of the scope of Article 56 TFEU, beyond that in *Laval*, would be required in order for unofficial action to be covered.

The second question – justification – is undoubtedly relevant where industrial action, aimed at the extension of terms and conditions to posted workers, is organised by a trade union or other association of workers. On this point, it is significant that the Court accepted the principle of such industrial action in its *Laval* judgment:

> the right to take collective action for the protection of the workers of the host State against possible social dumping may constitute an overriding reason of public interest . . . which, in principle, justifies a restriction of one of the fundamental freedoms guaranteed by the Treaty.[23]

The Court's two objections to the justifiability of the industrial action at issue in that case concerned the detail of the claims made of the posting

---

[21] *Laval* (above), para 98.
[22] It may also require that the industrial action be aimed at regulation of a sector: see Dashwood (2008, 535–536). For a different rationale, which focuses on the social power of collective action, see Azoulai (2008, 1343–1346).
[23] *Laval* (above), para 103.

employer. Firstly, it objected to the fact that the industrial action aimed at the extension of obligations which went beyond the subjects listed in the Posted Workers Directive.[24] Secondly, it considered that the intended obligations as regards pay were too uncertain, and for that reason amounted to a disproportionate interference with the employer's right to provide services in another member state.[25]

The industry agreement at issue in the Lindsey dispute may have risked non-compliance with the first of these objections.[26] That is because it covered matters not listed in Article 3(1) of the Directive, such as occupational pensions and grievance and disciplinary procedures. Nevertheless, the union's specific complaints regarding non-compliance with the agreement concerned rest breaks and the difficulty of verifying the amount of wages paid to the contractor's staff.[27] It is probable that each of these matters falls within the field of the Directive, as rest breaks and minimum wages are both referred to in Article 3(1), while verification arrangements would arguably be covered by the provision in Article 5 for 'adequate procedures' for 'workers and/or their representatives for the enforcement of obligations'.[28] In other words, the actual demands in the Lindsey dispute could probably have been tailored to meet the first of the objections in the *Laval* judgment. Meanwhile, the agreement appeared safe from the second objection in *Laval*, concerning transparency in wage claims, as it contained a comprehensive list of pay rates.[29]

In any event, the more significant legal constraints on industrial action aimed at the extension of terms of collective agreements again lie within

---

[24]   *Ibid.*, para 108.

[25]   *Ibid.*, para 110.

[26]   This was the 'National Agreement for the Engineering Construction Industry 2007–2010' (NAECI), available at http://www.njceci.co.uk/assets/downloads/NAECI%2020072010%20Final%20Printed%20Edition.pdf (accessed October 2010).

[27]   ACAS, *Report of an Inquiry into the Circumstances Surrounding the Lindsey Oil Refinery Dispute,* 16 February 2009, available at http://www.acas.org.uk/CHttpHandler.ashx?id=1019&p=0 (accessed October 2010).

[28]   See too Case C-60/03 *Wolff & Müller* [2004] ECR I-9553, para.30, where the Court stated that the member states had 'a wide margin of appreciation' in relation to enforcement procedures.

[29]   It has been suggested that the pay provisions of the NAECI agreement did not respect the *Laval* judgment, as it did not set out 'minimum' rates, which is what the Posted Workers Directive provides for: Kilpatrick (2009, 859). The assumption here is that, since the Directive permits the extension of collective agreements, the concept of a 'minimum' should be interpreted flexibly, to cover differentiated minimum rates typical of collective agreements.

British law.[30] That is because the legal protection given to industrial action excludes secondary industrial action from its scope. Since the Conservative Government's Employment Acts of 1980 and 1982, the trade dispute immunity from economic torts has been limited to industrial action taken by workers against their own employer, in pursuance of a dispute with that employer.[31] Accordingly, the immunity does not cover industrial action – such as in the Lindsey dispute – where workers aim to put pressure on their own employer in pursuit of a dispute with another employer operating at the same workplace.[32] By extension, the protection against dismissal given to individual workers taking industrial action is unavailable, as it is dependent on the availability of the trade dispute immunity.[33]

NATIONALITY DISCRIMINATION

In the preceding discussion of the extension of collective agreements, it was assumed for the purposes of discussion that the relative terms and conditions of contractors' staff were at the heart of the 2009 protests. That may not be a correct characterisation, however, given that the unifying theme of the protests was the complaint that workers of other European nationalities had been employed when local and/or British labour was available. In the specific case of the Lindsey dispute, moreover, a report by the Advisory Conciliation and Arbitration Service (ACAS) made clear that it was an 'impasse' over the recruitment of local labour in negotiations between the contractors and the union that had triggered unofficial action.[34]

This leads us to the second labour law topic raised by the events of 2009 – guarantees of equal treatment on grounds of nationality. These events

---

[30] The discussion here focuses on the aim of the industrial action, in the best-case scenario that it is called by a trade union after a valid ballot. The actual disputes in 2009 were also legally problematic because they were unsupported by a trade union (unofficial).

[31] See now Trade Union and Labour Relations (Consolidation) Act 1992, s 244(1) and 244(5).

[32] This follows from the lack of protection even where the two employers are 'associated', through having the same or inter-linked ownership: see *Dimbleby & Sons Ltd v. National Union of Journalists*, [1984] ICR 386 (House of Lords). The inability of workers of another employer at the same workplace to take lawful industrial action was an aspect of the Gate Gourmet strike of 2005: see Hendy and Gall (2006, 249–250).

[33] Trade Union and Labour Relations (Consolidation) Act 1992, s 238A.

[34] *Ibid.*, para 12.

show the possibility *both* of discrimination against workers from other EU member states *and* of discrimination against British nationals. Each will be covered in the discussion here, which provides a separate analysis of the position of British employers, of foreign-based employers and of participants in industrial action. We will see that the law in this area has changed in 2010, but that ultimately there remains considerable uncertainty as to the legal duties of each of these three categories of person.

British Employers

In the case of possible nationality discrimination by British-based employers, a first point is that EU law on the free movement of workers may be relevant. Migrant workers who are EU nationals are protected by the requirement of equal treatment on grounds of nationality in Article 45 TFEU. Since the *Angonese* decision in 2000, it has been clear that Article 45 TFEU is 'horizontally' effective against all employers.[35] It has also long been established that Article 45 TFEU prohibits both direct and indirect forms of discrimination.[36] An important limitation however is that Article 45 TFEU applies only to EU workers who wish to work in other member states (including their own, if they are proposing to move there), but does not apply to workers seeking to remain in their own state. For that reason, the more important question is the position in British law.

The outright refusal by a British employer to hire a worker on grounds of their nationality – having, or not having, British citizenship – is a fairly straightforward matter in the law of employment discrimination.[37] Until 30 September 2010, such a course of action would have been prohibited by the Race Relations Act 1976 ('RRA 1976'), which includes 'nationality' within its definition of prohibited 'racial grounds'. Since 1 October 2010, it has instead been prohibited by the Equality Act 2010, which defines the concept of 'race' for the purposes of discrimination law to include 'nationality'.[38]

---

[35] Case C-281/98 *Angonese* v. *Cassa di Risparmio di Bolzano* [2000] ECR I-4139.

[36] Leading cases on indirect nationality discrimination in the employment context are Case C-15/96 *Schöning-Kougebetopoulou* [1998] ECR I-47, Case C-350/96 *Clean Car* [1998] ECR I-2521 and *Angonese* (above).

[37] The discussion here concerns Great Britain alone. The Race Relations Act 1976 does not apply to Northern Ireland, but equivalent provisions were adopted in the Race Relations (Northern Ireland) Order 1997 (SI 1997 No 869), Article 10 (as amended). The substantive provisions of the Equality Act 2010 do not apply in Northern Ireland.

[38] Equality Act 2010, s 9.

Beyond that, what of employer practices which favour, or disfavour, *locally resident* workers? It is necessary to address this question because, in the events of 2009, it was generally assumed that a preference for local workers would benefit British citizens over nationals of other EU member states. Does an employer policy which is advantageous to local workers amount to indirect discrimination on grounds of nationality against foreign workers? Or, would an employer policy which discouraged local labour entail indirect discrimination against British citizens? These forms of indirect discrimination might arise from a recruitment *rule*, which either required, or precluded, applications by local workers.[39] Or, they might arise from an employer's recruitment *practice*, in soliciting job applications or advertising vacancies in some locations rather than others.

In answering these questions, a first step is to determine which employer practices are even potentially caught by discrimination law. Prior to the coming into force of the Equality Act 2010, if the alleged ground of discrimination was nationality, the RRA 1976 prohibited indirect discrimination only where there was a 'requirement or condition'.[40] That phrase was generally taken to require a bar on employment in order for a finding of indirect discrimination to be possible.[41] It followed that, until 1 October 2010, recruitment rules concerning local workers – for, or against – could have been challenged for indirect discrimination, whereas recruitment practices which merely favoured, or disfavoured, local workers, could not have been so.

The position in this regard has recently been transformed by the Equality Act 2010. The background was that three EU directives on equality treatment in 2000 and 2002 defined indirect discrimination in a broader manner, to mean that an 'apparently neutral provision, criterion or practice' put persons in a given category 'at a particular disadvantage'.[42] In line

---

[39] An example of a bar on local applicants is given by *Hussein v. Saints Complete House Furnishers* [1979] IRLR 337. In that case, the bar was motivated by the employer's belief that workers from the local area, and those with whom they associated, were undesirable on social grounds. As the business was located in an area with a relatively high non-white population, and the policy could not be justified, the industrial tribunal found that there had been unlawful indirect discrimination on racial grounds.

[40] RRA 1976, s 1(1)(b).

[41] *Perera* v. *Civil Service Commission (No.2)* [1983] ICR 428.

[42] See Directive 2000/43 implementing the principle of equal treatment between persons irrespective of racial or ethnic origin, OJ 2000 L 180/22, Article 2(2)(b); Directive 2000/78 establishing a general framework for equal treatment in employment and occupation, OJ 2000 L 303/16, Article 2(2)(b); and, Directive 76/207 on equal treatment for men and women, Article 2(2), as amended by Directive 2002/73, OJ 2002 L 269/15.

with the requirements of one of those directives (Directive 2000/ 43), the RRA 1976 had itself been amended in 2003, so that the grounds of race, ethnic origins or national origins – but not nationality – were covered by the broader standard.[43] What the Equality Act 2010 has done is to extend that broader standard to all equality grounds, including nationality discrimination.[44] For our purposes, an important consequence is to create the possibility of claims of indirect nationality discrimination where employer recruitment practices favour or disfavour local workers, without amounting to a 'requirement or condition'.

The next question is whether an employer can justify a recruitment condition or practice which favours, or disfavours, local workers. One approach to justification has focused on the needs of alleged discriminators. The original authority for that approach was the statement by the Court of Justice in *Bilka-Kaufhaus* – in a case concerning equal pay between men and women – that the 'means chosen by the employer . . . meet a genuine need of the enterprise'.[45] A needs-based approach was followed in the interpretation of the RRA 1976 in *Hampson* in 1989, when the Court of Appeal required 'an objective balance between the discriminatory effect of the condition and the reasonable needs of the party who applies the condition'.[46] Elsewhere, however, EU law – including Directive 2000/43 – has focused on whether a discriminator's practice has a 'legitimate aim'.[47] As a result of the Equality Act 2010, that test is now set out in British legislation for all discrimination grounds, including nationality discrimination.[48]

From an employer's perspective, it is arguable that the concept of a 'legitimate aim' is broader than that of 'reasonable need' or 'genuine need'.

---

[43]   RRA 1976, s 1(1A), inserted by the Race Relations Act 1976 (Amendment) Regulations 2003, SI 2003 No. 1626. Even though Article 3(2) of the Directive 2000/ 43 states that 'This Directive does not cover difference of treatment based on nationality', acts of nationality discrimination may be found to amount to direct or indirect discrimination on grounds of 'racial or ethnic origin'. An example is given by Case C-54/07 *Firma Feryn* [2008] ECR I-5187, which concerned an employer who was reported to have said that he would not hire 'Moroccans', and who claimed to have said that he would not hire 'immigrants'. At the national level, it was concluded that the employer's statement amounted to direct discrimination on grounds of ethnic origin.
[44]   Equality Act 2010, s 19.
[45]   *Bilka-Kaufhaus* [1986] ECR 1607, para 36.
[46]   *Hampson v. Department of Education and Science* [1989] IRLR 69, 75–76 (Balcombe LJ).
[47]   Directive 2000/ 43, Article 2(2)(b).
[48]   RRA 1976, s 1(1A)(c), inserted by the Race Relations Act 1976 (Amendment) Regulations 2003, SI 2003 No 1626 and Equality Act 2010, s 19(2)(d).

The difference might be thought to lie in the possibility for the employer to rely upon wider social objectives in justification of their rules or policies. If that were possible, for our purposes, it would lead to the question whether an employer's 'social responsibility' might justify a preference for local workers.[49] To date, however, the approach of the British courts has been to treat the two tests as identical, with the focus remaining on the needs of the alleged discriminator.[50] If that position is maintained, it will continue to be necessary for an employer to show that any recruitment policies it adopts are defensible by reference to its needs alone.

Applying a 'needs' test, a policy which favours, or disfavours, local residents is likely to be problematic. Firstly, a rule which either *requires* or *excludes* existing local residents will be difficult to justify, as it is hard to see what need the employer could have concerning the prior residence of prospective employees. At most, one might imagine an employer having an interest in local residence *after* hiring – but even that would probably have a greater effect on non-British workers, and so require justification with reference to the employer's organisational needs. Secondly, recruitment strategies which make it significantly more, or less, likely that local residents will apply, are also problematic. An employer would presumably have to explain why a particular strategy was adopted, having regard to its need for workers of a particular kind, the labour market circumstances, and its prior experience.[51] If one starts from employer needs, however, what appears *not* to be permissible is for an employer to pursue a policy of seeking to recruit local residents for social reasons, or because of pressure exerted by unions and others.

Employers Based in Other Member States

Further complexity is added where an employer is not based in Britain, but instead posts workers there. Any direct or indirect nationality discrimi-

---

[49] For a discussion of local labour clauses and 'corporate social responsibility' under EU public procurement law, see Barnard (2009, 262–275).

[50] *R (Elias) v. Secretary of State for Defence* [2006] EWCA Civ 1293, para.151 (Mummery LJ); approved by *R (E)* v. *Governing Body of JFS* [2009] UKSC 15, para.97 (Lord Mance).

[51] That justification may be not straightforward, can be seen from the 2009 decision of the Employment Appeal Tribunal in *Osborne Clarke Services v. Purohit* [2009] IRLR 341. The EAT found that it amounted to indirect nationality discrimination for an employer to refuse to consider an application from someone who required a work permit. In reaching that conclusion, it rejected the employer's attempted justification that it had assumed the immigration authorities would not grant a work permit.

nation in recruitment by such an employer may be actionable by virtue of the free movement of workers principle in EU law, or under the other state's laws. There are possible gaps, however, as the free movement of workers will not protect EU law or British workers who have remained in Britain, and there may be no other protection in the law of the state where the employer is based. For our purposes, the key question is again whether a posting employer may be liable to legal action under British discrimination law. In addressing that, it will though be necessary to have regard to the Posted Workers Directive, and in particular its Article 3(1), which requires the extension to posted workers of statutory rules on '(g) equality of treatment between men and women and other provisions on non-discrimination'.

In British law, the employment discrimination provisions of the RRA 1976 were amended in 1999 to bring them into line with what the Directive was thought to require. The result was the replacement of the previous rule that employment was excluded if it was 'wholly or mainly' outside Great Britain with a rule excluding employment only if it was 'wholly' outside that territory.[52] Later, that rule was stated positively, so that the 1976 Act applied to employment which was 'wholly or partly' in Great Britain.[53] It appeared therefore that the 1976 Act applied to hiring decisions in other states, both where it was anticipated that the employee would only work in Great Britain (here termed 'full' posting), but also where they would work for only some of the time there (here termed 'partial' posting).

In contrast, the Equality Act 2010 does not have an express statement as to its scope. The reason given by the then Government for this legislative silence was that it expected that the courts would fill the gap, as they had done for the Employment Rights Act 1996.[54] For our purposes, the problem is that the previous case-law dealt with post-employment litigation, where the place of work was already known, and may not provide a clear guide to the position where an individual complains about employer recruitment.[55] Given that the earlier case law has found that

---

[52] RRA 1976, s 8(1), as amended by the Equal Opportunities (Employment Legislation) (Territorial Limits) Regulations 1999, SI 1999 No. 316. For the link to the Directive, see the Explanatory Note to the Regulations.

[53] RRA 1976, s 8(1), as amended by the Race Relations Act 1976 (Amendment) Regulations 2003, SI 2003 No. 1626.

[54] *Equality Bill 2009: Explanatory Notes*, para 27. The territorial rule previously in section 196 of the Employment Rights Act was also abolished at the time of the implementation of the Posted Workers Directive: see section 32 of the Employment Relations Act 1999, and the explanation given by Trade and Industry Minister Lord Simon, *House of Lords Debates*, 8 July 1999, cols 1089–1090.

[55] The leading case is *Lawson v. Serco* [2006] UKHL 3, which concerned the reach of the unfair dismissal provisions.

employment law must apply to those who work in Great Britain, and are not peripatetic,[56] we may speculate that recruitment with a view to 'full' posting will be covered by the 2010 Act. The position with respect to recruitment with a view to 'partial' posting must however be considered uncertain.

What are the implications of the Posted Workers Directive for the application of discrimination law to hiring decisions abroad? An initial problem of interpretation concerns the fact that the phrase 'terms and conditions of employment' is used both in Article 3(1) of the Directive to define the duty on member states to extend the provisions of equality law to posted workers, and in Article 3(10) of the Directive, to define the scope of member state discretion to extend other 'public policy' measures to them. The difficulty is that that phrase would not ordinarily be thought to cover hiring decisions. If that ordinary reading were applied here, the consequence would be that the Posted Workers Directive did not protect the extension of equal treatment laws to recruitment decisions taken in other member states, either for 'full' or 'partial' posting. Member states would also be blocked under Article 56 TFEU, given the Court of Justice's apparent conclusion in *Commission v. Luxembourg*, that the Directive defines the limit of member states' power to extend their employment laws to posted workers.[57]

If the 'terms and conditions' obstacle were overcome, through a broad interpretation of the phrase, a further problem would be that Article 3(1) sets out a duty for member states only in relation to 'workers posted to their territory'. It is not clear that that formulation can cover individuals who have neither been hired nor sent to work in another member state. If there is no duty, might Article 3(10) of the Directive be invoked? The policy significance of the non-discrimination principle might lead one to conclude that the answer must be 'yes'. However, the judgment in *Commission v. Luxembourg* again poses a difficulty, as the Court there refused to allow Article 3(10) to be relied upon where other EU law provisions required the employer's *home* state to provide protection on the same subject.[58] The fact that EU law has a prohibition on nationality discrimination among EU workers – albeit an incomplete one, for the reasons set out above – might be thought to imply a similar conclusion in the case of an attempted export of obligations deriving from British discrimination law.[59] Alternatively,

---

56   *Ibid.*, paras 25–27 (Lord Hoffman).
57   See paras 65–67 of the judgment in *Commission v. Luxembourg*.
58   *Ibid.*, paras 40–42 and 60.
59   On this general question, see Barnard (2009).

there might be the untidy result that Britain's law could be applicable, but only to those not covered by Article 45 TFEU.

Industrial Action

A third question is the legal position where the aim of industrial action is to persuade an employer to discriminate (directly or indirectly) against foreign workers.[60] As things stand, a dispute of this kind appears to be protected by British law on industrial action. That is because the concept of a 'trade dispute' includes '(b) engagement or non-engagement . . . of one or more workers.'[61] Writing in the 1960s, Grunfeld gave disputes over the hiring of apprentices, or of non-union labour, as examples of the subjects covered by this provision.[62] Nevertheless, the formulation is broad enough to cover action taken against workers on grounds of their nationality, or place of usual residence.

As against that, both the RRA 1976 and the Equality Act 2010 have contained provisions making it unlawful to induce a person to commit an act of race discrimination (including on grounds of nationality), or to attempt to do so.[63] Under the 1976 Act, it was established that merely persuading someone to commit an act of discrimination was sufficient.[64] On that interpretation, industrial action with a discriminatory purpose would presumably have been in breach of the Act. The Equality Act 2010 has however made a significant change to the law in this area, by introducing a pre-condition to unlawfulness that the relationship between the person inducing and the person induced is such that the former could commit a breach of discrimination law in relation to the latter.[65] Since employees cannot commit acts of unlawful discrimination towards employers, it appears that the 2010 Act has removed the possibility that industrial action can fall foul of the provisions on inducement.

Because of the decision in *Laval*, EU law again has a potential role here. If the target of industrial action were a decision to use posted workers,

---

[60] The discussion here focuses on the objective of the action. In practice, the availability of the immunity requires that the industrial action be 'official', that is validly organised by a trade union.

[61] Trade Union and Labour Relations (Consolidation) Act 1992, s 244(1)(b).

[62] Grunfeld, C. (1966) *Modern Trade Union Law*, London: Sweet and Maxwell, p. 341.

[63] RRA 1976, s 31 and Equality Act 2010, s 111.

[64] *Commission for Racial Equality v. Imperial Society of Teachers of Dancing* [1983] ICR 473 (EAT).

[65] Equality Act 2010, s 111(7).

then *Laval* would obviously come into play. In such a case, it must be thought improbable that there would be room for justification of industrial action, as the action would go to the heart of the employer's right to engage in the cross-border provision of services under Article 56 TFEU. If the industrial action concerned the hiring of workers who were nationals of other member states, Article 45 TFEU would arguably be applicable, through the extension of its 'horizontal' effect to trade unions and other associations of workers, by analogy with *Laval*.[66] In the latter case, the difficult question would again be whether it was permissible to favour local residents. Given that (for the reasons indicated above) employers may struggle to justify 'local worker' policies under conventional discrimination law, it must however be considered unlikely that industrial action with an equivalent objective would be justifiable under the law on the free movement of workers.

CONCLUSION

Migrant employment has grown markedly over the past decade in Britain, with foreign-born persons estimated to have made up 13.3 per cent of the employed workforce in 2010.[67] The analysis of the 2009 protests in this chapter may be treated as a case-study of two kinds of challenge for labour law posed by increased migrant employment in Britain. Firstly, the addition of migrant workers may lead Britain's flexible labour law regime to appear problematic, whether for migrant workers, for previously resident workers, or for both.[68] In the events of 2009, that was seen in the lack of provision for the extension of the terms of collective agreements to non-parties, whether by statute, or through industrial action. The underlying point though is far broader, as it concerns the dilution of labour market regulation by Conservative governments in 1979–1997, and the choice of the succeeding 'New Labour' governments (1997–2010) not to reverse most of that deregulation.[69]

Secondly, migrant employment poses questions for the field which are migration-specific, in that they concern the legal and social status

---

[66] Also relevant in this regard is Case C-438/05 *Viking Line* [2007] ECR I-10779, concerning the freedom of establishment (Article 49 TFEU).

[67] Labour Force Survey data, available at http://www.statistics.gov.uk/statbase/TSDSeries1.asp (accessed October 2010). Space constraints preclude examination here of contemporary patterns of migrant employment in Britain.

[68] On this theme, see McKay and Rivers (2005).

[69] On the latter period, see Smith and Morton (2006).

of migrant workers. The particular problem for migrant workers shown in the 2009 events was the risk of direct and indirect discrimination in access to employment as a result of resident worker pressure on employers. Others concern the effects within the employment relationship of the public policy against irregular employment by those who lack a right to work.[70] These questions too are more likely to come to the fore with an increase in the employment of foreign workers.

Beyond questions for the content of labour law, increased levels of migrant employment may involve challenges for commentary on the field. The general issue for commentators is the avoidance of what has been termed 'methodological nationalism', which Andreas Wimmer and Nina Glick-Schiller have described as 'the naturalization of the nation-state by the social sciences'.[71] In this context, overcoming 'methodological nationalism' means giving due recognition to migrant workers' legitimate claims to take employment, and to be treated equally within the labour market. As the case-study in this chapter has hoped to show, viewing labour law through that prism may serve to cast familiar questions in a new light.

REFERENCES

Azoulai, L. (2008), 'The Court of Justice and the Social Market Economy: The Emergence of an Ideal and the Conditions for its Realization', *Common Market Law Review*, **45**, 1335–1356.
Barnard, C. (2009), 'The UK and Posted Workers: The Effect of *Commission v Luxembourg* on the Territorial Application of British Labour Law', *Industrial Law Journal*, **38** (1), 122–132.
Benedictus, R. and B. Bercusson (1987), *Labour Law: Cases and Materials*, London: Sweet and Maxwell.
Bercusson, B. (1978), *Fair Wages Resolutions*, London: Mansell.
Bercusson, B. (1996), *European Labour Law*, London: Butterworths.
Dashwood, A. (2008), '*Viking* and *Laval*: Issues of Horizontal Direct Effect', *Cambridge Yearbook of European Legal Studies,* **10**, 525–540.
Hendy, J. and G. Gall (2006), 'British Trade Union Rights Today and the Trade Union Freedom Bill', in K. Ewing (ed.), *The Right to Strike*, London: Institute of Employment Rights.
Kilpatrick, C. (2009), 'Laval's Regulatory Conundrum: Collective Standard-Setting and the Court's New Approach to Posted Workers', *European Law Review*, **34** (6), 844–865.
McKay, S. and A. Rivers (2005), 'Migrant Workers and Employment Law', in

---

[70]   See Ryan (2005).
[71]   Wimmer and Glick Schiller (2003, 576).

B. Ryan (ed.), *Labour Migration and Employment Rights*, London: Institute of Employment Rights.

Ryan, B. (2005), 'The Evolving Legal Regime on Unauthorized Work by Migrants in Britain', *Comparative Labour Law and Policy Journal*, **27** (1), 27–58.

Smith, P. and G. Morton (2006), 'Nine Years of New Labour: Neoliberalism and Workers' Rights', *British Journal of Industrial Relations*, **44** (3), 401–420.

Wimmer, A. and N. Glick Schiller (2003), 'Methodological Nationalism, the Social Sciences, and the Study of Migration: An Essay in Historical Epistemology', *International Migration Review*, **37**, 576.

Zahn, R. (2010), '"British Jobs for British Workers": The Problem of Collective Agreements in the United Kingdom', *Juridical Review*, 181–194.

6. What remedies for social derivatives and expansionism of the Court of Justice of the European Union?

Nikitas Aliprantis

OPENING REMARKS

In their anxiety to gradually create a common body of rules governing the European countries, the fathers of the current European Union (EU) established, among other things, the Court of Justice of the European Communities (CJEC, CJEU or ECJ today), and they endowed it with exorbitant judicial power, which is unique in the world.[1] They were obviously aware of this enormous attribution of competence envisaged by the then Article 164 of the EEC Treaty and which remains unchanged today in Article 19 of the Treaty of Lisbon (TEU). Under this provision the ECJ 'shall ensure that in the interpretation and application of the Treaties the law is observed'. It is clear that the 'law' is set up in a separate parameter distinct from the treaties and must 'inspire' their interpretation. Even if we ignore this formula which legitimates the Court's determination of what the 'law' is, the interpretation itself of the treaties is the uncontrolled and exclusive work of this Court. But then: *quis custodiat curiam?* Unfortunately, neither the original inspirers of the CJEC, nor the drafters of the new EU Treaty have provided 'safety valves' against disproportionate expansionism and against derived interpretations of the European jurisdiction.[2] This 'lacuna' is all the more serious as we witness for some time now how both of the dangers occur, especially at the social level. This allows us to measure the responsibility of the forces and European institutions that were recently animated by the desire to ensure and precipitate the ratification of the Treaty of Lisbon at all costs, instead of using the initial Irish 'no' to introduce safeguards against

---

[1] Its power is larger than, for example, that of the Supreme Court of the USA or the European Court of Human Rights.

[2] On the question of 'safety valve' see further in the text.

institutional slippages, current and/or virtual, including those of the ECJ.

That said, our intention here is not to make an inventory of the jurisprudential derivatives of the ECJ, but rather, from the evocation of some recent significant judgements, consider some remedies to the current state of affairs. These remedies are, on the one hand, of interpretative nature, and, on the other, institutional.

INTERPRETATIVE REMEDIES

The Court of Justice needs to acknowledge the current shortcomings and make the necessary changes in its jurisprudence. The changes are essential and concern the interpretation of some fundamental notions as well as the role ascribed to the national law of the EU Member States. Apart from these 'remedies' there exists an interpretative 'chance', which Article 16 of the Charter of Fundamental Rights opens before the ECJ.

The Necessary Abandonment of Erroneous or Outdated Conceptions

It is primarily a question of the Court's distancing itself from the three fundamental issues of its jurisprudence. First, ignoring the legal nature of social rights; second, not taking into account national laws; and finally, the contradiction concerning the conditions of the violation of legal rules, and in particular, those relating to economic freedoms.

The relevant case law under the three points raised has been sufficiently discussed elsewhere, so we limit ourselves here to proposing some 'remedies' in the order mentioned above.

1. It is crucial and urgent to make a fundamental change and recognize that social rights in the broadest sense – including rights related to work and rights to social security and protection – have their own legal value and are not just derogations or restrictions of economic freedoms, as the Court views them (among others in the well-known *Viking* and *Laval* judgements).[3] It is also important to reverse the terms of this rapport and acknowledge that it is the economic freedoms that constitute restrictions on social rights and not vice versa.[4] Far from

---

[3]   See comments in Blanpain and Swiatkowski (2009).
[4]   The idea was expressed by the late Brian Bercusson with regard to the mentioned judgements.

being revolutionary, this rapport is the result of common legal values and national constitutional rules. It would be useful to recall at this point what Robespierre first formulated in 1792 and make his conclusion a fundamental rule of Community law: 'What is the first of these rights (human rights)? The right to exist. *The first social law is the one which guarantees all the members of society the means to exist, all other rights are subordinate to the former*'.[5]

2. Not taking into account and/or putting aside national rules, even fundamental constitutional social rights for the benefit of the absolute priority given to economic freedoms of the primary or even secondary EU legislation, is also a severe error of the CJEC. Moreover, such ignoring of the 'national laws and practices' is directly contrary to the Charter of Fundamental Rights which, in an almost pedantic but justified manner, repeats the reference to them in the social provisions (Articles 27, 28, 30, 34 § § 1, 2, 3, 35). In view of the position taken by the Court so far, one realizes that it was indispensable to include systematic references to national laws and practices in the Charter, and that European trade unions were wrong to be opposed to this reference fearing that it might hamper social progress in Europe. It is known though that the trade unions objections were rejected by people like Guy Braibant, who rightly pointed out that 'in the current state of affairs, it is often Europe that acts in a way which slows down the development in the social field . . .'.[6] The arguments underlying the non-application of national rules are known and will be discussed briefly below. For now, we have drawn attention to this error and criticized the systematic attitude of the CJEC.

3. The concept of the violation of a rule, in this case economic freedoms, and in particular the freedom of establishment and the freedom to provide services (Articles 43 and 49 EC, today, respectively, Articles 49 and 56 of the Treaty of Lisbon), is a victim of a deformation with particularly serious consequences. The Court admits that the freedoms in question, and especially the latter, are restricted, therefore violated, as soon as there is an impediment, even potential, which might make their exercise less attractive or more difficult and possibly dissuade the interested parties (examples: judgements *Laval, Rüffert, Commission C. Luxembourg*).[7] However, the restriction of any freedom presupposes a

---

[5]   Speech delivered by Robespierre on 9 December 1792, shortly after the fall of the monarchy and the proclamation of the Republic.

[6]   Braibant (2001, 192).

[7]   Case C-341/05 *Laval un Partneri Ltd v. Svenska Byggnadsarbetareförbundet and Others*, of 18 December, 2007, point 99; Case C-346/06 Dirk *Rüffert*, in his

strong and constant pressure which either impedes the exercise of the freedom or aims at it. The fact that the exercise of a freedom might virtually become less attractive because of an impediment, which is itself hypothetical, could by no means constitute a prohibited restriction of the freedom. The constant contrary jurisprudence of the Court of Justice is one of its most serious legal errors.

The consequences of this erroneous approach manifest themselves at two essential levels and take two different forms, even antithetical:

a)   The fact of admitting the existence of a far-fetched violation of economic freedoms leads to dismissing a way too easily and too hastily of national social rules as contrary to EU legislation. It basically means restricting abusively and arbitrarily the legislative powers of the states, at least in their choices on social matters. An example deserves to be very briefly mentioned here. In *Commission v. Luxembourg* the Court rejected several Luxembourgian legal provisions which required a written contract or equivalent written document and obliged service providers to make available to labour inspectorates on demand basic information necessary for the monitoring of posted workers prior to the commencement of the work, and the requirement of an ad hoc agent residing in Luxembourg to retain the documents necessary to control the obligations falling on the enterprise. So, many 'benign' social rules were 'annihilated' as restrictive of the freedom to provide services,[8] and as a result, incompatible with the Community law, and the legislative powers of the national states were trimmed.[9]

---

capacity as liquidator of the assets of Objekt und Bauregie GmbH & Co. *KG v. Land Niedersachsen*, of 3 April 2008, point 37; Case C-354/05, *Commission v. Luxembourg*, of 18 May 2006, points 81, 85.

[8]   Also on the basis of other considerations, often confusing if not contradictory (see, points 38–41).

[9]   See, *mutatis mutandis, Othmar Michaeler and Subito GmbH v. Labour Inspectorate of the Autonomous Province of Bolzano* (joined cases C-55/07 and C-56/07, 24 April 2008) which declared contrary to the Community law, a provision, established by the Italian law, which required that copies of part-time employment contracts be sent to the authorities within 30 days of their signature and envisaged a penalty for failure to comply with that obligation in the form of an administrative fine for each worker concerned and for each day of delay. The reasoning of the Court was based on the argument that the obligation in question was likely to limit opportunities for part-time work which Directive 97/81 tends to promote, as if the state would not be able under its employment policy to privilege full-time contracts by establishing the notification procedure for this type of contract as well!

b) The excessive rigour applied to the notion of the restriction on the freedom to provide services (which also applies to the freedom of establishment) admits no justification for a restriction regarding the protection of workers. In *Laval, Rüffert* and *Commission v. Luxembourg* the Court continued and confirmed the distorted interpretation of the Posted Workers Directive (96/71), considering that it provides maximum standards (*Laval*)[10] and prohibits host states to establish working conditions which are more favourable to workers than the mandatory rules for minimum protection (*Rüffert*).[11] Moreover, the theory of effectiveness is put forward to justify the standardization of the minimum level of the conditions of work.[12] Ultimately, it seems that by following the logic of this jurisprudence we should conclude that any difference in the higher level of protection in one country in comparison with another constitutes a restriction on the freedom to provide services.

It is obvious that time has come to put an end to such errors and recall the jurisprudence of the Court which was anxious to prevent unfair competition and consequently, recognized the restrictions on the freedom to provide services.[13] To the interpretative remedies previously reported there should be added an interpretative 'chance', which is open before the ECJ by Article 16 of the Charter of Fundamental Rights, an article which deals with the freedom of enterprise.

The 'Interpretative Chance' and Freedom to Conduct a Business

The inclusion of this provision into the Charter, as it has been pointed out by some authors, 'has been belated but remarkable'.[14] While it is undoubtedly based on the jurisprudence of the Court[15] it has some essential elements of its own whose consequences though have not been brought to light so far. Thus, the freedom to conduct a business comprises several inherent elements: the pursuit of profit, which is its *raison d'être*, on the

---

[10] *Laval*, point 80.
[11] *Rüffert*, point 33; *Commission v. Luxembourg*, point 47.
[12] The *Rüffert* judgement has been widely commented upon. See, among others, in French, Lyon-Caen, A. RTD, 2008, p. 273; N. Moizard, Dr. soc. 2008, p. 866 and references herein.
[13] Some important judgements include judgement C-60/03 of 12.10.2004 and judgement C-244/04 of 19 January 2006.
[14] Braibant (2001, 137).
[15] See, among others, Braibant (2001).

one hand, and the economic risk, on the other hand. It is the entrepreneur who must assume the risk as an inherent part of the very freedom to conduct a business. The entrepreneur, therefore, cannot relieve himself of this responsibility by simply passing it on to others. This would be counter to the very nature of the freedom in question.

With regard to social aspects, this means that if the economic risk impacts on employees in a way which might lead to undermining their basic rights or affect important aspects and interests of their lives it would be contrary to the freedom to conduct a business.[16] This includes situations where working conditions are established – through Community or domestic legislation – in a very (too) flexible fashion, according to the needs of a business, changes in orders and/or movements of customers with a view to reducing or minimizing the economic risk of the business by shifting it onto the employees. Consider, for example, discontinuous working schedules, employment contracts (fixed-term, part-time, etc.) intermittent in irregular intervals, and so on, disrupting the normal organization of the life of the employee and his family. Consider also fixing the average work load on an annual basis, resulting in the elimination of increases in payments for overtime during peak periods and so on.

The arguments, presumably, of neoliberal origin, but factually put forward by the employers themselves, have resulted in gradually reconciling with the pseudo-truth that all this is related to the new forms of the organization of the business, and we deal here with measures which by their effect shift part of the economic risk onto the employees. Thus the idea that this risk should be entirely borne by the employer has been put aside and today there exists a danger of 'confusion of the kinds', namely, the respective legal positions of the entrepreneur (employer) and the employee. Yet it is important to re-establish the truth of things. As Rivero and Savatier (1991) put it, 'to employ entails corresponding profit and risks', and the obligation 'to pay the worker, even if ultimately no benefit is derived from the work' and the employee is 'entitled to a salary independently of the economic state of the enterprise'.[17] The roles of the employer and the employee are thus fundamentally different, unless we want to put into life the American slogan, tendentious, if not perverse, about 'the end of work of employees' and the subsequent transformation of everybody into entrepreneurs!

The Court of Justice in applying Article 16 of the Charter, should be vigilant to the need to ensure that the employer bears the economic risks

---

[16]   We see now how much wrong were the trade unions who had seen a kind of provocation in Article 16.

[17]   Rivero and Savatier (1991, 76).

and sanctions applied against actions contrary to the Community legislation (the invoked article), for example, Community law or practice and/or national practice, which results in a transfer of the economic risk onto the employees and has the reported effects.

Apart from the interpretative 'innovations' which are the responsibility of the Court of Justice, it is important to consider potential institutional remedies outside the EU.

NATIONAL CONSTITUTIONAL COURTS AS A POTENTIAL INSTITUTIONAL REMEDY

If the social errors and the current antisocial expansionism of the Court of Justice were to be perpetuated, one might wonder whether the Constitutional Courts of the Member States of the EU and other judicial bodies (for example, the French Constitutional Council, Supreme Courts) could represent a safety valve. They could in principle fulfil this role in their mission to preserve the fundamental social rights which are constitutionally guaranteed. Undoubtedly, there were many of those who believed that the fundamental legal values of the European countries – including social values – would constitute a common base and would be naturally recognized as community values. We now know that this hope was too hasty and contradictory. Another idea that the community law – thus also the judgements of the ECJ – would have precedence over national law, even constitutional, was reasonably well nourished by the same hope that we would have nothing to fear from the law of the Court of Justice. It is time, also in this aspect, to face the facts.

Indispensable Control

Taking into consideration the observations made, a control over the Court of Justice, at least in terms of fundamental social rights, would seem now indispensible to guarantee the future of social Europe. From this point of view, national and in particular constitutional judicial institutions, where they exist (Germany, Italy, Spain, Poland, France and so on) acquire enormous virtual importance. The proof is provided by the decision of 30 June 2009 of the German Federal Constitutional Court which, apart from some questionable formulas,[18] expressed some significant caveats. It

---

[18]   See critical observations from the institutional point of view in Koffmann and Wohlfahrt (2009, 443–446).

is important, in our opinion, to draw attention to the most characteristic ones from the social point of view:

1. The European integration could not be carried out 'in such a way that it leaves no space to its Member states on the political level, in the economic, cultural and social life' (point 249).
2. 'The Fundamental law assumes the responsibility of not only ensuring social objectives, against the background of supranational require-ments, but also linking European sovereignty – within the framework of the transferred functions – with the social responsibility . . .' (point 258).
3. That said, the key decisions in the social field must be made by the German legislative bodies within their competence. Especially the fact of ensuring the existence of every person – which is a requirement not only of the Social State but is also guaranteed in Article 1 of the Fundamental law[19] – must continue to remain a primary function of the Member States, although the harmonization is not excluded.
4. This would not run counter to . . . the participation of the German Republic in the realization of the united Europe project . . . if the Federal Constitutional Court, exceptionally and under particular and strict conditions, declared an aspect of EU law non-applicable in Germany (point 340).

With regard to the social field, the focus of the present chapter, the message is clear: any legal document, including a judgement of the ECJ, which disregards the national social rights might be ineffective in Germany.

If the Constitutional Courts and the supreme judicial institutions of the Member States assume a role of control and even of blocking legal docu-ments of the EU, including judgements of the ECJ, what risks could that entail and how could these be confronted?

Control of Virtual Risks

The major risk would certainly be a nationalist attitude which would question or block in an arbitrary way an EU legal act which would not be related to a breach of fundamental rights, especially social rights. Such an attitude would take the constitutional identity as a pretext to thwart the process of the European integration.

---

[19] It concerns the dignity of a human being.

How could one predict the outcome of such a conflict or yet another one, a justified one, affecting, *inter alia*, social rights? The question is of crucial importance because we can neither tolerate nationalist setbacks, nor accept disregarding fundamental social rights, taking place in the bodies of the EU and in particular in the ECJ which is the focus of our discussion.

Here is a major institutional topic upon which it would have been necessary to reflect and which it would have been necessary to regulate before the ratification of the Treaty of Lisbon. After this Treaty came into force it appeared wise, if not indispensible, to set up an informal body for resolving conflicts, following the model of conflict tribunals. This body could be a Committee of the Wise, composed of high level independent experts. Faced with uncontrolled expansionism and the prospect that the social errors of the ECJ might persist, such a body could become a vital safeguard. It seems neither prudent nor even permissible to have a European Court of Justice, in fact a constitutional court, that would be uncontrollable and which disregarded national constitutions based on the original sovereignty of the states. This observation is of particular importance in terms of social rights. Without solving the intractable problem '*quis custodiat custodes?*', the proposed Committee of the Wise could reduce the risk of the slippages of the ECJ as well as of national Constitutional Courts.[20] For as we know, and as aptly formulated by Immanuel Kant a person 'will always abuse his or her freedom if she or he has no one above him or her, who exerts a power according to the laws'.[21]

CONCLUSION

Confronted with the complexity of the problems, uncertainty about the future impact of the Charter of Fundamental Rights on social rights and the prospect of a European body for the resolution of potential conflicts between the ECJ and national constitutional courts, we would be rather tempted to say, to paraphrase Flaubert, that it would be stupid to want to conclude.

---

[20]   The compliance of the EU with the Revised European Social Charter could theoretically represent an important safeguard but the one which is fraught with many difficulties, well reported by O. De Schutter in his study published at the European University Institute, Badia Fiesolana, San. Domenico, 2004.

[21]   Immanuel Kant, 'Idee zu einer allgemeinen Geschichte in weltbürgerlicher Absicht', *Berlinische Monatsschrift*, November 1784, pp. 385–411, P. Menzer (ed.) (1911), *Sechster Satz*, Berlin, p. 210 et seq.

REFERENCES

Aliprantis, N. (2005), 'Social Rights are Full and Justiciable Rights', *Managerial Law*, **47** (6), 194; also published in French in *Droit social*, 2006, p.158.

Bercusson, B. (ed.) (2003), *Europäisches Arbeitsrecht und die EU-Charta der Grundrechte*, Kurzfassung, Brussels.

Blanpain, R. and A. Swiatkowski (eds) (2009), *The Laval and Viking Cases: Freedom of Service and Establishment v. Industrial Conflict in the European Economic Area and Russia*, Bulletin of Comparative Labour Relations, 69, Kluwer Law International.

Braibant, G. (2001), *La Charte des droits fondamentaux de l'Union européenne, témoignage et commentaires*, Paris: Editions de Seuil.

Davies, P. (1995), 'Market Integration and Social Policy in the Court of Justice', *Industrial Law Journal*, **24**, 49.

De Burca, G. and B. De Witte (2005), *Social Rights in Europe*, New York: Oxford University Press.

Flauss, J.-F. (ed.) (2002), *Droits sociaux et droit européen, Bilan et perspective de la protection normative*, Bruxelles: Bruylant.

Guy, L., E. Mazuyer and D. Nazet-Allouche (eds) (2006), *Les droits sociaux fondamentaux. Entre droits nationaux et droit européen*, Bruxelles: Bruylant.

Kocher, E. (2008), 'Fundamental Social Rights in Community Law and in the German Constitution-Equivalent Rights?', *The International Journal of Comparative Labour Law and Industrial Relations*, **24**, 385.

Koffmann, M. and C.Wohlfahrt (2009), 'Der gespaltene Wächter? Demokratie, Vorfassungsidentität und Interpretationsverantwortung im Lissabon-Urteil', *Zeitschrift für ausländisches Öffentliches Recht und Völkerrecht*, **69** (3), 443.

Koopmans, T. (1978), 'Legislature and Judiciary-Present Trends', in M. Cappelletti (ed.), *New Perspectives for a Common Law of Europe*, Leyden-London-Boston: Sigt Holf, p. 321.

Koukiadis, J. (2009), 'Les droits sociaux et les règles communautaires dérivées de l'Union Européenne', in N. Aliprantis (ed.), *Les droits sociaux dans les instruments européens et internationaux. Défis à l'échelle mondiale*, Bruxelles: Bruylant, p. 75.

Kravaritou, Y. (2009), 'Les Chartes de l'Union Européenne et les droits sociaux', in N. Aliprantis (ed.), *Les droits sociaux dans les instruments européens et internationaux. Défis à l'échelle mondiale*, Bruxelles: Bruylant, p. 55.

Maduro, M.P. (1998), *We The Court, The European Court of Justice and the European Economic Constitution*, Oxford: Hart Publishing.

Marcic, R. (1957), *Vom Gesetzesstaat zum Richterstaat*, Vienna: Springer.

Peers, S. and A. Ward (2004), *The European Union Charter of Fundamental Rights*, Oxford/Portland Oregon: Hart Publishing.

Rivero, J. and J. Savatier (1991), *Droit du travail*, 12th edn, Paris: Presses Universitaires de France.

PART II

The impact of fundamental rights on the
European social model: gender analysis

7. Carers, gender and employment discrimination: what does EU law offer Europe's carers?

Lisa Waddington

INTRODUCTION[1]

Caring is a gendered activity. Women are far more likely than men to be engaged in providing care within the home, and to provide care for longer periods of time. Recipients of care will frequently be children, but also older people and people with disabilities. In the case of the latter group, it may be more appropriate to speak of providing personal assistance rather than care; however, in this article the generic term 'care' will be used to refer to the unpaid support provided within the home. In spite of the commitments which caring tasks involve, many female (and male) carers are economically active and engaged in paid employment. In many cases, as a result of the commitment to caring in terms of time or energy, this employment is part-time or home-based. Such (atypical) work is naturally recognised as economic activity, and therefore falls within the scope of EU employment legislation. As a consequence, all individuals who combine caring tasks with paid employment, be it typical or atypical employment, are entitled to benefit from the full range of rights which are conferred by EU law, including the right not to be discriminated against

[1]   The author is very grateful to the Academy of European Law, the European University Institute and Prof. Marie-Ange Moreau for organising the Conference: 'Before and After the Economic Crisis: What Implications for the "European Social Model"?' in honour of Brian Bercusson and Yota Kravaritou, and to the participants at the conference for their comments on this paper.

This chapter was prepared and presented before the Treaty on the Functioning of the European Union (TFEU) came into force. The chapter has subsequently been adapted to take account of the new numbering of Treaty articles brought about by the TFEU. However, where appropriate for historical reasons, pre-TFEU Treaty articles are referred to. The chapter was completed in January 2010 and does not take account of subsequent developments.

on grounds such as gender, part-time worker status and disability and age.

The potential both for workers to be exposed to discrimination because of their domestic caring responsibilities, and for EU non-discrimination law to offer a remedy in such situations, has recently been revealed by the *Coleman* case.[2] The current chapter aims to explore the extent to which EU non-discrimination law prohibits discrimination which is directly or indirectly based on a worker's status as a carer. Carer status is not a prohibited ground of discrimination under EU law. However, a range of directives do prohibit (employment-related) discrimination on grounds such as sex, disability and age and part-time worker status. Since, as noted above, caring is mainly carried out by women (mothers, daughters, other female relatives and friends), it is important to consider the extent to which discrimination on the ground of caring status can be regarded as a form of indirect sex discrimination. In addition, since carers often work part-time, the protection offered to part-time workers is also worth considering. Lastly, since care is often provided to individuals because they are very young (children) or old, or because they have a disability, it is important to reflect on the question of how far non-discrimination law protects carers on the grounds that they associate with (care for) someone with a particular age or disability.

The chapter is structured as follows: the next section explores statistics which reveal that caring is a gendered activity in the EU, with women being far more likely than men to carry out caring-related tasks, and to be involved in caring for longer periods of time.

The chapter then examines the scope for interpreting EU non-discrimination law to include an explicit prohibition of discrimination on the grounds of carer status.

The chapter proceeds by reflecting on the extent to which EU law can protect carers, who are also in employment, from discrimination based on gender. The chapter covers both protection from discrimination for (female) carers, as well as the scope for positive action to benefit (female) carers. Such discrimination is based on a characteristic intrinsic to the carer, namely her own gender, rather than a characteristic intrinsic to the recipients of care.

The chapter continues by briefly considering the protection from discrimination provided to part-time workers. Such protection is important, given that the need to provide care within the home frequently prompts women to work part-time.

The next section considers how EU law can protect carers from

---

2   Case C-303/06 *Coleman v. Attridge Law* [2009] ECR I-5603.

employment-related discrimination which is based on a characteristic of the person they care for, such as age or disability. The focus here is on the phenomenon of 'discrimination by association', and this section will build on the ECJ's judgment in *Coleman*, which involved alleged discrimination against a woman on the grounds that she was the primary carer of her disabled child. Whilst gender is not directly at issue in such cases, women are far more likely than men to find themselves experiencing this kind of 'discrimination on association' on the grounds that they are more likely than men to be in a caring relationship.

Having stated what the chapter is 'about', it is also worth noting what the chapter is 'not about'. It does not attempt to explain why women are more likely than men to provide unpaid care to children and dependent relatives; nor does it directly address the consequences of caring for the careers or employment opportunities of women; and it does not reflect on how a more equal balancing of caring tasks between women and men could be brought about. These issues have received ample attention elsewhere.[3] Lastly, the chapter is not about the broad range of gender equality policies which the European Union has adopted, nor about the range of measures to promote 'family friendly policies', including the protection offered to pregnant women,[4] women on maternity leave and provisions relating to parental leave.[5] [6] Instead, the chapter acknowledges the current reality that women provide the majority of informal care within the home, and reflects on the extent to which EU law provides protection from employment discrimination to female (and male) carers.

THE GENDERED DIMENSION TO CARE

Women are more likely than men to be engaged in unpaid and informal caring activities. The likelihood that women's daily activities will include unpaid care for children varies from one Member State to the next but,

---

[3] See, for example, Drew (2000) which includes a good overview of the theoretical explanations for women's continued responsibility for household work and men's unwillingness to adapt their employment patterns to the demands of fathering and caring tasks. See also Crompton (2001).

[4] See Directive 92/85/EC on the introduction of measures to encourage improvements in the safety and health at work of pregnant workers who have recently given birth or are breastfeeding, [1992] O.J. L.348/1.

[5] See Directive 96/34/EC on parental leave [1996] O.J. L.145/4 as amended.

[6] For information on 'family friendly policies' in the EC, see the informative Chapter 6 by Catherine Barnard (2006).

in all Member States,[7] women are more likely than men to be involved in unpaid child care. For example, in 1999 the percentage of women in the EU-15 engaged in unpaid childcare on a daily basis ranged from 28 per cent in Portugal to 40 per cent in the Netherlands, whilst the figures for men ranged from 8 per cent in Portugal to 31 per cent in the Netherlands. On average, in the EU-15, 31 per cent of women and 19 per cent of men were engaged in unpaid childcare on a daily basis. The figures relating to the daily care of people other than children, including 'sick disabled or frail adults', reveal a similar gender imbalance, and also similar disparities between Member States.[8] In all Member States other than Denmark,[9] women were more likely to be involved in providing such care than men. Specifically, the figures relating to the percentage of the population who carry out unpaid care for adults on a daily basis ranged from 3 per cent of women in Denmark to 18 per cent of women in the United Kingdom and 1 per cent of men in Portugal, to 15 per cent of men in the United Kingdom. On average in the EU-15, 5 per cent of men and 8 per cent of women carried out such care on a daily basis.

More up to date indirect evidence is also provided by a set of Eurostat statistics on the average usual working hours of employed persons aged between 15 and 64 by regular care of other children or people in need of care, which dates from 2005. The survey reveals that, in the EU-27, women who combined employment and care spent an average of 34.2 hours per week in paid employment, whilst those men who also provided care, invested 41.5 hours in paid employment.

For women the figures ranged from 30.3 hours (Denmark) to 40.6 hours (Bulgaria), and for men from 38.6 hours (Denmark) to 45.1 hours (Greece).[10] This suggests women may be spending more time providing care within the home than men, thereby reducing the amount of time they can devote to paid employment.

---

[7]   This statement is based on material contained within Eurostat/European Community household panel users' database version, December 2002, reproduced in *Living Conditions in Europe*, Statistical pocketbook, Data 1998–2002, 2003 edition, European Commission/Eurostat, Office for Official Publications of the European Community, 2004, 112. The statistics in question cover EU-15 and relate to 1999. No date was given for Luxembourg and Sweden.

[8]   *Ibid.*, 112.

[9]   Where men and women are equally likely to be involved in providing such care. However, this figure does not reveal whether men and women invest similar number of hours in providing care, meaning that it is still possible that women carry the greater burden in terms of providing care within the home to dependent adults in Denmark.

[10]   Average usual working hours of employed persons between 15 and 64 years old by regular care of other children or people in need of care, Eurostat, 2004.

Taking the Netherlands as a case study, research from the Central Bureau of Statistics dating from the 2005, reveals the differing commitment to providing unpaid care by men and women. In 2005, 612,000 men in the Netherlands regularly spent one or more days per week caring for the children, compared to 1,333,000 women.[11] Of the 612,000 men who provided such care, 170,000 spent less than 12 hours on care; 154,000 spent 12–20 hours on care; 151,000 spent 21–40 hours on care, and 111,000 spent more than 40 hours on care. The comparable figures for women were 60,000 (less than 12 hours); 160,000 (12–20 hours); 376,000 (21–40 hours); and 679,000 (more than 40 hours). Therefore most men, when they did regularly care for children, invested less than 12 hours in caring, and the numbers of men caring for their children steadily decreased as the number of care hours measured increased. In contrast, most women invested more than 40 hours per week in caring for their children, and, as the number of care hours decreased, it became less likely that women were caring for that period. In short, women in the Netherlands who provided regular care to children were most likely to spend 40 or more hours doing this, whilst men who provided regular care for children were most likely to spend less than 12 hours doing this. Of the men who had children under the age of 13, 643,000 did not have at least one day a week which they regularly spent caring for their children, whilst the comparable figure for women was 131,000.[12]

With regard to care provided to a dependent adult, men and women in the Netherlands were equally likely to care for a partner or child over 12 within the home (44, 000 men compared to 45,000 women). However, women were far more likely to care for a parent (232,000 women compared to 124,000 men), or another family member, friend or child outside the home (99,000 women compared to 52,000 men). Women were also twice as likely to have to care for more than one person (18,000 women compared to 8,000 men).[13]

In terms of hours spent caring for a dependent adult, women in the Netherlands were likely to spend more time on caring tasks than men,

---

[11] Centraal Bureau voor de Statistiek, Netherlands, 'People aged 25–49 who regularly spend one or more days per week caring for children, 2005', questionnaire amongst the working population (Personen van 25–49 jaar naar vaste zorgdagen voor de kinderen, 2005).

[12] Centraal Bureau voor de Statistiek, Netherlands, 'People aged 25–49 who regularly spent one or more days caring for children according to care hours, 2005' (Personen van 25–49 jaar met vaste zorgdagen naar aantal zorguren voor de kinderen, 2005).

[13] Centraal Bureau voor de Statistiek, Netherlands, 'Persons aged 25–64 providing care to a dependent adult (over 12 years of age), 2005' (Personen van 25–64 jaar naar mantelzorg, 2005).

with women most likely to invest 4–11 hours on care (143,000 women), whilst men were most likely to spend less than four hours on caring tasks (106,000 men). Only 24,000 men cared for dependent relatives for 21 hours or more compared to 51,000 women.[14]

Whilst one can conclude that women are more likely than men to carry out unpaid care work within the home, and to provide such care for more hours per week than men, one should not conclude that all women are equally likely to be involved in care work. Clearly women (and men) in their 20s, 30s and 40s are most likely to care for young children, although one should note that grandmothers (and grandfathers) also provide such care. Research in the Netherlands also reveals that people in their 50s are most likely to care for a dependent adult relative, such as an elderly parent. Twice as many women as men provide such care in the Netherlands, and such care reaches its peak among the 50–54 age group.[15] Moreover, with the tendency for women to delay having children until a later age, the likelihood of women having to take on a 'double care task', involving both care for young children and dependent parents, is increasing.[16]

Finally, one should consider that cultural values which may be associated with ethnic origin or religious belief may also influence caring patterns. For example, in the Netherlands it seems that women (daughters and daughters-in-law) of Turkish and Moroccan origin are more likely to provide care to an elderly parent(-in-law) than is the case for women who are of Dutch or Western European origin. Research by the Centraal Planbureau dating from 2004 reveals that a half of Moroccan children, and a third of Turkish children, provide care for their parents.[17]

Lastly, European Union statistics reveal a gradual increase in the number of women in paid employment within the EU, in line with the Lisbon objectives of achieving 60 per cent female employment by 2010.[18] The increase is particularly marked at the level of part-time employment. However, this increase in female employment does not seem to have led to a change in the traditional role of women, as the primary care givers and

---

[14] Centraal Bureau voor de Statistiek, Netherlands, 'Persons aged 25–64 according to care hours for a dependent adult, 2005' (Personen van 25–64 jaar naar aantal uren mantelzorg, 2005).

[15] 'Vijftigers meest belast met mantelzorg', Centraal Bureau voor de Statistiek, Netherlands, Webmagazine, 25 September 2006.

[16] Maarten Alders and Ingrid Esveldt (2004) 'Zorg voor hulpbehoevende ouders', *Bevolkingstrends*, 3rd quarter, 75–79.

[17] See Sheila Kamerman (2009) 'Ouderen, Zorg voor Turkse en Marokkaanse ouderen is nog vooral een taak voor de kinderen, De schoondochters wacht een zware klus', *NRC Handelsblad*, 7 May, 2.

[18] See European Commission, 2009, 8.

providers of domestic work within the household. Even when women are in employment, they continue to carry out a greater share of domestic and caring responsibilities than men.[19] The increased employment of women, combined with their continued role as care givers, leads to a greater chance of women experiencing employment discrimination on grounds of their carer status. In short, the weakening of the 'male breadwinner model' and the rise of the 'dual breadwinner model', poses challenges for employment non-discrimination law.

EU LAW AND DISCRIMINATION ON THE GROUNDS OF BEING A CARER

As a result of the Amsterdam Treaty, the European Community acquired the competence, through Article 13 EC, to take action to address a variety of forms of discrimination. Under the Treaty on the Functioning of the European Union, this article has been renumbered Article 19 TFEU. The Article refers to a closed list of discrimination grounds, namely sex, racial or ethnic origin, religion or belief, disability, age or sexual orientation. Caring status is not mentioned. The Amsterdam Treaty also expanded the Community's competence to act under Article 141 EC (now Article 157 TFEU), to allow it to adopt legislation to address sex discrimination in matters of employment and occupation. These new competences were subsequently used to adopt Directive 2000/78/EC[20] (henceforth: the Employment Equality Directive), covering employment related discrimination on the grounds of religion or belief, disability, age and sexual orientation; Directive 2000/43/EC[21] (henceforth: the Racial Equality Directive); and Directive 2006/54/EC (Recast)[22] relating to gender based employment discrimination. As a result of these directives, direct and indirect discrimination on all 'Article 19 TFEU' grounds is prohibited with regard to employment.

---

[19] *Ibid.*, the table shows the average time spent per week in domestic and family work and in paid employment, in 2005 (by sex), 33.

[20] Directive 2000/78 /EC establishing a general framework for equal treatment in employment and occupation, [2000] O.J. L.303/16 (based on Article 13 EC).

[21] Directive 2000/43/EC implementing the principle of equal treatment of persons irrespective of racial or ethnic origin, [2000] O.J. L.180/22 (based on Article 13 EC).

[22] Directive 2006/54/EC on the implementation of the principle of equal opportunities and equal treatment of men and women in matters of employment and occupation (recast), [2006] O.J. L.204/23 (based on Article 141 EC).

As noted, discrimination on grounds of caring status is not a protected category under EU law. Moreover, the ECJ has already addressed the scope for extending the list of protected grounds through judicial interpretation, and found that only those grounds explicitly mentioned in Article 13 EC (now Article 19 TFEU) and a specific directive are covered by EU law.

In *Chacón Navas*,[23] which concerned adverse treatment on the grounds of sickness, the ECJ was asked to consider whether sickness could be added to the list of protected grounds found in the Employment Equality Directive. In response, the Court noted that the EC Treaty does not prohibit discrimination on grounds of sickness as such,[24] and moreover, since (the then) Article 13 EC did not refer to discrimination on grounds of sickness, it could not constitute a legal basis for Council measures to combat such discrimination.[25] Whilst noting that the general principle of non-discrimination forms part of the fundamental rights on which the general principles of Community law are based, the Court concluded that: 'it does not follow from this that the scope of Directive 2000/78 should be extended by analogy beyond discrimination based on the grounds exhaustively listed in Article 1 thereof.'[26]

As a consequence one can conclude that caring status, also, cannot currently be added to the list of protected grounds found in EU non-discrimination law. Nor can EU law be interpreted as directly prohibiting discrimination on the grounds of caring status.

EU LAW AND DISCRIMINATION BASED ON A CHARACTERISTIC OF THE CARER: GENDER

EU Non-Discrimination Law Relating to Gender

Having established that women are more likely than men to be involved in unpaid care, and that EU law does not prohibit discrimination against carers as such, we will now turn to EU non-discrimination law which addresses gender. In 2006 the EC consolidated (and amended) a number of earlier gender equality directives in Directive 2006/54/EC (henceforth:

---

[23]   Case C-13/05 *Chacón Navas v Eurest Colectividades SA* (Case C-13/05) [2006] ECR 1-6467. For commentary on this case see Waddington (2007).

[24]   *Ibid.*, para 54.

[25]   *Ibid.*, para 55.

[26]   *Ibid.*, para 56.

Recast Directive).[27] As a consequence, Directives 75/117/EEC (equal pay for men and women),[28] 76/207/EEC (equal treatment for men and women as regards access to employment, vocational training and promotion and working conditions),[29] 86/378/EEC (equal treatment for men and women in occupational social security schemes)[30] and 97/80/EC (burden of proof in cases of sex discrimination)[31] have been repealed, and the Recast Directive now implements 'the principle of equal opportunities and equal treatment of men and women in matters of employment and occupation'.

The Recast Directive prohibits direct and indirect discrimination on grounds of sex, harassment related to the sex of a person and sexual harassment. Moreover, it defines less favourable treatment of women related to pregnancy or maternity leave as a form of discrimination.[32] These prohibitions apply with regard to access to employment, including promotion, and to vocational training; working conditions, including pay; and occupational social security schemes.[33] In relation to caring tasks, Recital 11 of the preamble to the Directive notes that 'flexible working time arrangements[34] which enable both men and women to combine family and work commitments more successfully' can be used by the Member States and social partners to address gender-based wage differentials

---

[27]   Directive 2006/54/EC on the implementation of the principle of equal opportunities and equal treatment of men and women in matters of employment and occupation (recast), [2006] O.J. L.204/23.

[28]   Directive 75/117/EEC on the approximation of the laws of the Member States relating to the application of the principle of equal pay for men and women, [1975] O.J. L.45/19.

[29]   Directive 76/2007/EEC on the implementation of the principle of equal treatment for men and women as regards access to employment, vocational training and promotion, and working conditions, [1976] O.J. L.39/40. Directive as amended by Directive 2002/73/EC, [2002] O.J. L.269/15.

[30]   Directive 86/378/EEC on the implementation of the principle of equal treatment for men and women in occupational social security schemes, [1986] O.J. L.225/40.

[31]   Directive 97/80/EC on the burden of proof in cases of discrimination based on sex, [1998] O.J. L.14/ 6 as amended by Directive 98/52/EC, [1988] O.J. L.205/66.

[32]   Art. 2 of the Recast Directive.

[33]   Art. 1 of the Recast Directive. See also Art. 5 (occupational social security schemes) and Art. 14 (employment, vocational training and promotion and working conditions) for further elaboration of the fields in which the prohibition of discrimination applies.

[34]   The Recital goes on to give examples of such arrangements as including 'appropriate parental leave arrangements which could be taken up by either parent as well as the provision of accessible and affordable child-care facilities and care for dependent persons'.

and gender segregation on the labour market. Under Article 21 of the Directive, Member States are to encourage the social partners to promote 'flexible working arrangements, with the aim of facilitating the reconciliation of work and private life'. Specific provisions also address returning from maternity leave, and paternity and adoption leave.[35] However, the problem of discrimination experienced by (female) carers is not explicitly mentioned.

The Recast Directive exists alongside Article 157 TFEU, which has direct effect and provides for the equal pay of men and women. Article 157(4) moreover provides that 'the principle of equal treatment shall not prevent any Member States from maintaining or adopting measures providing for specific advantages in order to make it easier for the underrepresented sex to pursue a vocational activity or prevent or compensate for disadvantages in professional careers'.

Applying EU Gender Non-Discrimination Directives to Carers

Discrimination in employment

Many work-related requirements or practices can place individuals who have domestic caring commitments at a disadvantage. Carers will often need to be available to provide care at set times in the day – typically early in the morning and in the late afternoon, evening and night. Children will often be attending a crèche or school during the middle part of the day, whilst older or disabled people who are dependent on care, may be at day centres or receiving support through social services during this period. Employers can, however, require or request that their employees work outside these 'normal office' hours – either regularly, through shift work, with different shifts working throughout the day and night in the most extreme case, or on an ad hoc basis, with occasional requests for employees for example to work at weekends or in the evenings, or spend nights away from home. Such requirements or expectations can be impossible, or highly difficult, for carers to meet, especially where no respite or support care is available, and where the carer cannot easily share caring tasks with another, as may be the case with a single parent. As a result of this partial lack of availability, employers may decline to hire carers who are not able to work flexible schedules, decline to promote them to more senior positions, or even dismiss them. Moreover, women with caring responsibilities may only be able to work part-time, or in other atypical arrangements, and this is likely to have 'negative conse-

---

[35]   Arts. 15 and 16 respectively of the Recast Directive.

quences in terms of pay, career advancement and accumulated pension rights'.[36]

Research from Australia supports these arguments relating to the employment disadvantages experienced by female carers. Carney[37] has concluded that the inability of mothers to conform to the 'ideal worker' model, which involves workers being 'readily available to work and no consideration need[s] to be given to their lives away from work',[38] has resulted in them experiencing disadvantages. As noted, women often need to work part-time and take career breaks in order to attend to the care of children, and this results in disadvantage in terms of their career progression. Carney regards such disadvantage as 'systemic discrimination',[39] and argues that norms of 'ideal' behaviour are stronger in higher status occupations, meaning that mothers are at a greater risk of becoming excluded from employment within those occupations.

As noted above, given that caring work is disproportionately carried out by women, women are far more likely than men to be disadvantaged in employment by the aforementioned sorts of requirements. However, the gendered nature of caring also implies that work-related requirements that are likely to put carers at a disadvantage, can potentially amount to indirect discrimination on the grounds of sex.

The Recast Directive defines indirect discrimination as occurring:

> where an apparently neutral provision, criterion or practice would put persons of one sex at a particular disadvantage compared with persons of the other sex, unless that provision, criterion or practice is objectively justified by a legitimate aim, and the means of achieving that aim are appropriate and necessary.[40]

Requirements relating to availability for work, which do not single out carers, can clearly potentially amount to such a disadvantage for women who have caring responsibilities. Nevertheless, a 'provision, criterion or practice' which puts female carers at a disadvantage in practice, will be acceptable, and not amount to discrimination, if it meets the justification criteria set out in the Directive. As noted above, this requires that the measure in question must be:

---

[36] European Commission, 2009, 9.

[37] Carney (2009).

[38] Carney (2009, 117) describing the characteristics which make men 'ideal workers'.

[39] One question raised by this assertion relates to the capacity of EU law to address systemic discrimination. Such an issue lies outside of the scope of this paper. However, it seems that EU non-discrimination law is ill equipped to tackle such behaviour.

[40] Art. 2(1)(b) of the Recast Directive.

- objectively justified by a legitimate aim;
- the means of achieving the aim must be appropriate; and
- the means of achieving the aim must be necessary.

As a consequence, where the employer could, for example, excuse the worker from working 'unsocial hours' for the duration of her caring responsibilities, for example, until her children are old enough to be left unsupervised, by requiring that other workers cover such 'hours', then a requirement that she did work those hours could potentially amount to indirect discrimination. In these circumstances, whilst a requirement to work outside normal office hours may be objectively justified by a legitimate aim, and the requirement would be appropriate, it would not be necessary in the case of the individual worker. Clearly an employer with a larger workforce would be more likely than a small employer to have the flexibility and opportunity to excuse a limited number of workers from taking on certain duties or responsibilities, and to allow carers not to be available for work at a time when they need to carry out caring tasks.

The potential value of the prohibition of indirect discrimination to female carers has been revealed by the English case of *London Underground Ltd. v. Edwards (No. 2)* of 1998.[41] Ms Edwards was a train driver who worked for London Underground. The shift system which was in force when she took up her position enabled her to combine work with the care for her child, for whom she was the sole carer. The employer subsequently introduced a new shift system in order to reduce costs and increase efficiency. Under the new shift system Ms Edwards could only continue to work during the daytime, when her child was at school, if she was willing to work longer hours for no increase in pay. She was not prepared to accept such conditions, and resigned from her position and submitted a claim of indirect discrimination. She alleged that the new shift system was harder for single parents to comply with than was the case for other workers, and that the system amounted to indirect sex discrimination, given that women were far more likely than men to be single parents.

The case was considered and appealed before three tribunals and courts, and was finally heard in the Court of Appeal. Ms Edwards was successful before all three courts, but their reasoning was not identical. Ultimately the case turned on whether the new shift system created requirements which 'is such that the proportion of women who can comply with it is considerably smaller than the proportion of men who can comply with

---

[41]   *London Underground Ltd v. Edwards* [1999] ICR 494 (CA).

it'.[42] London Underground employed 2,023 male train drivers, all of whom could comply with the new requirements, and 21 female train drivers, of which one (Ms Edwards) or possibly two, could not comply. The employer argued that the proportion of women who could comply (92.5 per cent) was not 'considerably smaller' than the percentage of men who could comply (100 per cent). However, neither the Employment Appeal Tribunal nor the Court of Appeal accepted this argument.

Addressing this point, Potter LJ of the Court of Appeal found that:

> The figure of 100 men for every 1 woman indicated that it was either difficult or unattractive for women to work as train operators. Thus a condition which made it even more difficult for women to perform or continue such work was of particular significance. They [the Industrial Tribunal LW] were also entitled to take into account their own knowledge and experience that the burden of child care falls upon many more women than men and that a far greater proportion of single parents with care of children are women rather than men.[43]

Simon Brown LJ concurred, finding that

> it would seem to me wrong to ignore entirely the striking fact here that not a single man was disadvantaged by this requirement despite the vast preponderance of men within the group. Looked at in the round, this requirement clearly bore disproportionately as between men and women, even though only one woman was affected by it.[44]

The Court found that the employer could not justify the requirement, especially since it had, in principle, been willing to negotiate special arrangements for single parents with the trade union.[45] However, had the employer been able to justify the need to apply its new shift system to all workers, including single parents, in line with the requirements found in UK law (which are based on the aforementioned justification criteria found in EU law), Ms Edwards would not have been successful in her claim. Herein lies the weakness of a claim of indirect discrimination: even where it is established that a measure 'indirectly discriminates' against a group of women, or another covered group, the employer can still refer to an objective justification[46] which allows it to 'trump' any claim of discrimination, and continue with the measure.

---

[42]   This was a requirement for the establishment of indirect discrimination against women under the Sex Discrimination Act s. 1(1)(b).

[43]   Para. 20(i) and (ii) of the judgment.

[44]   *Ibid.*, para. 49.

[45]   However, such negotiations did not result in agreement, and no such special arrangements were ultimately made.

[46]   Leading to a measure that is also appropriate and necessary.

The measure at issue here related to flexible working time requirements and the obligation to work 'unsocial hours'. As noted above, these are exactly the kind of employment-related requirements which are most likely to disadvantage carers and, as evidenced here, single carers in particular. The case also reveals the potential protection offered to female carers by the prohibition of indirect discrimination, even in cases where the difference between the number of men who can comply with any requirement and the number of women seems to be comparatively small. However, whilst women are more likely than men to seek to combine care and paid employment, some men do take on such roles. A man finding himself in the position of Ms Edwards would not have been able to bring a claim of indirect sex discrimination, although he would have been entitled to claim equal treatment to any female single parents, should the employer have decided to make special arrangements for them.

Whilst it is likely that most adverse treatment experienced by female carers will potentially amount to indirect discrimination, it is also possible that an employer will directly discriminate against female carers. For example, an employer may decline to hire mothers of young children based on the assumption that they will be unreliable and less committed to their work than fathers of young children. Such action would clearly amount to direct sex discrimination, involving one person being treated 'less favourably on grounds of sex than another is, has been or would be treated in a comparable situation'.[47] However, where both male and female carers receive equally bad treatment, then a possible claim of indirect discrimination only remains open to female carers. This is a consequence of the failure of EU law to explicitly protect carers from discrimination.

Positive action in employment and benefits for female carers

EU law allows Member States the room to maintain or adopt measures 'providing for specific advantages in order to make it easier for the underrepresented sex to pursue a vocational activity or to prevent or compensate for disadvantages in professional careers'. This provision is found in Article 157(4) TFEU (and formerly, as of the Amsterdam Treaty, in Article 141(4) EC), with a similar provision included in the Recast Directive.[48] Previously 'positive action' with regard to sex was provided for in the (now repealed) Equal Treatment Directive (76/207/EEC).

---

[47]   Art. 2(1)(a) Recast Directive.
[48]   Article 3, which reads 'Member States may maintain or adopt measures within the meaning of Article 141(4) of the Treaty with a view to ensuring full equality in practice between men and women in working life'.

Article 2(4) of that Directive, which has been the subject of a number of rulings of the ECJ, provided that '[t]his Directive shall be without prejudice to measures to promote equal opportunity for men and women, in particular by removing existing inequalities which affect women's opportunities . . .'.

The ECJ considered the scope for positive action under Article 2(4) in Case C-476/99 *Lommers*.[49] At issue was a measure which gave priority when allocating subsidised nursery places to the children of female employees, in a situation in which women were significantly under-represented within the relevant government ministry (the employer) and where there was a shortage of available nursery places. Only those men who found themselves in an 'emergency' situation, e.g. single male parents, were to have equal access to women to the nursery places. The ECJ found that this preference did not fall foul of Article 2(4) of the Equal Treatment Directive. The measure was regarded as helping to tackle the extensive under-representation of women within the Ministry,[50] since women were more likely than men to give up work in order to care for their children where no alternative suitable care arrangements could be made.[51]

The Court acknowledged that such a scheme 'might nevertheless also help to perpetuate a traditional division of roles between men and women',[52] and seemed to feel that a preferable option would have been to allow both male and female employees to access subsidised nursery care. Indeed, in principle, the exclusion of men from the scheme breached the proportionality principle.[53] However in a situation such as at issue, where a shortage of nursery places existed and female workers were already significantly under-represented amongst the employer's staff, the Court felt the decision to target female employees, whose careers were more likely to be adversely affected when childcare was not available, was justified.[54]

---

[49] Case C-476/99 *Lommers v. Ministerie van Landbouw* [2002] ECR I-2891.
[50] *Ibid.*, para 50.
[51] *Ibid.*, para 37.
[52] *Ibid.*, para 41.
[53] *Ibid.*, para 42.
[54] With regard to childcare provisions see also Council recommendation 92/241/EEC of 31 March 1992 on childcare [1992] O.J. L. 123/16, and the agreement reached at the Barcelona European Council that, by 2010, Member States should provide childcare for at least 90 per cent of children between 3 years old and the mandatory school age, and at least 33 per cent of children under 3 years of age. In 2009 most Member States had not met these targets, see European Commission, 2009.

One can conclude that the provisions in Article 157(4) TFEU and the Recast Directive similarly allow for scarce resources, such as subsidised childcare places, to be directed towards female carers in preference to male carers, where women are under-represented in a particular category or field of employment. Such measures could complement other adaptations made to accommodate (female) carers, such as being excused from having to work certain 'unsocial' hours. Whilst the latter measures, where they are regarded as being necessary to avoid a situation of indirect discrimination against certain women (i.e. women with caring tasks), would also have to be extended to men in a similar position (i.e. comparable caring tasks), this is not necessarily the case for positive action measures. Where the positive action measures in question are designed to make it easier 'for the under-represented sex to pursue a vocational activity or to prevent or compensate for disadvantages in professional careers' then it is only necessary that members of the 'under-represented sex' are targeted.[55]

EU LAW AND DISCRIMINATION BASED ON A CHARACTERISTIC OF THE CARER – PART-TIME WORKER STATUS

Directive 97/81[56] prohibits discrimination against part-time workers. This Directive is important in the present context because the need to provide unpaid care prompts many women to work part-time.[57] In the words of a European Commission report: 'Although part-time and other flexible working arrangements may reflect personal preferences, the unequal share of domestic and family responsibilities leads more women than men to opt for such arrangements.'[58] In 2007 31.2 per cent of women employed in the

---

[55] Although, in line with the *Lommers* judgment, when a positive action measure favours female carers, men in particularly disadvantaged or exceptional circumstances would also need to be given access where appropriate.

[56] Directive 97/81/EC concerning the framework agreement on part-time work concluded by UNICE, CEEP and the ETUC, [1998] O.J. L. 14/9.

[57] For information on the connection between motherhood and part-time work see Carney (2009) writing in the Australian context. See also the ECJ's judgment in Case C-243/95 *Kathleen Hill and Ann Stapleton* v. *Revenue Commissioners* [1998] ECR I-9383, in which the Court states that most of the women who chose to job share did so 'in order to be able to combine work and family responsibilities which invariably involve caring for children', paras 41–2, cited in Barnard (2006, 463).

[58] European Commission, 2009, 8.

European Union worked part-time, compared to only 7.7 per cent of men. Women were most likely to work part-time in the Netherlands, where 75 per cent of women in employment worked part-time.[59]

Prior to the adoption of Directive 97/81, women who combined caring and part-time work had to rely on the prohibition of indirect sex discrimination if they felt they experienced discrimination as a result of their part-time worker status,[60] whilst men who worked part-time were, in principle, left without any remedy. In Case C-285/02 *Elsner-Lakeberg*,[61] the Court found that Article 141 EC (now Article 157 TFEU) (and the now repealed Equal Pay Directive) were capable of providing protection from discrimination to female part-time workers in certain circumstances. Ms Elsner-Lakeberg worked part-time as a teacher. The regional Civil Service Code, which regulated her working arrangements, provided that teachers who worked three hours or more in a month above their regular contractual hours, were entitled to compensation for the overtime worked. Lesser amounts of overtime did not result in any compensation. The 'three hour rule' applied to both full-time and part-time workers. Ms Elsner-Lakeburg's worked 2.5 hours overtime in a set month, and, in line with the Civil Service Code, her request for additional compensation relating to this work was refused. She challenged this decision before the courts, and a preliminary reference was made to the ECJ regarding the compatibility of the rule in the Civil Service Code with Article 141 EC and the Equal Pay Directive. The Court found that 'three additional hours is in fact a greater burden for part-time teachers than it is for full-time teachers',[62] and that '[s]ince the number of additional teaching hours giving entitlement to pay is not reduced for part-time teachers in a manner proportionate to their working hours, they receive different treatment compared to full-time teachers as regards pay for additional teaching hours'.[63] Turning to the issue of indirect sex discrimination, the Court found that if the rule which disadvantaged part-time workers affected considerably more women than men, and if there existed no objective justification unrelated to sex, or if the different treatment was not necessary to achieve the objective pursued, then the measure breached Article 141 EC and the Equal Pay Directive. It was for the national court to make such an assessment.

---

[59]   European Commission, 2009, see table: 'Share of part-time workers in total employment (persons aged 15 and over) in EU Member States – 2007', 20.

[60]   See Traversa (2003).

[61]   Case C-285/02 *Edeltraud Elsner-Lakeberg v. Land Nordrhein Westfalen* [2004] ECR I-5861.

[62]   *Ibid.*, para 17.

[63]   *Ibid.*

Today Directive 97/81 confers rights on part-time workers as such, including the right to non-discrimination. Part-time workers are defined as workers 'whose normal hours of work, calculated on a weekly basis or on average over a period of employment of up to one year, are less than the normal hours of a comparable full-time worker'.[64] Clause 4 of the Directive provides that:

1. In respect of employment conditions, part-time workers shall not be treated in a less favourable manner than comparable full-time workers solely because they work part-time unless different treatment is justified on objective grounds.

    Where appropriate, the principle of *pro rata temporis* shall apply.

As Barnard has noted, whilst the Directive marked a step forward, as discrimination on the ground of being a part-time worker was now prohibited, it also allowed for different treatment to be justified on (unspecified) objective grounds.[65] Therefore, unlike most of the 'Article 19 TFEU' grounds,[66] different (adverse) treatment directly based on the ground of being a part-time worker can be objectively justified.[67] Moreover, as Gerards has noted, most Member States seek to achieve equal treatment for part-time workers by means other than through non-discrimination legislation, for example by concluding collective agreements or amending or supplementing existing employment legislation. She notes that only a limited number of Member States have extended their non-discrimination legislation explicitly to cover part-time workers.[68] At the time this chapter was completed, ECJ case law explicitly addressing this matter under the Directive was still absent.[69]

---

[64]   Clause 3(1).

[65]   Barnard (2006, 477).

[66]   Some national legislation also allows for a, *de facto*, objective justification test in the case of alleged instances of direct discrimination on the ground of age. See also Article 6 of the Employment Equality Directive.

[67]   Barnard (2006, 478).

[68]   Gerards (2007, 155).

[69]   But see reference for a preliminary ruling from the Landesgericht Innsbruck (Austria) lodged on 12 November 2008 – *Zentralbetriebsrat der Landeskrankenhauser Tirols v. Land Tirol* (Case C-486/08) and reference for a preliminary ruling from the Corte d'appello di Roma (Italy) lodged on 12 September 2008 – *Istituto nazionale della previdenza sociale (INPS) v. Tiziana Bruno and Massimo Pettini* (Case C-395/08).

EU LAW AND DISCRIMINATION BASED ON A CHARACTERISTIC OF THE RECIPIENT OF CARE: DISABILITY AND AGE

EU Non-Discrimination Law

As noted above, since 1999 the European Union has had the competence to take action to combat discrimination based not only on sex, but also racial or ethnic origin, religion or belief, disability, age and sexual orientation. In 2000 the European Community adopted Directive 2000/43/EC implementing the principle of equal treatment between persons irrespective of racial or ethnic origin, and Directive 2000/78/EC establishing a general framework for equal treatment in employment and occupation. The latter Directive prohibits employment-related discrimination on the grounds of religion or belief, disability, age or sexual orientation. Both Directives prohibit direct and indirect discrimination, harassment and an instruction to discriminate.[70] Common definitions of these concepts are shared by the 2000 Directives and the Recast Directive, and these will be explored below in more detail. Both Directives also prohibit discrimination with regard to conditions of employment; vocational guidance and training; employment and working conditions; and membership and involvement in an organisation of workers or employers or professional organisation.[71]

Given that individuals are most likely to need care as a result of their age (dependent younger and elderly people) or because of a severe disability, the Employment Equality Directive is of most interest with regard to establishing levels of protection from discrimination experienced by carers. Recital 6 of the preamble to this Directive refers to the Community Charter of the Fundamental Social Rights of Workers, which recognises the importance of combating every form of discrimination, including the need to take appropriate action for the social and economic integration of elderly and disabled people. No explicit references are made to the situation of workers who also provide care to young, elderly or disabled people in the Directive. Nevertheless, as will be explored in the next section, in *Coleman* the ECJ held that a carer who experienced employment discrimination on the grounds that she cared for her disabled child, was able to rely on the protection provided by the Employment Equality Directive.

---

[70]   Art. 2 of both Directives.

[71]   Art. 3 of both Directives. In addition, the Racial Equality Directive covers social protection, including social security and healthcare; social advantages; education; and access to and supply of goods and services which are available to the public, including housing.

Applying the Employment Equality Directive to Carers

Discrimination by association and carers: *Coleman*[72]

Sharon Coleman worked as a legal secretary, and was the mother of a disabled child who required specialised care. She alleged that, on returning to work after having given birth to her child, she was treated less favourably than other employees in comparable positions because she was the primary carer of a child with a disability. She made a number of allegations of adverse treatment, including that she was not allowed to return to her original job following her maternity leave, whilst parents of non-disabled children were allowed to do this; she was not allowed the same flexibility regarding her working hours as parents of non-disabled children; she was described as 'lazy' for requesting time off to care for her child, and was threatened with dismissal when she occasionally arrived late because of the need to care for her child, when parents of non-disabled children were not treated in this way; and that highly abusive comments were made about her and her child. Ultimately Ms Coleman accepted voluntary redundancy, and subsequently lodged a claim before a UK Employment Tribunal that she had been the victim of direct discrimination and harassment because she was the primary carer of a disabled child.

As noted, the Employment Equality Directive prohibits direct discrimination and harassment on the grounds of religion or belief, disability, age or sexual orientation. Protection is not explicitly confined to individuals who possess these grounds or characteristics themselves, and Ms Coleman argued that, by virtue of using this language, the Directive prohibited 'associative discrimination' with regard to direct discrimination and harassment, and that the relevant British legislation[73] should also be interpreted in this way. The Employment Tribunal concluded that guidance from the European Court of Justice was required on this matter in order for it to proceed,[74] and forwarded a number of preliminary references which, in essence, asked whether the Employment Equality Directive prohibited direct discrimination and harassment against employees who, although not themselves disabled, are subject to the less favourable treatment on the grounds that they associate with a person who is disabled.

In its judgment, the Court began by recalling the purpose of the Directive, which it found to be 'to combat all forms of discrimination

---

[72] Case C-303/06 *Coleman v. Attridge Law* [2009] ECR I-5603. Parts of the text which follows are based on Waddington (2009).

[73] The Disability Discrimination Act 1995, as amended.

[74] Employment Tribunal, Case Number 2303745/2005, 17 February 2006.

on grounds of disability' with regard to employment and occupation.[75] Following its Advocate General, it noted that the 'principle of equal treatment . . . applies not to a particular category of person but by reference to the grounds mentioned in Article 1'.[76] However, the Court went on to note that some provisions of the Directive, and specifically Article 5 relating to reasonable accommodation and Article 7(2) addressing health and safety at work and positive action,[77] did only apply to disabled people. This had led some of the Member States[78] which intervened in the case to argue that the prohibition of direct discrimination contained in the Directive could also only be relied on by individuals who were themselves disabled. However, the Court distinguished such disability specific measures from the general scope of the protection provided by the Directive,[79] and held that the existence of such measures could not lead to the conclusion that the protection from discrimination provided by the Directive as a whole should also be confined to people who actually had a disability themselves.

The Court then addressed a second argument raised by some Member States:[80] that, in light of the Court's earlier judgment in *Chacón Navas*, the concept of disability should be interpreted very strictly. In response, the Court acknowledged that it had held that the personal scope of the Directive could not be extended beyond the grounds enumerated in the Directive and Article 13 EC (now Article 19 TFEU) in *Chacón Navas*. However, it stressed that, in that case, it had not held that the grounds that were covered by the Directive had to be interpreted strictly.[81]

The Court continued by considering the argument that the objectives and effectiveness of the Directive would be undermined if someone in Ms Coleman's position could not rely on the prohibition of direct discrimination. The Court recalled that Ms Coleman alleged that she suffered less favourable treatment on the ground of disability, and noted once again that the Directive functions by reference to the covered grounds, and not with regard to a particular category of person. The Court concluded that, when an employee suffers direct discrimination on the grounds of disability, an interpretation of the Directive which limited its application only to

---

75 Case C-303/06, para 38.
76 *Ibid.*
77 In the context of positive action, Article 7(2) refers to measures aimed at creating or maintaining provisions or facilities for safeguarding or promoting the integration of disabled persons into the working environment.
78 United Kingdom, Greece, Italy and the Netherlands.
79 *Coleman v. Attridge Law* [2009] ECRI-5603, para 42.
80 United Kingdom, Italy and the Netherlands.
81 *Coleman v. Attridge Law* [2009] ECRI-5603, paras 44–47.

people who had a disability themselves 'is liable to deprive that directive of an important element of its effectiveness and to reduce the protection which it is intended to guarantee'.[82]

Turning to the matter of harassment by association, the Court applied a similar line of reasoning as with regard to direct discrimination, and concluded its judgment by ruling that the protection from direct discrimination and harassment found in the Employment Equality Directive is not limited to people who are themselves disabled, but also applies when an employer directly discriminates against or harasses an employee, where that discrimination or harassment is based on the disability of the employee's child, whose care is provided primarily by the employee.

Applying *Coleman*: the value of prohibiting discrimination by association for carers

Direct and indirect discrimination by association, and carers   Based on the *Coleman* judgment, one can conclude that the Employment Equality Directive prohibits direct discrimination and harassment against carers on the grounds that the person they care for has a disability or, by implication, on the ground of the age of the person they care for. However, the behaviour which Ms Coleman alleged that she experienced was particularly brazen, and it is doubtful if most adverse treatment experienced by carers will fall into this category. As noted above in the context of gender, adverse treatment experienced by carers is more likely to be regarded potentially as a form of 'indirect discrimination'. Requirements relating to flexible working time, including availability for shift work or work during unsocial hours, are not expressly addressed to carers, but they can be more difficult for carers to comply with, than for those without such domestic commitments. As a consequence, such requirements can be regarded as an 'apparently neutral provision, criterion or practice' which puts workers who also care for individuals with 'a particular disability, a particular age ... at a particular disadvantage compared with other persons'. Indeed, some of the treatment which Ms Coleman alleged she experienced, such as punishment for arriving late and being refused permission to take time off work, would, in other circumstances also be regarded as 'indirect', where that treatment was not directly related to her caring tasks but the objective fact of late arrival or limited availability. The employer's alleged behaviour only became direct discrimination, because it was explicitly linked to the disability of Ms Coleman's child.

---

[82]   *Ibid.*, para 51.

Assuming that most adverse treatment experienced by carers will be of the nature described above (that is, requirements relating to flexible working time which cannot be complied with), and therefore only be 'indirectly' related to the age or disability of the person they care for, does the Employment Equality Directive also prohibit indirect discrimination by association?

In *Coleman* the Court did not address indirect discrimination by association. However, an initial reading of the Employment Equality Directive appears to suggest that it does not protect people from indirect discrimination on the grounds that they associate with someone with a disability or particular age. The Employment Equality Directive defines indirect discrimination as occurring where 'an apparently neutral provision, criterion or practice would put persons having . . . a particular disability . . . at a particular disadvantage compared with other persons . . .'. The definition therefore seems to provide protection from indirect discrimination only for 'persons having . . . a particular disability . . .' who are disadvantaged. As a consequence, it seems difficult to argue that an individual who is disadvantaged not because they have a disability, but because someone they associate with has a disability, is protected from indirect discrimination as a result of this association under EU law. Such protection would only be possible if, 'persons having . . . a particular disability' could be interpreted as including 'persons who associate with persons having a particular disability'.

In *Coleman*, Advocate General Poiares Maduro also noted the difference between, on the one hand, the prohibitions of direct discrimination and harassment, and, on the other, indirect discrimination in his Opinion. He concluded that, in the case of direct discrimination and harassment, there is a 'necessary relationship' between the adverse treatment and the 'suspect classification', with the covered ground being the direct motivating factor for the adverse treatment. He argued that the Directive prohibits the use of those classifications or grounds as a basis for any employment-related decision. He contrasted this situation with that existing under indirect discrimination, which involves apparently neutral measures which have a (usually) unintentional negative impact on members of the covered group.

> [W]hile the prohibition of direct discrimination and harassment operates as an exclusionary mechanism (by excluding from an employer's reasoning reliance on certain grounds) the prohibition of indirect discrimination operates as an inclusionary mechanism (by obliging employers to take into account and accommodate the needs of individuals with certain characteristics).[83]

---

[83] Opinion of Advocate General Poiares Maduro, delivered 31 January 2008, Case C-303/06 *Coleman v. Attridge Law* [2009] ECRI-5603, para 19.

He concluded that, even if one were to accept that this implied that discrimination by association fell outside the scope of the Directive with regard to indirect discrimination,[84] this did not mean this was also true in the case of direct discrimination and harassment. In contrast, interpreting these forms of discrimination as including a prohibition on discrimination by association 'is the natural consequence of the exclusionary mechanism through which the prohibition of this type of discrimination operates'.[85]

Whilst the Court did not reflect on the status of indirect discrimination in its judgment, it did make a strict separation between those Articles which cover only disabled people, such as Article 5 and Article 7(2), and those provisions which address discrimination 'on the grounds of disability', where the focus was on the characteristic which led to the disadvantage, rather than on whether the claimant actually possessed that characteristic. This may suggest that the Court also interprets protection from indirect discrimination as being confined to persons with a disability. However, the reasons given for restricting the benefits of Articles 5 and 7 to people who have a disability do not seem to apply in the context of indirect discrimination,[86] and the Court was silent on this issue.

Taking the opposing position, one could argue that the Court should, given the opportunity, interpret the prohibition of indirect discrimination as covering those who experience discrimination on the grounds that they associate with a disabled person or a child or elderly person (who they care for) – on the basis that this would be in line with the broad purpose of the Directives, even though it would not be in accordance with a literal interpretation of the wording. However, this would probably be a rather 'ambitious' interpretation by the Court. Nevertheless, in light of the Court's silence on the matter, it remains unresolved.

In conclusion, it seems unlikely that indirect discrimination by association is prohibited by the Employment Equality Directives or, indeed, other EU non-discrimination directives.

Finding a comparator carer   EU non-discrimination law requires that the person alleging discrimination is compared to another person. As a consequence, in order to establish direct discrimination, it must be shown[87]

---

[84]   As the United Kingdom government had argued. *Ibid.*, para 19.
[85]   *Ibid.*, para 19.
[86]   Unless one could argue that extending indirect discrimination to cover individuals who associate with others who possess one of the covered characteristics would prove to be disproportionate.
[87]   Subject to the rules relating to the burden of proof in cases of alleged discrimination.

that one person 'is treated less favourably than another is, has been or would be treated in a comparable situation'. Whilst the last phrase 'would be treated' opens the door to 'hypothetical comparators', an individual will clearly be able to make a much stronger case if they can refer to a real person in a comparable situation who has received better treatment.

One can wonder how often a carer alleging direct discrimination will be able to identify an appropriate comparator. Whilst Ms Coleman was in the fortunate position of having a good set of comparators, namely parents of young children without disabilities who, presumably, were equivalently affected by their caring responsibilities and who allegedly received better treatment at the hands of their employer, it is doubtful if most carers will be in this position. If Ms Coleman had needed, for example, more time off work than parents of non-disabled children, and this was because of the disability of her child, her situation could have been very different. In such a case the employer could have argued that Ms Coleman was not in a comparable position to other parents, and that any employee who took so much time off work would have been sanctioned. It would be left to a court to determine how far workers were in a comparable position, and how far the characteristics of the recipients of care, and the level of care needed, were comparable and, ultimately, if the facts justified a claim of direct discrimination at all.

In looking for a suitable comparator, carers who allege direct discrimination based on the characteristic of the person they care for must bear a number of things in mind. They will have to seek to compare themselves with someone else with caring responsibilities who receives better treatment because the person they care for has a different characteristic (such as lack of disability, a different age) and this difference is the reason for the different treatment. It is questionable how often such a scenario can be envisaged. Instead, employers may treat all carers with equal (in)tolerance and not seek to distinguish on the basis of the characteristics of the recipients of care. For example, it seems unlikely that employers frequently will treat parents of disabled children more badly than parents of non-disabled children, with regard to making allowance for caring tasks, although this may well have been what happened to Ms Coleman.

As was noted above in the context of gender discrimination, where an employer treats all carers equally badly, irrespective of, for example, the disability or lack of disability of the person they care for; the age of the person they care for; or the fact that the individual is caring for a heterosexual or homosexual partner, then no direct claim of discrimination is possible. However, a claim of indirect sex discrimination may be an option for female carers in such a situation.

CONCLUSION

Although the prohibition of (employment related) discrimination is a key element within the European Social Model, the discrimination experienced by carers has attracted no explicit attention at the legislative level[88] or, it seems, within the various (soft-law) instruments and publications adopted by the Community. Instead the focus within the latter is on the 'reconciliation of professional and private life' and 'striking the right balance between work and home lives'.[89] Rather, it has been left to the courts, at both the European and the national level, to address employment discrimination experienced by carers in an ad hoc manner, and through the prohibition of discrimination on grounds that are not explicitly related to the status of carer. In spite of some interesting and positive developments within case law,[90] it seems that discrimination and adverse treatment experienced by carers is worthy of a more focused and structured attention from European policy makers. This issue may become even more topical in light of the ongoing economic crisis. As national and local authorities cut back expenditure, it is likely that care and support services, both in the form of subsidised childcare places and care provided to dependent adults, will suffer, placing an even greater burden on family and friends in terms of unpaid and informal care giving.

Turning to the legislation and case law examined in this chapter, the headline-grabbing *Coleman* case has focused attention on the situation of carers who experience employment discrimination, at least amongst the media. However, it has been argued here that female carers are far more likely to be able to bring a successful claim of discrimination related to

---

[88] With the possible exception of the part-time work and fixed-term work directives – however, neither of these explicitly protect carers from discrimination.

[89] Both quotations are taken from European Commission, 2007. The introduction to the report refers to 'eliminating disincentives for women and men to enter and remain on the labour market', and refers to approaches which can facilitate this: working-time patterns, work organisation, flexibility of the workplace, crèches, after-school activities, care for the elderly and other dependents and tax incentives. Addressing discrimination experienced by carers who are also in employment is not mentioned at all (p. 5). In the same strain, Article 33(2) of the Charter of Fundamental Rights provides: To reconcile family and professional life, everyone shall have the right to protection for dismissal for a reason connected with maternity and the right to paid maternity leave and to parental leave following the birth or adoption of a child.

[90] It is worth noting that, in spite of arguing that the *Coleman* judgment is unlikely to lead to greater protection from discrimination for most carers, the author does regard the recognition, and protection from, 'discrimination by association' by the ECJ, as a very positive development.

their status as carers if they rely on the long-standing EU law prohibition of indirect sex discrimination. Such a claim would remain subject to the justification test provided for in cases of indirect discrimination. Bringing a successful claim of discrimination by association, and thereby following in the footsteps of Ms Coleman, presents many challenges. Firstly, as EU law currently stands, such a claim can only be brought with regard to direct discrimination and harassment – whereas it has been argued here that most adverse treatment experienced by carers is likely to be regarded as a potential form of indirect discrimination. Moreover, such a claim would involve the identification of a 'comparator' carer who is receiving better treatment. However, the reality may be that employers may not choose to differentiate between carers or will differentiate, but on the basis of factors such as availability for work, which is not a characteristic directly related to an attribute of either the carer or the recipient of the care. Lastly, examining the question from another perspective, it seems EU law allows Member States the freedom to permit employers to provide positive action measures targeted at female carers in order to facilitate their employment.

REFERENCES

Alders, M. and I. Esveldt (2004), 'Zorg boor hulpdehoevende ouders', *Bevolkingstrends*, 3rd quarter, 75.

Barnard, C. (2006), *EC Employment Law*, 3rd edn, Oxford: Oxford University Press.

Carney, T. (2009), 'The Employment Disadvantage of Mothers: Evidence of Systemic Discrimination', *Journal of Industrial Relations*, **51**(1), 113–130.

Centraal Bureau voor de Statistiek (Nederland) (2005), Personen van 25–49 jaar naar vaste zorgdagen voor de kinderen.

Centraal Bureau voor de Statistiek (Nederland) (2005), Personen van 25–49 jaar met vaste zorgdagen naar aantal zorguren voor de kinderen.

Centraal Bureau voor de Statistiek (Nederland) (2005), Personen van 25–64 jaar naar mantelzorg.

Centraal Bureau voor de Statistiek (Nederland) (2005), Personen van 25–64 jaar naar aantal uren mantelzorg.

Crompton, R. (2001), 'Gender Restructuring, Employment, and Caring', *Social Politics*, Fall, 266–290.

Drew, Eileen P. (2000), 'Reconciling Divisions of Labour', in S. Duncan and B. Pfau-Effinger (eds), *Gender, Economy and Culture in the European Union*, London and New York: Routledge Research in Gender and Society, pp. 87–112.

European Commission (2007), *Reconciliation of Professional and Private Life: Exchange of Good Practice*, Luxembourg: Office for Official Publications of the European Communities.

European Commission (2009), *A Comparative Review of 30 European Countries,*

European Commission's Expert Group on Gender and Employment Issues (EGGE), Luxembourg: Office for Official Publications of the European Communities.

Eurostat/European Commission (2004), *Living Conditions in Europe, Statistical Pocketbook, Data 1998–2002*, 2003 edition, Office for Official Publications of the European Community.

Gerards, J. (2007), 'Discrimination Grounds', in D. Schiek, L. Waddington and M. Bell (eds), *Cases, Materials and Text on National, Supranational and International Non-Discrimination Law*, Oxford and Portland, Oregon: Hart Publishing.

Souren, Martijn (2006), 'Vijftigers meest belast met mantelzorg', *Webmagazine*, Centraal Bureau voor de Statistiek.

Traversa, E. (2003), 'Protection of Part-time Workers in the Case Law of the Court of Justice of the European Communities', *International Journal of Comparative Labour Law and Industrial Relations*, **19** (2), 219–241.

Waddington, L. (2007), 'Case C-13/05, *Chacón Navas v. Eurest Colectividades SA*, Judgment of the Grand Chamber of 11 July 2006', *Common Market Law Review*, **44** (2), 487–499.

Waddington, L. (2009), 'Case C-303/06, *S. Coleman v. Attridge Law and Steve Law*, Judgment of the Grand Chamber of the Court of Justice of 17 July 2008', *Common Market Law Review*, **46** (2), 665–681.

8. Gender and 'plastic' citizenship in European social law

Anna-Maria Konsta

INTRODUCTION

This chapter offers a critical discussion of European social law from a gender perspective. The notion of plastic citizenship is developed. A process of transsubjectivation occurs in Foucaultian terms, which means a kind of transformation of the subject that can produce a new self. This transsubjectivation might be called plasticity.

Plastic citizenship creates plastic subjectivities for women in Europe today. In order to prove this thesis, selected European Union social policy areas – such as multiple discrimination, working time and migration policy – are treated to critical discussion. The relevant legal framework constructs the unprivileged legal subject in Europe today. The unprivileged legal subject is the bearer of rights and obligations provided by the plastic citizenship notion; a citizenship that is fluid and flexible, it changes according to the interests and needs of the states involved in each law-making process.

THEORETICAL CONTEXT

Hannah Arendt (1951) defines citizenship as the right to have rights. Thus, citizenship is a prerequisite for the enjoyment of human rights (*ibid.*). The condition of the excluded is defined by Arendt as 'statelessness'. And Sommers has established that today 'statelessness' does not mean only non-membership in a national community, but is applied also to the excluded (the poor, the unemployed), and that *de jure* citizenship does not automatically imply *de facto* citizenship (Sommers, 2008, 26–27). Giorgio Agamben makes the distinction between People (political body) and people (excluded bodies). The erasure of this division can restore humanity to those who are excluded and denied citizenship (Agamben, 1998, 177, 180). Jo Shaw views citizenship as 'full membership of any given community or polity', which means not only 'formal membership', but also 'practical access to the benefits of membership' (Shaw, 2007a, 18–20).

This broader conception of citizenship allows us to reflect on the concept of subjectivity.

A contemporary, differentiated, legal subjecthood, in a Member State (MS) and a European Union (EU) context opens the doors to political, economic, social and legal relations of great complexity which could be characterized by individuals whose legal status may become more and more differentiated from the so-called 'neutral', but predominantly 'male' legal subject of positive law.

In this context, recent European Union legislation on Equality and Non-discrimination goes beyond the boundaries of traditional citizenship rights, which are reserved only to EU and MS nationals and needs to take into account the transcultural legal subject, the bearer of rights and obligations deriving from various legal systems and legal cultures (see in relation to mobile subjects who respond to dynamic borderless market conditions, Ong, 1999). Women are often victims of multiple discrimination on the grounds of sex, race, ethnicity, religion, beliefs, economic or social status. The predominant role of economic migration in Europe today requires a new conception of citizenship rights and a proper institutionalization of the so-called European social citizenship (Magnusson and Stråth, 2004).

Migrant women enjoy a transnational subjectivity and a multiple belonging. For instance, migrant women may be transnational mothers, dividing their time between one site and country in which they work, and another in which they share time and space with family members. This mobility may be possible and at the same time limited by legal regulation.

EU migration law, arrayed in the ceremonial mantle of security considerations, is hostile towards migrants from non-EU countries, and it undermines the hesitant emergence of a European social citizenship (Marshall, 1950), or the future emergence of an automatic or ascriptive citizenship for all resident non-nationals in the Member States of the European Union (Rubio-Marin, 2000; Shaw, 2007b) which would encompass migrants as well (Kymlicka, 1995, 2000; Soysal, 1994). Instead, a plastic citizenship emerges, a citizenship that is fluid and flexible, easily altered by public authorities.

Malabou (2004) explains the concept of plasticity as follows:

> The subject is not supple and soft, and it is not rigid either; it is something in between. The subject is 'plastic'. The dictionary defines 'plastic' as having the property of being fluid but also resisting. Once formed, it cannot go back to its original state. For example, when the sculptor is working on the marble,

the marble, once sculpted, cannot be brought back to its original state. So, plasticity is a very interesting concept, because it means, at once, both openess to all kinds of influences, and resistance. (Vahanian 2008, 6)

As Benson (2006, 42) notes in reference to the word 'plastic' (*plastisch* in German):

Before it came to refer only to a cheap and brittle man-made material, this word had a long history in art criticism, where it referred to a sculptural style of moulded and solid forms, in contrast to a 'painterly' style of surface textures. In German, Malabou notes, the word can mean both 'capable of shaping' and 'capable of being shaped'. It thus expresses both the active and passive aspects of shaping.

The subject is plastic, not elastic, it never returns to its original form, it may be shaped, but in the process of being shaped, it undergoes a sort of transformation into something new. In Foucaultian terms, a process of trans-subjectivation of the subject occurs (Foucault 2004, 214), which can produce a new self. Plasticity might be the name of this trans-subjectivation (Vahanian 2008, 5).

According to Malabou, contemporary neurobiology offers a new perspective on subjectivity. It creates the so-called 'neuronal subject'. Malabou (2004, 6) adds:

In fact, the concept of 'plasticity' . . . characterizes a certain kind of organization, that of the system. Between the system of absolute knowledge or of absolute subjectivity in Hegel and the nervous system in neurobiology, the difference is not so dramatic. It is the same model of being, the same functioning, the same economy.

Plasticity is revealed in the European Union context both in the letter of the law and its actual implementation. Law provides a sort of exceptionalism for women who are third-country migrants, for example, and public authorities often apply regulation in a discriminating and marginalizing manner. Law creates life (*vitam instituere*) in the sense that it constructs identities (Douzinas, 2005). Law creates women's subjectivities. It may alter them, redefine them, reconstruct them or even abolish them.

Migrant women undergo a process of trans-subjectivation when they are granted limited citizenship rights, through the regularization process, for example. They are transformed into new subjects of law; they lose their old subjectivity, and new subjectivities emerge, differentiated from one another, which, even though one may think they are shaped by public authorities and remain static, unable to escape their newly created form, in fact incorporate seeds of resistance, which eventually will be revealed. Michel Foucault argues that power, the power over subjects, always creates resistance (Foucault, 1978, 96).

In this sense, if societies are closed structures that mould and shape subjectivities – and European society in relation to women is one of them – they cannot at the same time be contrary to freedom or any kind of personal achievements or resistance. Plastic citizenship in this respect creates plastic subjectivities for women.

Here the notion of plasticity in citizenship is applied, implying that it emerges when boundaries are blurred and processes of becoming or not are fluid, changing over time and influenced by notions of who should belong and who should not, who is entitled to what rights and who is not; at the same time, this plastic citizenship leads to a transformation of women's subjectivities into plastic subjectivities, which can resist and can have all kinds of possibilities to wiggle and escape from the rigidity of the societal structure (Konsta and Lazaridis, 2010, 368).

SELECTED AREAS IN EUROPEAN UNION SOCIAL LAW

In this section, the notion of plastic citizenship is applied to selected areas of European social law in its broader sense, including migration, multiple discrimination and working time in relation to gender.

Migrant Women

In the European Union context, different kinds of citizenship rights apply: regular European Union nationals' citizenship rights, rights of third-country nationals married to a European Union citizen, rights of non-European Union nationals. The two EU non-discrimination directives, the Race Directive 2000/43/EC and the Employment Directive 2000/78/EC, grant non-discrimination rights to non-European Union citizens as well. A kind of quasi-social citizenship on behalf of migrant women emerges in the context of these two directives, which is constantly undermined by migration legislation, which is restrictive of the rights of third-country migrants, and by the narrow stance taken by the Court of the European Union, which interprets non-discrimination legislation in relation to migrants. The predominant role of economic migration in Europe today requires a re-conceiving of citizenship rights and a proper institutionalization of the so-called European social citizenship, which would entail more consistency between non-discrimination and migration legislation in the direction of the protection of rights of all people living and working in the European Union territory.

Immigration laws in the Member States are largely adaptations to the requirements of two EU directives, one regarding family reunification of nationals of non-MS (2003/86/EC), and the other applying to long term residents in the EU (2003/109/EC). Both these directives allow MS to impose integration tests and conditions (e.g. proper use of native language) to migrants and their children, in order for them to acquire the status of long-term residents, or enjoy family reunification. Thanks to the social objectives of the Treaty of Rome, envisaged from the very beginning (articles 117ff.), it was possible to recognize the right to family reunification, involving spouses, the children of each spouse and their parents 'whatever their nationality' – forming part of the 'bonds of affection' which are recognized by Community social law (Kravaritou, 2002a).

The desire of a family to be reunited is a basic need for affection which, even if not explicitly stated as such, is protected by the concept of human rights precisely because it expresses a profound human need, and a reciprocal need in the sense that, in the case in question, it is felt both by the working parent, whether an immigrant or not, and the child (Kravaritou, 2008, 95).

In the case of the family reunification directive the European Parliament asked for the annulment of the directive (C-540/03, judgement 27/06/2006) on the basis that the provisions relating to family reunification of minor children of third-country nationals breached the fundamental right to respect for family life as recognized by art. 8 European Convention on Human Rights, the right of non-discrimination on grounds of age (art. 21 Charter of Fundamental Rights of the EU) and the obligation to have regard to the best interests of children as expressed in the Convention on the Rights of the Child.

The European Court in Luxembourg (ECJ), even if it recognized that the EU legal order is bound by these fundamental rights, refused to grant adequate protection to migrants by assuming that the directive is not in breach of these rights. The Court in this case took a very narrow-minded stance, bound politically by strict EU immigration policy to the detriment of a broader approach to EU citizenship that would encompass non-EU nationals as well. This restrictive approach to the rights of immigrants directly affects migrant women in the European Union. Immigration law is stripped of emotion and does not take into account bonds of affection. One of the greatest ordeals suffered by these women is the forced physical alienation from their children imposed by law.

There is a paradox here: gender equality and non-discrimination law in the EU context is a highly developed law, which has elaborated concepts that go beyond formal equality and direct discrimination, such as indirect discrimination and positive action. However, somehow this law is not meant to apply to migrant women to a full extent. Women who are EU nationals enjoy a full set of rights and privileges on the one hand, whereas migrant women face restrictions on these rights imposed by an austere immigration law. Here again there arises the issue of the differentiated legal subject.

The study of the concept of subjectivity seen in the light of John Stuart Mill's historical discussion of *The Subjection of Women*, draws attention to the contemporary discussion of legal culture in Europe, which historically has been a culture of privilege, which was dominated by legal regimes based upon special rights and privileges combined with general rights (Petersen et al., 2004, 43). European legal history is, thus, a history of different rights for different groups of people (estates and classes) including different rights for men and women (*ibid.*). Gender studies, in this context, need to shift the focus on to the unprivileged legal subject, and migrant women and their children are by definition *the* unprivileged legal subject in Europe today.

Gender and EU Citizenship Rights

Even if EU citizenship rights were initially designed to entail only market-based rights, the ECJ expanded citizenship by including also social rights for EU citizens, as in the case of Martinez Sala (C-85/96), where a Spanish mother who resided in Germany for many years, but had never worked there because of her childcare responsibilities, could claim welfare benefits in Germany. The Court went further in decoupling citizenship from market rules by granting direct effect to provisions on citizenship, namely article 18(1) EC protecting the right to reside within the territory of the MS for every EU citizen (*Baumbast*, C-413/99). Also, in this case the Court recognized the role of women in care work by taking into account that the refusal to renew the residence permit of Mr Baumbast's Colombian wife would leave their children without their primary carer. In the *Chen* case (C-200/02) the Court decided that the right of residence of a child who is an EU citizen would be meaningless if the prime carer of the child, as a non-EU citizen, is deprived of the right to reside in the host Member State. The court here implicitly recognized the predominant role of women as prime carers and enriched European social citizenship by performing a sort of judicial gender mainstreaming (Millns, 2007, 233ff).

The issue of differentiated subjectivities for women arises in this context as well. Migrant women who are mothers of EU citizens enjoy more social citizenship rights than migrant women who are not mothers of EU citizens. The right of residence in a MS is hierarchically superior for migrant women, since it is connected in many cases with their own and their families' biological survival, and there is no equal treatment in the enjoyment of this right for all migrant women. Law shapes migrant women's subjectivities in this respect. At the same time law connects social citizenship rights for migrant women to motherhood, perpetuating the division between the public and private spheres.

Gender Equality and Multiple Discrimination

The directives adopted under article 13 of the Treaty Establishing the European Community (now article 19 of the Treaty on the Functioning of the European Union), that is, The Race Directive (2000/43/EC), the Framework Employment Directive (2000/78/EC) (Bell 2002, 2008) and the Goods and Services Gender Directive (2004/113/EC), grant a sort of plastic citizenship to women by including certain rights on their behalf, and at the same time excluding others. Non-discrimination in relation to a woman's race and equality of treatment in employment are well-protected by formal EU social law. The limited application, however, of the Framework Employment Directive only to employment does not protect women when multiple discrimination occurs on other grounds besides gender outside the sphere of employment. Also, the Goods and Services Gender Directive's material scope is very limited and it excludes areas such as education, domestic violence, taxation and the media (areas which were initially inserted in the Draft Directive by the Commission, but were removed after it became clear that no consensus could be reached inside the Council on these matters (Masselot 2007, 153)). 'The limitation of the scope of anti-discrimination law on the basis of sex therefore sends the message that some forms of gender inequality and discrimination are acceptable, while others are not allowed as far as racial discrimination is concerned' (*ibid.*).

Of course, one should not forget that gender equality in the EU has taken the form of a fundamental right (especially after the ratification of the Lisbon Treaty, which makes article 23 of the Charter of Fundamental Rights of the EU (ECFR) legally binding. Article 23 of the Charter requires equality between the sexes to be ensured in all areas. As Yota Kravaritou states in the book *European Labour Law and the EU Charter of Fundamental Rights* (Bercusson, 2002):

> That equality 'must be ensured in all areas' means as much that men must assimilate to the social roles undertaken by women as vice versa. The emphasis on the global dimension of equality in article 23 – in the public, work and private spheres – indicates awareness of the breadth of problematic gender relations in European society.

Gender equality has a horizontal effect on all EU policy-making (gender mainstreaming) and it is accompanied by positive action measures in order to achieve not merely formal but substantive equality between the sexes. Nevertheless, the adoption in 2006 of the Gender Equality Recast Directive (2006/54/EC) did not enrich the existing rights conferred by previous directives and ECJ case law. Also, there is an ongoing debate as to whether soft law practices such as gender mainstreaming undermine the adoption of formal regulation as far as gender is concerned in the EU context, and often take the place of adoption of affirmative action measures on behalf of women (Stratigaki, 2005).

Gender and Working Time

The Marshallian concept of social citizenship, which deals mainly with redistribution of income and social security rights, needs to be enriched in the EU context through redistribution of social care services and unpaid care-giving activities (Bleijenbech et al., 2004, 311). Rights such as the right to time for caring (through paid leave or equal treatment in part-time work) and the right to be cared for (through social care services) are components of European social citizenship (*ibid.*).

The Part-Time Work Directive (1997/81/EC) fails to ensure a living wage to part-timers and to promote the redistribution of domestic responsibilities between men and women. Also, it does not include equality of treatment in social security issues. All working time legislation – Fixed Term (1999/70/EC), Temporary (2008/104/EC), Working Time (2003/88/EC) Directives – neglect this private/public sphere dichotomy, with the exception perhaps of the Parental Leave Directive (1996/34/EC as repealed by Directive 2010/18/EU), which still, however, does not provide for paid parental leave for both sexes. Article 33 para 2 of the EU Charter of Fundamental Rights relating to the reconciliation of family and professional life provides for a right to paid maternity leave and a right to a parental leave without specifying whether it would be paid or not, perpetuating, thus, the public/private divide.

CONCLUDING REMARKS

The relevant legal framework on European social law constructs the unprivileged legal subject in Europe today. The unprivileged legal subject is the bearer of rights provided by the plastic citizenship notion; a citizenship that is fluid and flexible, it changes according to the interests and needs of the EU and the states involved in each law-making process.

The perpetuation of the public/private divide by gender equality formal law and soft law in the EU context, the fragmented regulation and ECJ case law on issues that affect gender relations, granting limited gender equality rights to some groups of women, while refusing them to others – all these factors create plastic subjectivities for women in Europe today.

Citizenship cannot be viewed any longer in the narrow sense of political participation, but should encompass the enjoyment of social rights as well, which will be connected not only to working life, but to life itself. The right to time for caring and the right to be cared for, accompanied of course by a living wage, are integral parts of a European social citizenship model, expressing the *'liens affectifs'* or 'bonds of affection', as Yota Kravaritou (2002a) would say, in European social law.

REFERENCES

Agamben, G. (1998), *Homo Sacer, Sovereign Power and Bare Life*, translated by Daniel Heller-Roazen, Stanford, CA: Stanford University Press.

Aliprantis, N. (ed.) (2008), *Ta kinonika dikeomata se iperethniko epipedo ana ton kosmo* [*Social Rights at a Supranational Level around the World*], Athens: Papazissis Publications.

Arendt, H. (1951), *The Origins of Totalitarianism*, New York: Harcourt.

Bell, M. (2002), *Anti-discrimination Law and the European Union*, Oxford: Oxford University Press.

Bell, M. (2008), *Racism and Equality in the European Union*, Oxford: Oxford University Press.

Benson, P. (2006), 'The Future of Hegel by Catherine Malabou', *Philosophy Now*, issue 54.

Bercusson, B. (ed.) (2002), *European Labour Law and the EU Charter of Fundamental Rights*, Brussels: ETUI.

Bleijenbech, I., J. De Bruin and J. Bussemaker (2004), 'European Social Citizenship and Gender: The Part-time Work Directive', *European Journal of Industrial Relations*, **10** (3), 309–328.

Douzinas, K. (2005), *Nomos kai Aisthitiki: Logotechnia, Techni, Dikaio* [Law and Aesthetics: Literature, Art, Law], translated by C. Xanthopoulou, Athens: Papazisis.

Foucault, M. (1978), *The History of Sexuality*, translated by R. Hurley, New York: Random House.

Foucault, M. (2004), *The Hermeneutics of the Subject*, New York: Picador.

Konsta, A.-M. and G. Lazaridis (2010), 'Civic Stratification, "Plastic" Citizenship and "Plastic Subjectivities" in Greek Immigration Policy', *Journal of International Integration and Migration*, **11**, 363–382.

Kravaritou, Y. (2002a), *Liens affectifs et droit social européen*, Liber amicorum Jean-Victor Louis, Bruxelles: Bruylant.

Kravaritou, Y. (2002b), *Yia tin kinoniki Evropi kai to Dikeo tis* [On a Social Europe and its Law], Thessaloniki: Sakkoulas Publications.

Kravaritou, Y. (2002c), 'Kinonika dikeomata kai evropaiki kinoniki idiotita tou politi' [Social Rights and European Social Citizenship], 50 *Nomiko Vima* [Legal Forum], 1426ff.

Kravaritou, Y. (2008), 'Oi Hartes tis Evropaikis Enosis kai ta Kinonika dikeomata' [The Charters of the European Union and Social Rights], in N. Aliprantis (ed.), *Ta kinonika dikeomata se iperethniko epipedo ana ton kosmo* [Social Rights at a Supranational Level around the World], Athens: Papazissis Publications, pp. 77–98.

Kymlicka, W. (1995), *Multicultural Citizenship*, Oxford: Oxford University Press.

Kymlicka, W. (2000), 'Citizenship in Culturally Diverse Societies: Issues, Contexts, Concepts', in W. Kymlicka and W. Norman (eds), *Citizenship in Diverse Societies*, Oxford: Oxford University Press, pp. 1–41.

Magnusson, L. and B. Stråth (eds) (2004), *A European Social Citizenship? Preconditions for Future Policies from a Historical Perspective*, Brussels: Peter Lang.

Malabou, C. (2004), *The Future of Hegel: Plasticity, Temporality and Dialectic*, London: Routledge.

Marshall, T.H. (1950), *Citizenship and Social Class and Other Essays*, Cambridge: Cambridge University Press.

Masselot, A. (2007), 'The State of Gender Equality Law in the European Union', *European Law Journal*, **13** (2), March, 152–168.

Millns, S. (2007), 'Gender Equality, Citizenship, and the EU's Constitutional Future', *European Law Journal*, **13** (2), March, 218–237.

Ong, A. (1999), *Flexible Citizenship: The Cultural Logic of Transnationality*, Durham, NC: Duke University Press.

Petersen, H., A. Kronborg and I. Conradsen (2004), 'Transformations of Legal Subjectivity in Europe', in L. Paserini (ed.), *Gender Relationships in Europe at the Turn of the Millennium: Women as Subjects in Migration and Marriage*, GRINE final report for European Commission Directorate-General for Research, June, pp. 40–49.

Rubio-Marin, R. (2000), *Immigration as a Democratic Challenge: Citizenship and Inclusion in Germany and the United States*, Cambridge: Cambridge University Press.

Shaw, J. (2007a), *The Transformation of Citizenship in the European Union*, Cambridge: Cambridge University Press.

Shaw, J. (2007b), 'E.U. Citizenship and Political Rights in an Evolving European Union', *Fordham Law Review*, **75**, 2549–2579.

Somers, M.R. (2008), *Genealogies of Citizenship: Markets, Statelessness, and the Right to Have Rights*, Cambridge: Cambridge University Press.

Soysal, Y.N. (1994), *Limits of Citizenship. Migrants and Postnational Membership in Europe*, Chicago: University of Chicago Press.

Stratigaki, M. (2005), 'Gender Mainstreaming vs. Positive Action: An Ongoing Conflict in EU Gender Equality Policy', *European Journal of Women Studies*, **12** (2), 165–186.

Vahanian, N. (2008), 'A Conversation with Catherine Malabou', *Journal for Cultural and Religious Theory*, **9** (1), 1–13.

Vogel-Polsky, E. and M.N. Beauchesne (eds) (2001), *Les Politiques sociales: ont-elles un sexe?* Brussels: Editions Labour.

Section 1

From Equality to Dignity at Work and Social Citizenship

9. The reasonableness principle in the European Court of Justice age discrimination cases

Piera Loi

INTRODUCTION

In this chapter we will analyse the reasonableness principle in age discrimination cases in the light of the principles of the European Directive 2000/78/CE and the ECJ case law, which undoubtedly represent a new era and an innovative step in European discrimination law.

As in many European law systems (before the adoption of the Council Directive 2000/78/EC) age, unlike sex or race, was not expressly defined as a discriminating factor. Besides that, the previous anti-discrimination legislation was structured by way of identifying a discriminating factor and the consequent obligation of removing this factor from the decision-making process (Swift, 2006, 228), whereas the discriminating factor is also capable of identifying a minority group to be protected. The innovative feature of the anti-discrimination law complying with the Directive 2000/78/EC relies on the fact that some discriminating factors like age, since they represent a quality common to all, do not identify a minority group that should be protected (Fredman and Spencer, 2000, 37), especially in the case of age discrimination at work (Sargeant, 2006, 79) and that the decision-making process which refers to them is apparently objective. What is required by the Directive 2000/78/EC is then to verify if the decision-making criteria that appear objective are in actual fact age-related and the criteria have to be removed only if they are used for purposes which are illegitimate or if the consequences are disproportionate.

The aim of this chapter is to ascertain the role and functions of the reasonableness principle in discrimination cases on grounds of age, and more precisely, to verify how the European Court of Justice has used this principle in age discrimination case law. We will argue that the ECJ, through the use of the reasonableness principle in age discrimination cases, has *de facto* legitimated a competence of European institutions in the area of employment policies far beyond the limits recognised by art. 145 of the Treaty on the Functioning of the European Union. This could be seen as yet another tool in the hands of the European Court of Justice which through a balancing judgement in cases of discrimination on grounds of age, exercises a control over national employment policies, which in many cases, are aimed at tackling the economic crisis.

THE REASONABLENESS PRINCIPLE IN THE EQUALITY JUDGEMENT

The concept of reasonableness is used by lawyers and philosophers in very different ways and, like the concept of rationality to which it's strictly connected (Alexy, 2009, 5), it involves various consequences depending on its theoretical background. Since a description of the different theories on reasonableness would go beyond the scope of the present chapter, we will emphasise balancing as the prevailing feature of the reasonableness principle (Alexy, 2009, 8; MacCormick, 2005, 173). The idea of reasonableness as balancing is particularly useful when a plurality of values is at stake and provides answers incompatible with practical questions (Alexy 2009, 8).

One of the most frequent uses of reasonableness as balancing is in the equality judgement. As we all know the equality principle in the Aristotelian formula means that 'likes should be treated alike' and this is commonly described as the formal concept of equality, transposed in many constitutions as a principle 'everyone is equal before the law'. We all know that the other expression of the equality principle, typical of the welfare state, is the substantive equality principle which acknowledges that individuals start from different points of departure (depending on social, cultural situations and economic resources) and affirms the necessity to guarantee to everyone the same chances and the equality of opportunities. This concept admits, or better requires, the differentiation in treatment which should be justified in order to guarantee to every individual access to resources, welfare or well-being, or capabilities (Sen, 1992, 39) depending on the theory of justice behind the principle (Gosepath, 2008).

The equality principle imposes that all different treatments by the law should be justified on the basis of the differences of the situations to be regulated (where the categories of similar and different undoubtedly have not only a prescriptive but also a normative dimension) and of the reasonableness of the distinction that has been used. In other words, it should be demonstrated that the two situations in question are not similar and because of that the fact that they deserve a different treatment is reasonable (that is a consequence of the equality principle). Nonetheless, not all the factors legitimate a different treatment: a series of factors on the grounds of which we could admit a different treatment are considered suspect factors. The suspect factors are criteria which cannot be taken into account by the law or by individuals in order to justify different treatment and are, thus, identified by the anti-discrimination law. Suspect factors like sex, racial or ethnic origin, religion or belief, disability, age or sexual orientation could change in relation to the evolution of the legal systems and of the systems of values of each society.

We must admit that the reasonableness principle is a vague and indeterminate concept which nonetheless is frequently used by the constitutional courts to ascertain either that the law has treated differently situations which are analogous or that it has treated alike situations which are different. As a result, the law can be judged as unreasonable when it has treated differently situations which are analogous or when it has treated alike situations which are different. If the different treatment is not considered reasonable we are faced with a discrimination, since not all different treatment falls into the category of discrimination, but on the contrary to differentiate treatments could be a declination of the equality principle when situations are different. From this point of view, the reasonableness principle has the function of admitting or excluding the discriminatory nature of a different treatment. The function of anti-discrimination laws, in identifying grounds of discrimination which are forbidden, is then to inhibit the legislator (when the anti-discrimination law is at the constitutional level) or the individuals to justify a different treatment on grounds which are forbidden, since they represent suspect factors.

The reasonableness principle plays a fundamental role in the equality judgement (Cerri, 1991, 1) in the judicial review before the Constitutional Courts (Scaccia, 2000, 3) and also before the European Court of Justice. The structure of the judicial review changes if it involves a question of equality or discrimination. In the former case, the control technique is minimal: in the Spanish Constitutional Court this kind of control is called '*juicio de minimo*' (Mercader Uguin and Nogueira Guastavino, 2004, 1068) because there is a presumption of legitimacy of the different treatment introduced by the law. In the latter case, the control is strict, and it starts with the suspect nature of the factor on the ground of which the different treatment has been introduced. It follows a procedure and a structure of legal argumentation which rejects all the justifications which are not considered reasonable, that is a reason capable of limiting a fundamental right. Following the Spanish constitutional theory when in the difference of treatment one of the criteria described by the law as discriminatory is adopted (sex, race, age and so on) the legislator must show that it's aiming at pursuing a goal justifying limitations of fundamental rights.

In this case the principle of equality is transformed into the fundamental right not to suffer any discrimination (Mercader Uguin and Nogueira Guastavino, 2004, 1068).

The reasonableness principle use in equality judgements is not standardised, but we can nonetheless trace some common elements which frequently emerge in constitutional courts. We can also identify different steps (Morrone, 2009, 237). In the first step of the judgement, in order to establish if the two situations are treated by the law equally or differently, it is necessary to ascertain whether the situations regulated by the law are similar or different. This is not a mere factual operation but it is precisely a normative operation which contains an irreducible dose of arbitrariness (Supiot,1992, 212). When a law assumes that two situations are similar, it simply makes an abstraction of their different features and qualifies as relevant the feature that they have in common. The constitutional judge will ascertain if the legislator's choice of qualifying as similar or different the two situations is reasonable, and will make reference to the *ratio legis*, that is the objective goal of the law, which represents the so-called *tertium comparationis*. The second step is aimed at verifying the coherence of the *ratio legis*, which reconciles different treatments with the constitutional norms through the control of proportionality. This principle is strictly linked to that of reasonableness; and it is the principal criterion which is used in order to assess the State's intervention through legislation to ensure that any restriction of individual freedom aiming at attaining a specific goal is not manifestly excessive and does not go beyond what is necessary in order to attain it.

The principle of proportionality, following the German tradition (Alexy, 1992, 149) is composed of three sub-principles: suitability, which means that the restrictive measure is appropriate to achieve the aim that has to be achieved; necessity, which means that the adopted measure should not exceed what is necessary to achieve the objective and that a less restrictive measure does not exist; and, finally, *stricto sensu* proportionality, which means that the disadvantages caused by the measure do not outweigh the advantages which would justify the measure (Emiliou, 1996, 27; Van Gerven, 1999, 37). The more they affect fundamental rights, the greater weight should be given in the balancing to the reasons justifying the intervention (Alexy, 2002, 42).

In the words of the German constitutional court, 'The intervention must be suitable and necessary for the achievement of its objective. It may not impose excessive burdens on the individual concerned and must consequently be reasonable in its effect on him' (Van Gerven, 1999, 45).

The third step of the proportionality *strictu sensu* principle implies a balancing between interests and rights, between the sacrifices of the individuals caused by the measure, and the society as a whole or in identifiable groups.

At this point we should ask if the reasonableness test has different functions in an equality judgement and in a discrimination judgement. We could say that a norm defining a non-discrimination principle plays an instrumental function to the principle of equality. In its choice of the legislation or of the individuals, from the range of all the reasons that could justify any different treatment, it excludes those which are suspect. This traditional scheme is altered when the law forbidding a discrimination at the same time admits justifications when the reasons are objective and the aim is legitimate and proportionate: when the different treatment is reasonable.

In this case the judicial review and the reasonableness control have the function of subduing to the judiciary power the legitimacy of the legislator's choice of excluding a particular discriminating factor. In other words, in the equality judgement the judge will ascertain that the different treatment is reasonable. At the same time if there is a discrimination prohibited by the law admitting justifications, the judge will verify if it's reasonable to reconsider the suspect factor which would qualify the different treatment as a discrimination and turn it into a reasonable different treatment. The legislative technique of admitting justifications to discriminations is used by the Directive 2000/78/EC art. 2(2)(b) and, especially in case of discriminations on grounds of age, in art. 6(1).

THE USE OF THE REASONABLENESS PRINCIPLE BY THE ECJ

The reasonableness principle is also used by the ECJ as an interpretative criterion and as a general principle relevant both for the construction of the internal market and the sharing of competencies between the Community and the Member State, and for the protection of fundamental rights. In its case law the ECJ makes more often reference to the proportionality principle, than to the reasonableness principle (Adinolfi, 2009, 384). Notwithstanding that, the reasonableness principle has significantly been used in the area of discrimination law, which has reached an ever-growing importance in the construction of the EU legal order. Embodied in art. 5 TFEU, the ECJ not infrequently refers to the principle of proportionality (De Búrca 1994, 105) recognising that a measure is proportionate when, while appropriate for securing the attainment of the objective pursued, it does not go beyond what is necessary in order to attain it.

Given the manifold dimension of the reasonableness principle in

European Law we should concentrate on the use of this principle by the ECJ in the area of fundamental rights and discrimination law. What should be pointed out first of all is that the recourse to reasonableness in the ECJ case law differs from its use by national courts in legal systems where it is embodied into a constitution.

As far as the legal sources of the equality principle in European Union law are concerned, the academic debate on the expansion of the competencies of the European Union in the area of anti-discrimination based on ex art. 13 TEC (now art. 19 TFEU) (Bell, 2004, 242), derives from all the discussions on the existence in the treaties of a general principle of community law forbidding discrimination and producing direct effects. This explains different positions adopted with regard to the existence of a general principle of non-discrimination on grounds of age expressed by the ECJ in *Mangold* and more recently in *Kücükdeveci* and, with a contrary opinion, in *Bartsch*. The recognition by art. 6, n. 1 TUE that the Charter of Fundamental Rights has the same legal value as the treaties, would definitely reassess the role of equality in the EU legal order, since under art. 20 of the Charter everyone is equal before the law and under Article 21 (1) of the Charter any discrimination based on a series of grounds, including age, shall be prohibited.

As we have seen national courts and the ECJ take different approaches and adopt different legal reasoning in evaluating equality or non-discrimination cases. Rather than establishing a priority value (that of equality) the test of non-discrimination frequently used by the ECJ demands an appropriate justification of the violation of equality. In this sense the principle of non-discrimination provides for the balance of reasons by focusing upon supportive structures among reasons (Bengoetxea et al, 2001, 74).

When the suspect classifications (like the criteria set out in art. 19 TFEU) are involved there is a presumption of discrimination and the Court's judicial review will be rigorous and may extend to a strict examination of proportionality.

When a question of suspect classifications is not involved, and there's an equality judgement the Court chooses to restrain its judicial review competencies only 'to ascertaining whether there has been a manifest error of assessment in the legislative choices made . . . and verify the compatibility of the measure adopted with the general principles of Community law and, in particular, the principle of equal treatment'.

AG Poiares Maduro explains the self-restraint of the Court in equality judgements when a suspect classification is not involved, especially in the areas of economic and social regulation. He says that since all legislative activity entails choices and involves the redistribution of interests, in principle this inevitably favours certain social and economic categories over others. However, this choice does not necessarily constitute discrimination. If it is for the legislature to discuss, define and determine the configuration of interests and resources redistribution, a strict judicial scrutiny would subject the economic and social choices of the legislature to a second assessment, and this would call into question both judges' legitimacy and capacity to perform their judicial role. It's exactly the same category of arguments of the famous footnote four in the *United States v. Carolene Products Company* case. It discusses in which situations the legislation should be subject to a stricter judicial scrutiny:

> Nor need we inquire whether similar considerations enter into the review of statutes directed at particular religious . . . or national . . . or racial minorities: . . . whether prejudice against *discrete and insular minorities* may be a special condition, which tends seriously to curtail the operation of those political processes ordinarily to be relied upon to protect minorities, and which may call for a correspondingly more searching judicial inquiry.

Following this reasoning the AG admits that it is only where specific groups, often under-represented in the political decision-making process, are identified and protected by the law through a non-discrimination principle, that the courts should undertake a stricter review of the differences in the treatment decided upon by policy-makers. The question is then: how can we identify groups especially in age discrimination cases?

THE USE OF THE REASONABLENESS PRINCIPLE BY THE ECJ IN AGE DISCRIMINATION CASES

The reasonableness and proportionality test (questions arise as to whether the two concepts diverge: Della Cananea, 2009, 302) can be found in the European Court of Human Rights case law. Under art. 14 ECHR any differential treatment is discriminatory if it has no objective and reasonable justification unless there is a legitimate public aim and there is a relation of proportionality between the means employed and the aims pursued by the norm. The ECJ seems to have been influenced by this case law to which it expressly makes reference.

Following this scheme the reasonableness test is applied by ECJ in age discrimination cases and entails first of all verifying whether one person is treated less favourably than another person in a comparable situation because of age, and consequently whether this less favourable treatment could imply a direct or indirect discrimination.

The second step, when a less favourable treatment on grounds of age is ascertained, is to qualify that difference of treatment as a discrimination prohibited by the principle of non-discrimination or as a legitimate differential treatment. This implies an answer to the question of whether only indirect discrimination can be justified, whereas direct discrimination cannot admit derogations (Izzi, 2005, 62). The judicial argumentation of the ECJ has developed on this point following the *Age Concern* case where one of the preliminary questions raised was whether there was a significant practical difference between the test for justification set out in Article 2(2) of the directive in relation to indirect discrimination, and the test for justification set out in relation to direct age discrimination in Article 6(1) of the directive.

It is fundamental to distinguish cases of direct discrimination where by virtue of Article 2(2)(a) direct discrimination on grounds of age would occur where one person is, has been or would be treated less favourably than another person in a comparable situation. Art. 2(2)(b) of Directive 2000/78 defines indirect discriminations on grounds of age which take place where an apparently neutral provision, criterion or practice would put persons having a particular age at a particular disadvantage compared with other persons. Only provisions, criteria or practices liable to constitute indirect discrimination, by virtue of Article 2(2)(b) may be not classified as discrimination if, under Article 2(2)(b)(i), the 'provision, criterion or practice is objectively justified by a legitimate aim and the means of achieving that aim are appropriate and necessary'.

At the same time, in case of indirect discriminations the scheme of justifications put by art. 2 (2)(b) seems quite general and indefinite. In case of direct discriminations on grounds of age, the scheme of justifications is set out by art. 6(1) of Directive 2000/78, which authorises Member States to provide that certain differences of treatment on grounds of age do not constitute discrimination if, 'within the context of national law, they are objectively and reasonably justified by a legitimate aim, including legitimate employment policy, labour market and vocational training objectives, and if the means of achieving that aim are appropriate and necessary'. The second subparagraph of Article 6(1) lists specific examples of differences in treatment that, as a rule, may be regarded as 'objectively and reasonably justified' by a legitimate aim. The other scheme of justification for direct discriminations is given by art. 4(1) whereby a difference of treatment on grounds of age shall not constitute discrimination where, by reason of the nature of the particular occupational activities concerned or of the context in which they are carried out, such a characteristic constitutes a genuine and determining occupational requirement, provided that the objective is legitimate and the requirement is proportionate. As underlined by AG Kokott in the *Ole Andersen* case:

in case of direct discriminations on grounds of age the set of justifications is limited to arguments linked to legitimate employment policy, labour market and vocational training objectives or to legitimate and determining occupational requirement, so that only in exceptional cases direct discrimination can be justified and by specific arguments, following whereas in case of indirect discriminations on grounds of age the set of justifications could not be linked to labour market or employment policies argument.[1]

To summarise, we could say that justifications in case of direct discriminations on grounds of age must be subject to a very high standard of scrutiny.

The third step of the reasonableness test is aimed precisely at verifying the legitimacy of the aim pursued by the national measure from which a differential treatment on grounds of age is derived and the proportionality of the measure adopted. Through this last test of proportionality, as we have seen, it should be demonstrated that the measure is appropriate and necessary. The test of adequacy or of appropriateness means that the measure is not manifestly inadequate to reach the legitimate aim. Then it should be demonstrated that the measure is necessary to reach the aim. This is the last step of the proportionality test which implies that a different treatment is considered reasonable, when it is demonstrated that it is not possible to adopt any other measure to reach the legitimate aim. But even if the measure was considered as necessary, there's a supplementary test, which in reality is the proportionality *strictu sensu* test, and it has been applied by the ECJ since the *Palacios de la Villa* case.[2] This step implies a balancing between the sacrifices suffered by the individuals because of the measure, and other identifiable groups. Notwithstanding its importance, it is precisely the identification of groups that is highly controversial. While unequal treatment can readily be established in comparison based on specific individual cases, it is less apparent in an abstract comparison based on age groups. This last argument is especially useful to solicit a deeper reflection on the definition of classes and groups identified by the discrimination EC law and particularly by the Directive 2000/78/EC which indicates age as a discriminating factor, since it represents a quality common to all and does not identify a minority group that should be protected. How can we justify, then, a deeper judicial scrutiny of the ECJ, and what kind of balance could be reached and between the interests of which groups? The difficulties and, at the same time, the necessity of identifying minority groups whose rights and interests should be balanced with rights

---

[1] Opinion of Advocate General Kokott, delivered on 6 May 2010, Case C-499/08, point 31.
[2] Case C-411/05 *Palacios de la Villa* [2007] ECR I-8531.

and interests of other groups is well underlined by AG Kokott in the *Ole Andersen* case, but it simply renders potentially more controversial all judicial review on age discrimination cases.

THE ECJ RULINGS IN AGE DISCRIMINATION CASES AND EUROPEAN EMPLOYMENT POLICY

We should not forget that the Directive 2000/78/EC is limited to the field of employment and occupation and is aimed at combating discrimination against disadvantaged groups in order to increase their participation in the labour force. It is for this reason that it emphasised the need to pay particular attention to supporting older workers. We should think about the fact that discriminations on grounds of age are not considered wrong or bad per se, as in the case of sex discrimination, but only if they lack any justification, especially those justifications linked to labour market arguments. In other words, age is a discriminating factor not in every situation or in every sector of life but only in this specific institution which is the labour market, where the problem of distribution of resources is at stake.

It seems that in the case of age discrimination economic or market reasons impose 'differentiation of treatment' and that admitting or forbidding this differentiation is possible and necessary in order to exercise a control in the labour market which otherwise will produce its own discrimination not permitting to some categories to enter the labour market. That's why the anti-discrimination principle is a powerful regulatory instrument, as underlined by Advocate General Geelhoed in the *Chacón Navas* case.[3] It risks altering the equilibrium in the distribution of competencies between the Community and the Member States:

> So broad an interpretation of Article 13 EC and of the rules adopted by the Community legislature on the implementation of that article results, as it were, in the creation of an Archimedean position, from which the prohibitions of discrimination defined in Article 13 EC can be used as a lever to correct, without the intervention of the authors of the Treaty or the Community legislature, the decisions made by of the Member States in the exercise of the powers which they – still – retain.

Seen from this point of view, the reasonableness principle is used by the ECJ as a tool to enlarge EU competencies in employment policies. This

---

[3] Case C-13/05, *Sonia Chacòn Navas v. Eurest Colectividades SA*, [2006] ECR I-6467.

is a step perfectly admissible through the justification principle set by the directive 2000/78/CE which excludes any discrimination on grounds of age when differences in treatment are justified by legitimate employment policy, labour market and vocational training objectives. On the other hand, it's clearly admitted in Article 25 of the directive that: 'The prohibition of age discrimination is an essential part of meeting the aims set out in the Employment Guidelines and encouraging diversity in the workforce.'

To put it differently, the non-discrimination principle on grounds of age is functional to reach the aims set out by the European Strategy for Employment, since in all the national labour markets age is considered as a disadvantaging factor that should be re-balanced by a specific employment policies measure. Through the Employment Guidelines EU identifies the cohorts of people (workers) of different ages whose age is considered a factor hindering their access to the labour market. Through the reasonableness principle the ECJ and the EU institutions enlarge the competencies recognised by art. 145 TFUE in developing a coordinated strategy for employment.

The same kind of questions can be raised as far as the EU competencies in the field of social security and social protection of workers are concerned. The ECJ rulings in age discrimination cases can be considered as an attempt to enlarge EU competencies or as an alternative way to attain the ambitious objectives of adequate and sustainable pensions, defined lately in the Green paper *Towards Adequate, Sustainable and Safe European Pension Systems*.[4] The ECJ in *Palacios de la Villa* and *Age Concern* cases deals with national legislation which permits employers to dismiss employees aged 65 or over by reason of retirement and seeks to ascertain whether directive 2000/78/CE precludes this kind of national legislation according to the 14th recital in the preamble to Directive 2000/78 which says that the directive is to be without prejudice to national provisions laying down retirement ages. However, in *Palacios de la Villa* the Court interpreted that recital narrowly, holding that it 'merely states that the directive does not affect the competence of the Member State to determine retirement age' and that it does not 'in any way preclude the application of that directive to national measures governing the conditions for termination of employment contracts where the retirement age has been reached'.

Following the Court's reasoning in *Palacios de la Villa* the legislation permitting the automatic termination of an employment relationship once the worker's retirement age of 65 has been reached affects the duration of

---

4   European Commission Green Paper (2010) *Towards adequate sustainable and safe European pension systems*, Brussels, COM (2010) 365 final.

the employment relationship between the parties and, more generally, the engagement of the worker concerned in an occupation by preventing his future participation in the labour force, so that such legislation falls within the meaning of Article 3(1)(c) of Directive 2000/78 establishing rules relating to 'employment and working conditions, including dismissals and pay'.

The same position is confirmed in the *Age Concern* case. What is indeed impressive in these rulings is that the ECJ declares with vagueness that a national rule which permits employers to dismiss employees aged 65 or over if the reason for dismissal is retirement can in principle be justified under Article 6(1) of Directive 2000/78 because it is not apparent that the means put in place to achieve that aim of public interest are inappropriate and unnecessary for the purpose of promotion of full employment by facilitating access to the labour market.

It is clear that by this interpretation a great deal of autonomy is left to Member States as far as the reasonableness of the differentiation of treatment leaves space to an heterogeneity of justifications with no substantial criteria of interpretation by the ECJ. We should ask which are the different interests to be taken into account and to be balanced in a test whose meaning is to verify to what extent the principle of equal treatment should be sacrificed? In this specific case we should ask if the right to stability of employment of older workers should be sacrificed to be balanced with whose other interest? Younger workers' interests? First of all, it should be evident that reducing job security for older workers means more jobs for younger people. Otherwise it should be admitted that this is simply a technique to offer flexible workforce at a lower cost in order to give more advantages to enterprises. But even if the rationale was to enhance job opportunities for younger workers it should be admitted that by this we transfer some labour market risks from one category (younger) to the other (older). We should then admit that the Directive 2000/78/EC establishes the principle that a less favourable treatment is not a discrimination when the disadvantages suffered by a category are transformed into (measurable) advantages for another category. The vagueness of the ECJ in applying those principles leaves too much discretion to the legislator and national Courts (Baker, 2008, 305) which will not apply the rigorous scrutiny required by EU Discrimination Law.

REFERENCES

Adinolfi, A. (2009), 'The Principle of Reasonableness in European Union Law', in G. Bongiovanni, G. Sartor and C. Valentini (eds), *Reasonableness and Law*, Dordrecht; Heidelberg; London; New York: Springer, pp. 383–404.

Alexy, R. (1992), 'Rights, Legal Reasoning and Rational Discourse', *Ratio Juris*, 143–152.

Alexy, R. (2002), 'Collisione e bilanciamento quale problema di base della dogmatica', in M. La Torre and A. Spadaro (eds), *La ragionevolezza nel diritto*, Torino: Giappichelli, pp. 27–44.

Alexy, R. (2009), 'The Reasonableness of Law', in G. Bongiovanni, G. Sartor and C. Valentini (eds), *Reasonableness and Law*, Dordrecht; Heidelberg; London; New York: Springer, pp. 5–15.

Baker, A. (2008),'Proportionality and Employment Discrimination in the UK', *Industrial Law Journal*, **37**, 305–328.

Barnard, C. and B. Hepple (2000), 'Substantive Equality', *Cambridge Law Journal*, **59**, 562–585.

Bell, M. (2004), 'Equality and the European Union Constitution', *Industrial Law Journal*, **3**, 242–259.

Bengoetxea, J., N. MacCormick and L. Moral Sorano (2001), 'Integration and Integrity in the Legal Reasoning of the European Court of Justice', in G. De Burca and J. Weiler (eds), *The European Court of Justice,* Oxford: Oxford University Press, pp. 43–82.

Cerri, A. (1991), 'Ragionevolezza delle leggi', in *Enciclopedia Giuridica, agg. XIV*, Roma: Treccani.

De Búrca, G. (1994), 'The Principle of Proportionality and its Application in EC Law', *Yearbook of European Law*, **13**, 105–150.

Della Cananea, G. (2009), 'Reasonableness in Administrative Law', in G. Dongiovanni, G. Sartor and C. Valentina (eds), *Reasonableness and Law*, Dordrecht; Heidelberg; London; New York: Springer, pp. 295–310.

Emiliou, N. (1996), *The Principle of Proportionality in the European Law: A Comparative Study*, London; The Hague; Boston: Kluwer Law International.

Fredman, S. and S. Spencer (eds) (2003), *Age as an Equality Issue. Legal and Policy Perspectives*, Oxford: Hart Publishing.

Gosepath, S. (2008), 'Equality', in N. Zalta Edward (ed.), *The Stanford Encyclopedia of Philosophy*, Fall Edition, available at http://plato.stanford.edu/entries/equality/ (accessed December 2010).

Izzi, D. (2005), *Eguaglianza e differenze nel rapporto di lavoro. Il diritto antidiscriminatorio tra genere e fattori di rischio emergenti*, Napoli: Jovene.

MacCormick, N. (2005), *Rhetoric and the Rule of Law*, Oxford: Oxford University Press.

Mercader Uguin, J. and M. Nogueira Guastavino (2004), 'El fin de la validez de las cláusulas convencionales de jubilación forzosa: Comentario a la SSTS 9 marzo 2004 [RJ 2004, 841 y RJ 2004, 873]', *Aranzadi Social*, **5**, 1063–1086.

Morrone, A. (2009), 'Constitutional Adjudication and the Principle of Reasonableness', in G. Bongiovanni, G. Sartor and C. Valentini (eds), *Reasonableness and Law*, Dordrecht; Heidelberg; London; New York: Springer, pp. 215–240.

Sargeant, M. (2006), *Age Discrimination in Employment*, Aldershot: Gower Publishing.

Scaccia, G. (2000), *Gli 'strumenti' della ragionevolezza nel giudizio costituzionale*, Luiss-Collana di Studi Giuridici, Milano: Giuffrè

Schiek, D. (2006), 'The ECJ Decision in Mangold: A Further Twist on Direct Effect of Directives and Constitutional Relevance of Community Equality Legislation', *Industrial Law Journal*, **35**, 329–341.

Sen, A. (1992), *Inequality Re-Examined*, New York: Clarendon Press.
Supiot, A. (1992), 'Principi di eguaglianza e limiti della razionalità giuridica', *Lavoro e Diritto*, **2**, 210–220.
Swift, J. (2006), 'Justifying Age Discrimination', *Industrial Law Journal*, **35**, 228–244.
Van Gerven, W. (1999), 'The Effects of Proportionality on the Actions of Member States. National Viewpoint from Continental Europe', in E. Ellis (ed.), *The Principle of Proportionality in the Laws of Europe*, Oxford and Portland, Oregon: Hart Publishing.

10. The principle of non-discrimination within the Fixed-Term Work Directive

Mark Bell

Since the early 1980s, the European Union has been actively engaged in a debate about how labour law should respond to the variety existing amongst employment contracts. The archetype is traditionally regarded as the individual who works full-time, on an open-ended contract and who is directly engaged by the firm that provides employment. Reflecting the assumption that this is the standard form of employment relationship, the label 'atypical' has been applied to those forms of employment which deviate from the norm, such as part-time, temporary or agency work. These forms of employment have tended to increase over time,[1] hence making it more pressing for labour law to adapt to such contractual diversity.

In relation to temporary employment contracts, the initial trajectory of EU policy was to seek to limit their growth through close regulation of the circumstances under which a fixed-term employment contract could be created.[2] Although this reflected the approach in some domestic labour law systems at the time,[3] it did not receive sufficient support within the Member States and there followed a long period of stalemate. A breakthrough first arrived in relation to part-time work (Directive 97/81).[4] This was followed by Directive 1999/70 on fixed-term work[5] and, after

---

[1] In 2008, 18.2 per cent of workers in the EU were employed part-time, whilst 14 per cent were employed on fixed-term contracts: 'Employment in Europe 2009', Luxembourg: Office for Official Publications of the European Communities, 2009, 155.

[2] [1982] OJ C128/2.

[3] See Countouris (2007), Chapter 3.

[4] Directive 97/81/EC concerning the framework agreement on part-time work concluded by UNICE, CEEP and the ETUC [1998] OJ L14/9.

[5] Directive 1999/70/EC concerning the framework agreement on fixed-term work concluded by ETUC, UNICE and CEEP [1999] OJ L175/43.

some delay, Directive 2008/104 on temporary agency work.[6] The main regulatory method adopted by each of these Directives is to invoke the principle of non-discrimination as a tool for ensuring appropriate protection of these workers. Put crudely, part-time workers should be treated equally to full-time workers, fixed-term workers should be treated equally to permanent workers, and agency workers should be treated equally to those recruited directly by the user undertaking.

It is perhaps unsurprising that the principle of non-discrimination eventually proved an acceptable point of consensus for the Member States. Equality is one of the most powerful and evocative principles in contemporary law and politics. It can also be regarded as a cornerstone of labour law, with its inherent struggle to redress the inequality of bargaining power between management and workers.[7] This chapter explores what meaning is attached to the principle of non-discrimination in the Fixed-Term Work Directive. This Directive was selected for further scrutiny because, unlike the Part-Time Work Directive, it is not closely connected to any element of pre-existing EU equality law. Moreover, it has been the subject of cases within both national courts and the Court of Justice, whereas the Agency Work Directive is yet to enter into force. The chapter begins by considering the diverse meanings that can be attributed to non-discrimination. It then proceeds to consider what concept of non-discrimination is evident within the Directive and the subsequent case-law.

INTERPRETING EQUALITY AND NON-DISCRIMINATION

Non-discrimination, equal treatment and equality are interlinked concepts that are difficult to distinguish and the choice of one term or another does not, by itself, provide a sufficient indicator of what the legislator intended. The Part-Time and Fixed-Term Work Directives refer to 'the principle of non-discrimination', whereas the Agency Work Directive adopts the term 'principle of equal treatment'. It would be rash, though, to assume that this implies that the underlying concept is intended to be different. As is well-established in the academic literature, equality takes a wide variety of forms and its meaning is often contested.[8] A general principle of equality can be found within most European constitutions and the Court of

---

6   Directive 2008/104/EC on temporary agency work [2008] OJ L327/9.
7   Vigneau et al. (1999, 148).
8   See for example, More (1999).

Justice has repeatedly recognised that this is one of the general principles of EC law. In this context, equality is highly malleable and it amounts to little more than a test of rationality.[9] The general principle of equality can be applied as a constraint on arbitrary rules within labour law. An illustration is provided in *Cordero Alonso v Fondo de Garantía Salarial*.[10] This case concerned the recovery of payments where the employer was insolvent. Following his dismissal, compensation of EUR 5,540 for Mr Cordero Alonso was agreed under a judicially-supervised conciliation settlement. When his employer became insolvent, he requested the sum from the Spanish guarantee authority. Full payment was refused on the basis that this was a conciliation settlement; full payment was only provided for compensation awarded in a court judgment. The Court of Justice held that the Spanish courts had to ensure: 'observance of fundamental rights, which include inter alia the general principle of equality and non-discrimination . . . That principle precludes comparable situations from being treated in a different manner unless the difference of treatment is objectively justified.'[11]

On the facts, the Court deemed that Mr Cordero Alonso's situation was comparable to that of workers awarded compensation via a court judgment and there were no grounds for treating him differently in relation to his entitlement to receive the payment. Equality, in this manifestation, is an instrument for promoting fairness between all workers.

At the other end of the spectrum, equality can be interpreted with more rigour, typically described as the pursuit of substantive equality. Here equality is not concerned with mere consistency in the treatment of comparable categories. Instead the starting point is recognition that certain groups in society experience sustained socio-economic inequality. Overcoming these engrained patterns of disadvantage will not flow from simply trying to root out arbitrary behaviour and irrational prejudice. Compensatory measures are needed to redress the effects of a history of inequality. By their nature, these measures are targeted at groups that experience inequality and this implies a departure from formal equal treatment.[12]

Within EU law, it is debatable whether the goal of substantive equality has been fully embraced. The EU has a well-established body of legislation that regulates in some detail discrimination on grounds of sex, racial or ethnic origin, religion or belief, age, disability and sexual orientation.[13]

---

9   McCrudden and Kountouris (2007, 75).
10   Case C-81/05 [2006] ECR I-7569.
11   *Ibid.*, para 37.
12   McCrudden (2007, 513).
13   For an overview, see Ellis (2005).

This legislation is premised on the assumption that general constitutional principles of equality are an inadequate response to the patterns of inequality and disadvantage linked to these characteristics. The various Directives, which will be collectively referred to in this chapter as 'anti-discrimination legislation', move beyond the loose rationality test and seek to place firm limits on the circumstances where unequal treatment can be permitted. Furthermore, the Directives tentatively recognise that taking positive action may be necessary 'with a view to ensuring full equality in practice'.[14] Although this is not a decisive commitment to pursuing substantive equality, the legislator has treated unequal treatment based on these personal characteristics as demanding more than the flexible standards of fairness and consistency within the general principle of equality.

One explanation lies in the apparent connection to fundamental human rights. This perspective elevates the social and legal significance of differences of treatment based on personal characteristics. The anti-discrimination Directives explicitly link their objectives with human rights protection. The preamble of the Racial Equality Directive, for example, refers to the fact that the Union is founded on the principle of respect for human rights and cites a range of international human rights instruments that recognise equality as a 'universal right'.[15] The 'recast' Directive on gender equality couches its fundamental rights foundation in the equality rights located in the EU Charter of Fundamental Rights.[16] It is also arguable that differences of treatment based on certain personal characteristics are set apart by their capacity to infringe human dignity. Within the anti-discrimination Directives, this connection is found in the definition of harassment, which includes violation of dignity as one of its constituent elements.[17]

The question which arises from this short discussion is where the principle of non-discrimination within the Fixed-Term Work Directive should be located along the equality spectrum. Should it be assimilated to discrimination based on personal characteristics, or is it more appropriately viewed as an emanation of the general principle of equality, as applied to the labour law domain? The answer matters because it is likely to shape

---

[14] For example Art. 3, Directive 2006/54 on the implementation of the principle of equal opportunities and equal treatment of men and women in matters of employment and occupation (recast) [2006] OJ L204/23.

[15] Recitals 2–4, Directive 2000/43/EC implementing the principle of equal treatment between persons irrespective of racial or ethnic origin [2000] OJ L180/22. See also, Recitals 1, 4, 5, Directive 2000/78 establishing a general framework for equal treatment in employment and occupation [2000] OJ L303/16.

[16] Recital 5, Directive 2006/54.

[17] For example Art. 2(1)(c), Directive 2006/54.

the intensity of judicial scrutiny when courts confront distinctions between fixed-term and permanent workers. The remainder of this chapter will consider various aspects of the Directive, and its judicial interpretation, in order to begin to answer this question.

THE FIXED-TERM WORK DIRECTIVE AND FUNDAMENTAL RIGHTS

As mentioned above, the fundamental rights vocation of the EU anti-discrimination Directives is clearly proclaimed. In contrast, fixed-term work does not appear in the list of protected characteristics found in international human rights instruments or in the EU Charter. Indeed, this is rather barren terrain even in those instruments devoted to fundamental social rights. The ILO has adopted conventions on part-time work and agency work,[18] but no dedicated convention applies to fixed-term work.[19] Similarly, there is no express reference to fixed-term work within the Revised European Social Charter. Nevertheless, the Fixed-Term Work Directive does provide one indication that it touches upon the realm of fundamental rights. Recital 3 states:

> Point 7 of the Community Charter of the Fundamental Social Rights of Workers provides, *inter alia*, that 'the completion of the internal market must lead to an improvement in the living and working conditions of workers in the European Community. This process must result from an approximation of these conditions while the improvement is being maintained, as regards in particular forms of employment other than open-ended contracts, such as fixed-term contracts, part-time working, temporary work and seasonal work.'

Although the 1989 Charter is not legally-binding, the Court of Justice has recognised its relevance for interpreting provisions of EU labour law. In *BECTU*,[20] the Court provided an early indication that the treatment of fixed-term contract workers could engage fundamental rights. In that case, the British legislation implementing the Working Time Directive only extended the entitlement to paid holidays to workers with more than 13

---

[18] Convention on Part-Time Work (No. 175) and Convention concerning Private Employment Agencies (No. 181).

[19] This may, however, flow from the assumption that all ILO Conventions apply to fixed-term workers, unless expressly excluded: Countouris (2007, 152).

[20] Case C-173/99, *R v Secretary of State for Trade and Industry, ex parte Broadcasting, Entertainment, Cinematogaphic and Theatre Union (BECTU)* [2001] ECR I-4881.

weeks of continuous employment. The Court drew upon the 1989 Charter, alongside other international sources of labour law, to recognise that paid annual leave was 'a social right directly conferred by that Directive on every worker'.[21] Notably, the Court rejected arguments to the effect that labour market flexibility should qualify the extent to which fixed-term workers should be entitled to this fundamental social right.[22]

The emphasis on the rights of fixed-term workers continues to be evident in the case-law under the Fixed-Term Work Directive. The case of *Del Cerro Alonso*[23] involved the entitlement of a public health service worker to a length of service allowance in respect of periods worked on a temporary contact. In its preliminary observations, the Court stated that the equal treatment rights within the Fixed-Term Work Directive 'must be deemed to be of general application since they are rules of Community social law of particular importance'.[24] Later in the judgment, the Court reiterated that the equal treatment of fixed-term and permanent workers is a 'principle of Community social law [which] cannot be interpreted restrictively'.[25] The language used appears to imply that the Court is elevating the status of the Directive (or at least its equal treatment provisions) in the direction of a fundamental social right.[26] One weakness, however, in the *Del Cerro Alonso* judgment is that Court fails to provide any concrete explanation of why the non-discrimination provisions in the Directive are a rule of 'particular importance'.

In *IMPACT*,[27] the Court goes a little further in explaining its rationale for attaching particular importance to this Directive. This case was brought by an Irish trade union against various practices in the Irish civil service, including alleged unequal treatment of fixed-term workers in employment conditions. Specifically, the Court had to consider whether clause 4 (the principle of non-discrimination) extended to cover access to occupational pensions. The Court's starting point, as in *Del Cerro Alonso*, was that the rights conferred should not be interpreted restrictively.[28] In justifying this approach, the Court locates the

---

21   *Ibid.*, para 47.
22   McCann (2008, 126).
23   Case C-307/05, *Del Cerro Alonso v. Osakidetza-Servicio Vasco de Salud* [2007] ECR I-7109.
24   *Ibid.*, para 27.
25   *Ibid.*, para 38.
26   Sciarra (2007, 21).
27   Case C-268/06, *IMPACT v Minister for Agriculture and Food and others* [2008] ECR I-2483.
28   *Ibid.*, para 114.

Framework Agreement (annexed to the Directive) in a broader social rights context:

> The Framework Agreement, in particular clause 4, thus follows an aim which is akin to the fundamental objectives enshrined in the first paragraph of Article 136 EC as well as in the third paragraph of the preamble to the EC Treaty and Article 7 and the first paragraph of Article 10 of the Community Charter of the Fundamental Social Rights of Workers to which Article 136 EC refers . . .[29]

The Court reiterates this statement in the subsequent case of *Angelidaki*,[30] even though that case was not concerned with the non-discrimination provisions of the Framework Agreement, but instead clause 8(3) on non-regression. Moreover, in *Angelidaki*, Advocate-General Kokott links the Framework Agreement to the Council of Europe's European Social Charter and describes it as an expression of 'fundamental social policy objectives of the Community'.[31]

The overall message emerging is that the Court regards the Fixed-Term Work Directive as enjoying an enhanced status and this leads it in the direction of a relatively robust interpretation of its provisions. Yet a close textual reading of the judgments reveals that the Court has still not adopted rights-based language, preferring instead to call it a 'principle of Community social law'.[32] This contrasts with the anti-discrimination case-law, where the Court has expressly referred to 'fundamental human rights'.[33] It is risky to read too much into this subtle difference in wording, but it does suggest that the status of the Fixed-Term Work Directive is something of a half-way house between run-of-the-mill secondary legislation and the EU fundamental rights *acquis*.

THE CONCEPT OF NON-DISCRIMINATION WITHIN THE FIXED-TERM WORK DIRECTIVE

Another means of evaluating the principle of non-discrimination within the Directive is to look in more depth at its approach to defining the

---

[29]   *Ibid.*, para 112.
[30]   Cases C-378/07 to C-380/07, *Angelidaki and others* [2009] ECR I-3071, paras 112–113.
[31]   Para 63, Opinion of Advocate-General Kokott, 4 December 2008.
[32]   Para 114, *IMPACT*.
[33]   For example para 19, Case C-13/94, *P v. S and Cornwall County Council* [1996] ECR I-2143; paras 26–27, Case 149/77, *Defrenne v. SABENA (III)* [1978] ECR 1365.

concept of discrimination. Within EU anti-discrimination legislation, there is a settled approach to discrimination which rests upon a four-fold definition. The Directives distinguish between (i) direct discrimination; (ii) indirect discrimination; (iii) harassment; and (iv) instructions to discriminate. Looking at the Fixed-Term Work Directive, there are several respects in which it is set apart from this framework: a monolithic concept of discrimination; the requirement for a comparator; objective justification of direct discrimination.

A Monolithic Concept of Discrimination

The term 'discrimination' is not actually used within the Framework Agreement, except in the heading attached to Clause 4. The operative provision is clause 4(1): 'In respect of employment conditions, fixed-term workers shall not be treated in a less favourable manner than comparable permanent workers solely because they have a fixed-term contract or relation unless different treatment is justified on objective grounds.'

This definition does not refer to the concepts of direct or indirect discrimination. The Framework Agreement's silence in this respect is not decisive; the original Article 119 EEC did not refer to direct or indirect discrimination on the ground of sex in remuneration, but the Court of Justice recognised these concepts through its case-law.[34] A stumbling block in the pathway of such an evolution is the requirement that the less favourable treatment is 'solely' because the worker has a fixed-term contract. Vigneau argues that this will make it difficult to mount indirect discrimination claims.[35] The nature of an indirect discrimination claim would be that a measure applies to more than just fixed-term workers, but it has the effect of placing fixed-term workers at a particular disadvantage.

The Court of Justice has yet to consider this issue, but it has arisen in UK domestic case-law. In *Coutts*,[36] a bank decided to pay all 'permanent staff' a bonus worth 5 per cent of basic salary following the completion of a merger. 'Non-permanent staff' covered a variety of contractual arrangements, such as on-call working, but 3,000 of the 6,000 non-permanent staff were employed on fixed-term contracts. The question arose whether the exclusion of fixed-term employees from the bonus was less favourable treatment 'solely' because of their fixed-term status. The bank contended that various groups of staff were excluded, not 'solely' those on fixed-

---

[34] Craig and de Búrca (2007, 886).
[35] Vigneau (1999, 145).
[36] *Coutts & Co, Royal Bank of Scotland v. Cure and Fraser* [2005] ICR 1098.

term contracts. In the end, the matter was resolved by recourse to the wording used in the national implementing legislation. The British legislation omitted the phrase 'solely' and instead referred to treatment 'on the ground that the employee is a fixed-term employee'.[37] The Employment Appeal Tribunal held that this was a more generous test than the wording used in the Directive and, accordingly, it was sufficient to show that the rule disadvantaged fixed-term employees, irrespective of whether there were also other groups of employees similarly disadvantaged.[38] Although a positive outcome for the litigants, the case illustrates how the restrictive wording of the Directive may hinder indirect discrimination claims.

The Requirement for a Comparator

Using comparators in order to establish that discrimination has occurred is a common feature of discrimination litigation, but it is not prescribed in detail by EU anti-discrimination legislation. The standard definition states that 'direct discrimination shall be taken to occur when one person is treated less favourably than another is, has been or would be treated in a comparable situation'.[39] This definition allows considerable flexibility regarding what constitutes another person in a 'comparable situation', a point reinforced by the express possibility for hypothetical comparisons ('would be treated').[40] Once again, the Framework Agreement departs from the model common to anti-discrimination legislation by requiring, in clause 4(1) that less favourable treatment is measured in relation to 'comparable permanent workers'. Clause 3(2) elaborates on the characteristics of this comparator:

> [T]he term 'comparable permanent worker' means a worker with an employment contract or relationship of indefinite duration, in the same establishment, engaged in the same or similar work/occupation, due regard being given to qualifications/skills.
>
> Where there is no comparable permanent worker in the same establishment, the comparison shall be made by reference to the applicable collective agreement, or where there is no applicable collective agreement, in accordance with national law, collective agreements or practice.

---

[37]   Reg 3(3)(a), Fixed-Term Employees (Prevention of Less Favourable Treatment) Regulations 2002, SI 2002/2034.

[38]   Paras 50–51, *Coutts*.

[39]   For example Art. 2(2)(a), Directive 2000/43.

[40]   The approach taken to comparators is different in respect of equal pay for women and men, see Ellis (2005, 158), however, it should be noted that Directive 2006/54 may permit hypothetical comparators in this field: Arts 2(1)(a) and 4.

The first part of this paragraph imposes a rather stringent test of locating another worker in a similar situation in the same establishment. This creates the obvious risk that if an employer relies entirely upon fixed-term workers for a particular occupational activity, then those workers will struggle to find any appropriate comparator. Furthermore, the reference to qualification/skills is puzzling. This suggests that even if there is a permanent worker performing the same work, this worker might not be comparable based on differences in their qualifications or skills. This seems to conflate the comparator question with the objective justification of the difference in treatment. If two employees are performing the same work, the fact that one has better qualifications cannot truly be regarded as rendering their work non-comparable. The employer might wish to argue that there are justifications for rewarding more generously those with better qualifications (for example, encouraging professional development), but this does not seem relevant to the preliminary definition of what constitutes comparable work.[41]

The second part of clause 3(2) opens the door for a somewhat broader range of comparators. It is, though, relatively vague in terms of how widely, or narrowly, this can be interpreted within domestic implementing legislation. Where no applicable collective agreement exists, clause 3(2) allows comparisons based on national 'law' or 'practice'. This could be interpreted as embracing the typical approach in domestic law to the question of finding a comparator, thus forming a bridge to anti-discrimination legislation.[42]

Objective Justification of Direct Discrimination

Whether or not clause 4(1) extends to indirect discrimination, it is certainly applicable to instances of direct discrimination between fixed-term and permanent workers. EU anti-discrimination legislation does not normally permit justification of direct discrimination,[43] so it is striking that the Framework Agreement expressly permits different treatment 'on objec-

---

[41]   Admittedly, in its case-law on equal pay, the Court of Justice has accepted the argument that the level of qualifications can be relevant to determining whether or not workers are in a comparable situation, even though the work performed is 'seemingly identical': para 20, Case C-309/97, *Angestelltenbetriebsrat der Wiener Gebietskrankenkasse v. Wiener Gebietskrankenkasse* [1999] ECR I-2865.

[42]   For an argument to this effect, see McColgan (2003, 196); Lorber (2008, 317).

[43]   The most notable exception is Art 6, Directive 2000/78 in relation to age discrimination.

tive grounds'. The rigidity or leniency with which this is interpreted will evidently determine the strength of the principle of non-discrimination. In *Del Cerro Alonso*, the Court was asked whether the different treatment of fixed-term and permanent workers, in respect of a length of service allowance, could be justified on the mere basis that the rule was laid down in legislation or in a collective agreement. The Court firmly rejected this notion, holding that it was necessary to show that the 'unequal treatment in fact responds to a genuine need, is appropriate for achieving the objective pursued and is necessary for that purpose'.[44] Subsequent cases have not focused on clause 4, but the Court has reiterated this formula in its interpretation of 'objective reasons' as regards the justification for renewal of a fixed-term contract.[45]

The Court does not cite any particular source for this interpretation of objective grounds, however, it is not difficult to see echoes of the objective justification test found within anti-discrimination law. To take a classic example, in *Bilka*, the Court held that indirect sex discrimination in pay would be justified if 'the measures chosen by the employer correspond to a real need on the part of the undertaking, are appropriate with a view to achieving the objectives pursued and are necessary to that end'.[46] These three elements (real need, appropriate, necessary) mirror the test established by the Court in *Del Cerro Alonso*. Although it is tempting to conclude that this is a clear sign that the Court is assimilating the Fixed-Term Work Directive to EU anti-discrimination legislation, it must be conceded that this style of justification test is not unique to anti-discrimination law; it is also found in the Court's approach to justifications of restrictions to free movement.[47] A more overt alignment of anti-discrimination law concepts and the Fixed-Term Work Directive can be found in *Zentralbetriebsrat der Landeskrankenhäuser Tirols v. Land Tirol*.[48] This case concerned, in part, the exclusion from a range of employment rights of those working under contracts with less than six months' duration. The provincial authorities argued that this could be justified on administrative grounds, but the Court rejected this on the basis that 'rigorous personnel management is a budgetary consideration and cannot therefore justify discrimination'.[49] Given the flexible scope for justifying less favourable

---

[44]   Para 58, *Del Cerro Alonso.*
[45]   Clause 5(1)(a); for example para 100, *Angelidaki and others.*
[46]   Para 36, Case 170/84, *Bilka-Kaufhaus GmbH v. Weber von Hartz* [1986] ECR 1607.
[47]   Craig and de Búrca (2008, 889).
[48]   Case C-486/08, judgment of 22 April 2010.
[49]   *Ibid.*, para 46.

treatment of fixed-term workers, it was far from obvious prior to this decision that serious financial reasons could not be invoked as objective justification. Notably, the Court cites case-law on the equal pay of women and men as authority for reaching this conclusion,[50] thereby reading across principles of anti-discrimination law into the interpretation of the Fixed-Term Work Directive.

REGULATING FIXED-TERM WORK VIA NON-DISCRIMINATION

This chapter commenced by positing a range of interpretations of the concept of non-discrimination. These varied from loose judicial oversight designed to restrain arbitrary behaviour, through to intense judicial scrutiny in the pursuit of substantive equality. Although the Fixed-Term Work Directive is heavily shaped by the principle of non-discrimination, it remains an open question as to whether that is viewed as an expression of the flexible, general principle of equality, or whether it can be assimilated to the more stringent standards of anti-discrimination legislation.

The material presented above suggests that the Fixed-Term Work Directive does not fit neatly into the category of EU anti-discrimination legislation. On the face of it, the Directive has a narrow definition of non-discrimination with considerable scope for objective justification. This contrasts unfavourably with the multifaceted and mature concept of discrimination found within the anti-discrimination Directives. The Court of Justice appears to be striding a middle path in its interpretation of the Fixed-Term Work Directive. It has not yet elevated it to the status of a fundamental rights instrument, but it has indicated that it contains norms of particular importance. This is reinforced by a relatively rigorous interpretation of the concept of objective justification for less favourable treatment of fixed-term workers. Nevertheless, the extent to which the Court conceptually aligns non-discrimination in the Fixed-Term Work Directive with EU anti-discrimination legislation remains ambiguous. This uncertainty is reinforced by the Court's decision in *Commission v. Luxembourg*.[51]

The case concerned infringement proceedings related to Luxembourg's implementation of the Posted Workers Directive.[52] Article 3(1) of the

---

[50]   Joined Cases C-4/02 and C-5/02, *Schönheit and Becker* [2003] ECR I-12575.
[51]   Case C-319/06 [2008] ECR I-4323.
[52]   Directive 96/71/EC concerning the posting of workers in the framework of the provision of services [1997] OJ L18/1.

Directive enumerates areas of national labour law that are to be applied to posted workers temporarily working in a Member State, provided these are laid down in national legislation, or collective agreements and arbitration awards that have been declared universally applicable. Article 3(1)(g) specifies that this includes 'equality of treatment between men and women and other provisions on non-discrimination'. In Luxembourg, its legislation provided that domestic 'rules on part-time and fixed-term work' would apply to posted workers. This was challenged by the Commission as going beyond the requirements permitted by Article 3(1). The Court agreed, tersely commenting that the rules on part-time and fixed-term work were 'a matter which is not mentioned in the list in the first subparagraph of Article 3(1)'.[53] Although there is no elaboration in the judgment, the assumption by both the Commission and the Court that rules on fixed-term work were not 'provisions on non-discrimination' reveals a particular mindset about where the boundaries of non-discrimination legislation lie.

The apparent reluctance on the part of the Court to assimilate the Fixed-Term Work Directive to the anti-discrimination Directives may lie in its underlying *raison d'être*. Clause 1 casts the principle of non-discrimination in an instrumental light: 'the purpose of this framework agreement is to: (a) improve the quality of fixed-term work by ensuring the application of the principle of non-discrimination'. In this guise, non-discrimination emerges as a tool for changing labour market practices, rather than an autonomous objective in its own right. This ambivalence reflects the undercurrent of the Framework Agreement, which arguably seeks to restrain recourse to fixed-term contracts. General Consideration 6 includes the important statement of principle that 'employment contracts of an indefinite duration are the general form of employment relationships and contribute to the quality of life of the workers concerned and improve performance'. While it has been argued that the Framework Agreement is 'latently permissive' of fixed-term contracts,[54] it clearly seeks to place them within boundaries and to reaffirm the exceptionality of this type of contract. From the standpoint of equality, this makes it difficult to equate the Fixed-Term Work Directive with EU anti-discrimination Directives. There is no sense in which the latter have any hostility to the protected characteristic; indeed it is evident that they are designed to ensure that hitherto marginalised groups, such as ethnic minorities, are fully integrated into the labour market so that they can enjoy full equality in practice. In contrast, the Fixed-Term Work Directive does not seek to use the

---

[53] Para 57, *Commission v. Luxembourg.*
[54] Murray (1999, 273).

principle of non-discrimination as a way of rendering fixed-term contracts equal in status to open-ended contracts. This interpretation is unavoidable given the limits placed on the successive use of fixed-term contracts.

Acknowledging the paradoxical position of non-discrimination at the heart of the Directive reawakens an old debate on whether non-discrimination rights are the most effective means of regulating fixed-term work. Critics have highlighted that the formal equal treatment model is handicapped by its dependency on a comparison with the supposedly standard worker on a permanent contract.[55] This assumes that the problems faced by fixed-term workers can be effectively redressed simply by treating them in the same way as permanent workers. Yet for fixed-term workers a key source of precariousness is the short and fragmented duration of the employment relationship, leading to exclusion from the array of statutory rights, social security entitlements and workplace benefits that tend to be linked to length of service thresholds.[56] The constricted principle of non-discrimination found within the Fixed-Term Work Directive does not seem to be equipped to tackle this underlying source of disadvantage for fixed-term workers.

REFERENCES

Countouris, N. (2007), *The Changing Law of the Employment Relationship – Comparative Analyses in the European Context*, Aldershot: Ashgate.

Craig, P. and G. de Búrca (2007), *EU law – text, cases and materials*, 4th edn, Oxford: Oxford University Press.

Ellis, E. (2005), *EU Anti-Discrimination Law*, Oxford: Oxford University Press.

Lorber, P. (2008), 'Achieving the Fixed-Term Work Directive's Aims: United Kingdom Implementation and Comparative Perspectives', in F. Pennings, Y. Konijn and A. Veldman (eds), *Social Responsibility and Labour Relations – European and Comparative Perspectives*, Boston: Wolters Kluwer, pp. 311–329.

McCann, D. (2008), *Regulating Flexible Work*, Oxford: Oxford University Press.

McColgan, A. (2003), 'The Fixed-Term (Prevention of Less Favourable Treatment) Regulations 2002: Fiddling while Rome Burns?', *Industrial Law Journal*, **32**, 194–199.

McCrudden, C. (2007), *Buying Social Justice – Equality, Government Procurement, and Legal Change*, Oxford: Oxford University Press.

McCrudden, C. and H. Kountouris (2007), 'Human Rights and European Equality Law', in H. Meenan (ed.), *Equality Law in an Enlarged European Union – Understanding the Article 13 Directives*, Cambridge: Cambridge University Press, pp. 73–116.

---

[55] Vosko (2006).

[56] Vigneau (1999, 177).

More, G. (1999), 'The Principle of Equal Treatment: From Market Unifier to Fundamental Right', in P. Craig and G. de Búrca (eds), *The Evolution of EU law*, Oxford: Oxford University Press, pp. 517–553.

Murray, J. (1999), 'Normalising Temporary Work: The Proposed Directive on Fixed-term Work', *Industrial Law Journal*, **28**, 269–275.

Sciarra, S. (2007), 'Il lavoro a tempo determinato nella giurisprudenza della Corte di giustizia europea. Un tassello nella "modernizzazione" del diritto di lavoro', Working Papers Centro studi di diritto del lavoro europeo 'Massimo D'Antona', 52/2007, Catania, University of Catania.

Vigneau, C. (1999), 'The Principle of Equal Treatment of Temporary and Permanent Workers', in C. Vigneau, K. Ahlberg, B. Bercusson and N. Bruun (eds), *Fixed-term Work in the EU: A European Agreement Against Discrimination and Abuse*, Stockholm: National Institute for Working Life, pp. 135–184.

Vosko, L. (2006), 'Gender, Precarious Work, and the International Labour Code: The Ghost in the ILO Closet', in J. Fudge and R. Owens (eds), *Precarious Work, Women, and the New Economy*, Oxford: Hart Publishing, pp. 53–75.

11. A dual European social citizenship?

Claire Marzo

INTRODUCTION

Professor Bercusson was one of the first authors to argue for a social citizenship at the EU level. In his manifesto,[1] he foresaw its possible evolution at a time when European citizenship was still considered an empty shell.[2] He argued in favour of a social citizenship: he believed that the European Union could be given a social turn and fought his whole life to make this come true.[3]

European citizenship has indeed been transformed. Instead of reflecting only political rights, it has been associated with the freedom of movement of workers.[4] After the *Martínez Sala* case, it was given a social content.[5] Article 21 FEU (formerly Article 18 EC) concerning the freedom of movement of European citizens and Article 18 FEU (formerly Article 12 EC) concerning the principle of non-discrimination on grounds of nationality were associated to extend rights formerly limited to workers. Social benefits were given to European citizens on

---

[1] Mückenberger, U., B. Bercusson,S. Deakin, P. Koistinen, Y. Kravaritou, A. Supiot and B. Veneziani (1997), 'Manifesto for a Social Europe', European Law Journal, **3** (2), 189–205.

[2] Jacqueson, C. (2002), 'Union Citizenship and the Court of Justice, Something New under the Sun? Towards Social Citizenship', European Law Review, **3**, 260–281

[3] Bercusson, B. (1993), 'EU Citizenship and Fundamental Social Rights: Community Law, European Law, National Law', in P. Rodière (ed.), La citoyenneté européenne face au droit social et au droit du travail, Trèves, ERA Bundesanzeiger, Vol. 14, Série de publications de l'Académie de Droit européen de Trèves, pp. 9–21.

[4] See Articles 17 and 18 EC (now Articles 20 and 21 FEU), Chalmers, D., C. Hadjiemanuil, G. Monti and A. Tomkins (2006), European Union Law, Cambridge: Cambridge University Press, pp. 574 ff.

[5] Case C-85/96, *Martínez Sala/Freistaat Bayern*, [1998] ERC I-2691.

the sole condition of their nationality associated with their movement to another Member State. European citizenship has, then, been used on many occasions by the Court of Justice of the European Union. It was finally given a legislative meaning by Directive 2004/38 on the freedom of movement of European citizens. It is further found in the new proposal for a directive on the application of patients' rights in cross-border healthcare.[6]

Today, citizenship is even used beyond its case-related scope to be found in other social fields. The existing European social citizenship thus appears to be two-fold: on the one hand, it is drawn from the European citizenship of Article 21 FEU (formerly Article 18 EC). On the other hand, it is derived from the idea of participation in unrelated fields such as active citizenship,[7] European services of general interest[8] and non-discrimination of article 19 FUE (formerly 13 EC).[9] This appears for instance in Article 170 §1 FEU (formerly Article 154 TEC) which states that in order:

---

[6]   In its conclusions of 1 and 2 June 2006, the Council of the European Union has 'recognized the particular value of an initiative on cross-border healthcare ensuring clarity for European citizens about their rights and entitlements when they move from one Member State to another in order to ensure legal certainty'. See Proposal for a Directive of the European Parliament and of the Council on the application of patients' rights in cross-border healthcare {SEC(2008) 2163} {SEC(2008) 2164} {SEC(2008) 2183}, COM (2008) 414 final – COD (2008)142, p. 1. It follows case C-158/06, Kohll Union des caisses de maladie, [1998] ERC I-1931 and case C-120/95, Decker/Caisse de maladie des employés privés, [1998] ERC I-1831.

[7]   Communication from the Commission to the Council on European policies concerning youth – Addressing the concerns of young people in Europe – implementing the European Youth Pact and promoting active citizenship, SEC (2005) 693, COM (2005) 206 and Communication from the Commission to the European Parliament, the Council, the European Economic and Social Committee and the Committee of the Regions – An updated strategic framework for European cooperation in education and training {SEC(2008) 3047} {SEC(2008) 3048}, COM (2008)865 final, p. 6 and p. 10 ff.

[8]   See Article 170 and 174 FEU and Micklitz, H. (2008), 'SGEI's in Energy: A National or European Concept? Consumer Rights or Citizenship?', Services of General Economic Interest in the Single Market: What Role for Europe?, Florence: European University Institute.

[9]   This tendency appears in Article 2 of Regulation (EC) No 1922/2006 of the European Parliament and of the Council of 20 December 2006 on establishing a European Institute for Gender Equality, OJ L 403, 30.12.2006, pp. 9–17 which states the objective to 'contribute to the promotion of equality between men and women' and 'to raise the awareness among EU citizens' and in Article 3 §2 of Council Directive 2000/43/EC of 29 June 2000 implementing the principle of equal treatment between persons irrespective of racial or ethnic origin, OJ L 180, 19.7.2000, pp. 22–26.

to help achieve the objectives referred to in Articles 26 FEU [about the common market] and 174 FEU [about economic, social and territorial cohesion] and to enable *citizens of the Union*, economic operators and regional and local communities to derive full benefit from the setting-up of an area without internal frontiers, the Union shall contribute to the establishment and development of trans-European networks in the areas of transport, telecommunications and energy infrastructures.

Several texts have consequently followed the constitutional mandate and given new rights to the citizens.[10]

Two social citizenships appear – one has been developed by the case-law of the European Court of Justice, the other is to be found in Directive. In terms of personal scope of application, the first one is limited to nations of Member States whereas the second one seems to be more universal and open to European citizens, but also to world citizens. The analysis of these two social citizenships raises several interesting questions such as that of the links between citizenship and welfare state,[11] the normative interest of such a coordination at a national[12] and European level,[13] its legitimacy[14] and its democratic implications.

In this short chapter, I want to focus on one single question: how do we justify the co-existence of these two social citizenships? I try to understand why the European institutions have relied on two different concepts both named after citizenship and more precisely why they have two different personal scopes of application.

---

[10] A more detailed analysis is available in Marzo, C. (2010), La dimension sociale de la citoyenneté européenne, Aix-Marseille: Presses universitaires d'Aix-Marseille.
[11] For instance, UK: Marshall, T.H. (1992), Citizenship and Social Class, London: Pluto Perspectives; EU: Shaw, J. (1997), 'Citizenship of the Union: Towards Post-National Membership?', 6 Jean Monnet Working Papers, New York: New York University School of Law.
[12] Rimlinger, G.V. (1966), 'Welfare Policy and Economic Development: A Comparative Historical Perspective', Journal of Economic History, **56**, 556–571; Ashford, D.E. (1986), The Emergence of the Welfare States, Oxford: Blackwell, Chapters 2 and 3.
[13] For instance, De Búrca, G. (2005), EU Law and the Welfare State. In Search of Solidarity, Oxford: Oxford University Press, Introduction; Johnson, A. (2005), European Welfare States and Supranational Governance of Social Policy, London: Palgrave, Chapter 4.
[14] See specifically De Búrca, G. (2005), 'The Future of Social Rights Protection in Europe'; De Witte, B., 'The Trajectory of Fundamental Social Rights in the European Union'; Moreau, M.-A. (2005), 'European Fundamental Social Rights in the Context of Economic Globalization', all in De Búrca, G. and B. De Witte (eds) (2005),Social Rights in Europe, Oxford: Oxford University Press.

THE HISTORICAL JUSTIFICATION

A first explanation for the differing personal scopes of European citizenship and the other form of citizenship – that is open citizenship – could relate to the limits resulting from compromises between the EU and the Member States. It was proposed on several occasions that EU citizenship should be based on residence and not on nationality. If another choice was then made in Article 17 EC, it was the result of negotiations between the Member States. One could draw from this that the European Union has always had some universal ambition, but it found limits when it was given a reality. This would explain that this second or open citizenship is more broadly open than European citizenship which focuses on equality and rights awarded by Member States. This echoes the opposition between residence and nationality which appears clearly from the study of the evolution of the notion of citizenship, mainly before it was enacted.

Before 1992, when European citizenship did not exist yet and was called 'special rights', it included economic and social rights which were open to anybody. In the first report about the idea of European citizenship, it was stated that it would be interesting to 'examine the extent to which civil rights given to all foreigners and all rights deriving from the EC treaties could be better protected if they were reserved to nationals of Member States'.[15] The European Commission and the European Parliament both considered that European citizenship should not be limited to Member States' nationals. In 1987, the Parliament appeared in favour of a right to vote in local elections awarded to Member States' nationals, but also to third country nationals who are long-term residents.[16] In 1990, it proposed to give not only economic and social, but also political rights to workers, whatever their nationality.[17]

Since then, the European Commission has had a more nuanced discourse. It has always been in favour of a better integration of third-country nationals and is still willing to give them economic and social rights.[18] For a while it argued for residents to be given the right to vote in

---

[15] 'Towards a Europe of Citizens', European Commission report about the implementation of point 11 of the final report of the Paris Summit, 9–10 December 1974, Report given by the European Commission to the European Council on 3 July 1975, Bull. E.C. Suppl. 7/75, p. 28.

[16] Resolution of 15 December 1987 OJEC 13, 18 January 1988, p. 26, point 8.

[17] Resolution of the European Parliament on migrant workers of third countries, 14 June 1990, OJEC C 175/180, 16 July 1990.

[18] All the regulations about labour law and social security issues are applicable to all persons notwithstanding their nationality.

local elections.[19] But, it changed its approach when political rights alone were considered: they should be reserved to nationals of Member States.[20] Consequently, the Directive[21] and the proposition which preceded it,[22] limited the right to vote in the European Parliament to Member State nationals. This approach would shape EU citizenship in the Maastricht Treaty in 1992 and have an influence on some social rights.

However, in 1989, this tendency appears again in texts about EU citizenship. At the European Council of Madrid, the presidency focused under the title 'Citizenship' on the question of third-country nationals' integration. In a paragraph about 'Freedom of movement of persons and Europe of citizens', the European Council wished to establish an inventory of the national positions with regards to immigration.[23] It analysed the efficiency of external border controls. The same year, the resolution about the Declaration of fundamental rights and freedoms showed the wide reach of the European citizen. If this Charter should be 'the expression of common values of the citizens of Europe',[24] it gave rights 'to all persons' in each of its Articles.[25] Only a few rights are limited to European citizens.[26]

When the Maastricht Treaty was being drafted, the Spanish delegation proposed a memorandum entitled 'Towards a European citizenship'[27] which based a foreign policy and common security, as well as a mon-

---

[19] Action Program in Favour of Migrant Workers and Their Families, Bull. EC suppl 3-76, p. 13, spec. p. 23; Draft Council resolution on guidelines for a community policy migration, COM(1985) 48 final.

[20] Voting rights in local elections for community nationals residing in a Member State other than their own (report from the commission to the European Parliament transmitted to the Council for information, 26 September 1986), COM (86) 487 final.

[21] Council Directive 94/80/EC of 19 December 1994 laying down detailed arrangements for the exercise of the right to vote and to stand as a candidate in municipal elections by citizens of the Union residing in a Member State of which they are not nationals, OJ L 368, 31.12.1994, pp. 38–47, modified but on this question by Directive 96/30/EC and Directive 2006/106/EC.

[22] Proposal for a Council directive on voting rights for community nationals in local elections in their member state of residence, OJ C 246, 20.9.1988, p. 3, COM (1988) 371 final.

[23] European Council of Madrid, conclusions of the presidency, 26–27 June 1989, Bull. EC. 12-1989, pp. 10–11.

[24] Resolution on the adoption of the declaration of fundamental rights and freedoms, OJ C 120, 16/5/1989, p. 51.

[25] Ibid., p. 51 and f.

[26] Specially, Article 17 is about democracy; ibid.

[27] Text presented the 25 September 1990, reproduced in French in Europe documents, 2 October 1990, no 1653.

etary and economic union, on European citizenship.[28] It proposed a 'common space where the European citizen would have a central role'.[29] This statement shows that it was already foreseen that European citizenship is bound to have a broad scope of application, whether personal or material. The European Parliament considers that 'in this context, legal residents who are third-country nationals should also be given economic and social rights'.[30] What is original is the fact that these rights are part of European citizenship. European citizenship cannot completely deny its association with residence. And often, even nowadays, one can see that, in the name of citizenship, the situation of third-country national legal residents is taken into account more[31] or less[32] explicitly. We see already that European citizenship was fluctuating between a closed and an open personal scope of application which would then lead to two citizenships: that of the case-law limited to Member States nationals and that more open one.

Finally, the Charter of Fundamental Rights is ambivalent concerning the inclusion of third-country nationals. It adds in a second paragraph of Article 45 that 'freedom of movement and residence may be granted, in accordance with the Treaties, to nationals of third countries legally resident in the territory of a Member State'. This shows that, in a similar manner to those of European citizens, legal residents' rights are progressively made more concrete.

The EU's hesitations are corroborated by doctrinal proposals in favour

---

[28] This proposal is repeated in the Treaty of Lisbon. Article 3 § 2 TEU states that 'the Union shall offer its citizens an area of freedom, security and justice without internal frontiers, in which the free movement of persons is ensured in conjunction with appropriate measures with respect to external border controls, asylum, immigration and the prevention and combating of crime'.

[29] Solbes Mira, P. (1991), 'La citoyenneté européenne', Revue du marché commun et de l'Union européenne, **345,** 168–170.

[30] Point H of the Resolution on Union Citizenship, 16/12/1991, R. Bindi, OJ C 326, 21/11/1991, pp. 205–206.

[31] The same idea appears again in the Catania report, 30 June 2005, PE 360.098v01-00. This document proposed a residence citizenship. It was not adopted by the Parliament.

[32] For instance, in a paragraph about 'a Union closes to its citizens', and more precisely about the establishment of an area of freedom, security and justice, the European Parliament approved the transfer of competences regarding asylum and immigration and the third country nationals' status from the third to the first pillar. European citizens and third-country nationals are given an increasingly similar status. This tendency also appeared in the fifth report on European citizenship, ibid., COM(2008) 85 final, SEC(2008) 197, p. 4.

of a residence-based citizenship.[33] Some authors propose to integrate foreigners (nationals of other Member States and third-country nationals) by application of the principle of non-discrimination drawing on, without explaining it, an isopolitical citizenship.[34] Others link these rights to the right to work, which frees one from relying on the condition of nationality.[35] Finally, some authors develop the idea of a post-national citizenship which not only exists at a supranational level (i.e. European), but is also based on foundations other than nationality.[36] Ferry and Shaw develop this citizenship in the field of political rights.[37] Habermas develops the concept of constitutional patriotism to underline the schism between the feeling of belonging of national citizenship and its practice at a supranational level.[38] Considering immigration in the 1960s and focusing on non-European populations, Soysal proposes a post-national citizenship implying the adoption of international norms on grounds of residence and not legal citizenship.[39] All these discourses recommend a new model of citizenship.[40]

---

[33]   Oger, H. (2003), 'Residence as the New Additional Inclusive Criterion for Citizenship', Web Journal of Current Legal Issues, **5**, available at http://webjcli. ncl.ac.uk/2003/issue5 /oger5.html (accessed May 2011).

[34]   Chevallier, J. (2004), L'État post modern, Paris: LGDJ.

[35]   Supiot, A. (2006), 'Azione normativa e lavoro decente. Prospettive nel campo della sicurezza sociale', Giornale di diritto del lavoro e di relazioni industriali, **28** (112), 625–655; Mavridis, P. (2003), La sécurité sociale à l'épreuve de l'intégration européenne, Etude d'une confrontation entre libertés du marché et droits fondamentaux, Bruxelles: Bruylant.

[36]   Kastoryano, R. (1996), La France, l'Allemagne et leurs immigrés: négocier l'identité, Paris: Armand Colin.

[37]   Ferry, J.-M. (1991), 'Pertinence du postnational', Esprit, **11**, 80–94; Shaw, J. (2007), The Transformation of Citizenship in the European Union: Electoral Rights and the Restructuring of Political Space, Cambridge: Cambridge University Press.

[38]   Habermas, J. (1996), 'The European Nation State: Its Achievements and its Limitations. On the Past and Future of Sovereignty and Citizenship', Ratio Juris, **9** (2), 125–137; Lenoble, J. and Dewandre, N. (1992), L'Europe au soir des siècles, coll. Esprit, Paris: Editions du Seuil, pp. 17–39.

[39]   Soysal, Y. (1994), Limits of Citizenship. Migrants and Postnational Membership in Europe, Chicago: Chicago University Press, pp. 143 ff.

[40]   'The new democratic politics is about negotiating this complex relationship between the rights of full membership, democratic voice and territorial residence', in Benhabib, S. (2004), The Rights of Others: Aliens, Citizens and Residents, Cambridge, Conference sponsored by CRASSH, University of Cambridge; Farkas, O. and O. Rymkevitch (2004), 'Immigration and the Free Movement of Workers after Enlargement: Contrasting Choices', The International Journal of Comparative Labour Law and Industrial Relations, **20** (3), 369–397; Supiot, A. (2009), 'Justice sociale et libéralisation du commerce international', Droit Social, **2**, 131–146.

Even if it is only in the early stages, it is often proposed that European citizenship should be based on residence.[41] The fact that European citizenship is based on nationality does not correspond to any clear necessity.[42]

This ambiguity between nationality and residence explains well the recent developments in the field of social security and education: European citizenship is limited to Member States' nationals and their families, but also to a condition of residence of a certain duration in the host Member State. It also explains why, while the rights linked to the four economic freedoms are limited to European citizens, there is also another type of citizenship which shows an 'increasing trend towards a kind of integration and focuses less on formal data such as nationality and more on factors such as residence, employment and social integration' because the European citizenship from the case-law is so limited, there is a need for another one more inclusive.[43] But, residence and nationality are part of the explanation; the next question is to determine why the rights associated with European citizenship are more limited than the others. Two justifications will be examined in turn: an institutional one and a doctrinal one.

THE INSTITUTIONAL JUSTIFICATION

The distinction between the two European social citizenships could be linked to the action of the Court of Justice of the European Union. The Court has traditionally focused its attention on the application of the principles of free movement and non-discrimination, thus relying on the nationality of the Member States to give rights. On the contrary, the European Commission, the Council and the Parliament have had a broader approach through legislative means, thus creating a more open citizenship applicable to more persons.

The first category, European citizenship, has been given a broad field

---

[41] Oger, H. (2006), Constitutionalising Multi-Level Euro-Denizenship, Florence: European University Institute; Benlolo Carabot, M. (2007), Les fondements juridiques de la citoyenneté européenne, Bruxelles: Bruylant.

[42] Diez-Picazo, L.M. (2003), 'Citoyenneté et identité européennes', in G. Cohen-Jonathan and J. Dutheil de la Rochère (eds), Constitution européenne, démocratie et droits de l'homme, Actes du colloque des 13 et 14 mars 2003, Bruxelles: Bruylant, Nemesis, pp. 165–182, esp. 173.

[43] Condinanzi, M., A. Lang and B. Nascimbene (2008), Citizenship of the Union and Freedom of Movement of Persons, Leiden: Martinus Nijhof.

of application by the Court. It consists in a control by the Union ensuring that the Member States are treating the nationals of other Member States similarly to the way they treat their own citizens. It is an extensive application of the principle of non-discrimination on grounds of nationality which goes back to the Rome treaties.[44] The Court has systematically ensured that Member States would respect the nationals of other Member States. For example, it developed the notion of social advantages before regulation 1612/68 repeated it.[45] It also developed an extensive understanding of the worker.[46] More recently, it has given a content to European citizenship. More precisely, with and after the *Martínez Sala* case, it contradicted Directive 93/96 to enhance the free movement of students and allow them to remain in the country even when they do not have sufficient resources.[47]

The Court has always been seen as *avant-garde* in the protection of the European competences and the compliance of the Member States. This position has allowed it to rely on the new concept of European citizenship to expand the freedom of European citizens to move. It triggered Directive 2004/38 to limit these expansions. Through the application of the principle of non-discrimination on grounds of nationality, it has ensured that Member States applied their national rules to European citizens without distinction as soon as they were in their country. It was not about creating new rules, but controlling their applications. For instance, in the *Tas-Hagen* and *Nerkowska* cases, the Court ruled that a Member State could not refuse to give a war-related benefit to its nationals on the ground that they no longer lived in the country but in another Member State.[48] It is thus logical that national rules are only going to be applied to the nationals of other Member States who have moved to another EU country.

Conversely, wider citizenship was developed by the legislative European institutions. It is not so much the Court of Justice which has ensured the application of national laws to European citizens, but the creation of new acts applicable first to European citizens, and also, more generally, to everybody. European services of general interest, active citizenship

---

[44]   Robin, Olivier S. (1999), Le principe d'égalité en droit communautaire: étude à partir des libertés économiques, Aix-en-Provence: Presses universitaires d'Aix-Marseille.

[45]   Regulation (EEC) No 1612/68 of the Council of 15 October 1968 on freedom of movement for workers within the Community, OJ L 257, 19.10.1968, pp. 2–12.

[46]   Case C-456/02, Trojani, [2004] ERC I-7573; case C-138/02, Collins, [2004] ERC I-2703.

[47]   Case C-184/99, Grzelczyk, [2001] ERC I-6193; case C-209/03, Bidar, [2005] ERC I-2119; case C-158/07, Förster, [2008] ECR I-8507.

[48]   Case C-192/05, Tas-Hagen and Tas, [2006] ERC I-10451, Case C-499/06, Nerkowska, [2008] ERC I-3993.

and anti-discrimination laws are good examples. Without any link to European citizenship in the Treaty, these areas are now metamorphosed by a new starting point: citizenship. The objectives are to show 1) the care that the EU takes about its inhabitants, and 2) to foster participation. These two reasons give the institutions an aim for transforming the existing policies.

One argument questions this justification. It has to do with the constant effort of the *Court* to extend the circle of beneficiaries of the rights of horizontal citizenship. It has developed an increasingly broader concept of the family of the European citizen which has subsequently been expanded by Directive 2004/38.[49] The Court gave a generous interpretation of family members. It even included descendants aged over 21, together with ascendants and divorced partners.[50] The Court has also considered the need to take into account persons born in Europe but deprived of the nationality of a Member State. Such is the case in Germany where the *jus sanguinis* system limits German nationality to the children of German nationals. In the *Orfanopoulos* case, the Court decided that the expulsion of a third-country national – in this case a Turkish national – could only be executed if the context was considered, specifically, the fact that the claimant was born in Germany and had never left the country meant that he should only be expelled under very restricted conditions.[51] This extension might lead one to consider that horizontal and vertical citizenship will one day have the same personal scope of application. But this would not be realistic as this extension is nonetheless limited. The family is a closed concept. If Article 8 ECHR allows this enlargement, it is very unlikely that there will be an extension to all residents. So, even though in this case non-European citizens are given the same rights as European citizens, the application of the non-discrimination principle is still quite limited.

This justification appears efficient; it is, moreover, supported by a theoretical justification.

---

[49] Case C-127/08, Metock e.a., [2008] ERC I-6241.and Directive 2004/38/EC of the European Parliament and of the Council of 29 April 2004 on the right of citizens of the Union and their family members to move and reside freely within the territory of the Member States amending Regulation (EEC) No 1612/68 and repealing Directives 64/221/EEC, 68/360/EEC, 72/194/EEC, 73/148/EEC, 75/34/EEC, 75/35/EEC, 90/364/EEC, 90/365/EEC and 93/96/EEC (Text with EEA relevance), OJ L 158, 30.4.2004, pp. 77–123.

[50] Case C-127/08, Metock e.a., [2008] ERC I-6241.

[51] Cases C-482/01 and C-493/01, Orfanopoulos and Oliveri, [2004] ERC I-5257.

THE THEORETICAL JUSTIFICATION

The justification of the two different fields of application of the two types of citizenship raises the wider questions of belonging to a society and of access to citizenship rights. A prescriptive analysis proposed by Rubio Marin identifies several justifications for the group (a state or an international organization such as the EU) granting social rights, or more generally citizenship rights, to a human being.[52] The first ground is solidarity. The notion of community or collective identity justifies the participation of an individual member of the community in its organization.

This justification implies excluding people who are not part of the community. The second ground is not linked to solidarity, but to human dignity. It is an individualistic vision of the person who owns rights by the reason only of his/her existence on earth. His/her status is linked to his/her humanity. All men and women have a right to dignity and fundamental rights. Hence the idea of a minimum standard of social rights.

This justification recalls the eternal dilemma of security versus justice.[53] A territorial unit (the state or, in this case, the European Union) wants to be safe by opposing other territories which might endanger it politically as well as socio-economically. It creates a minimum standard of social rights granted to its members (the European citizens). This creation is built on the difference between people who do and those who do not belong to its territory. It contradicts by essence the equality between all persons, here called 'justice'.

These two approaches are not contradictory: they can be juxtaposed. The second one gives a minimal standard to everybody, which does not prevent a community from giving more rights to its citizens on grounds of solidarity, sharing the common good. The first justifies a European social citizenship whereas the second justifies an open social citizenship.

On the one hand, an old citizenship built on the model of the Member States only gives national rights. The beneficiaries are the nationals of other Member States. The aim to limit access is justified by the limited quantity of goods to share. Access to social security, education and health care are

---

[52]　Workshop on the understanding of Social rights in European countries and institutions, organized on behalf of the EUI working group on European social and labour law and University Paris Ouest Nanterre, European University Institute, 26 June 2009, Florence, Italy. See also Rubio Marin, R. (2000), *Immigration as a Democratic Challenge*, New York: Cambridge University Press.

[53]　See Jordan, B. and F. Duvall (2003), *Migration: the Boundaries of Equality and Justice*, Cambridge: Polity.

expensive public services.[54] They are mostly closed to non-nationals and, to a certain extent, open to migrant nationals of other Member States. It corresponds to the theory that T.H. Marshall proposed in the 1950s in the United Kingdom. He not only distinguished between civil, political and social citizenship, but he also drew links between the members of the community. According to him, the conscience of community had grown from a local territory to a bigger one, the state. And the different generations of rights had made this societal conscience possible. He made his proposal in the context of the United Kingdom, but he did not define the link between the citizens. It could as easily be nationality or residence.[55] In any case, it is solidarity which limits the access to citizenship.[56]

On the other hand, an open citizenship is making the EU ideals real. The aim is to claim the European values and enforce them in and beyond Europe. It concerns everybody. It represents a transnational citizenship which is superimposed on the limited solidaristic version of citizenship, but which nonetheless exists. This citizenship follows newer paths such as the humanization of rights, or the growing recognition of human rights and their universality. This citizenship develops under the protection and the influence of the European Court of Human Rights: all men should have a minimum standard of rights.

Two remarks should be made. First, the question of financial contribution to the national system would appear to be an interesting one. It would correspond to the open citizenship as all persons are touched upon by the measures, but only the ones who pay to access the public services such as transport or electricity can actually enjoy it. It could also fit into the solidaristic approach as the condition of residence can be founded on the idea that only people who lived in the country and thus contributed to its financial system would have a right to enjoy it.[57] This analysis might obliterate the previous distinction. Nonetheless, the distinction stands where it

---

[54] They are sometimes run by private services, but that is not the point. For EU influence also in private sectors, see case C-11/06, Morgan, [2007] ERC I-9161.

[55] In the Beveridge report, it is not clear whether the citizens (beneficiaries of social security) are nationals or residents, see Beveridge, S.W. (1942), Social Insurance and Allied Services, New York, Toronto: The Macmillan Company of Canada, p. 299, also available at: http://news.bbc.co.uk/2/shared/bsp/hi/pdfs/19_07_05_beveridge.pdf (accessed May 2011).

[56] What this suggests is that some sense of historical community and shared destiny of citizenship is a prerequisite for social rights. See Marshall, Citizenship and Social Class.

[57] Thomas, R. (2002), 'Who Belongs? Competing Conceptions of Political Membership', European Journal of Social Theory, **5** (3), 323–349, at p. 323.

supports that the financial contribution proposition shall not account for European citizenship to be limited to nationals. It is superimposed on the two citizenships, but it does not question it.

Secondly, it is interesting to see that some rights fall into the two categories. For instance, active citizenship can be compared to educational rights. If the differences are clear – as active citizenship is a simple EU programme whereas education is a clear competence in each Member State – links can be made, not only because education is a shared competence, but also because some elements of active citizenship could be realized through national education. This does not prevent us from establishing a clear distinction. The possible confusion shows that a different situation could have occurred and that other institutions might have followed other paths.[58] These three justifications explain the historical developments and the existing framework. The next question is to decide whether the distinction can be normatively justified and think about its future: it is not unlikely that these two citizenships could be reconciled or at least coordinated.

The institutional justification shows a previous development, but does not exclude an evolution. One might even consider that it has already started when looking at Directive 2004/38 which codifies the Court's rulings. Similarly, it is likely that the Court is going to be asked to judge on questions previously only dealt with by regulations. The *Kohll* and *Decker* cases indicate an evolution in this direction.[59]

Similarly, the more theoretical justification explains a state of the art and the two underlying conceptions, but does not exclude an evolution. The two approaches can be superimposed.[60]

REFERENCES

Ashford, D.E. (1986) *The Emergence of the Welfare States*, Oxford: Blackwell.
Benhabib, S. (2004), *The Rights of Others: Aliens, Citizens and Residents*, Cambridge, Conference sponsored by CRASSH, University of Cambridge.

---

[58]   One might think that it is for the existing democratic authority to decide which rights should be given to which persons. Rubio Marin, R. (2000), Immigration as a Democratic Challenge, New York: Cambridge University Press.

[59]   See also the Court's influence on the understanding of the four freedoms: Tryfonidou, A. (2010), 'Further Steps on the Road to Convergence among the Market Freedoms', European Law Review, **35**, 36–56.

[60]   For a plea in favour of a reunion of the two types of citizenship, see Marzo, C.(2010), La dimension sociale de la citoyenneté européenne, Aix-Marseille: Presses universitaires d'Aix-Marseille, Chapter 7 and conclusion.

Benlolo Carabot, M. (2007), *Les fondements juridiques de la citoyenneté européenne,* Bruxelles: Bruylant.

Bercusson, B. (1993), 'EU Citizenship and Fundamental Social Rights: Community Law, European Law, National Law', in P. Rodière (ed.), *La citoyenneté européenne face au droit social et au droit du travail,* Trèves, ERA Bundesanzeiger, Vol. 14, Série de publications de l'Académie de Droit européen de Trèves, pp. 9–21.

Beveridge, S.W. (1942), *Social Insurance and Allied Services,* New York, Toronto: The Macmillan Company of Canada, also available at http://news.bbc.co.uk/2/shared/bsp/hi/pdfs/19_07_05_beveridge.pdf (accessed May 2010).

Chalmers, D., C. Hadjiemanuil, G. Monti and A. Tomkins (2006), *European Union Law,* Cambridge: Cambridge University Press.

Chevallier, J. (2004), *L'État post modern,* Paris: LGDJ.

Condinanzi, M., A. Lang and B. Nascimbene (2008), *Citizenship of the Union and Freedom of Movement of Persons,* Martinus Nijhof.

De Búrca, G. (2005), *EU Law and the Welfare State. In Search of Solidarity,* Oxford: Oxford University Press.

De Búrca, G. (2005), 'The Future of Social Rights Protection in Europe', in G. De Búrca and B. De Witte (eds), *Social Rights in Europe,* Oxford: Oxford University Press.

Diez-Picazo, L.M. (2003), 'Citoyenneté et identité européennes', in G. Cohen-Jonathan and J. Dutheil de la Rochère (eds), *Constitution européenne, démocratie et droits de l'homme, Actes du colloque des 13 et 14 mars 2003,* Bruxelles: Bruylant, Nemesis, pp. 165–182.

Farkas, O. and O. Rymkevitch (2004), 'Immigration and the Free Movement of Workers after Enlargement: Contrasting Choices', *The International Journal of Comparative Labour Law and Industrial Relations,* **20** (3), 369–397.

Ferry, J.-M. (1991), 'Pertinence du postnational', *Esprit,* **11**, 80–94.

Habermas, J. (1996), 'The European Nation State: Its Achievements and its Limitations, on the Past and Future of Sovereignty and Citizenship, *Ratio Juris,* **9** (2), 125–137.

Jacqueson, C. (2002), 'Union Citizenship and the Court of Justice, Something New under the Sun? Towards Social Citizenship', *European Law Review,* **3**, 260–281.

Johnson, A. (2005), *European Welfare States and Supranational Governance of Social Policy,* London: Palgrave, Chapter 4.

Jordan, B. and Duvall, F. (2003), *Migration: the Boundaries of Equality and Justice,* Cambridge: Polity.

Kastoryano, R. (1996), *La France, l'Allemagne et leurs immigrés: négocier l'identité,* Paris: Armand Colin.

Lenoble, J. and N. Dewandre (1992), *L'Europe au soir des siècles,* coll. Esprit, Paris: Editions du Seuil, pp. 17–39.

Marshall, T.H. (1992), *Citizenship and Social Class,* London: Pluto Press.

Marzo, C. (2010), *La dimension sociale de la citoyenneté européenne,* Aix-Marseille: Presses universitaires d'Aix-Marseille.

Mavridis, P. (2003), *La sécurité sociale à l'épreuve de l'intégration européenne, Etude d'une confrontation entre libertés du marché et droits fondamentaux,* Bruxelles: Bruylant.

Micklitz, H. (2008), 'SGEI's in Energy: A National or European Concept? Consumer Rights or Citizenship?', *Services of general economic interest in the single market: what role for Europe?,* Florence: EUI.

Moreau, M.-A. (2005), 'European Fundamental Social Rights in the Context of Economic Globalization', in G. De Búrca and B. De Witte (eds), *Social Rights in Europe*, Oxford: Oxford University Press.

Mückenberger, U., B. Bercusson, S. Deakin, P. Koistinen, Y. Kravaritou, A. Supiot and B. Veneziani (1997), 'Manifesto for a Social Europe', *European Law Journal*, **3** (2), 189–205.

Oger, H. (2003), 'Residence as the New Additional Inclusive Criterion for Citizenship', *Web Journal of Current Legal Issues*, **5**, available at http://webjcli. ncl.ac.uk/2003/issue5 /oger5.html (accessed May 2011).

Oger, H. (2006), *Constitutionalising Multi-Level Euro-Denizenship*, Florence: EUI.

Rimlinger, G.V. (1966), 'Welfare Policy and Economic Development: A Comparative Historical Perspective', *Journal of Economic History*, **56**, 556–571.

Robin Olivier, S. (1999), *Le principe d'égalité en droit communautaire: étude à partir des libertés économiques*, Aix-en-Provence, Presses universitaires d'Aix-Marseille.

Rubio Marin, R. (2000), *Immigration as a Democratic Challenge*, New York: Cambridge University Press.

Shaw, J. (1997), 'Citizenship of the Union: Towards Post-National Membership?', Jean Monnet Working Papers, No.6, New York: New York University School of Law.

Solbes Mira, P. (1991), 'La citoyenneté européenne', *Revue du marché commun et de l'Union européenne,* 345, 168–170.

Soysal, Y. (1994), *Limits of Citizenship. Migrants and Postnational Membership in Europe*, Chicago: Chicago University Press.

Supiot, A. (2006), 'Azione normativa e lavoro decente. Prospettive nel campo della sicurezza sociale', *Giornale di diritto del lavoro e di relazioni industriali*, **28** (112), 625–655.

Supiot, A. (2009), 'Justice sociale et libéralisation du commerce international', *Droit Social*, **2**, 131–146.

Thomas, R. (2002), 'Who Belongs? Competing Conceptions of Political Membership', *European Journal of Social Theory*, **5** (3), 323–349.

Tryfonidou, A. (2010), 'Further Steps on the Road to Convergence among the Market Freedoms, *European Law Review*, **35**, 36–56.

Section 2

Trade Union Action and Workers' Participation

12. Toward new synergies through worker representatives?

Sylvaine Laulom

For Brian Bercusson (2004), participation of workers through their representatives was without doubt, part of the European Social Model. According to him:

> Contrasting the presence and role of trade unions and workers' representative organisation in the USA with European experience illustrates the singularity of the European model of employment and industrial relations. Its manifestation, in all its diversity at both EU and Member States levels, in the form of macro-level national dialogue, collective bargaining at intersectoral and sectoral levels, and collective participation in decision-making at the workplace is the most salient quality distinguishing the European model of employment and industrial relations.

In another article he wrote that 'EU law is shaping an economic model incorporating mandatory information and consultation of employees and their representatives' (Bercusson, 2002).

The building of a European model of workers' participation started in the 1970s (Laulom, 2005). The Community's first Social Action Program of 1974 had three main objectives. One of them was the increased involvement of management and labour in the economic and social decisions of the Community and of workers in companies. After the adoption of the first social directives in 1975 and 1977 dealing with workers' participation and restructurings of enterprises,[1] workers' participation has been one of the main areas of European intervention along with gender and discrimination and health and safety. The importance given to workers'

---

[1] Council Directive 75/129/EEC of 17 February 1975 on the approximation of the laws of the Member States relating to collective redundancies, OJ L048, 22.02.1975, p. 29 and Council Directive 77/187/EEC of 14 February 1977 on the approximation of the laws of the Member States relating to the safeguarding of employees' rights in the event of transfers of undertakings, businesses or parts of undertakings or businesses, OJ L 61, 5.3.1977, p. 26.

representatives and to social partners is reflected by the social dialogue at the European level. It is an important part of the Community acquis. But the European Union also stresses the important role workers' representatives should play in enterprises. Several directives have now been adopted. The Charter of fundamental rights of the European Union also recognizes the fundamental rights of workers or their representatives to be informed and consulted. The European Employment Strategy and flexicurity approach further stresses the role that the social partners, at various levels, should play in these processes.

Since the 1970s, European references to workers' representation have always been linked to economic changes and restructuring of enterprises. Thus the first rights recognized to workers' representatives were about collective dismissals and transfer of undertakings. More recently, the Commission staff working paper published in July 2008, on restructuring and employment, states that 'the importance of a joint approach by the social partners with regard to anticipation and management of change should be underlined'.[2]

The current financial and economic crisis has affected all Member States and it has had severe effects on employment as a consequence of a rising number of companies being forced to restructure their activities. The crisis raises questions related to the issue of workers' participation:

- How has the European model of workers' participation 'operated' when restructuring fell on enterprises?
- How has the economic crisis challenged this model of European workers' participation?

Indeed, the economic and financial crisis illustrates the potentiality but also the limits of a European system of workers' participation that started to be elaborated in the 1970s and that is an almost coherent system.

THE BUILDING OF A EUROPEAN FRAMEWORK OF WORKERS' PARTICIPATION

If we compare the building of the European framework of workers' participation to the national systems, some characteristics appear. First, the European Union is more interested in workers' participation than

---

[2]   SEC(2008)2154 of 2 July 2008, 2/07/2008, *Restructuring and Employment, the Contribution of the European Union*, Commission staff working paper.

in workers' representation. The European Union has granted national workers' representatives various rights to be informed and to be consulted without defining who these workers' representatives are. Second, the various steps to build this European framework vary widely from the national ones. Instead of defining general rights to workers' representatives first, the European Union has first granted specific rights to be informed and consulted to national workers' representatives and then it has dealt with the recognition of transnational representation in European companies; finally some general rights to be informed and consulted have been recognized by the 2002 Directive. Therefore it is only indirectly that this Directive generates a statutory structure for employees' representation in companies.

Specific Rights to be Informed and Consulted

The first directives dealing with workers' participation were adopted in 1975 and 1977. They were about collective redundancies and transfer of undertakings. Both of them were adopted, according to their preamble to 'protect workers'.[3] This protection is accomplished by granting workers' representatives, at enterprise level, the right to be informed and consulted on the restructuring of the enterprise. The directives define the information to be delivered to workers' representatives and the moment when the information and consultation should take place. Moreover, the directives do not only provide information and consultation but also a right to be consulted 'in good time with a view to reaching an agreement'. Thus a true right to negotiate on the restructuring and on the social measures to be defined is provided by the directives.[4]

The ECJ has recently delivered two interesting decisions on the collective redundancies Directive that show that even if it was adopted more than 30 years ago, the Directive is still relevant. In the first,[5] the ECJ held that:

---

[3]   Both directives were respectively modified in 1992 and 1998 and codified in 1998 and 2001 (Council Directive 98/59/EC of 20 July 1998 on the approximation of the laws of the Member States relating to collective redundancies, OJ L 225, 12.8.1998, p. 16 and Council Directive 2001/23/EC of 12 March 2001 on the approximation of the laws of the Member States relating to the safeguarding of employees' rights in the event of transfers of undertakings, businesses or parts of undertakings or businesses, OJ L 82, 22.3.2001, p. 16).

[4]   See ECJ, C-382/92 and C-383/92, *Commission v. United Kingdom*, and ECJ, C-188/03, *Junk*.

[5]   ECJ, C-12/08, *Mono Car Styling SA*, 16 July 2009, see Laulom (2010a).

it is clear, first of all, from the text and scheme of Directive 98/59 that the right to information and consultation which it lays down is intended for workers' representatives and not for workers individually . . . It must therefore be held that the right to information and consultation provided for in Directive 98/59, in particular by Article 2 thereof, is intended to benefit workers as a collective group and is therefore collective in nature.

This is an important precision. Of course, as a result, individuals could remain restricted from individually seeking to enforce the collective redundancy consultation obligations. However, it confirms a point which is sometimes not so clear in some other directives: the priority that must be given to workers' representatives in the process of information and consultation.

In the second case, the ECJ has clarified at what moment the consultation process shall begin.[6] Under article 2(1) of Directive 98/59, 'the employer shall begin consultations with the workers' representatives in good time with a view to reaching an agreement', when he/she is 'contemplating collective redundancies'. For the ECJ, the obligation arises when there is an intention to make collective redundancies. This intention will be deemed to form when the employer adopts 'strategic decisions' or 'changes in activity' compelling the employer to contemplate or plan for redundancies. The ECJ also confirmed that the obligation to consult does not depend on the employer being able to supply the employees' representatives with all the information required by the Directive. The employer may supply that information during the consultation as and when it becomes available.

Since the adoption of the 1975 and 1977 Directives, almost every social directive contains a reference to an intervention of workers' representatives on the issue it deals with. Sometimes directives just contain a recommendation. This is the case, for example, of Directive 97/81 on part-time work. The Directive only states that 'As far as possible, employers should give consideration to . . . the provision of appropriate information to existing bodies representing workers about part-time working in the enterprise'. But sometimes directives provide an obligation to inform and to consult workers' representatives. This is, for example, the case of the framework directive on health and safety at work. This is also the case of the recent directive on temporary agency work.[7] Its article 8 provides that the user undertaking must provide suitable information on the use of temporary agency workers when providing information on the employment situation.

---

6 ECJ, C-44-08, *Akavan*, 10 September 2009, note *ibid*.
7 Directive 2008/104 of 19 November 2008, OJ L327, 5.12.2008, p. 9.

The Recognition of a Transnational Level of Representation

The next step in the building of the European framework on workers' participation was the adoption in 1994 of the directive on European works councils. In this directive the relationship between restructuring and workers' participation is explicit. According to the preamble:

> the functioning of the internal market involves a process of concentrations of undertakings, cross-border mergers, take-overs, joint ventures and, consequently, a transnationalization of undertakings and groups of undertakings; whereas, if economic activities are to develop in a harmonious fashion, undertakings and groups of undertakings operating in two or more Member States must inform and consult the representatives of those of their employees that are affected by their decisions.
>
> Appropriate measures must be adopted to ensure that the employees of Community-scale undertakings are properly informed and consulted when decisions which affect them are taken in a Member state other than that in which they are employed.

As is well known, the 1994 Directive organizes a negotiation between a special negotiating body, representing the workers of the transnational company, and the management of the company to determine, by agreement, the nature, the composition, the functions and the procedure of European works councils. Therefore the 1994 Directive recognizes a specific right to negotiate at the level of transnational company and it defines the method to set up the organ representing the workers of the transnational company. For Elodie Bethoux (2008):

> it gives the example of a legally structured negotiation at the European level (even though, in parallel, the social partners have a considerable extent of contractual freedom). It gives also the example of negotiation processes that rest, with the set up of special negotiating bodies (SNBs), on the existence of a new transnational negotiation agent.

The directive also provides, according to the subsidiary provisions, the right of the European instance of workers' representation to be regularly informed and consulted on the employment situation of the company. However, contrary to the other directives, the European works councils set up according to the standard rules (in the event of failure of negotiations) are not granted a right to negotiate on a restructuring of the transnational company.

The Directive on workers' involvement in the European Company is based on the same model as the 1994 Directive, even if there are some specificities with regard to the question of board-level representation of employees. However, the representative body (set up according to standard rules) has more power in case of restructuring ('where there are exceptional circumstances affecting the employees' interests to a considerable extent, particularly in the event of relocations, transfers, the closure of establishments or undertakings or collective redundancies'). In this case, the Directive provides that the representative body has a right to meet at its request the competent organ of the European Company. Where the competent organ decides not to act in accordance with the opinion expressed by the representative body, this body shall have the right to a further meeting with the competent organ of the SE 'with a view to seeking agreement'. Therefore, the representative body has a right to negotiate on the restructuring even if the subsidiary requirements add that 'the meetings referred to above shall not affect the prerogatives of the competent organ'.

A General Right to be Informed and Consulted

The completion of the European framework of workers' representation has been realized with the adoption of the 2002 Directive establishing a general framework for informing and consulting employees. Here again information and consultation are viewed as tools to accompany the restructuring of enterprises as noted in the preamble:

> There is a need to strengthen dialogue and promote mutual trust within undertakings in order to improve risk anticipation, make work organisation more flexible and facilitate employee access to training within the undertaking while maintaining security, make employees aware of adaptation needs, increase employees' availability to undertake measures and activities to increase their employability, promote employee involvement in the operation and future of the undertaking and increase its competitiveness.
>
> (8) There is a need, in particular, to promote and enhance information and consultation on the situation and likely development of employment within the undertaking and, where the employer's evaluation suggests that employment within the undertaking may be under threat, the possible anticipatory measures envisaged, in particular in terms of employee training and skill development, with a view to offsetting the negative developments or their consequences and increasing the employability and adaptability of the employees likely to be affected.
>
> (9) Timely information and consultation is a prerequisite for the success of the restructuring and adaptation of undertakings to the new conditions created by globalisation of the economy, particularly through the development of new forms of organisation of work.

The adoption of this Directive was indeed essential for the effectiveness of the other European texts. It represents the missing element to complement the existing fragmented community system providing for the right of workers' representatives to be informed and consulted in special situations in the life of their undertaking. The Directive applies either to undertakings employing at least 50 employees or establishments employing at least 20 employees. It provides for a general, ongoing and regular right to information and consultation which shall cover information on the recent and probable developments of the undertaking's activities and economic situation, information and consultation on the situation, structure and probable developments of employment within the undertaking and on any anticipatory measures envisaged and information and consultation on decisions likely to lead to substantial changes in work organization or in contractual relations.

An indirect but essential consequence of the 2002 Directive is that a system of employees' representation has to be provided in each Member State, even though direct involvement cannot be excluded if not otherwise decided by the workers themselves (see point 16 of the preamble of the Directive). The Directive generates a statutory structure for employees' representation and workers' participation becomes an essential aspect of a European Social Model.

The effectiveness of a right to be informed and consulted on specific situations such as redundancies depends first on the position of national workers' representatives in the undertakings. As demonstrated by the United Kingdom case,[8] the directives on collective redundancies and transfer of undertakings cannot play their role if there are no representatives to be consulted. Thus the 2002 Directive, in providing a general right of information and consultation in undertaking employing at least 50 employees, obliges the Member States to recognize a general system of workers' representation in the undertaking.

The European Framework of Workers' Participation

If we look now at these directives altogether, the main features of the European framework of workers' participation appear. Workers' representatives have a general right to be informed and consulted on the situation of their undertaking and more specifically on the employment's situation, under the Directive 2002. Under this directive they also have a right to negotiate on 'decisions likely to lead to substantial changes in work

---

8   ECJ, C-382/92 and C-383-92, *Commission v. United Kingdom*, 8 June 1994, see Davies (1994).

organisation or in contractual relations'.[9] They have rights to be informed, consulted and to negotiate on specific situations such as collective redundancies and transfer of undertaking. They also have specific rights to be informed on the subjects treated by the other social directives (temporary work, fixed-term contracts, health and safety, non-discrimination, etc). The transnational structures of globalized companies are taken into account with the 1994 Directive and the European works councils should be associated with decisions dealing with transnational restructurings.

This European framework is linked to the European policy on restructuring. Clearly, European law supports the involvement of workers' representatives in restructuring, at national and transnational level, in order to facilitate them. Information and consultation procedures have two main aims: on the one hand, the improvement of what is now called risk anticipation in defining measures to increase the employability of employees and, on the other hand, the management of restructuring, the information and consultation being seen as a prerequisite for the success of the restructuring.

From this perspective, there is an obvious instrumentalization of information, consultation and negotiation rights conceived as tools of employment policy. There is also a direct link between these rights and the European flexicurity policy. According to the Commission, 'active involvement of social partners is key to ensure that flexicurity delivers benefits to all'. The directives granting rights to workers' representatives can be seen as instruments of the European Employment Strategy.

However, the directives also refer in their preamble to the Community Charter of Fundamental Social Rights of Workers, more precisely to its article 17 under which 'information, consultation and participation for workers must be developed along appropriate lines, taking account of the practices in force in different Member States'. Information and consultation are also recognized as fundamental rights in the Charter of Fundamental Rights of the European Union.[10] The reference to fundamental rights in the directives is important, as the directives are first instruments of realization of fundamental rights, providing that the interests of

---

[9]   According to Article 4.4, 'consultation shall take place . . . with a view to reaching an agreement on decisions within the scope of the employer's powers referred to in paragraph 2(c)', i.e., 'decisions likely to lead to substantial changes in work organisation or in contractual relations'.

[10]   See Article 27: 'Workers or their representatives must, at the appropriate levels, be guaranteed information and consultation in good time in the cases and under the conditions provided for by Community law and national laws and practices.'

workers are taken into account in the restructuring of enterprises and that workers' representatives could influence the decision making process.

The economic and financial crisis illustrates the potentiality but also the limits of the European framework on workers' representation.

POTENTIALITIES AND LIMITS OF THE EUROPEAN SYSTEM OF WORKERS' REPRESENTATION

Toward New Synergies through Workers' Representatives

The European directives have created common obligations for the Member States and have contributed to the definition of minimum standards of protection in cases of national and transnational restructurings. Regularly informed and consulted, workers' representatives should know the economic and social situation of the enterprise and could contribute to the definition of anticipatory measures. They have a right to negotiate the social consequences of national restructuring. These rights of information and consultation are no longer limited to the national borders of the company as the European works councils should also have information on the economic and social situation of the company in its transnational composition. They should also be informed and consulted on transnational restructuring.

The development of a transnational collective negotiation also seems to be linked to the set up of European works councils as they are the main actors of these negotiations. They have concluded or negotiated most of the transnational company agreements dealing with restructuring issues. Thus, the European works councils have contributed to the definition of European norms granting some rights for workers employed in transnational companies.

Some of these agreements are dealing with the issue of restructuring and have contributed to the development of new synergies. Sometimes European Works Councils have been key actors in reorganization processes. 'Management and workers' representatives in an increasing number of multinational companies have moved ahead of the EU regulatory framework and developed their own tools and mechanisms to deal with organisational change'.[11] At the beginning of 2008, 37 joint texts signed in

---

[11] See Carley, M. (2008), *Report of the Restructuring Forum on Transnational Agreements at Company Level*, 13 November, French Presidency Restructuring Forum, Lyon.

a total of 22 companies were dealing with restructuring and/or anticipation on change, in a specific, general or brief manner.[12] The report identifies four groups of agreements. In the first, agreements are specifically dedicated to the social consequences of an announced restructuring plan. The second group comprises agreements laying down principles and general rules to be applied in the event of a (potential) restructuring plan. The third group consists of agreements specifically or mainly dealing with the anticipation of change. Texts of the fourth group are global agreements making a reference to restructuring and/or anticipation of change. Most of the texts are essentially frameworks containing guidelines, policies, principles or general rules that have to be implemented at lower levels within the multinational concerned. However, a few lay down concrete measures and detailed provisions that do not appear to need further concretization to be applied.[13] The texts negotiated specifically in response to a European restructuring project refer to four main subjects: avoiding redundancies, transfer and redeployment guarantees, other accompanying measures (such as early retirement, voluntary separation or outplacement assistance) and procedural rules on employee representation and social dialogue.

Some new agreements have been signed recently. For example, an agreement on restructuring and anticipation of changes is going to be signed in ArcelorMittal, a transnational company.[14] In June 2009, the Thales Group and the EMF also signed an agreement seeking to improve the professional development of the group's European employees. Employee representatives are expected to be closely involved in the anticipation process. The content of the agreement is detailed and it provides for coordination mechanisms between the group level and the national entities.

The development of these voluntary practices has been very well analysed and discussed and the European Commission has played an important role in the diffusion of the knowledge on the texts signed. This could have positive impact in generalizing these practices. The same can be said on restructuring processes. The European policy on restructuring with the

---

[12] Schmitt, M. (2008), *Restructuring and Anticipation Dimension of Existing Transnational Agreements: Analysis and Overview Table*, Report for the European Commission, Brussels.

[13] For example, the international agreement concluded in October 2001 by Danone and the international trade union organization for foodworkers (IUF) sets out the social provisions to be applied in the context of the company's restructuring plans for its European biscuits division. It contains a number of commitments, including a pledge not to make any compulsory redundancies, to try to find new owners for sites due to close, to provide appropriate training and to guarantee salary levels for a year.

[14] Liaisons sociales Europe no 234, October 2009.

set up of the restructuring task force and the organization of restructuring forums on various important facets of restructuring has also contributed to a better knowledge of restructuring processes and a diffusion of this understanding.[15]

However, the economic crisis also shows some of the limits of the European approach. With the economic crisis, companies announced massive restructurings with delocalization, losses and job cuts. Even if there is an increase, the number of transnational company agreements is still very low compared with the number of restructurings. The crisis also shows that it is not possible to anticipate all changes and that social management of restructuring operations is not common practice. If some companies have negotiated new agreements dealing with restructuring and defining new rights for the workers, in many companies there was nothing more to negotiate than redundancy payments. There were also important collective conflicts and strikes like, for example, the six-week strike in Caterpillar in France.

The Limits of the European Framework of Workers' Participation

The first is directly linked to the structure of the Directives themselves. All the European Directives recognize some rights to workers' representatives leaving to the Member States the choice of their designation. The definition of employees' representatives, or the absence of definition, is the same in all directives: 'employees' representatives means the employees' representatives provided for by national law and/or practices.' Of course, the competence here given to the Member States is perfectly understandable. It will be very difficult to directly interfere with the national system of workers' representation and the directives leave it for the Member States to decide if information and consultation rights are granted to elected works councils, elected employees' representatives or elected or recognized trade unions. There is no explicit preference in the directives between a single channel of representation or multi channels. Another important issue is that very few Member States provide for a duty for the employer to establish a representative body within the undertaking. It is up to the workers to establish a representative body.[16] It may happen that in some workplaces information and consultation will not be enjoyed because there will be no representatives.

The competences given here to Member States have important

---

[15] See the final report on the AGIRE (Anticiper pour une Gestion Innovante des Restructurations en Europe) project which proposes a deep analysis of European restructurings.

[16] Ales (2007).

consequences: the effectiveness of the rights granted by the directives depends in the end on the strength of national systems of workers' representation; it depends on their capacity to exercise in right time their social and economic prerogatives.

The directives give some rights to these representatives, like the right to an 'adequate protection' or a right to training. However, as reported by the Implementation report of Directive 2002/14/EC, generally, 'the resources granted to employees' representatives in carrying out their mandate vary considerably from one Member State to the next and are reduced to the minimum in the new Member States'.[17] The 2002 Directive could reinforce the position of workers' representatives at enterprise level. An indirect consequence of the directive is that a system of employees' representation has to be provided in each Member State. However, the application of the Directive will necessarily depend on the position of workers' representatives in the enterprise and this position could be very weak. A report of the European Parliament (Committee on Employment and Social Affairs) of 29 January 2009 calls for a 'gradual strengthening of the process of informing and consulting employees within the EU' and it regrets that some 'Member States have confined themselves to transcribing certain aspects of its minimum applicable provisions'.

It is also possible to argue that the *Laval* and *Viking* cases, when limiting the right to strike, can weaken the position of national workers' representatives.

The second limit has to do with some of the ambiguities and gaps of the European approach. This can be very well illustrated by the new directive on the European Works Councils.[18] The aims of the revision were to ensure:

> the effectiveness of employees' transnational information and consultation rights, to increase the proportion of European works Councils established, to resolve the problems encountered in the practical application of Directive 94/45/EC and to remedy the lack of legal certainty resulting from some of its provisions or the absence of certain provisions and ensure that the Community legislative instruments on information and consultation of employees are better linked.

In fact, as reported by the Commission,[19] the right to transnational information and consultation lacks effectiveness, as the European Works

---

[17] Schömann et al. (2006).
[18] Directive 2009/3/EC of 6 May 2009.
[19] COM(2008) 419 final, 7/02/2008.

Council is not sufficiently informed and consulted in the case of restructuring. Very often, they are simply informed and sometimes after the restructuring has been decided.[20] If approximately 820 European Works Councils are active, representing 14.5 million employees, European Works Councils have been set up in only 36 per cent of undertakings falling within the scope of the Directive. There are legal uncertainties, particularly with regard to the relationship between the national and transnational levels of consultation, and in cases of mergers and acquisitions. One of the main problems raised by the application of the Directive is the articulation and the timing between the national and the European procedures.

Unfortunately, it is possible to argue that the new directive failed to address these various questions (Laulom, 2010b). First, it is doubtful that the new directive will facilitate the establishment of new European works councils. Second, the issues of the coordination of national and European procedures and of the precise moment of the intervention of the EWC are still not very well defined. There will be no real consultation if the EWC is not consulted prior to the restructuring decision.

Interpreting the Directive 98/59 on collective redundancies, the ECJ has recently clarified at what moment the consultation process shall begin.[21] However, the new EWC's Directive does not explicitly provide for a preliminary consultation. The preamble of the Directive reflects this ambiguity when it states that: 'Informing and consulting the European Works Council should make it possible for it to give an opinion to the undertaking in a timely fashion, without calling into question the ability to adapt.' The notion of consultation implies that it takes place before the decision. As the Advocate General states in its conclusions under *Akavan*: 'The employer is required to begin those consultations in good time, that is to say at a moment when, because of its function, consultation will enable the workers' representatives to participate effectively in those negotiations' (point 53). But there is still a lack of clarity in the new directive on that issue, which can undermine the position of the European Works Council (EWC) when a restructuring occurs.

Another uncertainty relates to the coordination between information and consultation at national level and information and consultation at European level. The 1994 Directive did not give any indication of what should be the chronology of these procedures. The new Directive leaves it to the agreements to resolve this issue. According to Article 6, the agreement concluded to establish EWC shall determine 'the arrangements for

---

20   Moreau (2006); Moreau and Paris (2008).
21   ECJ, 10 September 209, C-44-08, *Akavan*.

linking information and consultation of the EWC and national employee representation bodies, in accordance with the principles set out in article 1(3)'. Article 1(3) limits the competence of EWC to transnational issues. Article 12 of the Directive also states that 'information and consultation of the EWC shall be linked to those of the national employees representation bodies, with due regard to the competences and areas of action of each and to the principles set out in Article 1(3)'. Here again the Directive does not give any clear indication on how to define when the consultation of the EWC and of the national bodies should take place. Article 12 seems also to consider both procedures to be independent from each other while they shall be conceived in their complementarities. The EWC can have a more general and global view of the restructuring, it is possible to argue that it should be consulted prior to national bodies. In a very limited way, the preamble seems to recognize this link:

> For reasons of effectiveness, consistency and legal certainty, there is a need for linkage between the Directives and the levels of informing and consulting employees established by Community and national law and/or practice ... National legislation and/or practice may have to be adapted to ensure that the European works Councils can, where applicable, receive information earlier or at the same time as the national employee representation bodies, but must not reduce the general level of protection of employees.

It would certainly have been better for effectiveness and legal certainty if this rule had been formulated in clearer terms and had been included into the directive itself and not only in the preamble. However, it could give a guideline to interpret the Directive.

Another gap in the European Framework on workers' participation is the absence of a legal framework for transnational company agreements. In 2004, the European Commission introduced the idea of setting up an 'optional framework' for negotiating European collective agreements, having noted the development of these practices. Since then there has been no real progress on this very controversial issue. A legal framework could ensure some legal certainty and could support the negotiation of transnational company agreements. For example, as there is no legal framework, it is necessary for the negotiation of each agreement to define who will be the employees' representatives. Thus specifying who is empowered to negotiate and sign agreements in a legal framework could bring certainty. But this is of course a controversial issue.

CONCLUSION

The European framework on workers' participation has contributed to the definition of minimum standards applying to every Member State. This framework should not be undervalued but it is not sufficient. Some clarifications, like the right for the EWCs to be informed and consulted prior to the restructuring and the definition of the coordination between the competences of European workers' representatives and national ones, are needed. Moreover, it is not enough to grant rights to be informed and consulted to workers' representatives without taking into account the effectiveness of these rights in the national systems. The economic crisis also highlights the importance of individual rights for workers affected by a restructuring operation. At European level, some minimum and individual standards have already been recognized. The directive on transfer of undertakings provides for an individual right: in case of a transfer of an economic entity, the contracts of employment are automatically transferred to the new employer. The insolvency directive aims at guaranteeing payment of outstanding claims to employees in the event of their employer's insolvency. With the current economic crisis, some old instruments have been rediscovered such as temporary short-time working arrangements which are now supported by the Commission.[22] It also reveals the European Commission's renewed interested in measures to protect workers affected by restructuring operations.

REFERENCES

Ales, E. (2007), 'Studies on the Implementation of Labour Law Directives in the Enlarged European Union. Directive 2002/14/EC', Synthesis Report, available at ec.europa.eu/social/BlobServlet?docId=2451&langId=en (accessed 15 July 2010).

Bercusson, B. (2002), 'The European Social Model Comes to Britain', *Industrial Law Journal*, **31** (3), 209–244.

Bercusson, B. (2004), 'The Institutional Architecture of the European Social Model', in T. Tridimas and P. Nebbia (eds), *European Union Law for the Twenty-First Century. Volume 2, Rethinking the New Legal Order*, Oxford: Hart publishing, pp. 311–331.

Bethoux, E. (2008), 'Transnational Agreements and Texts Negotiated or Adopted at Company Level: European Developments and Perspectives. The Case of Agreements and Texts on Anticipating and Managing Change', Background paper for the facilitation of a meeting of the Restructuring Forum devoted to

---

[22] A Shared Commitment for Employment, COM(2009) 257 of 3 June 2009.

transnational agreements at company level, available at ec.europa.eu/social/Blo bServlet?docId=4968&langId=en (accessed 15 July 2010).

Davies, P. (1994), 'A Challenge to Single Channel', *Industrial Law Journal*, **23** (3), 272ff.

Laulom, S. (2005), 'Le cadre communautaire de la représentation des travailleurs dans l'entreprise', in S. Laulom (ed.), *Recomposition des systèmes de représentation des salariés en Europe*, Presses Universitaires de Saint-Etienne, pp. 23–66.

Laulom, S. (2010a), 'Actualité du droit social de l'Union européenne', *Semaine Sociale Lamy*, 1444, 15–20.

Laulom, S. (2010b), 'The Flawed Revision of the European Works Council Directive', *Industrial Law Journal*, **39**, 202–208.

Moreau, M-A. (2006), 'Restructurations et comité d'entreprise européen', *Droit Social*, 308–318.

Moreau, M.-A. and J.-J. Paris (2008), 'Le rôle du comité d'entreprise européen au cours des restructurations, Expériences et prospectives', *Semaine Sociale Lamy*, suppl. no 1376, 33–45.

Schömann, I., S. Clauwaert and W. Warneck (2006), 'Information and Consultation in the European Community, Implementation Report of Directive 2002/14/EC', ETUI-REHS, available at http://www.etui.org/research/Media/Files/Reports/2006/06_ReportDirective97_EN (accessed April 2011).

13. Toward a de-fundamentalisation of collective labour rights in European social law?

Antonio Lo Faro

INTRODUCTION

A sort of double antithesis is emerging within the juridical representation of Europe. *Social rights v. Economic freedoms* is the first; *Individual employment rights v. Collective labour rights* is the second. Whereas many comments have been devoted to the former, scarce attention has been given to the latter.

Though, a certain degradation of collective labour rights is precisely one of the main side-effects of the new 'post-enlargement' jurisprudence steadily put forward by the European Court in cases such as *Laval, Viking* and *Rüffert*. A streak of cases which seems to be further prolonged by the recent *Germany* case,[1] an infringement procedure – addressed to a German law allowing to award service contracts related to occupational pensions to bodies designated by collective agreements – which the Court decided according to the statement that 'the exercise of the fundamental right to bargain collectively must [therefore] be reconciled with the requirements stemming from the freedoms protected by the FEU Treaty'.

Most probably, it was not by mere chance that the lesser status of social rights *vis-à-vis* economic freedoms has been stated by the Court precisely in cases where a collective aspect of the labour relations was at stake: the right to strike in the two 'Nordic' cases; the right to collective bargaining

---

[1]   Case C-271/08 of 15 July 2010, *European Commission v. Federal Republic of Germany*. Having recalled that 'the terms of collective agreements are not excluded from the scope of the provisions on freedom of movement' and that 'the right to bargain collectively enjoys in Germany the constitutional protection conferred, generally, by Article 9(3) of the German Basic Law', the Court however reaffirms that 'the fact remains that, as provided in Article 28 of the Charter, that right must be exercised in accordance with European Union law' (quotations from points 41–44 of the judgment).

in the two German cases. Would the Luxembourg judges have decided in a similar way should an individual employment right be at issue? Would they have considered – say – a national anti-discrimination measure as an unlawful restriction to free movement, in the same way as they did for the right to strike?

The answers to such questions are not entirely obvious. In the following pages, I will suggest that beyond the specific circumstances of the three notorious cases – the *Viking-Laval-Rüffert* jurisprudence exceeds the reassuring rhetoric of constitutional balancing, to impinge upon a more significant process of labour law de-collectivization. As Brian Bercusson put it in his last essay, the whole history of labour law as we know it, might have found in the current ECJ jurisprudence its 'judgement day' (Bercusson, 2007).

COLLECTIVE RIGHTS AND EQUAL TREATMENT IN THE POST-LAVAL INTERNAL MARKET: THE FORGOTTEN EVIDENCE

I will use as a starting point an argument that is linked to a personal remembrance of Yota Kravaritou and Brian Bercusson, whose memory we honour in this book. Back in 1991, when I was a PhD student at the European University Institute, Yota and Brian organized a joint seminar on an issue that was of their deep intellectual concern: that is equal treatment in labour law, and namely in collective labour law.

My point is that although they may appear far-away issues, equal treatment has indeed something to do – or should have something to do – with the right to collective action and with the way it is currently recognized, or not recognized, within the EU legal system. At the very foundation of the present ECJ understanding of the right to strike there is an equal treatment problem: the core of the *Laval-Viking-Rüffert* jurisprudence – or, to be more precise, the essence of their outcome in terms of practical consequences – is a judicial acceptance of a set of clear inequalities.

Discriminating Workers

To begin with, a *discrimination among workers*: employees of the host country's undertakings who may benefit from the domestic labour legislation and collective agreements, and employees of the posting undertaking, who may – or should – be treated differently although performing the same job in the same place at the same time. This kind of inequality is not specifically due to the most recent and highly disputable ECJ case-law, rather being owed to an established jurisprudence dating back to the *Säger* case[2] (see §. 2.1) and to the subsequent choice to include into the notion of 'national restriction' indistinctly applicable measures too. As a result, the very same rights legislatively conferred to a host country's workers, become unjustified 'obstacles' when claimed by posted workers against their home country's undertakings.

Discriminating Undertakings and Differentiating Rights

When talking of the ECJ version of the right to strike, however, a different inequality comes at stake: that is a *discrimination among undertakings* operating within the same territory. On the one hand, those undertakings against which a right to strike exists (the host country's undertakings); on the other hand, those who are immune from any strike (the posting undertaking). It is precisely in this different kind of inequality that the groundbreaking character of cases such as *Laval* and *Viking* becomes manifest.

What is at stake in such a new perspective is no longer – as in the first kind on inequality – the applicability of domestic labour law to foreign posted workers; but rather the applicability of domestic labour law to national workers. The question is no longer 'should Latvian worker posted to Sweden earn Swedish salaries?', but rather 'can Swedish workers continue to exercise, in Sweden, the right to strike that the Swedish Constitution confers upon them?'

In fact, such a situation can be read two-fold, depending on the side from which it is observed.

1. If considered from the point of view of 'Capital', that is of the undertakings involved, it is an irrational disparity of treatment, based on the representation of the foreign provider as an untouchable sacred cow of the internal market. The foreign undertaking providing a service abroad is covered by a total immunity[3] against any kind of collective action,[4] which is not given to national undertakings, and which that very same international undertaking would not have granted

---

[2] Case C-76/90 of 25 July 1991.
[3] When talking about strikes, immunity is not an unfamiliar concept. In some national systems, 'immunity' traditionally indicates protection of strikers against negative consequences deriving from their actions. The immunity we are talking about here is completely different: it is an immunity protecting undertakings, not workers.
[4] And toward public procurement social clauses, as in *Rüffert*.

within its own national borders.[5] What can be charged to domestic contractors in terms of duties and costs cannot be equally imposed on foreign undertakings, up to the point of configuring a true reverse discrimination in damage of the former.

2. If considered from the point of view of 'labour', that is of the workers' rights at issue, it turns out to a denial of their *fundamental* character, notwithstanding the opposite allegation of the Court of justice.[6] What is evident, thus, is an inequality affecting the way the very same right to collective action is conceived when it is addressed against a national undertaking, and also when on the contrary it is addressed against an international undertaking. How can a right be declared fundamental when such obvious disparities are permitted – or rather required – in its application? Can the content and the limits of a fundamental right change according to the person toward which it is exercised? Or even according to the geographical place in which that person is temporarily located? Should not a 'European' fundamental right be such, irrespective of the national or geographical qualities of the addressee?

What is mostly questionable, then, is not – in *absolute* terms – that a social right succumbs to an economic freedom; but rather – in *relative* terms – that such a succumbing is stated, within a single legal order, exclusively with regard to certain undertakings. A hypothetical national law allowing strikes only against foreign undertakings and not against national ones, would be clearly contrary to an elementary principle of equal treatment. Why is not the opposite true?

Maybe the following sounds like a paradox, but it is not: the ECJ rulings on collective rights would have been more acceptable if their principles were generally applicable: that is, if the pre-eminence of market freedoms (or rights) over collective action had been been affirmed with regard to all the strikes which do not pass the proportionality test, and not with exclusive regard to those which are called against a foreign provider of services.

Paradoxes apart, however, it remains difficult to comprehend how a

---

5   It is debated whether a similar immunity of the posting undertaking exists also with regard to strikes called *by its own workers* posted abroad within the provision of a service. Indeed, any collective action limiting the undertaking's freedom to provide a service – even if coming from its own employees – risks to be labelled as an 'obstacle' within the meaning of current ECJ jurisprudence.

6   The statement according to which 'the right to take collective action, including the right to strike, must [therefore] be recognised as a fundamental right which forms an integral part of the general principles of Community law', is present in both the *Laval* and *Viking* rulings.

fully integrated market within a legal order 'founded on the value of . . . equality' where 'any discrimination on grounds of nationality shall be prohibited',[7] could be built – as occurs in the ECJ perspective – upon such patent inequalities. And one may legitimately wonder how a quite fatalistic acceptance of such clear inequalities can coexist with the energy that the same Court employs in combating other kinds of discrimination.

The allusion is to a series of recent cases in which the Luxembourg Court has demonstrated the highest responsiveness toward sexual orientation and disability related discrimination. In *Maruko*,[8] for instance, it stated that the same-sex surviving partner must receive the same benefit granted to a surviving spouse. In *Coleman*,[9] it pioneered the notion of 'discrimination by association', by declaring that prohibition of discrimination covers also people who are not themselves disabled but take care of a disabled relative. And a similar sensitivity the Court has demonstrated in *Del Cerro Alonso*,[10] where it extended the scope of equal treatment principle between fixed-term and permanent workers, by also including pay discrimination, notwithstanding the exclusion of pay from the sphere of EU competencies.

Consistently inexorable toward sexual orientation, type of contract and disability-based discriminations; indulgently tolerant toward those based on nationality of the posted workers and of the host country's undertakings.

A MATTER OF (EQUAL TREATMENT) PRINCIPLE

However – and in spite of the general consensus assisting the ECJ 'market access' doctrine[11] – the connections linking workers' mobility within the provision of a service and equal treatment are too obvious to be ignored. And indeed, they were not ignored by the European Parliament, which in a recent resolution correctly brought back the flaming debate on the three cases to the real essence: equality of treatment.

While acknowledging that freedom to provide services is a 'cornerstone' of the whole European project, the parliamentary assembly 'recalls' that

---

7   Respectively, Art. 2 TUE and Art. 21.2 Charter of Fundamental Rights of the European Union.
8   Case C-267/06 of 1 April 2008.
9   Case C-303/06 of 17 July 2008.
10   Case C-307/05 of 13 September 2007.
11   On the relationships between market access jurisprudential doctrine and regulatory competition policies, see Barnard and Deakin (2002).

'equal treatment is a fundamental principle of the European Union'. After reminding that 'freedom of movement for workers entails the abolition of any discrimination based on nationality between workers of the Member States as regards employment, remuneration and other conditions of work and employment', it concludes by stressing the 'need to safeguard and to strengthen equal treatment and equal pay for equal work in the same workplace as laid down in Articles 39 and *12*[12] of the EC Treaty', to the extent that 'in the framework of freedom to provide services or freedom of establishment, the nationality of the employer, or of employees or posted workers cannot justify inequalities concerning working conditions, pay or the exercise of fundamental rights such as the right to strike'.

If one only considers that analogous concerns have been expressed by (some of) the social partners in their most structured analysis of the ECJ rulings,[13] it is enough to restate – as has been already outlined – that the true 'victim' of an internal market hegemonized by an unconditional 'free movement axiology', is not an outdated remainder of 19th-century industrialism as the right to strike, but rather an advanced key pillar of 21st-century societies as the principle of equal treatment.

A sort of interim conclusion could now be drawn before continuing along the line of argument I'm trying to follow in this chapter. Although clearly involving equal treatment issues, the *Market freedom v. Social rights* question has been dealt with by the Court without any attention paid to that very same equal treatment principle which in other occasions the Court demonstrated itself to be very sensitive to.

Why so?

Two possible kind of answers could be given to such a question, depending on the kind of inequalities previously sketched out: on the one hand, those inequalities jeopardizing the possibility of posted workers to be granted the same rights as those applied to national workers (§. 2.1). On the other hand, those jeopardising both the possibility for national workers to exercise their rights toward posting undertakings (*Laval* and *Viking*), and the possibility for national legislators to impose on posting undertakings the same obligations it imposes on national undertakings (*Rüffert*) (§. 2.2).

---

[12]   Author's emphasis.

[13]   'Report on Joint Work of the European Social Partners on the ECJ rulings in the Viking, Laval, Rüffert and Luxembourg cases', 19 March 2010, where the ETUC observes that 'all actors on the internal market, workers as well as companies, should not be discriminated against because they come from another Member State' (p. 11).

The Unfair Consequences of *Säger* in the Post-enlargement Internal Market

With regard to the first profile – not particularly connected to collective rights – it should be noted that the exclusion of temporarily posted workers from accessing the entire labour legislation of the receiving country is by no means an inescapable requirement of the treaties, but rather the result of a given interpretation of those treaties, which the Court of justice only began to implement from the beginning of the 1990s.

It was only in 1991 that the notorious *Säger* formula was coined, stating that 'Art. 49 requires not only the elimination of all discrimination on grounds of nationality, but also the abolition of any restriction, even if it applies without distinction to national providers and to those of other Member States'. With that formula, the era of regulatory competition has *de facto* been initiated, thus relegating Member States' ambitions to grant equal treatment to national and posted workers into the sphere of 'protectionist' measures. It is on these rather questionable grounds that rights have become obstacles or restrictions, and that unequal treatment for the same job at the same time in the same place has become the rule of the internal market.

However, that this is a long-standing and well-established principle does not mean that it cannot be disputed: is it really inevitable to consider national social rights as obstacles to the free movement across borders, once it is assured that they are equally addressed to domestic and foreign undertakings?

Not even the invocation of an unquestioned keystone of EU equality law such as indirect discrimination, could suffice to modify the severe criticism that the *Säger* approach seems to deserve. A fundamental difference hinders, in fact, the possibility to drive the *Säger* jurisprudence on the same conceptual tracks of indirect discrimination and its remedies. True, in both cases there is a formally neutral behaviour (i.e. the application to posted workers of the same rule provided for national workers) risking to determine negative consequences upon certain subjects (i.e. the posting undertakings, which may have more difficulty to access the host country market). But whereas in indirect discrimination cases the removal of the formally neutral behaviour determines a situation of equality, what is left as a result of the *Säger* formula is nothing but another discrimination (to the detriment of the posted workers).

More importantly, it cannot be underestimated that it was one thing to enforce the *Säger* formula in the 1991 internal market, that is in a context characterized by a substantial socio-economic homogeneity among the then 12 Member States. But it is a totally different thing to keep those principles in a post-enlargement internal market characterized by a high socio-economic fragmentation among the old and the newcomers. It is precisely in such a context that social dumping risks become evident, and that – therefore – Member States should be allowed to exercise their 'right not to discriminate',[14] by permitting them to apply *indistinctively* their own social standard to all those who operate within their territory.

By definition, jurisprudential principles are not perpetual. After 20 years maybe the time has came to put *Säger* to one side and to affirm that national social measures cannot be considered as restrictions of economic freedoms to the extent that they are indistinctively applicable.[15]

'Keynes at Home, Smith Abroad': An Outdated Formula?

In the first paragraph of this chapter it was mentioned that the *Laval* and *Viking* cases cannot be merely classified as umpteenth episodes of the posted workers rights' jurisprudential story.

Unlike other cases which came to the attention of the Court, what is at stake here is not a possibility for a Member State to apply domestic labour rules to foreign workers temporarily posted within its own territory, but rather the different question of verifying if and how that Member State could claim to apply its own rules to its own nationals within its own territory. The slogan 'Swedish law in Sweden' – inscribed on the placards held by workers protesting against *Laval un Partneri* – was an incomplete one. 'For Swedish workers' should have been added to that slogan.

This is the reason why the 'Scandinavian' cases immediately stunned a large proportion of observers: because they mark the translation in legal terms of a debate, which for some time had been filling the doctrinal and the political agendas; that is: where is the room for the preservation of national social models in the time of an internal market requiring the removal of any 'restriction'?

This is the major constitutional dilemma to be faced in the years to

---

[14]   Contrary to a certain way of understanding the rationale subtending the Posted Workers Directive, it became rapidly clear at the end of the 1990s that what is at stake in the social aspects of free movement is not the *duty* of the host State to apply domestic rules to posted workers, but rather its *interest* to do it. That kind of rationale was clearly outlined in one of the first analyses of the Directive. In the words which Davies (1997, 590) dedicated to the 1996 Directive: 'Member States were given a permission to extend their domestic regulation to posted workers rather than the posted workers being given a right to equal treatment with employees of host State establishments.'

[15]   The opportunity to revise the *Säger* formula is indicated in a number of recent essays. See Bruun (2006); Meulman and de Waele (2006); Deakin (2008).

come. It is one thing to renounce any ambition to uniformity; something which has been clear since the 1980s at least. It is a very different thing to discard the original founding compromise according to which Member States had accepted the removal barriers to international trade only on the condition of preserving their respective social sovereignties (Giubboni, 2006). 'Keynes at Home, Smith Abroad' – the catchphrase of the embedded liberalism subtending the European integration dawn – risks becoming an outdated formula in post *Laval-Viking-Rüffert* Europe.

COLLECTIVE RIGHTS AS NOT SO FUNDAMENTAL RIGHTS

It is widely known that within the intense debate anticipating the Luxembourg verdicts, a large number of the commentators had evoked the fundamental nature of the right to strike as a factor capable of orientating the ECJ decision.

In particular, reference had been made to the *Omega* and *Schmidberger* cases[16] as examples of how the protection of a constitutionalized right could be qualified as a legitimate obstacle to a European market freedom.[17] If human dignity and freedom of expression – but also the protection of childhood, as it occurred in the less-renowned but equally significant *Dynamic Medien* case[18] – are considered as legitimate justifications for a restriction on a fundamental freedom, why should it not be the same with regard to the right to strike or the right to collective bargaining?

As it is well-known, those expectations were left unattended and things went differently. Was it only a matter of dissimilar results of different 'ad hoc balancing'[19] processes, which on a case-by-case basis may let one or the other right prevail? Or rather, are *Laval* and *Viking* the end result of less contingent and more structural circumstances, entailing a lesser status for collective labour rights?

---

[16] Respectively, case C-36/02 of 14 October 2004, and case C-112/00 of 12 June 2003.

[17] For an analysis of the ECJ fundamental rights case-law with particular regard to the role assigned to the Charter of fundamental rights, see Caruso and Militello (2009).

[18] Case C-244/06 of 14 February 2008.

[19] The notion of constitutional 'ad hoc' balancing, as opposed to that of 'definitional' balancing, has been introduced in the American legal debate by a celebrated essay of Nimmer (1968). See also Aleinikoff (1987).

It has been noted by many that within the line of reasoning followed by the European Court a sort of logical inversion is detectable with regard to what usually happens in national courts when a decision about the limits of the right to strike is to be made. Whereas national courts estimate whether the constitutional right to strike can be limited by other rights or interests, the ECJ has followed the inverse path: it has indeed evaluated whether the fundamental freedom to provide a service could be limited by the right to strike. Rather than a *limitable* right, the strike has thus appeared to the Court as a *limiting* right.

Far from being a sheer inversion of the terms not influencing the substance of the question, such a circumstance does reveal an approach which cannot be underestimated: to the extent that the ECJ task is to 'ensure that in the interpretation and application of the *Treaties* the law is observed' (Art. 19 TUE), the main object of its hermeneutical activity could only have been the economic freedom provided for by Art. 49 of the Treaty,[20] not the right to strike, for the simple reason that within the Treaties there is no such a thing as the right to strike.

The true object of the ECJ decision, therefore, has been economic freedoms, not the right to strike, whose formal recognition as a 'fundamental right which forms an integral part of the general principles of Community law' was not able to modify the ECJ inertial application of its own previous 'market access' jurisprudence. Evidence of that is given by the use on the part of the Court of the conceptual schemes and of the terminology itself of its 'national restrictions' case law. Notwithstanding its alleged *European* and fundamental nature, hence, the right to strike has been utterly understood by the Court in the same way as one of those 'imperative reasons of general interest' which in the past it had evoked in order to provide a justification for *national* measures limiting free movement. This is precisely what the right to strike is, according to the ECJ: not a European fundamental right, but rather a national obstacle to the full achievement of a Treaty provision. More than an operation of constitutional balancing between equally ranked rights, then, what the ECJ has accomplished resembles rather a more traditional application of the doctrine of EU law *primacy*.

It is precisely in that respect that the difference between the two groups of cases – *Omega* and *Dynamic Medien* on the one side; *Viking* and *Laval* on the other – emerges. In the former two cases the Court acknowledged not only the fundamental nature of the rights at issue, but also a considerable degree of national autonomy in determining their actual

---

[20] Now Art. 56 TFUE.

meaning, extension and intensity. As the Court stated in one of those cases:

> it is not indispensable that restrictive measures laid down by the authorities of a Member State to protect [fundamental] rights correspond to a conception shared by all Member States. As that conception may vary from one Member State to another on the basis of, inter alia, moral or cultural views, Member States must be recognized as having a definite margin of discretion.

And yet again:

> the mere fact that a Member State has opted for a system of protection which differs from that adopted by another Member State cannot affect the assessment of the proportionality of the national provisions enacted to that end. Those provisions must be assessed solely by reference to the objective pursued and the level of protection which the Member State in question intends to provide.[21]

What seems clear from such quotations is that when the Court accepted the sacrifice of fundamental market freedoms on the altar of fundamental rights, it has done so not through a balancing of equally ranked constitutional EU rights, but rather by accepting that a national rule (the fundamental right) prevails over an EU rule (the fundamental freedom). To put in another way, in *Omega* and *Dynamic Medien* human dignity and childhood's safeguard prevailed over freedom of movement not as *Community* rights which 'won' the battle of balancing over freedom of movement; but rather as *national* rights which in that specific occasion the Court chose to consider as a legitimate justification to a limitation of a fundamental freedom.

This kind of deferential attitude towards Member States' individual choices concerning those fundamental rights which are considered as essential components of their respective constitutional traditions,[22] was not responded to in *Laval* and *Viking*.

It only remains to be seen why.

---

21 Quotations from points 44 and 49 of the *Dynamic Medien* ruling.
22 Such a stance is clearly detectable also in the following argument, proposed by the Court in *Omega*: 'It is not indispensable ... for the restrictive measure issued by the authorities of a Member State to correspond to a conception shared by all Member States ... the need for, and proportionality of, the provisions adopted are not excluded merely because one Member State has chosen a system of protection different from that adopted by another State'. Quotations extracted from point 37–38 of the *Omega* ruling.

DE-COLLECTIVIZING LABOUR LAW?

Why then, when talking about collective labour rights did the Court reveal such a meagre sensitivity? Certainly scarcer than the attention it has reserved for other individual fundamental rights, either labour (*Maruko, Coleman, Del Cerro Alonso*) or not labour (*Omega, Schmidberger, Dynamic Medien*) related?

It must be observed, first, that such a lesser status of collective rights cannot be explained through the well-known statement according to which social rights do have a constitutional status which cannot but be different – and inevitably minor – than the one assigned to human and civil rights. Social rights, it is alleged, are unavoidably 'expensive' (*droits à prestation*), whereas human and civil rights are not. It follows that only the latter may be considered complete rights, whilst the enforcement of social rights is inescapably subordinated to other circumstances. In this sense, social rights would always be subordinate rights (*diritti condizionati*).

However – and leaving the question of its general acceptability aside – such a traditional allegation cannot be of any help in explaining the lower status conceded to collective labour rights by the recent ECJ case-law. The right to strike, indeed, is a social right with the same structure of a civil right: as it has been said, 'it is self-sufficient and operational by itself' (Luciani, 2009).

The reason for such a poor treatment of industrial rights must therefore be found elsewhere. My impression – not further demonstrable as any impression may be – is that the weak appraisal of collective rights within the Luxembourg jurisprudence might be attributable to motivations connected with the overall cultural climate into which the market building process in post-1989 and post-enlargement Europe has submerged.

What is easily detectable in this rather settled jurisprudential attitude is indeed a general devaluation of the collective side of labour law to the advantage of its individual aspects.[23] In such a perspective, the most recent ECJ pronouncements coherently persist along the line initiated some time ago with the *Albany* ruling,[24] in which – behind the facade of an apparent deference – the Court had accorded to collective bargaining only a sort of 'probation freedom'.[25]

However, an adverse cultural environment cannot by itself be con-

---

[23]   For a comprehensive analysis of labour law development in the last decades, see Wedderburn (2007).
[24]   Case C-67/96 of 21 September 1999.
[25]   The definition was given by Pallini (2000).

sidered an exhaustive explanation of the Court's positions. More than a detrimental hostility, the judicial depreciation of collective rights may most likely be due to the Court's failure to grasp the essential regulatory function that some national systems traditionally assign to collective autonomy and to its instruments: strike and collective bargaining (and the correlated rights).[26] Voluntarism, functional connection between collective bargaining and strike, relationships between legislation and collective agreements, deep motivation driving toward a centralization and/ or decentralization of industrial relations, possible (inverse) correlation between union density and general application of collective agreements; all of these profiles of collective labour law – each explaining and affecting national industrial relations systems – have been completely overlooked by the Court's reasoning.

By way of conclusion, one further comment could be made. The weak status of collective labour rights emerging from the ECJ case law is all the more controversial in so far as it bluntly clashes with the EU rhetoric of social dialogue and social partnership as pillars of supranational new governance. The 'openness' of the Open Method of Coordination should consist precisely in a strategy of social partner participation in the internal market regulation. But social partners do perform their role precisely through collective autonomy and collective action. Neither are quite comforted, let alone promoted, by the current ECJ inclination. Not good news for a European social policy which – as someone predicted some years ago – is increasingly 'left to the Judges and the Markets' (Leibfried, 2005).

REFERENCES

Aleinikoff, T.A. (1987), 'Constitutional Law in the Age of Balancing', *The Yale Law Journal*, **96** (5), 943–1007.

Barnard, C. and S. Deakin (2002), 'Market Access and Regulatory Competition', in C. Barnard and J. Scott (eds), *The Law of the Single European Market: Unpacking the Premises*, Oxford: Hart Publishing, pp. 197–222.

Bercusson, B. (2007), 'The Trade Union Movement and the European Union: Judgment Day', *European Law Journal*, **13** (3), 279–308.

Bruun, N. (2006), 'The Proposed Directive on Services and Labour Law', in R. Blanpain (ed.), *Freedom of Services in the European Union*, The Hague: Kluwer Law International, pp. 19–35.

Caruso, B. and M. Militello (2009), *The Charter of Nice in the Law in Action: An Investigation into the Judges' Statements of Reasons (2000–2008)*, WP C.S.D.L.E. (Working Papers of the Centro Studi di Diritto del Lavoro

---

[26] See Sciarra (2008).

Europeo), 'Massimo D'Antona.INT – 74/2009', available at http://www.lex.
unict.it/eurolabor/en/research/wp/wp_it_en.htm (accessed April 2011).
Davies, P. (1997), 'Posted Workers: Single Market or Protection of National
Labour Law Systems?', *Common Market Law Review*, **34** (3), 571–602.
Deakin, S. (2008), 'Regulatory Competition after Laval', *Cambridge Yearbook of
European Legal Studies*, **10**, 581–609.
Giubboni, S. (2006), *Social Rights and Market Freedom in the European
Constitution: A Labour Law Perspective*, Cambridge: Cambridge University
Press.
Leibfried, S. (2005), 'Social Policy. Left to the Judges and the Markets?', in H.
Wallace, W. Wallace and M. Pollack (eds), *Policy-Making in the European
Union*, Oxford: Oxford University Press, pp. 243–278.
Luciani, M. (2009), 'Diritto di sciopero, forma di Stato e forma di governo',
Argomenti di diritto del lavoro, **15** (1), 1–25.
Meulman J. and H. de Waele (2006), 'A Retreat from *Säger*? Servicing or Fine-
Tuning the Application of Article 49 EC', *Legal Issues of Economic Integration*,
33 (3), 207–228.
Nimmer, M.B. (1968), 'The Right to Speak from Times to Time: First Amendment
Theory Applied to Libel and Misapplied to Privacy', *California Law Review*, **56**
(4), 935–967.
Pallini, M. (2000), 'Il rapporto problematico tra diritto della concorrenza e
autonomia collettiva nell'ordinamento comunitario e nazionale', *Rivista italiana
di diritto del lavoro*, **19** (2), 225–244.
Sciarra, S. (2008), 'Viking e Laval: diritti collettivi e mercato nel recente dibattito
europeo', *Lavoro e diritto*, **22** (2), 245–272.
Wedderburn, B. (2007), 'Labour Law 2008: 40 Years On', *Industrial Law Journal,*
36 (4), 397–424.

14. How the European Court of Human Rights gave us *Enerji* to cope with *Laval* and *Viking*

Filip Dorssemont

INTRODUCTION

The Life of Brian: In Search of a *Right* to Strike

In the autumn of 2008, the European Trade Union Institute and the Expert group on Transnational Trade Union Rights took the decision to honour the memory of the late Brian Bercusson by editing a book containing his selected writings on *Labour Law and Social Europe.*[1] Brian had founded this expert group in 1999[2] and chaired it for nearly a decade until his death in the summer of 2008. His selected writings consolidate and disseminate an important part of his academic legacy. Brian's way to animate and inspire the debate and his generous inability to say 'no' to those seeking for advice and academic co-operation corroborated his natural and invisible authority to chair this group.

Though the selected writings cover a wide range of issues, it is interesting to consider[3] that the oldest as well as the most recent contributions dwell on Brian's discomfort with the case law restricting the right to take collective action. In 'One Hundred Years of Conspiracy and Protection of Property: Time for Change' (1977)[4] the author criticised a decision of the

---

[1]   Unknown editor (2009).
[2]   The expert group at present is composed of Th. Blanke, N. Bruun (chair), S. Deakin, F. Dorssemont, A.T.J.M. Jacobs, C Kollonay-Lehoczky, K. Lörcher, B. Veneziani and C. Vigneau. It has been assisted by two researchers of the ETUI: S. Clauwaert (1996–2002) and I. Schömann (2002–present). Shortly after Brian Bercusson passed away, the group had to overcome the loss of Yota Kravaritou, one of its founding members.
[3]   The observation was made earlier by Niklas Bruun in his 'Introduction' to the first Chapter (Institutional and legal framework) of the *Selected Writings*.
[4]   B. Bercusson (1977, 268–292).

Court of Appeal in *Hubbard v. Pitt* which outlawed picketing. He indicated that salvation should come from a *statutory* recognition of picketing. In what has been one of his last contributions 'The Impact of the Case-Law of the European Court of Justice upon the Labour Law of the Member States',[5] he criticises the infamous judgements *Laval*, *Viking* and *Rüffert*. According to Brian, the Court invented an EU law on workers' collective action which undermined legal certainty for those having recourse to such an action. As he indicated in *The Trade Union Movement and the European Union: Judgement Day*,[6] which Brian published prior to the judgements in *Laval* and *Viking* the approach adopted by the Court was far from inevitable. To the contrary, the Court had to overcome a lot of conceptual hurdles in order to arrive at its questionable 'balancing operation'. In his last footnote to the contribution dealing with the impact of the Court's case law, Brian seems to relinquish his hope in the Luxembourg Court as a fountain of justice. He criticised the *Laval* and *Viking* judgements for reflecting doctrines long superseded in national legal discourse.[7]

He stated that the 'nineteenth century doctrinal ghosts of the dominance of market freedoms have returned to haunt EU labour laws of the twenty first century'.[8] [9]

Brian's disappointment over the CJEU needs to be situated against the background of his 'great expectations'. In a contribution which was published while the *Laval* and *Viking* cases were still pending, he pondered on the question of whether 'European laws' constituted 'Help or Hindrance'.[10] He considered that the UK law on industrial action revealed an important defect, in so far as its reliance on *immunities* needed to be contrasted with a continental European tradition of the assertion of a fundamental right of workers to take collective action, often protected by national constitutions of the EU member States. The *Monti*-Regulation[11] still pays witness to the underlying distinction between a right and a freedom to collective action.[12] The author still had high hopes for the

---

[5] B. Bercusson (2009).

[6] B. Bercusson (2007, 279–308).

[7] Unknown editor (2009, 462).

[8] *Ibid.*

[9] A recent publication of the Institute of Employment Rights dedicated to Brian Bercusson, refers to this passage of Brian: K. Ewing and J. Hendy (2009, 111).

[10] B. Bercusson (2006, 221–246).

[11] See Article 2 of EC Regulation 2679/98.

[12] In *European Commission on Human Rights, National Association of Teachers in Further and Higher Education v. The United Kingdom*, 16 April 1998 (Application No. 28910/95), the applicant union referred to 'a paper by professor Bercusson'

CJEU. He genuinely or methodically believed that the incorporation of the EU Charter enshrining fundamental workers' rights which are vital to industrial relations would create a momentum for the CJEU to 'adopt interpretations consistent with international labour standards, where again national labour laws may fall short'.[13] He expressed the hope that the EU Charter provided 'a further means whereby the Court can promote European integration, this time in the social and labour field'.[14] Brian audaciously suggested that the EU Charter promised a renewal of labour law, both at European trans-national level and *within* the Member States of the EU.[15] It is not entirely irrational to assume that these hopes included the UK. In this perspective, the EU Charter was considered to be a lever or a catalyst to grant a genuine *right* to strike. Hence, the strike would cease to be a *'un droit contraire au droit'*,[16] in need of some immunity to persist.

A Posthumous Case: *Enerji Yapi Yol Sen*

The optimist in action *did* offer a wide range of short, medium and long term pathways to overcome the general feeling of defeat which haunted many labour lawyers. The majority of his long term and indeed more 'structural' solutions urge for an amendment of the Lisbon Treaty, introducing the legal prerequisites for socio-economic governance.[17] In sum, whereas Brian suggested a 'legislative' *revanche sur la judiciaire* in 1977 to overcome judicial restrictions to picketing, he suggested a 'constitutional' *revanche sur la judiciaire* to overcome *Laval* and *Viking.*

Brian could hardly know that by the end of 2008 the Grand Chamber of the European Court of Human Rights in *Demir and Baykara*[18] would review its outdated view on the freedom of collective bargaining as not being an essential element of the freedom of trade union association,

---

stating 'that the *right* to strike is not guaranteed in the United Kingdom, either expressly or implicitly, and that in a survey of most member states of the European Union, only the United Kingdom has a requirement to provide information on strikers'.

[13]   B. Bercusson (2006, 225).

[14]   *Ibid.*

[15]   *Ibid.*

[16]   See the *bon mot* of M. Planiol, annotation of Cour de Bourges, 19 June 1894, *Dalloz Périodique* II, 441.

[17]   Unknown editor (2009, 459–490).

[18]   European Court of Human Rights, 12 November 2008, *Demir and Baykara v. Turkey*, no. 34503/97.

paving the way for an unprecedented ruling in *Enerji*.[19] Despite its inability to qualify the right to strike as an *essential* means to protect workers' interests, the Court did construe the right to strike to be interwoven with the freedom of association. The Court approved of the ILO's Freedom of Association Committee's assessment that the right to strike is indeed a 'corrolaire indissociable' of the freedom of association. If the right to strike cannot be dissociated from the freedom of association, it would better have to be requalified as 'essential' to the latter. The clue to this judicial revolution was the very methodological tool of interpretation which Brian suggested to the CJEU, *id est* 'interpretations consistent with international labour standards, where again national labour laws may fall short'.[20] In *Demir and Baykar II* the ECHR ruled that:

> The Court, in defining the meaning of terms and notions in the text of the Convention, *can* and *must* take into account elements of international law other than the Convention, the interpretation of such elements by competent organs, and the practice of European States reflecting their common values. The consensus emerging from specialised international instruments and from the practice of Contracting States may constitute a relevant consideration for the Court when it interprets the provisions of the Convention in specific cases.[21]

In sum, we can now add another pathway to Brian's inventory. *Strasbourg* could lead the way for the European Union in re-balancing economic freedoms and genuine fundamental rights. The answer to the question how the European Union gets to Strasbourg is enshrined in the Lisbon Treaty. The Treaty urges and requires the Union to accede to the European Convention on Human Rights. The pathway is essentially different from the proposals Brian formulated. The Lisbon Treaty does not need to be amended. It has been ratified and entered into force. It is now up to the Member States to provide proof of good faith and to agree to the accession.

In this chapter, I will try to reconstruct the case law of the European Court of Human Rights related to strike and collective action. By means of contrast, I will examine the poor and eventually bad record of the CJEU in the field of upholding the freedom of association. In a subsequent step, I will ponder on the potential added value the accession of the European

---

[19]   European Court of Human Rights, 21 April 2009, *Enerji Yapi-Yol Sen*, no. 68959/01.

[20]   B. Bercusson (2006, 221–246).

[21]   European Court of Human Rights, 12 November 2008, *Demir and Baykara v. Turkey,* no. 34503/97, § 85.

Union to the EConvHR might have for the recognition of a genuine right to strike, indeed of collective action, and for the shielding of such a right against a detrimental clash with so-called fundamental freedoms.

THE EUROPEAN COURT OF HUMAN RIGHTS AND THE STRIKE: FROM DESPAIR TO HOPE

The EConvHR has seldom been a key reference in academic legal doctrine related to the right to organise. Individuals rather than trade unions have been the driving actors in a vast majority of the cases. Until recently, the case law has primarily dealt with applications made by individuals (including employers) *not* willing to organise or by trade unions *not* recognised as being representative. In a contribution on the 'Implications of Wilson and Palmer', Ewing referred to a lack of confidence and a 'debit balance' which the Wilson and Palmer judgement was able to restore or rebalance.[22] During the entire twentieth century, the Court was reluctant to identify a hard core of means which a Contracting State should guarantee in order to allow trade unions to protect their members' interests. In fact, it was only in 2008 (*Demir and Baykara II*) that the Court finally recognised the right to bargain collectively as an essential element of the right to form and join trade unions. The more timid recognition of the right to strike as a corollary right which cannot be dissociated from the freedom of association dates back to 2009 (*Enerji Yapi-Yol Sen*).

The EConvHR does not refer to the existence of a right to take collective action. The important ILO Conventions Nos 87 and 98 likewise do not include an explicit reference to the right to collective action. The ILO's supervisory Freedom of Association Committee has developed the right to strike as an essential aspect of the freedom of association as early as 1952.[23] Hence, the question arises whether the European Court of Human Rights has recognised the right to collective action as such a corollary right of the right to form and join trade unions.

The issue of whether the right to strike is necessarily inherent in Article 11 of the EConvHR came to the forefront in *Schmidt and Dahlström*.[24] Both litigants were members of two 'belligerent' unions which had

---

22   Ewing (2003, 4).
23   See, in this connection, Novitz (2003, 192–203).
24   European Court of Human Rights, 6 February 1976, *Schmidt and Dahlström v. Sweden*, no. 5589/72. See the following passage in § 36: 'their right to strike which is, in their submission, an "organic right' included in Article 11 of the European Convention'.

organised a strike after the expiry of a collective agreement applicable to Swedish State employees. When a new agreement for the public sector was being concluded which was made universally applicable through a Royal Order, a 'Strike breaks retro-activity principle' was being introduced. The members of the belligerent trade unions were refused the benefit of retro-activity. Both applicants argued that the refusal by the employer to apply certain benefits in a collective bargaining agreement retroactively to them had a chilling effect on the use of the strike threat. The Court unambiguously stated that the right to strike is one of the most important means to protect workers' interests. It considered however that the strike was by no means the only means to do so.[25] Indeed, restriction of the right to strike did not result in the unions' complete inability to defend the interests of workers adequately. The right to strike was in no way seen as an indispensable tool for defending workers' interests. Contracting parties have a free choice to regulate the means available to unions and their members to defend the members' interests adequately. From this perspective, restrictions on the right to strike never seem to deprive trade unions of any means to protect workers' interests. This observation does not hold true in two hypothetical situations. In the first situation, the State prevents the union from employing alternative tactics to defend the workers' interests adequately. In the second situation, the limitation on the right to strike is applied in a discriminatory manner.

The judgement in *Schmidt and Dahlström* is not a textbook example of judicial activism. The *Schmidt and Dahlström* judgement seems to have had a chilling effect on trade unions and workers. In fact, it took nearly a quarter of a century before restrictions on the right to strike were challenged again before the Court on the basis of Article 11 of the European Convention. The British union Unison lodged an application on 20 October 1999. Unison is a union for civil servants. Various employees of the University College London Hospital (UCLH) were members of this union. As part of the 'Whitley Councils', the union participated in the discussions about employment conditions in the health care sector. The UCLH was considering transferring parts of the hospital from the 'public' to the 'private' sector. Unison demanded guarantees that the transferred workers and the new workers recruited by the transferee would be assured the same employment conditions set forth in one of the transferor's collective bargaining agreements for more than 30 years. Pressure was put on the transferor to lay down these guarantees in the acquisition agree-

---

[25]   European Court of Human Rights, 6 February 1976, *Schmidt and Dahlström v. Sweden*, no. 5589/72, § 36.

ments. The transferor refused to include such a clause. After an internal vote among the members, Unison gave notice of a strike. The UCLH went to court to prohibit the strike. A critical factor was the finding that the employer subjected to the strike was considered to be a 'third party' in the conflict. The industrial dispute was conceived as one between the union and transferee. A provision in the British Trade Union and Labour Relations (consolidation) Act (TULRCA) made the immunity of unions dependent on the requirement that the trade dispute at hand involved a dispute between employees and 'their employer'. Unison argued that the structural prohibition on strikes impeded it from effectively defending the interests of its workers during the strategically crucial time period of the negotiations regarding the transfer. The union claimed that the right to strike was not just one means among others to defend the interests of its workers. The right to strike was regarded as an indispensable means of defending workers' interests. The strike prohibition affected the very heart of the right to organise. The applicant pointed to the close interrelationship between the right to organise and right to collective action in the reports and conclusions of the ILO's and Council of Europe's supervisory bodies.

The Court decided on 10 January 2002 that this application was inadmissible, given that it was manifestly ill-founded.[26] At first blush, the judgement appears to affirm *Schmidt and Dahlström*. The Court reiterated its well-known view on the margin of appreciation which States have in regulating trade union freedom. It distanced itself from the proposition that the right to collective action was indispensable to defending worker interests. Consistent with the reasoning in *National Union of Belgian Police*, the Court could have merely examined whether the limitation on the right to strike was discriminatory in nature. A violation of Article 14 of the EConvHR was not, however, alleged by Unison. The Court could have therefore sufficed with the statement that the right to strike is not an indispensable element of the right to organise. Such an approach would have been in line with the existing case law. The Court was innovative in characterising the strike prohibition as a restriction of the unions' power to protect the interests of its members. That conclusion was determinative. It expressly did not go along with the British government's assertion that those interests could only be defended within the narrow context of 'trade union disputes'. It explicitly reviewed such restrictions against principles governing restrictions in Article 11 § 2 EConvHR. This passage constitutes

---

[26]   European Court of Human Rights, 10 January 2002, *Unison v. UK*, no. 53574/99.

a revolution.[27] Previously, the Court limited itself to merely reviewing against Article 11 §2 EConvHR those restrictions which are part of the basic core.

The elements of these restriction principles are well-known. They must be 'prescribed by law'. They must be justified by a legitimate objective referred to in Article 11 § 2. Such a restriction must be 'necessary in a democratic society'. However legitimate certain objectives may be a sense of proportionality is expected from the Member States. In the case in question, the restriction of the right to strike was set forth in an explicit statutory provision of TULRCA. The Court described the particular economic interest that the business had in the continuity of its services and the exercise of freedom of contract as a legitimate objective for restricting the right to strike. The Court seems to have endorsed the view espoused by the British government that these 'interests' fall under the 'rights of others' within the meaning of Article 11 § 2 EConvHR.

Unison's infamous course was extended further in *Federation of Offshore Workers' Trade Unions.*[28] At issue in that case was another prohibition on strikes which was imposed through a compulsory administrative measure. Notwithstanding that such a procedure to prohibit a strike in a non-essential service was considered by the ILO Freedom of Association Committee *and* the European Committee on Social Rights to be irreconcilable with ILO standards and Article 6.4 in conjunction with Article 31 of the European Social Charter, the application was deemed manifestly ill-founded by the Court. The gap between the restriction principles of Article 31 of the Charter and Article 11.2 of the Convention was never illustrated more poignantly.

In *Dilek and others*[29] the Court continues to follow the path traced in *Unison* and *Swedish Federation of Offshore Workers' Trade Unions.* The Court refuses to qualify the right to strike as an essential means to protect workers' interests, but does assess whether a restriction can be justified under Article 11 § 2. The case did not relate to a statutory restriction of the right to strike, but was related to a clear cut statutory prohibition for civil servants to have recourse to any kind of collective action which could suspend, obstruct or slow down the functioning of the public service. A number of civil servants had left their post for a couple of hours at a 'service de péage' which had to charge automobile drivers passing the

---

[27]   To this effect, see also Ewing (2003, 18).
[28]   European Court of Human Rights, 27 June 2002, *Federation of Offshore Workers' Trade Unions and Others v. Norway*, no. 38190/97.
[29]   European Court of Human Rights, 28 April 2008, *Dilek and others v. Turkey*, nos 74611/01, 26876/02 and 27628/02.

Bosporus river. They wanted to protest against the working conditions applicable to them. The Turkish government and the applicants disagreed on whether the action concerned could qualify as a strike action or not. The Court felt reluctant to enter into such a semantic debate. It considered the question of the definition of strike action to be irrelevant, in so far as the action concerned constituted a 'collective action within the context of the exercise of trade union rights' in the generic meaning of the word.[30] The assessment of the restrictions to the right to have recourse to collective actions were considered to be prescribed by law and to pursue a legitimate goal, *id est* the proper functioning of the public service. The restriction concerned which entailed a civil liability of the civil servants was considered to be disproportionate in view of the fact that it was imposed on the entire civil service and because the Turkish government was unable to prove how the trade union was able to defend the workers' rights in a peaceful way.[31]

In *Enerji Yapi Yol Sen*[32] the Court had to rule on the legitimacy of a circular which recapitulated the prohibition for civil servants to have recourse to any kind of collective action based upon the same statutory provisions that had been scrutinised in *Dilek and others*. Despite the fact that the circular had been addressed to civil servants rather than to any trade union likely to organise the strike, this was not a reason for the Court to decide that the application was inadmissible. The judgement of the Court was delivered less than seven months following the *Demir and Baykara II* ruling. The Court explicitly refers to the binding methodological tools for interpretation developed by the Grand Chamber. Thus, it examines the relation between the right to strike and two rights which fall within the ambit of the European Convention on Human Rights. These rights are the right to organise and the right to bargain collectively. The specific reference to the right to bargain collectively is natural in so far as this right has been construed as an essential element of the right to join and form trade unions. This relation is being examined in the light of two major human rights instruments of international law. The Court primarily refers to the ILO Convention no. 87. Despite the fact that the provisions of this Convention are mutant on the right to strike, the Court does take into account the interpretation given to this instrument by the ILO's

---

[30]   European Court of Human Rights, 28 April 2008, *Dilek and others v. Turkey*, no. 74611/01, 26876/02 and 27628/0257, § 57.
[31]   European Court of Human Rights, 28 April 2008, *Dilek and others v. Turkey*, no. 74611/01, 26876/02 and 27628/02, § 72.
[32]   European Court of Human Rights, 21 April 2009, *Enerji Yapi-Yol Sen*, no. 68959/01.

supervisory bodies. In this respect, the Court observes that these bodies have considered the right to strike to be interwoven with the freedom of association ('un corrolaire indissociable'). Furthermore, the Court observes that Article 6 § 2 of the European Social Charter establishes a functional link between the right to bargain collectively and the right to strike. In so far as the right to bargain collectively is necessarily inherent in the freedom of association and in so far as the right to bargain collectively is deprived of its substance, it can be argued that the right to strike does constitute an essential aspect of the right to organise by means of association. In our view, the reference to the case law of the ILO describing the right to strike as a 'corrolaire indissociable' further warrants the thesis that the Court implicitly has recognised the right to strike as an essential element of the right to trade union association. Thus, the Court does not even examine whether the trade unions had alternative means to 'have their voice heard'. Unfortunately, the Court unlike the vocabulary in *Demir and Baykara II* sticks to the formula of *Schmidt and Dahlström* describing recourse to strike action as 'just' an important means to protect workers' interests. The Court assesses the restriction (*id est* prohibition) of the right to have recourse to strike action as being unjustified. Contrary to *Dilek and others* it doubts whether there was a legitimate goal. However, it prefers to tackle the justified character of the prohibition under the angle of proportionality. A generic prohibition affecting the entire public sector was considered to be disproportionate.

The fact that the Court relates the recognition of the right to strike to the freedom of (trade union) association inevitably raises the question of whether the European Convention guarantees a right for workers to have recourse to 'spontaneous' or 'wild cat strikes' which are neither recognised nor organised by trade unions. The ILO's Freedom of Association Committee has been reluctant to recognise such a right and has held that the ILO Conventions do not prevent a State from prohibiting wild cat strikes.[33] The European Committee on Social Rights has consistently refused to construe the right to (organise a) strike as an exclusive trade union's prerogative.[34] In view of the individualistic stance that the Court has taken in respect of the right *not* to organise, it seems doubtful it would not be able to recognise that individuals have the right to have recourse to collective action without trade union recognition. In absence of a provi-

---

[33] International Labour Office, *Freedom of association, Digest of Decisions and Principles of the Freedom of Association Committee of the Governing Body of the ILO*, Geneva, 2006, no. 524.

[34] Swiatkowski (2007, 233).

sion which explicitly recognises the right to strike, such a recognition can only be based either upon a broad interpretation of the notion of 'trade union' or on a broad interpretation of the freedom of peaceful assembly. In this respect, it is worthwhile to consider that the Court did consider that the circular was problematic insofar as it prohibited the civil servants to exercise their freedom of peaceful assembly.[35]

THE EUROPEAN COURT OF JUSTICE AND THE RIGHT TO ORGANISE, INCLUDING THE RIGHT TO STRIKE

Until recently, the European Court of Justice had a poor record in upholding fundamental trade union rights. Ever since *Laval* and *Viking,* it has a bad record.

References by the Court to the right to organise as a general principle of EU law have been extremely rare. The Court of Justice has been primarily concerned with the recognition of the freedom of association as a principle of 'Labour Law', *id est* in its jurisprudence related to staff cases.[36] In the *Bosman case,* the Court did recognise the freedom of association, enshrined in Article 11 of the European Convention on Human Rights, as being one of the fundamental rights which are protected as general principles of EU law.[37] Though the case undoubtedly refers to a labour dispute, the freedom of association was not invoked by the employee involved, neither could the associations concerned be considered as 'employer's associations' in the classical meaning of the word. In sum, the case has no bearing on the issue of the right to organise in a context of industrial relations, *id est* the right to trade union association. On the other hand, the AG Jacobs in *Albany* did consider a more specific right to form and join trade unions to be a general principle of EU law.[38] The AG did base that reasoning on the principles laid down in the *Bosman* and the *Maurissen*

---

[35]   European Court of Human Rights, 21 April 2009, *Enerji Yapi-Yol Sen,* no. 68959/01, § 32.

[36]   See *inter alia*: CJEU, 8 October 1974, *Union syndicale, Massa and Kortner,* C-175/73, CJEU, 18 January 1990, *Henri Maurissen and Union syndicale,* C-193/87 and C-194/87.

[37]   CJEU, 15 December 1995, *Union royale belge des sociétés de football association ASBL contre Jean-Marc Bosman,* C-415/93, § 79.

[38]   Joined opinion of Mr Advocate General Jacobs delivered on 28 January 1999. *Albany International BV v. Stichting Bedrijfspensioenfonds Textielindustrie.* Reference for a preliminary ruling: Kantongerecht Arnhem – Netherlands, Case C-67/96, § 139.

judgement. Since the latter is a staff case, it is hazardous to state that the Court was in fact developing 'general' principles of EU law.

The only immediate tribute to the freedom of association in the context of industrial relations was made in the *Werhof* case.[39] The Court did construe that the freedom of association entailed a negative right of employers not to organise. Furthermore, it ruled that such a right was at stake insofar as employers were being forced to apply employment conditions enshrined in a collective agreement signed by employers' organisations to which they were not affiliated. The judgement needs to be criticised in so far as the Court pretends that *Gustafsson* would warrant the thesis that an obligation to apply a collective agreement to which he is not a party would affect an employer's negative freedom to organise.[40] In fact, a closer reading of *Gustafsson* reveals quite the opposite. The reasoning by the Court could in fact turn out to be dramatic in view of the obligation of a foreign service provider to apply collective agreements which were made generally applicable.

The record of the Court of Justice with regard to the freedom of collective bargaining is even more troublesome. In *Albany* the Court did not take the freedom of collective bargaining into consideration in order to assess the question of whether competition rules could restrict the validity of collective agreements declared universally applicable.[41] The Advocate General Jacobs did deny that the freedom of collective bargaining could be deduced from the recognition of the freedom of association as a general principle of EU law. He stated that 'it cannot be said that there is sufficient convergence of national legal orders and international legal instruments on the recognition of a specific fundamental right to bargain collectively'.[42]

Instead, he argued that the collective bargaining process, like any other negotiation between economic actors, is '. . . sufficiently protected by the general principle of freedom of contract. In our view, such an approach is questionable. It neglects the quintessential difference between individual and collective autonomy.'[43]

---

[39] CJEU, 9 March 2006, *Hans Werhof v. Freeway Traffic Systems GmbH & Co. KG.* C-499/04.

[40] CJEU, 9 March 2006, *Hans Werhof v Freeway Traffic Systems GmbH & Co. KG.* C-499/04, § 33.

[41] See CJEU, 21 September 1999, *Albany International BV v. Stichting Bedrijfspensioenfondstextielindustrie*, C-67/96.

[42] Joined opinion of Mr Advocate General Jacobs delivered on 28 January 1999. *Albany International BV v. Stichting Bedrijfspensioenfonds Textielindustrie.* Reference for a preliminary ruling: Kantongerecht Arnhem – Netherlands. Case C-67/96, § 160.

[43] Joined opinion of Mr Advocate General Jacobs delivered on 28 January

In *Ueapme*, the Court of First Instance did interpret the Maastricht Agreement on Social Policy as precluding an enforceable right to take part in the negotiations which could amount to an agreement concluded at community level.[44] The Court construed the bargaining process as being based on the '*mutual* willingness to initiate the process provided for in Article 4 of the Agreement'. In sum, the Court highlighted the voluntary character of the bargaining process based upon mutual recognition of the social partners. The voluntary nature of the bargaining process is consistent with the case law of the European Court of Human Rights as well as with the approach of the freedom of collective bargaining under the European Social Charter. Unfortunately, the Court did not refer to this conceptual framework.

In a recent case,[45] *Commission v. Germany*, the Court could not avoid the question whether the right to bargain collectively constituted a general principle of EU Law. The Commission had started an infringement procedure against the German Republic since local authorities and local authority undertakings had awarded service contracts in respect of occupational old-age pensions directly, without a call for tenders at European Union level. The Commission argued that this constituted a violation of Council Directive 92/50/EEC of 18 June 1992 relating to the coordination of procedures for the award of public service contracts (OJ 1992 L 209) and Directive 2004/18/EC of the European Parliament and of the Council of 31 March 2004 on the coordination of procedures for the award of public works contracts, public supply contracts and public service contracts (OJ 2004 L 134, p. 114).

The German Republic replied that these decisions were based upon collective agreements which because of their nature and subject-matter, fell outside the field of application of Directives 92/50 and 2004/18 in view of the so-called *Albany immunity* which shields collective agreements from competition rules. The Court did not accept this argument and was thus forced to consider whether the application of these directives had to be balanced against the right to bargain collectively. It did recognise that the right to bargain collectively had to be recognised as a general principle of EU law. The Court in this respect referred to the fact that this right had been enshrined in Article 6 of the European Social Charter and in the provisions of instruments drawn up by the Member States at Community

---

1999. *Albany International BV v. Stichting Bedrijfspensioenfonds Textielindustrie.* Reference for a preliminary ruling: Kantongerecht Arnhem – Netherlands. Case C-67/96, § 161.

[44] CJEU, 17 June 1998, *Ueapme v. Council of the European Union*, T-135/963.

[45] CJEU, 15 July 2010, C-271/08.

level or in the context of the European Union, such as Article 12 of the Community Charter of the Fundamental Social Rights of Workers (9 December 1989) and Article 28 of the Charter of Fundamental Rights of the European Union ('the Charter'). The Court explicitly indicated that the latter constituted an instrument to which Article 6 TEU accords the same legal value as the Treaties.

In the infamous *Viking* and *Laval*, the Court did recognise a right to have recourse to collective action as a general principle of EU law.[46] The Court construes the right to have recourse to collective action partially by reference to ILO instruments related to the freedom of association and partially by reference to the European Social Charter.[47]

'YES, WE SHALL', SO 'YES, WE CAN': A CONSTITUTIONAL BRIDGE TO THE EUROPEAN COURT OF HUMAN RIGHTS

Due to the ratification of the Lisbon Treaty, the consolidated Treaty on European Union now provides that 'The Union *shall* accede to the European Convention for the Protection of Human Rights and Fundamental Freedoms'.[48]

The accession to the EConvHR constitutes a more far reaching step in the constitutional recognition of fundamental rights within the European Union. In our view, it goes beyond a recognition of fundamental rights as mere general principles of the Union's law. In fact, Article 6 § 3 TEU already recognises such an impact of the fundamental rights, as guaranteed by the European Convention on Human Rights.

Due to the accession, the status of the fundamental rights enshrined in EConvHR will differ fundamentally from those enshrined in the Charter of Fundamental Rights. In fact, at its best, the rights enshrined in the Charter have the same *legal value* as conflicting fundamental freedoms enshrined in the EU Treaties. Furthermore, the Charter itself has upgraded some of the fundamental freedoms which have the potential to conflict with fundamental (workers') rights. Thus, Article 15 of the Charter has consecrated the freedom of establishment and the freedom to provide services as proper 'fundamental freedoms'. In *Viking* and *Laval,* both freedoms

---

[46]   CJEU, 11 December 2007, C-483/05 (*Viking*) and 18 December 2007, C-341/05 (*Laval*).
[47]   For a previous analysis, see F. Dorssemont (2009b, 45–104).
[48]   Article 6 § 2 TEU.

have been considered to justify restrictions to the fundamental right to strike and the fundamental freedom of collective bargaining. Last but not least, Article 16 of the Charter has consecrated the freedom to conduct a business. The only international Court to interpret the Charter will be the CJEU. For the CJEU, it will be one among other 'constitutional' principles to be taken into account.

In sum, in my view, the prospects that the Treaty reference to the Charter of Fundamental rights might provoke a shift in the way the Court deals or even has to deal with potential conflicts between the right to strike and so-called fundamental (economic) freedoms are extremely weak.

The prospects stemming from the accession to the EConvHR for changing the economic constitution of the European Union or at least adding a flavour of economic governance are more promising.[49] The accession to the EConvHR might add some relief to the flat juxtaposition of fundamental freedoms and fundamental rights integrated into one Charter. It puts genuine fundamental (workers') rights at the heart of the matter. Since the EConvHR is corroborated by a judicial supervision, it will force all European institutions, including the CJEU to abide by the judgements delivered in Strasbourg. As opposed to Luxembourg, Strasbourg will not dwell on the question whether human rights can restrict fundamental economic freedoms. It will assess whether and to what extent these fundamental economic freedoms can actually restrict genuine fundamental rights. It will force the European institutions to justify restrictions to citizens' rights, instead of forcing citizens to justify the exercise of their human rights.

The accession to the EConvHR is is by no means a fact. Though Article 6 TEU provides that the Union shall accede, article 218, § 8 of the Treaty on the functioning of the European Union provides that such a decision needs to be taken unanimously by the Council. The contrast between the wording of Article 6 and Article 218 § 8 TFEU is reminiscent of a similar contrast which characterises the implementations of European (collective) agreements concluded between management and labour at Community level in the meaning of Article 139 TEC. In the first edition of his *European Labour Law*, Brian insisted on the obligatory nature of the implementation procedure.[50] He pointed out that Article 139 TEC in both the French and the English version emphasised the obligatory character of the transposition procedure which can be operated through

---

[49]   In the same vein comparing the impact of the Charter and the accession to the EConvHR: Syrpis (2008).

[50]   B. Bercusson (1996, 543–552).

an autonomous and a heteronomous avenue. The English version refers to 'shall be implemented', whereas the French version refers to 'la mise en oeuvre intervient'. Franssen questioned the obligatory nature of the heteronomous avenue *ex absurdo* by pointing out that the distinction in the old Article 137 § 2 TEC between the qualified majority or the unanimity would be 'nonsensical'.[51] Indeed, in so far as the implementation is obligatory, such a distinction appears to be problematic. It would boil down to an obligation to decide with a qualified majority or with unanimity according to the subject matter covered by the agreement. In our view, this objection is less problematic, in the case of the accession to the European Convention on Human Rights. The request of unanimity does not as such provide an argument for Member States to question the obligatory nature of their constitutional duty under the Treaty on the functioning of the European Union to decide in favour of the accession. Article 238 § 8 TFEU does indicate that the ratification of the Lisbon Treaty as such is not sufficient to guarantee that the decision of the Council enters into force. The article provides that the decision will enter into force solely 'after it has been approved by the Member States in accordance with their respective constitutional requirements'. The procedure described in the Treaty needs to be distinguished from the requirements put forward in the European Convention on Human Rights. Thus, Article 59 EConvHR states that the Convention is open to ratification by the members of the Council of Europe.

PROSPECTS

The question arises whether the accession of the European Union to the EConvHR creates a momentum to rebalance the conflict between fundamental freedoms and genuine fundamental rights, such as the right to take collective action and the freedom of collective bargaining. In the landmark judgements of *Demir and Baykara* as well as in *Enerji*, the Court had to assess the conformity of provisions under Turkish law which deprived civil servants of the right to have recourse to any kind of collective action and to constitute trade unions. The judgements do not deal with restrictions based upon conflicting rights and freedoms. These recent judgements do not provide sufficient guidance to predict anything whatsoever.

In two judgements of the Strabsourg Court (*Unison* and *Federation of Offshore Workers' Trade Union*) which preceded both the landmark judge-

---

[51]   E. Franssen (2002, 287–288).

ments the Court did adopt a broad interpretation of the conflicting private and public interests which could justify restrictions to the right to take collective actions. Hence, at first sight the prospects look bad. As shown earlier on, the Court in *Demir and Baykara* did indicate that the Court was under an obligation to interpret Article 11 of the EconvHR in the light of 'international law other than the Convention, the interpretation of such elements by competent organs, and the practice of European States reflecting their common value'.

Since both judgements were ruled in disrespect of the ILO's supervisory bodies as well as of the jurisprudence of the European Committee on Social Rights, the persuasive authority of these 'precedents' is poor. In this respect, it is worthwhile recalling that the European Committee on Social rights has refused to take into account mere business interests as a justified restriction for the right to take collective action. Thus, it refuted that a 'proportionality test' was compatible with the exhaustive character of the restrictions under Article 31 ESC.[52] In the same vein, the ILO's Committee of experts has recently considered that 'it has never included the need to assess the proportionality of interests bearing in mind a notion of freedom of establishment or freedom to provide services'.[53] The Committee considered that the 'doctrine that is being articulated in these CJEU judgements is likely to have a significant restrictive effect on the exercise of the right to strike in practice in a manner contrary to the Convention'.

Irrespective of the accession of the European Union to the EConvHR, the European Court of Human Rights will be a competent forum to challenge national legislation and case law which has been influenced by the CJEU case law in *Laval* and *Viking*. In so far as domestic courts will refer to these cases to restrict the right to have recourse to collective action, this case law can be challenged. Thus, the Court will have the opportunity to scrutinise the CJEU in an indirect way. Unfortunately, the Court is known for being extremely cautious in assessing whether the action by contracting Parties to the EConvHR based upon EU law is contrary to that convention.[54]

---

[52] See in this respect, ECSR, XVI-1, Conclusion with regard to Belgium. For the situation in Belgium, see Dorssemont (2009a, 167–202).

[53] Report III (1A) Report of the Committee of Experts on the Application of Conventions and Recommendations, International Labour Conference, 99th Session 2010, 209.

[54] In this respect, see *inter alia* Douglas-Scott (2006, 638–640) and Unknown editor (2005, 581–585). The leading case is European Court of Human Rights, 30 June 2005, *Bosphorus Hava Yolları Turizm ve Ticaret Anonim Şirketi v. Ireland*, §§ 155–156. See about this case in Lawson (2005, 380–382).

The recent report of the ILO expert Committee is an inspiring example of a more courageous stance. The ILO's Committee refused to accept the defence of the British government which disclaimed any responsibility whatsoever for the attitude adopted by the judiciary, 'because any adverse impact of Viking and Laval would be a consequence of European Union law to which the United Kingdom is obliged to give effect, rather than of any unilateral action by the United Kingdom itself'. The Committee stated that it was in no position to judge the correctness of the CJEU holdings as such, but that it did have to 'examine whether the impact of these decisions at national level are such as to deny workers' freedom of association rights under Convention nr 87'.[55]

REFERENCES

Bercusson, B. (1977), 'One Hundred Years of Conspiracy and Protection of Property: Time for Change', *The Modern Law Review*, 268–292.
Bercusson, B. (1996), *European Labour Law*, London: Butterworths.
Bercusson, B. (2006), 'The European Laws: Help or Hindrance?', in K. Ewing (ed.), *The Right to Strike: from the Trade Disputes Act 1906 to a Trade Union Freedom Bill 2006,* Liverpool: The Institute of Employment Rights, pp. 221–246.
Bercusson, B. (2007), 'The Trade Union Movement and the European Union: Judgement Day', *European Law Journal*, **13** (3), 279–308.
Bercusson, B. (2009), 'The Impact of the Case-Law of the European Court of Justice upon the Labour Law of the Member States', in O. Schulz and U. Becker (eds), *Die Auswirkungen der Rechtsprechung des Europäischen Gerichtshofs auf das Arbeitsrecht der Mitgliedstaaten,* Baden-Baden: Nomos.
Dorssemont, F. (2009a), 'La (non) conformité du droit belge relative à l'action collective par rapport à la Charte sociale européenne', in *Actualités du dialogue social et du droit de grève,* Kluwer, Waterloo, pp. 167–202.
Dorssemont, F. (2009b), 'The Right to Take Collective Action v. Fundamental Economic Freedoms in the Aftermath of *Laval* and *Viking*', in M. De Vos (ed.), *European Union Internal Market and Labour Law: Friends or Foes*, Antwerpen; Oxford: Intersentia, pp. 45–104.
Douglas-Scott, S. (2006), 'A Tale of Two Courts: Luxembourg, Strasbourg and the Growing European Human Rights Acquis', *Common Market Law Review*, 629–665.
Ewing, K. (2003), 'The Implications of Wilson and Palmer', *Industrial Law Journal*, **32** (1), 1–22.
Ewing, K. and J. Hendy (2009), 'The New Spectre Haunting Europe', The Institute of Employment Rights.

---

[55] Report III (1A) Report of the Committee of Experts on the Application of Conventions and Recommendations, International Labour Conference, 99th Session 2010, 209

Franssen, E. (2002), *Legal Aspects of the European Social Dialogue*, Antwerpen: Intersentia.

Lawson, R. (2005), 'The Impact of the EU Constitution on the Relationship between Strasbourg and Luxembourg', in D. Curtin, A.E. Kellermann and S. Blockmans (eds), *The Constitution, the Best Way Forward?*, The Hague: TMC Asser Press, pp. 377–395.

Novitz, T. (2003), *International and European Protection of the Right to Strike*, Oxford: Oxford University Press.

Swiatkowski, A. (2007), *Charter of Social Rights of the Council of Europe*, Alphen aan den Rijn: Kluwer Law International.

Syrpis, P. (2008), 'The Treaty of Lisbon: Much Ado ... But About What?', *Industrial Law Journal*, **37** (3), 233–234.

Unknown editor (2005), 'Relations between International Courts and Community Courts: Mutual Deference or Subordination?', *Common Market Law Review*, **42**, 581–585.

Unknown editor (2009), *Labour Law and Social Europe. Selected Writings of Brian Bercusson*, Brussels: ETUI.

PART III

The changing legal framework of the
European social model

15. Towards a post-*Viking/Laval* manifesto for Social Europe

Ulrich Mückenberger

THE TWO MANIFESTOS FOR SOCIAL EUROPE

Brian Bercusson was one of the eight European scholars who were deeply involved in the elaboration of the two manifestos for Social Europe drawn up with the support of the European Trade Union Institute (ETUI – at that time directed by Reiner Hoffmann). They consisted of an approximately 15-page manifesto proper (published in nearly all European languages and signed by some hundred European labour scholars) and a manifesto book (in numerous languages) which gave political, economic and legal background analyses (Bercusson et al., 1996; Mückenberger, 2001).

Manifesto 1 (with a view to the Intergovernmental Conference (IGC) resulting in the Amsterdam Treaty) was meant to take a step against the EFTAisation of Europe and to strengthen a tendency which, in T.H. Marshall's words (1950), was based on political, civil and social rights of European citizenship and tended towards a democratised Social Europe. It coincided with Tony Blair's victory in the UK which made it possible to end the 'two-speed European labour law' by converting the social protocol into the social policy chapter and adding the employment chapter to primary law, in 1997. Manifesto 2 tried to move beyond the Amsterdam Treaty by concretising it, still on the basis of the citizenship approach, through instruments of industrial citizenship (European collective bargaining), gender equality and the quest for legally binding fundamental rights combined with legal tools for their implementation and enforcement. Common to both manifestos was the idea that Europe needed a properly functioning 'public sphere' allowing for political, social and cultural discourse and dispute concerning Europe's future – a discourse carried out in an open, transparent and transnational way.

The vision of Europe which we developed in the Manifestos was a set of political and strategic choices which Brian Bercusson also maintained later – although he changed the focus of his legal activity. This is why I try to keep Brian Bercusson's perspective in mind, what the main focuses of a new manifesto would be – after the enlargement and re-marketisation of the EU and the anti-social change in ECJ jurisprudence.[1]

AN INITIAL 'FOUNDING PACT' IN CAPITALIST SOCIETY: SOCIAL JUSTICE AND PRODUCTIVITY

The first insight is that labour law in general and European labour law in particular are characterised by a certain tension between 'the economic' and 'the social' – a tension which is integrated in what Alain Supiot called the 'founding pact' (2009). In post-war capitalist societies, the creation of employment has always been accompanied by a historic compromise. On the one hand, trade unions and left parties came to accept that, in both the socialist and the capitalist world, workers should be subjected to a scientific organisation of labour responding exclusively to the imperatives of efficiency, not of justice. On the other hand, big businesses eventually internalised the idea that improving the incomes and economic security of their employees was not only a legitimate goal, but brought increased efficiency in terms of productivity and market openings. This is why the issue of social justice has mainly been perceived as redistribution and as a sort of compensation of an inevitable alienation in the world of work.

A similar type of founding pact can be discerned at the European level, at least from the mid-1970s onward. Until recently, the distinguishing feature of the EC, compared to other customs unions, was that it did not confine itself to the free movement of goods and capital, but rather set itself the goal of creating a 'social Europe'. The Treaty of Rome stated that the free movement of people would go hand in hand with the 'need to promote improved working conditions and an improved standard of living for workers, so as to make possible their harmonisation while the improvement is being maintained' (art. 117 EEC). Despite the weakness and imperfections of this European social model, the EC remained faithful to the ideals of liberty and social justice of the postwar period, rejected from the outset by the Communist states as well as by the Anglo-Saxon countries and their continental epigones. In some respects, at least till the enlargement phase, this model has proved astonishingly robust.

There were five elements which Brian Bercusson and his co-authors agreed upon when working out the Manifestos for Social Europe –

---

[1] Some of the initial considerations take up issues raised by Alain Supiot and myself in a contribution in memory of Brian Bercusson; see Mückenberger and Supiot (2009).

elements meant to be the cornerstones of a new founding pact of Europe:

1. citizenship implies civil, political and social rights and integration;
2. the legal concept of capability combines and orders the status security of the people with their capability to act freely;
3. collective voice means autonomous collective bargaining structures and voluntary collective associations, in particular trade unions;
4. the subsidiarity principle should postulate, rather than policies of non-intervention and de-regulation, vertical as well as horizontal proactive European intervention in favour of the weak; and
5. Europe provides for an equilibrium of the public and the private spheres as a precondition of Western European legal, social and state culture. The European public sphere underpins the development of the 'societal' within the framework of a European civil society, and is not restricted to the link of the 'public' to the nation state.

In political terms, this original pact stems from the fact that Europe, with its sometimes tragic and bloody history, bears a heavy responsibility. Europe should learn from its mistakes and from an awareness of its own diversity, to find the means for making a different voice heard, and the ambition to become a crossroads of civilisations (rather than a bulwark against the 'rest of the world'). One of the essential 'values' that have characterised Europe since the Age of Enlightenment has been the faith in the capacity of people to govern themselves, and to be the architects of their own destiny. The EU should remain faithful to this legacy by becoming a democratic arena in which it is possible to debate and choose between the different possible Europes.

THE EROSION OF THE FOUNDING PACT

This founding pact has never been fully respected and has been constantly eroded in recent years. This was partly due to the free movement of capital and the resulting globalised competition among the workers of the North and between those of the North and the South. It was equally due to technical progress and its impact on the nature and the organisation of work.

The reasons for the failure of the founding pact were multifold.

1. The accession of the former Communist countries offered a historic opportunity to refound Europe on the basis of solidarity between its peoples, and give fresh impetus to the social model. In practice, the enlargement has simply meant the annexation of the East by the West.

Whereas a reunification of Europe would have required the sealing of a new social and political pact, taking account of existing inequalities between the Member States and aiming to 'equalise upwards', the enlargement undermined the political foundations of an already fragile European social model.

2.   The neoliberal offensive has led to initiatives, facilitated by the European Commission and a number of academics in its environment, which allow investors and firms to escape from the laws of the countries they operated in and to choose others more favourable to them.

3.   The European Commission's promotion of a policy of 'flexicurity' in fact follows the opposite path to what we called the founding pact of social Europe – considering people as 'human capital' who need to ensure their 'employability'.

4.   The European Court has made a turn towards free market fundamentalism. Until recently characterised by sensible prudence in the social sphere, the ECJ has become a spearhead for enforcing downward competition between European workers since the appointment of several judges from ex-Communist countries. It has now set about allowing businesses in those countries to make full use of their 'comparative advantages' in the social sphere, mainly by banning strikes against relocations, exempting firms from the collective agreements of other countries in which they operate and dismissing the right to national minimum wages and certain standards in working conditions (*Viking* 2007; *Laval* 2007; *Rüffert* 2008; *France* 2006; *Luxembourg* 2008).

This jurisprudence entails one capital mistake. The civil 'freedoms' contained in European primary law – freedom of movement, of establishment, of services – are regarded as a given, as a 'rule' and an absolute starting point for interpretation. The social 'rights' newly introduced into primary law – right of association, right to bargain collectively, right to strike – are recognised. However, they are treated as an 'exception from the rule' with only relative (relative to the absolute 'freedoms') legal force. Social rights have to respect civil freedoms – not the other way round. This is a capital mistake of interpretation because both civil freedoms and social rights enjoy the same legal force as parts of European primary law.[2] They have

---

[2]   This has recently been correctly stated by Advocate General Verica Trstenjak in her opinion delivered on 14 April 2010 in Case C-271/08 *European Commission v. Federal Republic of Germany*. Cf. no. 81: 'In the case of a conflict between a fundamental right and a fundamental freedom, both legal positions must be presumed to have equal status. That general equality in status implies, first, that, in the interests of fundamental rights, fundamental freedoms may

to be interpreted in a mutually compatible fashion rather than in a 'rule – exception mode',[3] the latter being pre-democratic. A further breach of the original contract seems to lie in the ominous 'Protocol on the Internal Market and Competition', which was appended to the Lisbon Treaty overnight, so to speak. There, the High Contracting Parties considered 'that the internal market as set out in Article 2 of the Treaty on European Union includes a system ensuring that competition is not distorted' and agreed that 'to this end, the Union shall, if necessary, take action under the provisions of the Treaties, including under Article 308 of the Treaty on the Functioning of the European Union'. It is true that this protocol took up the issue and wording of Article 3 para. 1 (g) EC: 'For the purposes set out in Article 2, the activities of the Community shall include, as provided in this Treaty and in accordance with the timetable set out therein: . . . (g) a system ensuring that competition in the internal market is not distorted.' It is equally true that this shift took place under pressure from the French President to eliminate free market and competition from the enumeration of EU objectives. However, whereas Art. 3 para 1 EC contained all other Community objectives, the protocol isolated the free market objective and did not contain any other one. Actually, this protocol was hailed by Conservatives all over Europe as a legal document avoiding a plurality of objectives of the European Union by giving priority, over all other objectives, to that of achieving the internal market and protecting competition against any distortion. Here, too, the assumption was to declare the free

---

be restricted. However, second, it implies also that the exercise of fundamental freedoms may justify a restriction on fundamental rights.' That Trstenjak, in the *alternative*, takes a restrictive view within the proportionality test (nos 175 ff.), cannot be discussed here.

[3]   In the pre-enlargement jurisprudence, the ECJ seemed to be aware of that. In the Albany sequence, e.g. in the Brentjens' Handelsonderneming BV judgment of the Court of 21 September 1999 (Joined cases C-115/97 to C-117/97), the Court ruled that a collective agreement restricts competition, but, given the co-existence of antitrust provisions and social policy provision in European primary law, is not void because it does not fall within the scope of Art. 85 para 1 of the EC-Treaty (nr. 62). So the Court recognised the equal primary law force of civil and social rights within the EC Treaty (see Bercusson, 2009, 660 ff.). However, the *Brentjens'* and the *Viking/Laval* cases differed in that Brentjens' dealt with a problem of 'demarcation' between coverage of civil rights and social rights – whereas *Viking/Laval* dealt with the problem of 'conflict' between rights of the two areas. If the Court in the latter case, too, would have chosen the approach of the Brentjens' judgment, it would have been obliged to mutually 'weigh' und 'reconcile' the two conflicting rights of equal legal force. Instead the Court mistakenly introduced the criticised 'rule – exception from the rule' approach between civil freedom and social right. This again has to be regarded and criticised as a breach of the original pact.

market as a given 'rule' and any other community objective as the 'exception from the rule' which has to be narrowly interpreted and properly justified.

This assumption is based on the same capital legal mistake as observed in the *Viking/Laval*-decisions of the ECJ. A protocol to a Treaty, though of the legal force of primary law (Riley, 2007), cannot, with legal force, set aside other norms of primary law expressing different policy objectives. The right to strike and the provisions of the Charter of Fundamental Rights, recognised throughout the Community, cannot be set aside and outlawed as 'distortions of competition' by a protocol. They form equal parts of a unitary Treaty structure and have the same legal force as other freedoms and rights. This is why the competition protocol (as interpreted by its Conservative apologists) contains a legal error – but, again, the effort to prioritise free market over other primary law objectives has to be regarded and criticised as a breach of the original contract.

OUTLINES OF A FORTHCOMING MANIFESTO

Against the background of the multifold rupture of the original contract, the new manifesto has to reconsider the renewal of Social Europe. In my view, this implies four steps. First, the democratisation process of Europe has to be promoted (see below) (against the German Constitutional Court). Second, 'the social' has to be freed from the nature of an 'appendix' to the economic, instead, it has to be recognised as an integrative essential of 'the political' and 'the economic' (see below). Therefore, third, the European polity has to be construed from its humane constituency (see below). And, fourth, Europe has to be understood not in a 'fenced-in' but rather in a cosmopolitan manner (see below).

Democratisation Beyond the Nation State: Voice/Entitlement Nexus

Globalisation in general and Europeanisation in particular are challenging the democratic foundation which was hitherto focused on the nation state. The implication of the traditional models of democracy is a nexus between voice (participation, representation) and entitlement (rights, duties, protection etc.) – viewed schematically for three groups of 'centres': political (e.g. state, community), economic (e.g. work place, company) and socio-cultural (e.g. family, household, neighbourhood) (see Mückenberger, 2008, 2010). For a democratic reinvention of Europe, however, it is increasingly necessary to call this nexus into question. The power of the national state is shifting and thereby benefitting suprana-tional agencies – and this implies a partial loss of sovereignty. And it is shifting to sub-national actors and agencies, resulting in – if not a loss of sovereignty – at least a decrease in central regulating powers (and law enforcement powers). In some instances the economic activities reach beyond the territory of state law and therefore escape its monopoly of power. In some cases, globalisation leads to competition among legal systems. Decentration of economy, occupation and work systematically weakens the state's regulatory powers over the economic actors. Self-regulating power, a fundamental prerequisite for the autonomy of the social partners, has lost many of its 'centres': centralised companies and company-based industries as agents in charge of negotiations with respect to their employees and unions are increasingly being replaced by individual 'regime hopping' of corporations or through individual nego-tiation results within the company – both of which are incompatible with traditional governance. This draws attention to the necessity of investigat-ing the possibility and the implementation of universal basal rights and guarantees.

This leads to the conclusion that the creation of a social Europe requires a democratised Europe. Up to now, Europe has been a 'limited democ-racy' within which questions of wealth distribution are removed from the political discussion, to be governed by the 'spontaneous order' of the market. A return to 'the political' is a precondition for posing the neces-sary question of how to oppose mass pauperisation. European democracy must cease to be an empty phrase. For example, rather than the European Parliament being elected on the basis of national constituencies, voting for MEPs should take place on a truly European scale. Party lists of candi-dates from all Member States should be pitted against one another, with each putting forward a project for Europe that would transcend national borders. Similar proposals have been made with a view to direct election of the President of the European Commission. It could be in this way that a new nexus between voice and entitlement could be established – re-inventing democracy on a European level.

Excursus: German Federal Constitutional Court: too much democratisation of Europe a breach of the German constitution?
So far, whenever the democratic deficit of the European Union has been asserted, measures have been considered to bring about steps towards its elimination: a real Europeanisation of the mode of election of the European Parliament, a direct election of the President of the Commission, and so on. This is not the case with the Lisbon verdict issued by the German Federal Constitutional Court (Bundesverfassungsgericht – BVerfG) on

30 June 2009.[4] The court did not reject the Lisbon Treaty. However, it made strict reservations concerning a further democratisation of Europe: if the Treaty of Lisbon had effectively eliminated the EU's democratic deficit, the court would have had to establish its unconstitutionality. It is the world turned upside down: how can it be that the democratic deficit – viewed with respect to the constitutionality of the Lisbon Treaty – does not constitute a weakness, but is in fact one of the EU's strong points? The paradox results from the starting point assumed by the court. As 'an association of sovereign national states (Staatenverbund)', the EU is not a state by itself – it derives its sovereign authority exclusively from the legislative power of its Member States. Its powers depend on the sum of limited single conferrals of power through the Member States. Its law does not gain supranational scope because of the authority of its legislative bodies (Council, European Parliament), but because of the sum of acts of 'conferral exercised in a restricted and controlled manner by the Member States' by which EU legal measures gain legally binding effect. That is why the exclusive authority to evaluate whether or not (*ultra vires*) the course of action adopted by the EU remains within the boundaries of the limited single conferrals of power granted by Germany and the other Member States – and to establish its constitutionality or unconstitutionality and possibly to suspend it in Germany – continues to lie exclusively with the BVerfG.

A democratic EU would not fit the court's concept. The Member States have to be democratic. They have to make sure that the EU is (and remains) compatible with their, the Member States', democratic nature. To the court, Europe does not have to be – in fact must not be – more democratic than this. If the EU had been constituted as a democratic entity by a European sovereign, the EU would no longer be a union of states but a federal state with independent and underived authority ('competence-competence'). For this, however, constitutive action by the European sovereign peoples would be required. If the European actors were to make an effort to fully democratise the EU by making changes, they would position themselves outside of the scope of constitutional validity. The BVerfG would declare the ratification of such a treaty unconstitutional and might order the Federal Republic of Germany to leave the EU should it undergo such a change.

---

[4]   Bundesverfassungsgericht, Az. 2 BvE 2/08, 2 BvE 5/08, 2 BvR 1010, 1022 and 1259/08, 2 BvR 182/09, Urteil vom 30 Juni 2009; English press release No. 72/2009 of 30 June 2009 – in the following, verbatim citations are taken from the official English press release.

In this way the EU's weakness of not being democratic mutates into a strength. If the insistence on the continuity of the democratic deficit by the highest German court becomes a common perspective, the belief in a Europe constituting an area that is beyond the national concept of democracy is going to vanish. Why should the citizens of the Union cast their votes in elections for the European Parliament if they are confronted with the fact that the European citizenship is not a real citizenship status and the European Parliament is no real parliament?

Many people, including many politicians as well as economic, social and cultural associations, are in favour of overcoming the European democratic deficit – instead of its perpetuation. The BVerfG's Lisbon verdict states that such efforts and such a perspective are, in fact, misguided – an erroneous projection of a federalist concept on to Europe. Is this a constructive contribution to the debate regarding the European polity – and to the fight against the emerging indifference when it comes to Europe?

The very fact that the court reduces the democratic requirement to the equal electoral right of each citizen shows decisionistic features. Direct involvement of the citizens of the Union as well as their parliamentary representation becomes something that is 'added' to the national vote – an accessory that one could basically do without. Instead, the assumption has to be that there is a variety of democratic rights and practices of which the equal electoral vote of each citizen is a highly important part, but not the exclusive one. The court remains trapped in the concept of a 'Westphalian state' – that is a concept of states with only a single level of sovereignty and, hence, only a national requirement (and admissibility) of democracy. In this age of political multi-level systems such as Europe and new hybrid constellations in politics, economy and civil society, it is no longer possible to operate on the basis of a uniform understanding of nation-state sovereignty and democracy without disregarding reality. Today we cannot say that *either* Germany *or* Europe is the sovereign to whom democratic demands have to be addressed. Within multi-level systems, we have to learn how to deal with shared and cooperatively executed sovereignties as well as with the regulated cooperation of public and private exertion of power. It is no longer an option to turn back to the Westphalian understanding of sovereignty and democracy represented by the nation state.

The Social: Not Epitheton but Essential Ingredient of Europe

On the basis of a democratised political Europe the issue of 'Social Europe' can be addressed anew. Up to now, Social Europe has been something like an appendix. Europe is essentially a free-market order – to which certain social buffers have to be added to make it more acceptable to the people.

This appendix can be or not be, can be improved or removed – but it always remains an appendix. Here we identify again the secret hierarchical order given by the ECJ to civil freedoms vs. social rights ('rule – exceptions from the rule'). Historically, this appendix theory may have to do with the origin of the European Economic Community as a free market, with the neofunctionalist hopes for a social spill-over; it may also have to do with a new emphasis on 'the economic' after the EC enlargement.

Nevertheless, this understanding of the social as an epitheton has always been wrong and nowadays shows more weakness than ever before. Wealth and social cohesion have always had their sources in human activity and cooperation. Neoliberalism has caused two fundamental errors which are both responsible for the appendix-theory of the social. Markets are not – as neoliberal deregulators and market radicals would have us believe – autonomous and self-organising but an artificial product of political, legal and social invention and intervention. And, therefore, 'the economic' is not an independent dominant variable but rather an artefact of interdependently cooperating ingredients. These observations are incompatible with an externalised and de-valued view of 'the social as an appendix' theory.

This is all the more true in our current state of affairs – in and after the financial crisis. High-wage and high-productivity economies like most of the European ones depend heavily on labour, cooperation and innovation (which all forms part of 'the social'). The recovery after the financial crisis seems to be due to an increase in high-quality commodity exports– which again underlines the importance of the humane in the economy.[5]

Only an integrated view on wealth production which recognises the social as a necessary lever and link of wealth is able to grasp this crucial character of 'the social' and 'social regulation'. This is why we should not speak about a Europe to which a 'social Europe' may or may not be appended. On the contrary, for her proper and sustainable existence, Europe has to be socially embedded – which implies a European polity construed from the humane, not an allegedly prioritarian 'economic' or 'market'.

European Polity Construed from the Humane

With the recent developments in mind, it is necessary to construct Europe from the humane. A new manifesto for Social Europe which takes this

---

[5]   The expression 'the humane in the economy' seems to be more accurate than the expression 'human capital' which from the outset commodifies human capabilities. Nevertheless, the increasing interest of business studies in human capital also hints at the origin of wealth in social relations.

as a starting point implies a double perspective and a double opposition against current developments. From a personal point of view, it has to encourage and strengthen human dignity, capabilities and creativity and defend them against fashionable concepts of 'flexicurity'. From a collective point of view, it has to strengthen the voice and self-regulation of working people – be it in a plant or in an enterprise, on the territorial level, or in the field of freedom of association, collective bargaining and strike – and to defend them against tendencies towards market supremacy, deregulation and privatisation which are now hegemonic in the EU policies.

As a starting point, the construction of a European polity from the humane primarily refers to 'work', not 'labour'. Labour is the com-modified form of human productivity whereas work equally includes those human activities which do not go through the formal labour market and are therefore not gainful. Care for children or the elderly, but also the informal sector (particularly outside the OECD, see Teklè, 2010) form essential parts of social well-being and cohesion, yet are not commodified (see Standing, 2009). One of the short-comings of the labour society is to neglect this type of work. Construing Europe from the humane cannot ignore work which is societally necessary, but not recognised as labour. It would have to allow for statutes of working people which involve areas of paid and unpaid work and which ensure adequate recognition and remu-neration (Supiot, 2001, 2010).

Within the areas of work, the humane approach involves democra-tisation at work, equal opportunitites for both sexes, a time allocation which makes work-life-balance and sustainability feasible, and protection against social exclusion (see Mückenberger, 2002). However, the protec-tion and encouragement of human dignity is not limited to labour law (hence 'labour'). It also covers areas of work which are not labour. This involves a mainstreaming gender orientation. The labour society often takes the male breadwinner as the point of reference for regulation. This is why the standard employment relationship systematically excludes or discriminates against female work – in the developed and, still more so, in the less developed worlds. A new manifesto therefore would have to clearly establish where labour regulations discriminate against 'work' and therefore have to be changed.

This humane approach is opposed to the European Commission's pro-motion of a policy of 'flexicurity'. Despite the charming title, flexicurity in fact follows the opposite path to what I have called a European polity con-strued from the humane. The practical consequence of flexicurity is that people are regarded as 'human capital', who need to ensure their 'employ-ability' rather than their human dignity and creativeness.

From a collective point of view, the construction of a new European polity as envisaged by the manifesto would take 'voice' as a basis for concepts and regulations. This will involve participation and self-regulation at all levels where work is being done. Given the interdependent and collaborative nature of work, participation will in most cases take the shape of a collective – direct or indirect – inclusion of stakeholders in decision-making. After the *Viking/Laval* earthquake the argument has to be put forward that, on the level of EU primary law, freedoms may not be allowed primacy over social rights, but that the latter are of equal status and even require predominance if 'the economic' is understood in the embedded way (above). This has to be made precise and concrete in the areas of plant, enterprise, territory, sector where work is done. It was mentioned already that 'voice' is equally the linkage between political participation and social rights and can, therefore, not be limited to the sphere of labour.

It goes without saying that this approach to a collective voice opposes many of the recent trends in Europe. Most obviously it criticises the subordination of social rights under economic freedoms as observed in the ECJ jurisprudence. But it would equally go against tendencies of the European Commission which in its recent governance approaches cares more about the 'acceptance' than about the 'transparency' of their politics.

Europe Embedded in Cosmopolitan Solidarity

Globalisation nowadays is oscillating between the utopia of a world which completely opens its borders for the free circulation of commodities and capital and the establishment of a 'Fortress Europe' with barricades and 'gated communities'. We have to find a way out of this deadlock. Europe should, simultaneously, protect and open itself. With a view to the non-OECD worlds it should play the role of a motor for re-thinking the relationships between the worlds in the light of the objective of international social justice as proclaimed by the Declaration of Philadelphia at the end of the Second World War (see Supiot, 2010). This cannot end with the mere proposition of universal social standards or human rights (a proposition which frequently has, even if unintended, protectionist implications). This proposition has to be accompanied by actions and measures encouraging the capabilities to implement and enforce universal standards everywhere in the world. This would be a credible cosmopolitan approach to life and work in the 21st-century world.

REFERENCES

Bercusson, B. (2009), *European Labour Law*, 2nd edn, Cambridge: Cambridge University Press.
Bercusson, B., S. Deakin, P. Koistinen, Y. Kravaritou, U. Mückenberger, A. Supiot and B. Veneziani (1996), *A Manifesto for Social Europe*, Brussels: European Trade Union Institute.
Marshall, T.H. (1950), *Citzenship and Social Class and Other Essays*, Cambridge: Cambridge University Press.
Mückenberger, U. (ed.) (2001), *Manifesto Social Europe*, Brussels: European Trade Union Institute.
Mückenberger, U. (ed.) (2002), *Le travail au seuil du 21e siècle: Propositions pour un nouveau régime de travail*, Bruxelles: Institut syndical européen.
Mückenberger, U. (2008), 'Alternative Mechanisms of Voice Representation', in B. Bercusson and C. Estlund (eds), *Regulating Labour in the Wake of Globalisation*, London: Hart Publishing, pp. 227–252.
Mückenberger, U. (2010), 'Civilising Globalism: Transnational Norm-Building Networks as a Lever of the Emerging Global Legal Order?', *Transnational Legal Theory*, **1** (4), 523–573.
Mückenberger, U. and A. Supiot (2009), 'Europe – A Still Unfulfilled Promise. In Memory of Brian Bercusson', in *Zeitschrift für ausländisches und internationales Arbeits- und Sozialrecht*, **23**, 171–181.
Riley, A. (2007), *The EU Reform Treaty & the Competition Protocol: Undermining EC Competition Law*, Centre for European Policy Studies (CEPS) Policy Brief, no. 142, September.
Standing, G. (2009), *Work after Globalisation. Building Occupational Citizenship*, Cheltenham, UK, and Northampton, MA, USA: Edward Elgar.
Supiot, A. (1999/2001), *Au delà de l'emploi. Transformations du travail et devenir du droit du travail en Europe*, Paris: Flammarion; English version (2001), *Beyond Employment. Changes in Work and the Future of Labour Law in Europe*, Oxford: Oxford University Press.
Supiot, A. (2009), 'Possible Europe', interview with M.-O. Padis, *New Left Review*, **57** (May–June), 57–65.
Supiot, A. (2010), *L'esprit de Philadelphie. La justice sociale face au marché total*, Paris: Éditions du Seuil.
Teklè, T. (ed.) (2010), *Labour Law and Worker Protection in Developing Countries*, Oxford: Hart Publishing; Geneva: ILO.

16.   European labour law after *Laval*

Catherine Barnard and Simon Deakin

INTRODUCTION

Brian Bercusson was the first scholar 'convincingly to make the case for European labour law as a wide-ranging discipline in its own right, with a distinct identity separate from national labour law systems, but influenced by them'.[1] In his landmark treatise on the subject, Bercusson saw the core of European labour law as the symbiosis between EU level norms and those operating at the level of national labour law systems.[2] EU level norms on labour law matters were both a reflection of, and a shaping influence on, the traditions of the national regimes. EU labour law drew on the experience of the Member States in such matters as the working environment, information and consultation and aspects of employment protection (acquired rights and collective redundancies), consolidating existing national laws and extending their effects within the 'social space' of the internal market. At the same time, EU law was innovative both in terms of its subject matter, as in the case of the impulse it gave to the extension of the principle of equal treatment in employment, and in its methods, through the development of the techniques of social dialogue and the open method of coordination as applied in the areas of employment policy and social cohesion.

It seemed that European labour law, so conceived, had achieved a certain legitimacy notwithstanding the neglect of social policy issues in the Treaty of Rome, an omission only partly remedied by later developments. The original EEC Treaty regarded labour above all as a resource of production in respect of which the principle of free movement was to apply. This was to treat labour as a commodity, directly contradicting the philosophy and methods of the ILO.[3] Subsequent Treaty amendments and the emergence of a body of secondary legislation in the form of

---

[1]   Ewing (2009, ix).
[2]   Bercusson (2009, 28).
[3]   *Ibid.*, 5.

various directives and other instruments helped to adjust this perspective on labour issues, but nevertheless, by the late 2000s, no comprehensive labour code had emerged at EU level. Whole areas of labour law which were intensively regulated at Member State level, in particular the right to strike, were formally excluded from the legislative competences of EU law-making bodies.[4] Other areas of labour law, including individual rights on termination of employment, were within the competences of the Union, but had failed to become embedded in EU-level norms because of a lack of political will. Despite this, it could be convincingly argued that European labour law was a distinctive body of norms and principles which had achieved 'an identity going beyond [EU] law and national labour law systems'.[5]

The Court of Justice's judgments in *Viking* and *Laval*[6] in late 2008 undoubtedly came as a shock to the system of European labour law. Their repercussions are still being worked through. The question we consider here is how far these judgments require a rethinking of the idea of a European labour law system. The nature of the relationship between EU level norms and national level labour laws has been, on the face of it, fundamentally altered by the Court's assertion of the power to review the operation of labour laws and institutions at national level against criteria implied by the law of free movement. This possibility was not entirely new, but prior to *Viking* and *Laval* it had been confined in various ways. *Viking* and, in particular, *Laval*, lifted some of those constraints, and in doing so created new opportunities for court-led deregulation of national labour laws.

Laval disturbed an uneasy compromise dating back to the foundation of the EEC in the 1950s, whereby the absence of formal legal harmonization of labour law rules at European level was accepted, in return for protection of national level regimes from the potentially destabilizing influence of free movement law. The implication of *Laval* was that national-level labour law rules could in future be levelled down in the name of removing restrictions on free movement, at the same time as political deadlock continued to prevent the emergence of a Europe-wide labour code.

To explore these themes, we will briefly examine, in the next section, the nature of the compromise initially embodied in the Rome Treaty, and consider how it was subsequently maintained up to the point of the *Viking*

---

⁴ Art. 153(5) TFEU.
⁵ Bercusson (2009, 15).
⁶ Case C-438/05 *Viking* [2007] ECR I-10779 and Case C-341/05 *Laval v. Svenska Byggnadsarbetareförbundet* [2007] ECR I-11767.

and *Laval* judgments. Then we will analyse in more detail the significance of those judgments, and related decisions, for the relationship between EU-level norms and the labour laws of the Member States. Our discussion will cover the implications of the Court's judgments for the stability of national labour law regimes and the reaction to them at Member State level. In the concluding section we will argue that the medium- to long-term effects of *Viking* and *Laval* are likely to take the form of a deepening of the integration process, a process within which transnational labour standards will continue to have a critical role to play.

THE COMPROMISE BETWEEN LABOUR LAW AND FREE MOVEMENT PRIOR TO *VIKING* AND *LAVAL*

The story of how the case for legally-driven harmonization of labour laws was rejected by the nascent EEC at the time of the Rome Treaty is by now well known,[7] but it is worth revisiting certain aspects of it in order to put *Viking* and *Laval* in context. The Ohlin Report,[8] commissioned from the ILO, concluded that a European labour code was unnecessary. This was because, in the first place, a levelling-up of labour standards and welfare state provision could be expected to occur spontaneously through the operation of the common market. Secondly, differences in wage costs largely reflected variations in productivity across the different Member States, and so would cancel each other out through the operation of exchange rates. Where this was not the case, the Ohlin Report accepted that intervention at transnational level was needed. Flexible exchange rates would not work to cancel out distortions of competition which arose from variations in levels of productivity within, as opposed to between, national systems.[9] This view was accepted by the Spaak report which formed the basis for the EEC Treaty,[10] and became the justification for the inclusion within that Treaty of the well known provisions relating to equal pay, as well as the now largely forgotten and superseded ones concerning working time.

A third reason given by the ILO experts for rejecting harmonization is of

---

[7]   See Deakin (1996); Barnard (2006, Ch. 1); Bercusson (2009, Part II); Kenner (2003).

[8]   The report is reproduced in International Labour Office, 'Social Aspects of European Economic Cooperation' (1956) *International Labour Review*, **74**, 99.

[9]   *Ibid.*, p. 107.

[10]   Comité intergouvernemental créé par la Conférence de Messine (1956) 'Rapport des Chefs de Délégation aux Ministres des Affaires Étrangères', Brussels. An English-language version appeared in Vol. 405 of the journal *Planning* (1956).

most relevance for our current discussion. Ohlin accepted that the removal of barriers to the movement of goods and resources across national borders would have a disruptive effect, revealing inefficiencies and removing the artificial effects of subsidies. These changes would lead, overall, to faster economic growth, but they required compensating measures at the level of social policy. Critically, Ohlin thought that these measures would operate most effectively at national level. The labour law and welfare state regimes of the original six Member States were extensive, enjoyed wide political support and were, in varying degrees, constitutionally embedded. Economic progress was dependent not simply on 'the more efficient international division of labour' implied by the common market, but also on 'the strength of the trade union movement in European countries and . . . the sympathy of European governments for social aspirations'.[11]

It took a long time for the potential deregulatory effects of the Treaty provisions on free movement to unsettle national social policy. At first, the Court was able to deflect such challenges through the use of the non-discrimination test. Perhaps the earliest example of this can be seen in *Commission v. France*:[12]

> The absolute nature of this prohibition [against discrimination], moreover, has the effect of not only allowing in each state equal access to employment to the nationals of other member states, but also, in accordance with the aim of Article 177 of the Treaty [sic[13]], of guaranteeing to the state's own nationals that they shall not suffer the unfavourable consequences which could result from the offer or acceptance by nationals of other Member States of conditions of employment or remuneration less advantageous than those obtaining under national law, since such acceptance is prohibited.

In other words, by applying the principle of equal treatment, the terms and conditions of employment of nationals of the host state would be protected against undercutting by migrants. The use of the non-discrimination approach, as the underlying test for the application of the free movement provisions, therefore effectively immunized national labour law from challenge under EU law. Provided national labour law rules were non-discriminatory they would be compatible with EU law. If they did discriminate either directly or indirectly, the discriminatory element had to be removed but the underlying rule remained intact.

---

[11] International Labour Office, 'Social Aspects of European Economic Cooperation', p. 112.

[12] Case 167/73 [1974] ECR 354, para. 45.

[13] The French language version uses 'Art. 117' EEC (now Art. 151 TFEU) which is more likely to be correct in the context.

However, the Court's embrace in the 1990s of the *Säger*[14] 'market access' approach (more recently referred to as the 'restrictions' approach) instead of the discrimination analysis threatened to undermine the careful balance between the preservation of national labour law and EU rules on free movement. While the non-discrimination model adopts a comparative approach looking to see how both nationals and migrants are treated (and only if there is a difference in treatment is there a potential illegality), the market access/restrictions approach considers only the perspective of the out-of-state actor. It asks whether the national rule hinders/restricts the ability of the out-of-state actor to gain access to the market or to exercise freedom of movement.

While there is a lively debate in the literature as to what precisely the market access test means and how it should apply to rules which 'structure the market' such as labour law rules, rules on taxation, environmental laws and so on,[15] the upshot of it is that national labour law rules potentially become liable to challenge as a restriction to free movement even where they are non-discriminatory. This can be seen in *Commission v. France (performing artists)*[16] where the Court said that French law which presumed artists had 'salaried status', resulting in them being subject to the social security scheme for employed workers, constituted a restriction on freedom to provide services. The Court said that the French system was 'likely both to discourage the artists in question from providing their services in France and discourage French organisers of events from engaging such artists'.[17] The rules were therefore presumptively unlawful unless they could be justified and were proportionate (which was not the case on the facts). A full-scale application of the market access test therefore risked jeopardizing the entire edifice of national labour law.

Nevertheless, in the late 1990s/early 2000s the Court showed a willingness to protect social law from the full force of the restrictions approach by

---

[14]   Case C–76/90 [1991] ECR I–4221, para 12. Article 56 required '*not only* the elimination of all discrimination against a person providing services on the ground of his nationality *but also* the abolition of any restriction, even if it applies without distinction to national providers of services and to those of other Member States, when *it is liable to prohibit or otherwise impede* the activities of a provider of services established in another Member State where he lawfully provides similar services'.

[15]   See for example Snell (2010); Barnard and Deakin (2002); Davies (2010); Spaventa (2004, 757–758).

[16]   Case C-255/04 *Commission v. France (performing artists)* [2006] ECR I-5251, para 38.

[17]   *Ibid.*, para 38.

using a number of techniques.[18] For example, it was willing to accept the argument that the labour law rule under challenge was too remote from affecting free movement to engage the Treaties,[19] or that the rule was not a restriction at all.[20] It also used the principle of solidarity to take the subject matter outside the scope of the Treaties. Therefore, in *Sodemare*[21] the Court said that Italian rules insisting that only non-profit-making private operators could participate in the running of its social welfare system did not breach Articles 49 and 54 TFEU on freedom of establishment because, as the Court noted, the system of social welfare, whose implementation is in principle entrusted to the public authorities, was based on the principle of solidarity, as reflected by the fact that it was designed to assist those who are in a state of need.[22] Even in cases where the Court found the labour law rule to be a restriction on free movement, it said that the rule could be justified on grounds of worker protection, and that the rule was proportionate, with the Court generally taking a fairly generous approach towards the Member States on the proportionality question.[23]

Perhaps, most famously, in *Rush Portuguesa* the Court gave an unreasoned but resounding endorsement to a host state applying all of its labour law rules to workers posted to that state (the so-called territorial application of labour law):[24]

[Union] law does not preclude Member States from extending their legislation, or collective labour agreements entered into by both sides of industry, to any person who is employed, even temporarily, within their territory, no matter in which country the employer is established; nor does [Union] law prohibit Member States from enforcing those rules by appropriate means.[25]

---

[18]   For full details, see Barnard (2010, 243–5).

[19]   Case C-190/98 *Graf v. Filzmozer Maschinenbau GmbH* [2000] ECR I-493. The Court explained that the entitlement to a termination payment was not dependent on the worker's choosing whether or not to stay with his current employer but on a future and hypothetical event (being dismissed). In paragraph 25 the Court concluded that '[s]uch an event is *too uncertain and indirect* a possibility for legislation to be capable of being regarded as liable to hinder free movement for workers'. Thus, paragraph 25 of *Graf* indicates that the event was too remote to be considered liable to affect free movement. It may not have been coincidental that *Graf* was in essence a claim for the levelling up of labour standards: see Deakin (2008, 607).

[20]   Case C-285/01 *Burbaud v. Ministère de l'Emploi et de la Solidarité* [2003] ECR 8219, para 96. Joined Cases C-51/96 & C-191/97 *Deliège v. Ligue Francophone de Judo et Disciplines Associés* [2000] ECR I-2549, para. 64.

[21]   Case C-70/95 *Sodemare v. Regione Lombardia* [1997] ECR I-3395.

[22]   *Ibid.*, para 29.

[23]   Case C-279/80 *Webb* [1981] ECR I-3305.

[24]   Case C-113/89 [1990] ECR I-1417.

[25]   Citing Joined Cases 62/81 and 63/81 *Seco SA and Another* [1982] ECR 223.

Even in the field of competition law, the Court indicated its willingness to ring-fence labour law from the rigours of Articles 101 and 102 TFEU. *Albany*[26] is perhaps the best-known example of this where the Court held that collective agreements are excluded from the scope of Article 101 TFEU, despite the restrictions of competition inherent in them, provided that two conditions are satisfied: the agreement must (1) have been concluded in the framework of collective negotiations, and (2) with a view to improving conditions of work and employment. Thus, a collective agreement which set up a supplementary pension scheme managed by a pension fund to which affiliation was compulsory did not fall within Article 101(1) TFEU.

THE IMPLICATIONS OF *VIKING* AND *LAVAL* FOR THE RELATIONSHIP BETWEEN NATIONAL AND EU-LEVEL NORMS

The Decisions

The decisions in *Viking* and *Laval* and their progeny, *Rüffert* and *Luxembourg*,[27] unsettled the general deference by the Court to national labour law rules. It will be recalled that these cases concerned a challenge by employers to industrial action taken by trade unions protesting about the re-registering of a Finnish vessel in Estonia (*Viking*) and about the refusal by a Latvian service provider to respect Swedish collectively agreed terms and conditions (*Laval*). The Court refused to extend the *Albany* principle to these situations and so found that free movement law did, in principle, apply to the cases. It then applied the *Säger* market access approach and found that the collective action was a 'restriction' on free movement in both cases and so breached Article 49 TFEU (*Viking*) and Article 56 TFEU (*Laval*). The collective action could possibly be justified on the grounds of worker protection (although this was unlikely on the facts in *Viking*) but, in the view of the Court, the collective action was probably not proportionate in *Viking*, and was definitely not in *Laval*.

There is now an extensive body of literature considering every aspect of these cases.[28] For the purposes of this chapter we want to highlight three

---

[26]   Case C-67/96 [1999] ECR I-5751.
[27]   Case C-346/06, *Dirk Rüffert v. Land Niedersachsen* [2008] *ECR* I-1989; Case C-319/06 *Commission v. Luxembourg* [2007] ECR I-4323.
[28]   See for example Chapters 17–22 of *Cambridge Yearbook of European Legal Studies 2007–2008*, 10, as well as Malmberg and Sigeman (2008); Kilpatrick (2009); Syrpis and Novitz (2008).

points about these judgments. First, the decision in *Albany* looks increasingly confined to competition cases and to the narrow fact pattern of that case. This point was emphasized in *Commission v. Germany (occupational pensions)*:[29]

> Furthermore, the fact that an agreement or an activity is excluded from the scope of the provisions of the [Treaties] on competition does not automatically mean that that agreement or activity is also excluded from the obligation to comply with the requirements stemming from the provisions of those [Directives 92/50 and 2004/18 on public procurement] since those two sets of provisions are to be applied in different circumstances.[30]

Second, although the Court claimed to be striking a balance between economic and social rights,[31] in practice the structure of the *Säger* market access approach inevitably prioritizes the economic right over the social interest. Once a rule is found to be a restriction it is presumptively unlawful. The burden then shifts to the defendant (in *Viking* and *Laval* the trade unions and in *Rüffert* and *Luxembourg* the state authorities) to show not only that the collective action or law in question can be justified in principle, now according to significantly tightened criteria, but also that taking collective action is proportionate.

Third, in these cases the Court identified the right to strike as a fundamental right. However, it then appeared to strangle that right at birth. It did this in two ways. On the one hand, it did not protect the right to strike as such. Rather, it protected the 'notion – inherent in that fundamental right – of protection of workers'.[32] On the other hand, the Court interpreted the limitations on the right in such a way as largely to subsume the right. The limitations, as identified in Article 28 of the Charter, are that the right to strike is subject to the rules laid down by national law *and* EU law. The limitations laid down by national law rules relate to, for example, balloting and notice requirements. Following *Viking* and *Laval* the limitations laid down by EU law are potentially more difficult for a trade union to satisfy: the strike can be justified only where jobs or conditions of employment are 'jeopardized or under serious threat' (*Viking*) or where the terms of the complex Posted Workers Directive are satisfied (*Laval*)), and where the trade unions have exhausted all other means

---

[29]   Case C-271/08 *Commission v. Germany* [2010] ECR I-000.
[30]   *Ibid.*, para 48.
[31]   E.g. *Laval*, para 105.
[32]   Trstenjak AG, Case C-271/08 *Commission v. Germany* [2010] ECR I-000, para 181.

(*Viking*). As the British Airlines Pilots Association (BALPA) discovered to its cost in the High Court of England and Wales, it is difficult to satisfy these thresholds and the liability in damages is potentially enormous.[33] No wonder John Monks, General Secretary of the European Trade Union Confederation (ETUC) said to the European Parliament in February 2008 that '. . . we are told that the right to strike is a fundamental right but not so fundamental as the EU's free movement provisions. This is a licence for social dumping and for unions being prevented from taking action to improve matters.'[34]

Deterritorialization of Labour Law, Preemption and Regulatory Competition

Brian Bercusson argued that the combined effects of the *Viking* and *Laval* judgments were 'bad for trade unions (as employers exploit unpredictability) and bad for the courts (arbitrating on the merits of social dumping)'.[35] Their implications for the operation of national labour law systems are also far-reaching. In *Laval* and in its later judgment in *Rüffert*, the Court overturned the presumption in favour of the territorial effect of labour legislation, at least in the context of freedom to provide services, which it had previously accepted in *Rush Portuguesa*. Laval was essentially arguing to be allowed to keep the competitive advantage of less protective (and hence less costly) Latvian labour laws and collective agreements while, through its subsidiary, it operated on Swedish territory.[36] In *Rüffert* the issue was whether Polish subcontractors working in Germany should 'lose the competitive advantage which they enjoy by reason of their lower wage costs'.[37] In deciding in favour of the service providers in these cases, the Court appeared to treat corporate location in a low-cost jurisdiction as a matter of competitive advantage, which it was the role of the free movement principle to protect.

The justifications given for doing this were highly contestable. Supporters of the Court's approach argued that as it was applying the test of 'restriction' or 'market access', rather than the discrimination test, it was irrelevant that suppliers based in the host state, and as such subject to the

---

[33]   Apps (2009).

[34]   See http://www.etuc.org/IMG/pdf_ETUC_Viking_Laval_-_resolution_070 308.pdf (accessed 26 August 2008).

[35]   Bercusson (2009, 486, 689).

[36]   See the Opinion of Mengozzi AG in *Laval* at para 133.

[37]   This was the way the issue was put by the referring court. See *Rüffert*, Opinion of Bot AG, at para 41.

normal application of its laws and collective agreements, were being placed at a competitive disadvantage with regard to out-of-state service providers who were established in a low-cost Member State.[38] Yet, the claim that differences in labour standards across the Member States gave rise, in and of themselves, to a restriction on free movement, opened a Pandora's Box.[39] This was precisely the argument rejected by the authors of the Spaak Report in 1956. They had foreseen the need to consider whether, 'leaving aside cases of overt discrimination and interventions aimed at favouring certain firms or modes of production, legislative and regulatory provisions may have such an impact on costs and prices' that the results would be to 'distort conditions of competition among the national economies as a whole or in particular branches of economic activity'.[40] The Spaak Report concluded, however, that simple differences in regulatory regimes could not amount to a distortion of competition, insisting that to think otherwise was to 'misunderstand' the way international trade worked. This was because 'competition does not necessarily require a complete harmonization of the different elements in costs'; rather, 'it is only on the basis of certain differences – such as wage differences due to productivity – that an equilibrium can be established and trade develop'.[41] The Spaak Report took this line in order to forestall arguments for (among other things) a comprehensive labour code at European level, but precisely the same argument applies, *mutatis mutandis*, to attempts to bring about the 'negative harmonisation' or levelling down of labour laws through free movement jurisprudence.

Federal systems, as well as quasi-federal entities such as the EU, can and do perfectly well combine an internal market based on free movement for economic resources, with the retention of jurisdiction over labour law and other matters of social policy at state or local level. Differences in labour law regulation across US states do not give rise to a prima facie breach of the Commerce Clause requiring justification by reference to a proportionality test, as *Viking* and *Laval* would have them do in the equivalent EU context of Articles 49 and 56 TFEU.[42] In principle, diversity of regulatory regimes is desirable as it makes it possible for labour law rules to be matched to local conditions, reflecting political priorities and social compromises at state level. Such diversity also facilitates learning

---

[38] Reich (2008).
[39] Eklund (2008, 572).
[40] Comité intergouvernemental créé par la Conférence de Messine (1956) at p. 60 (authors' translation).
[41] *Ibid*.
[42] Deakin (2008, 608).

across systems, an important aspect, more generally, of open coordination methods within the EU's emergent federal regime.[43] At the same time, a floor of rights at transnational level can be useful in preventing a 'race to the bottom'. Social policy directives generally contain minimum standards provisions and non-regression clauses with this end in mind. However, given their minimum standards content, they have not been interpreted as having a pre-emptive effect, that is, one which would prevent states from enacting standards which are more favourable to labour than those set out in the relevant transnational measure.[44] This was, however the interpretation given to the Posted Workers' Directive 96/71 in *Laval*, *Rüffert* and *Luxembourg*. It is possible that the Court's view on pre-emption of state level labour laws is confined to the Posting Directive, which, in terms of its Treaty base at least, is not a social policy measure,[45] but this remains to be seen.

Is a Race to the Bottom Inevitable?

While the Court's judgments in *Viking* and *Laval* opened the way for greater regulatory competition and for the destabilization of national labour law regimes, it does not follow that they will have this effect in practice. A first reason for caution on this point is evidence of the continuing will and capacity of Member States to pursue social policy goals at national level and to take steps to limit the impact of the *Viking* and *Laval* judgments. This is clearest in the case of the immediate reaction of the Nordic systems to *Laval* and in the regional German response to *Rüffert*. The Nordic reaction has essentially involved reaffirmation of the role of the social partners in setting market-wide labour standards through collective bargaining, a core feature of those systems which complements their widely praised active labour market policies.[46] The Swedish legislation which came into force in April 2010, although promoted by a Conservative-led government, was premised on the goal of allowing 'as far as possible the application of the Swedish labour market model to

---

[43]   See Deakin (2009).

[44]   *Ibid.*, 593–603.

[45]   Barnard and Deakin (forthcoming).

[46]   See also Chapter 2 in this volume. The Commission Green Paper, *Modernising Labour Law to Meet the Challenges of the Twenty-First Century*, COM(2006) 708, highlighted flexible employment law and active labour market policy as important elements of the Nordic model, but market-wide labour standards play a critical role in complementing these mechanisms: see McLaughlin (2008).

workers posted to Sweden from another country'.[47] It permits industrial action to support the application to posted workers of a sector-level collective agreement that is applied throughout national territory to workers of the relevant description, under the terms of Article 3(8) of the Posted Workers Directive. Although only minimum conditions of employment as set out in Article 3(1) may be enforced this way, the law can be seen as a limited accommodation of *Laval*. In Denmark reforms have been undertaken to confirm the legality of strike action in support of multi-employer collective agreements even in cases of minimum wages above subsistence level, and in Norway the courts have so far regarded powers to extend the effects of sector-level collective agreements by legal decree as compatible with *Laval*, a view also adopted by the EFTA Surveillance Authority.[48] Meanwhile, in reaction to *Rüffert*, the Land of Lower Saxony has enacted a law which requires compliance with *erga omnes* collective agreements, again under Article 3(8) of the Directive, and generally leaves the law on the application of market-wide labour standards stronger than it was before.[49]

A second reason to be cautious on the race to the bottom scenario is the role which sectoral social dialogue can play in responding to the Court's interventions. In 2009 a Council Directive was adopted giving effect to a framework agreement made by the European-level federations of employers' associations and trade unions in the maritime sector, governing terms and conditions of employment of workers affected by the use of flags of convenience. The Directive is intended to come into force alongside an ILO Convention which was adopted in 2006.[50] While by no means reversing *Viking*, these developments indicate the scope for norms based on transnational collective bargaining to fill the void left by court-led deregulatory initiatives.

A New Balance?

Brian Bercusson concluded his discussion of *Viking* and *Laval* with the following observation:[51]

---

[47] Rönnmar (2010, 285).

[48] Skjeie (2010).

[49] Sciarra (2010, 240).

[50] See Council Directive 2009/13 implementing the agreement concluded by the European Community Ship Owners' Associations and the European Transport Workers' Federation, OJ [2009] L 124/30; ILO Convention No. 186 on Maritime Labour, adopted 23 February 2006; Sciarra (2010, 232–233).

[51] Bercusson (2009, 698).

> The role of the ECJ in the future of European labour law depends on whether it can recover from the self-inflicted blows of its decisions in *Viking* and *Laval*. One lesson of *Viking* and *Laval* is that creating European labour law is too serious a matter to be left to judges.

However, as he noted, 'the unsatisfactory result produced by the ECJ in these cases was not inevitable'. As we shall now see, the decision in *Commission v. Germany (occupational pensions)*, read in conjunction with some of the changes introduced by the Lisbon Treaty in 2009, gives grounds for optimism that the Court might be able to redeem itself and help re-establish the idea of a European labour law system.

For our purposes, the Lisbon Treaty introduced three important changes: it gives legal effect to the Charter of Fundamental Rights 2007, which includes the chapter on solidarity; it requires the EU to accede to the ECHR which, following some recent judgments of the Court of Human Rights, now adopts a more positive approach to collective rights;[52] and it introduces, in Article 3(3) TEU, the objective for the Union to achieve 'a highly competitive social market economy'.[53] These three developments suggest that the time has come for a break with the pure market orientation of the past by the EU and an attempt to achieve a more genuine balance between the economic and the social. Advocate General Cruz Villalon appeared to accept this logic in *Santos Palhota*.[54] Having referred to Article 3(3) TEU, he said: 'The entry into force of the Lisbon Treaty requires that, if working conditions constitute an imperative reason in the public interest justifying a derogation from the free movement of services, it must no longer be interpreted in a restrictive manner.' In other words, where worker protection is used to justify a breach of the Treaties – as in *Viking* and *Laval* – it should no longer be considered an exception and thus interpreted restrictively.

---

[52] See for example *Demir and Baykara v. Turkey*, Application No 34503/97, 12 November 2008; *Enerji Yapi-Yol,* Application no. 68959/01; Ewing and Hendy (2010).

[53] For a discussion of this term, see Joerges and Rödl (2004, 19), who argue that 'this concept contained an ordo-liberal basis which was complemented by social and societal policies, whose aims and instruments were supposed to reply on market mechanisms'. According to Working Group XI on Social Europe (CONV 516/1/03 REV 1), at para 17, the objectives of the Union should refer to the concept of the 'social market economy' in order to underline the link between the economic and social development and efforts made to ensure greater coherence between economic and social policies.

[54] Case C-515/08 *Santos Palhota* [2010] ECR I-000, paras 51–53 (authors' translation).

In *Commission v. Germany* Advocate General Trstenjak went further in advocating a greater balance between fundamental economic and social rights. She said that the approach to fundamental rights adopted in *Viking* and *Laval* 'sits uncomfortably alongside the principle of equal ranking for fundamental rights and fundamental freedoms'.[55] She continues:

> Such an analytical approach suggests, in fact, the existence of a hierarchical relationship between fundamental freedoms and fundamental rights in which fundamental rights are subordinated to fundamental freedoms and, consequently, may restrict fundamental freedoms only with the assistance of a written or unwritten ground of justification.[56]

She rejects the existence of any such hierarchical relationship[57] and argues that it is possible to find an equilibrium between the economic freedoms and fundamental rights, as the Court did in *Schmidberger*,[58] using the principle of proportionality:[59]

> A fair balance between fundamental rights and fundamental freedoms is ensured in the case of a conflict only when the restriction by a fundamental right on a fundamental freedom is not permitted to go beyond what is appropriate, necessary and reasonable to realise that fundamental right. Conversely, however, nor may the restriction on a fundamental right by a fundamental freedom go beyond what is appropriate, necessary and reasonable to realise the fundamental freedom.

Commission v. Germany concerned a failure by Germany to respect the public procurement Directives. A number of local authorities in Germany had entered into a collective agreement with the trade unions concerning the conversion of earnings into pension savings. The collective agreement identified a limited list of pension providers entrusted with implementing the salary conversion measure. Given the existence of this agreement, the local authorities did not issue a call for tenders, as required by the Public Procurement Directives, thereby denying other pension providers the chance to offer their services.

The case therefore pitted the fundamental social right to engage in collective bargaining, combined with the autonomy of the social partners, against the fundamental economic freedoms, freedom of establishment and free movement of services. The Court is much less explicit about how

---

55 *Ibid.*, para 183.
56 *Ibid.*, para 185.
57 *Ibid.*, para 186.
58 Case C-112/00 *Schmidberger* [2003] ECR I-5659.
59 Case C-271/08 *Commission v. Germany* [2010] ECR I-000, para 190.

to achieve the balance but does appear to take inspiration from the words of its Advocate General:

> Exercise of the fundamental right to bargain collectively must therefore be reconciled with the requirements stemming from the freedoms protected by the FEU Treaty, which in the present instance Directives 92/50 and 2004/18 are intended to implement, and be in accordance with the principle of proportionality . . .[60]

Then, without referring to the usual *Säger* market access approach but citing *Schmidberger* instead, the Court said that reconciling the competing interests entails verification as to whether, when establishing the content of the collective agreement:

> a fair balance was struck in the account taken of the respective interests involved, namely enhancement of the level of the retirement pensions of the workers concerned, on the one hand, and attainment of freedom of establishment and of the freedom to provide services, and opening-up to competition at European Union level, on the other.[61]

The Court found that this balance had not been struck because the effect of the collective agreement was 'to disapply the public procurement rules completely, and for an indefinite period, in the field of local authority employees' pension saving'.[62] Rejecting the German government's argument that the public procurement directives should not be applied because (1) they did not provide room for worker participation; and (2) the collective agreement was a manifestation of the principle of solidarity (with good risks offsetting the bad), the Court said that the 'application of the procurement procedures [do not] preclude the call for tenders from imposing upon interested tenderers conditions reflecting the interests of the workers concerned'[63] nor do the directives preclude 'a local authority employer from specifying, in the terms of the call for tenders, the conditions to be complied with by tenderers in order to prevent, or place limits on, workers interested in salary conversion being selected on the basis of medical grounds.'[64] It added that the preservation of 'elements of solidarity is not inherently irreconcilable with the application of a procurement procedure'.[65]

---

[60] *Ibid.*, para 44.
[61] *Ibid.*, para 52.
[62] *Ibid.*, para 53.
[63] *Ibid.*, para 56.
[64] *Ibid.*, para 58.
[65] *Ibid.*

And in reaching this conclusion, the Court incidentally addressed the vexed question of how much space there is in any procurement process for social factors to be taken into account. The answer seems to be: much more than was first thought.

CONCLUSION

Brian Bercusson argued that European labour law formed a significant part of 'the unfolding dynamic of European integration'.[66] The *Viking* and *Laval* judgments are best seen, we suggest, as part of that continuing dynamic. By subjecting national labour law regimes to new forms of scrutiny, carried out in the name of free movement for economic resources, they created the potential for a deepening of the integration process. But as the dust settles and the nature of the response to the judgment becomes clear,[67] it can be seen that they are unlikely to lead to the marginalization of labour law within the wider European project. Individual Member States are not about to abandon their distinctive approaches to social policy, while, at transnational level, sectoral social dialogue may be growing in importance as a source of norms. Meanwhile, there are the first signs of a doctrinal adjustment, post-*Viking* and *Laval*, which will see fundamental social rights put on more level footing with economic freedoms. While few could have anticipated, prior to the autumn of 2007, the sharp right-turn which the Court was about to take, it is perhaps not surprising, in retrospect, that tensions between economic and social policy, which have proved controversial throughout the history of national labour law systems, should have surfaced at EU level. This was, perhaps, the coming of age of European labour law that Brian Bercusson had predicted.

REFERENCES

Apps, K. (2009), 'Damages Claims against Trade Unions after *Viking* and *Laval*', *European Law Review*, **34**, 141–154.

---

[66] Bercusson (2009, 641).

[67] One of the 12 proposals identified by the Commission in its Single Market Act (COM(2011) 206) is: 'Legislation aimed at improving and reinforcing the transposition, implementation and enforcement in practice of the Posting of Workers Directive 55, which will include measures to prevent and sanction any abuse and circumvention of the applicable rules, together with legislation aimed at clarifying the exercise of freedom of establishment and the freedom to provide services alongside fundamental social rights.'

Barnard, C. (2006), *EC Employment Law*, Oxford: Oxford University Press.

Barnard, C. (2010), *The Substantive Law of the EU: The Four Freedoms*, 3rd edn, Oxford: Oxford University Press, pp. 243–245.

Barnard, C. and S. Deakin (2002), 'Market Access and Regulatory Competition', in C. Barnard and J. Scott (eds), *The Legal Foundations of the Single Market: Unpacking the Premises*, Oxford: Hart Publishing.

Barnard, C. and S. Deakin (forthcoming), 'Social Policy and Labour Market Regulation', in A. Menon, E. Jones and S. Weatherill (eds), *Oxford Handbook on European Union Law*, Oxford: Oxford University Press.

Bercusson, B. (2009), *European Labour Law*, 2nd edn, Cambridge: Cambridge University Press.

Davies, A.C.L. (2006), 'One Step Forward, Two Steps Back? The *Viking* and *Laval* Judgments in the ECJ', *ILJ*, **37** (2), 126–148.

Davies, G. (2010), 'Understanding Market Access: Exploring the Economic Rationality of Different Conceptions of Free Movement Law', *German Law Journal*, **10**, 671–704.

Deakin, S. (1996), 'Labour Law as Market Regulation', in P. Davies, A. Lyon-Caen, S. Sciarra and S. Simitis (eds), *European Community Labour Law: Principles and Perspectives. Liber Amicorum Lord Wedderburn*, Oxford: Oxford University Press.

Deakin, S. (2008), 'Regulatory Competition after *Laval*', *Cambridge Yearbook of European Legal Studies 2007–2008*, **10**, 581–609.

Deakin, S. (2009), 'Reflexive Harmonisation and European Company Law', *European Law Journal*, **15** (2), 224–245.

Eklund, R. (2008), 'A Swedish Perspective on *Laval*', *Comparative Labour Law and Policy Journal*, **29** (4), 551–572.

Ewing, K. (2009), 'Preface', in B. Bercusson, *European Labour Law*, 2nd edn, Cambridge: Cambridge University Press.

Ewing, K. and J. Hendy (2010), 'The Dramatic Implications of *Demir and Baykara*', *Industrial Law Journal*, **39** (1), 2–51.

Joerges, C. and F. Rödl (2004), '"Social Market Economy" as Europe's Social Model?', European University Institute Working Paper Law No. 2004/8.

Kenner, J. (2003), *EU Employment Law: From Rome to Amsterdam and Beyond*, Oxford: Hart Publishing.

Kilpatrick, C. (2009), '*Laval's* Regulatory Conundrum: Collective Standard-Setting and the Court's New Approach to Posted Workers', *European Law Review*, **34** (6), 844–865.

Malmberg, J. and T. Sigeman (2008), 'Industrial Actions and EU Economic Freedoms: The Autonomous Collective Bargaining Model Curtailed by the European Court of Justice', *Common Market Law Review*, **45**, 1115–1146.

McLaughlin, C. (2008), 'On the Productivity Enhancing Impacts of the Minimum Wage: Evidence from Denmark and New Zealand', *British Journal of Industrial Relations*, **47**(2), 327–348.

Reich, N. (2008), 'Free Movement Versus Social Rights in an Enlarged Union: the *Laval* and *Viking* cases before the European Court of Justice', *German Law Journal*, **9**, 125.

Rönnmar, M. (2010), '*Laval* Returns to Sweden: The Final Judgment of the Swedish Labour Court and Swedish Legislative Reforms', *Industrial Law Journal*, **39**, 28.

Sciarra, S. (2010), 'Notions of Solidarity in Times of Economic Uncertainty', *Industrial Law Journal*, **39**, 323.

Skjeie, T. (2010), 'European Economic Integration: a Threat to the Scandinavian Labour Law Systems?', LL.M. Dissertation, University of Cambridge.

Snell, J. (2010), 'The Notion of Market Access: A Concept or a Slogan?', *Common Market Law Review*, **47**, 437–472.

Spaventa, E. (2004), 'From *Gebhard* to *Carpenter*: Towards a (Non-)Economic European Constitution', *Common Market Law Review*, **41**, 743–773.

Syrpis, P. and T. Novitz (2008), 'Economic and Social Rights in Conflict: Political and Judicial Approaches to their Reconciliation', *European Law Review*, **33**, 411.

17. The future of European social dialogue

Christophe Vigneau

To discuss industrial relations within the EU, scholars generally use the expression 'social dialogue'. This formula covers a wide range of rules and practices occurring at European level. Social dialogue has a long tradition in European integration and its role has been growing over the years. At the outset, social dialogue found an institutionalized agora with the European Economic and Social Committee. It also developed at sectoral level in the 1960s with the establishment of joint committees. At cross industry level, in the 1970s, the Standing Committee on Employment was set up for the Commission, the Council and the social partners to discuss employment. During the 1980s and under the auspices of the Commission, the informal meetings of Val Duchesse developed. In 1986, the European Single Act introduced a provision in the Treaty which formally obliges the Commission to promote social dialogue. Within this new framework, the Commission plays a decisive role, encouraging the so-called social partners to negotiate and conclude agreements. However, in the late 1980s and 1990s social dialogue remained relatively weak in terms of results, and marginal in determining European social policy.

A new and fundamental impetus is given to social dialogue by the Social Protocol attached to the Maastricht Treaty.[1] From 1992 onwards, social partners have been given a primary role in defining European social policy making. Prior to any proposal regarding social policy, the Commission must consult the social partners both on the opportunity and the content of a European instrument. Further to this, social partners may decide to negotiate and reach an agreement implemented through a Council decision which has in practice been a directive. Therefore, social dialogue becomes the primary source of European labour law. A new form of subsidiarity appears at European level.[2] Legislation through the

---

[1] Bercusson (1992, 177–190); Lyon-Caen (1993).
[2] Langlois (1993); Lyon-Caen (1997).

classic procedure is given a secondary place, when social partners refuse to negotiate or fail to reach an agreement. Statutory legislation is considered subsidiary to collective agreements. It is important to recall that this new institutional device for the production of European labour law originates from the social partners themselves. Indeed, the content of articles 138 and 139 of the Treaty derives from an agreement signed on 31 October 1991 between the ETUC, BusinessEurope and the CEEP.[3]

This new institutional arrangement raised high expectations for the development of European Social Policy. However, results may be considered disappointing to a certain extent. Paradoxically, this does not mean that social dialogue is diminishing in the European governance. On the contrary, social dialogue has never been so dynamic at European level. But its strong activity shows few regulatory results.

Social dialogue is not as widely used at national level as it is at European level. Within national industrial relations systems, social dialogue had been originally conceived from the narrower perspective of collective bargaining. Even if collective agreements have a different status within national legal orders, collective bargaining originated as a traditional and common regulatory instrument for trade unions and employers. It is historically linked to the ability of trade unions to create a power struggle with employers and to settle conflicts through collective agreements at plant levels. Even now, collective bargaining provides a technique to accommodate opposite interests and solve conflicts between employees and employers. Collective bargaining is considered in many national industrial relations systems as an important and autonomous regulatory technique for labour relations and constitutes therefore a substantial dimension of social dialogue mainly because it provides regulatory norms. It demonstrates the capacity of social partners to regulate labour relations without the intervention of the State.

For many reasons, it is difficult to speak about collective bargaining and collective agreements at community level. The undeniable vitality and expansion of social dialogue in European governance hides a major ambiguity as to its purpose and its scope. In particular, it seems necessary to think about the respective place and scope of social dialogue and collective bargaining. What do collective bargaining and social dialogue consist of? This exercise requires a definition of the characteristics of collective bargaining with respect to social dialogue. Collective bargaining is generally considered as one aspect of social dialogue which encompasses a larger variety of formal and informal relationships between employ-

---

[3]   On this agreement, Didry and Mias (2005).

ers' organizations and trade unions. In fact, social dialogue is a rather vague concept in terms of actors, procedures and objectives. Collective bargaining, on the other hand, refers to more precise relationships with a limited number of actors, defined procedure and objectives. Social dialogue includes concertation processes without a limited number of participants while collective bargaining remains a bipartite process. But the main difference between collective bargaining and social dialogue lies in the fact that while the first foresees a regulatory objective, the second does not necessarily have this aim. In other words, collective bargaining has a legal dimension, which is not the case with social dialogue.

At European level, social dialogue does not seem to be used for setting legal rules. At any rate, social dialogue takes place in a context of a soft approach of regulation at EU level regarding social policy. This conception has prevailed and will probably constitute the future of social dialogue. Therefore one major challenge for the European social dialogue would be its transformation into a collective bargaining system.

FROM SOCIAL DIALOGUE . . .

European social dialogue has become a keyword in European governance. It has been growing strongly over the last 20 years. This development has taken place at different levels and in various forms. It has produced a variety of instruments.

A Keyword in European Governance

On many occasions, the Commission has reaffirmed the central role of social dialogue. Since 1996, the Commission has issued four communications promoting social dialogue. In its 1996 communication,[4] the Commission examined different roles and the place social dialogue should take in European Governance. This document, followed by another communication in 1998, shows that the Commission wished to develop social dialogue at all levels.[5] Former informal structures are transformed in order to give more efficiency to social dialogue in particular at sectoral

---

[4] Commission Communication concerning the Development of the Social Dialogue at Community Level, COM (96), 448 final.
[5] Commission Communication on Adapting and Promoting the Social Dialogue at Community level, COM (98) 322 final.

level. Social partners are given three main prerogatives in the European Governance: information, consultation and negotiation.

Social dialogue is envisaged as a central element of the European governance where social democracy compensates for the deficiencies of political democracy. It provides increased legitimacy for European social policy and European integration. At the same time, it has also transformed the ETUC and BusinessEurope into the mains actors of this policy. This constant promotion of social dialogue in European governance found a consecration in Article 152 of the Treaty of the functioning of the EU which lays down that the Union 'recognizes and promotes the role of the social partners at its level, taking into account the diversity of national levels'.

Theoretically, social dialogue is presented as taking two possible forms within EU governance. It may be either bipartite or tripartite, the third actor being the Commission or the Council. In fact, the distinction is not as obvious in practice.

The tripartite form was the initial framework when social dialogue took place mainly in the cross-industry advisory committees. This is still the case in the tripartite Social Summits for Growth and Employment established in 2003 and which provides an official tripartite form of dialogue.

A tripartite form of social dialogue can be also identified in the open coordination processes on employment, inclusion or social protection. Regarding employment, social partners are consulted by the Employment Committee. The Council decision setting up the Employment Committee foresees that it should establish contacts with the social partners represented on the Standing Committee on Employment. Within this institutional framework, social partners are consulted on the employment guidelines.[6]

Social dialogue is presented as 'a force for economic and social modernisation'.[7] It is important to observe that in the tripartite relationship, the social partners are required to contribute to a policy defined elsewhere and in particular by European institutions. This has been the case particularly in the implementation of the Lisbon Strategy and the achievement of its various objectives. As indicated by the Commission in its 2002 communication called 'The European Social Dialogue, a Force for Innovation and Change':[8] 'the European social dialogue could constitute a tool for the modernisation announced at the Lisbon European

---

6   De la Porte (2003); De la Rosa (2005).
7   Communication from the Commission, 'The European Social Dialogue, a Force for Innovation and Change', COM (2002) 341 final.
8   *Ibid.*

Council for all key issues on the European agenda'. Thus, social partners are asked to present an annual report on their contributions to the Lisbon strategy.

Other forms of social dialogue, described as bipartite, take place at different levels. They exist at cross industry level between the ETUC, BusinessEurope and the CEEP. At sectoral level, this social dialogue occurs in the sectoral social committees. However, it is clear that the European institutions and in particular the Commission intervenes in the functioning of these committees. Firstly, the Commission has structured the sectoral social dialogue by creating these committees. At present, there are 36 sectoral committees. Secondly, the Commission may influence their activity. Its action was explicit in the 2002 communication where the Commission mentions that it will 'orientate the activities of the sectoral social dialogue committees to dialogue and negotiation only, excluding information and consultation activities which can be carried out in multisectoral forums, with the exception of specific sectoral consultations' and 'give priority support to committees whose work culminates in practical results representing their contribution to implementation and monitoring of the Lisbon strategy'.[9] From this it is clear that the Commission envisages sectoral dialogue as a tool for implementing the objectives pursued by the Council. In its 2004 communication,[10] the Commission also invited the social partners to contribute to achieving various objectives (flexicurity in order to improve adaptability of workers, investing in human capital and job quality, attracting more people to the labour market, delivering reforms).

At company level, the adoption of a directive in 1994, revised in 2009,[11] has provided a new framework for social dialogue. Here again, the social dialogue is conceived by the Commission as a means to introduce and develop orientations that have been decided by the European institutions. In the communication of 2004, social partners in multinationals are requested to contribute in particular to corporate social responsibility.

All these spheres of social dialogue produce a variety of instruments.

A Variety of Instruments

It is common to emphasize the dynamism of the social dialogue in the light of the results achieved so far. More than 300 texts have been concluded by

---

[9]   *Ibid.*

[10]   Communication from the Commission, 'Partnership for Change in an Enlarged Europe – Enhancing the Contribution of European Social Dialogue', COM (2004) 557 final.

[11]   Directive 2009/38.

the social partners. This high production of instruments clearly expresses the force of social dialogue at European level. However, the undeniable results of social dialogue must be analysed closely and put into perspective.

From a quantitative point of view, the number of texts has remained stable for the last 10 years. At sectoral level, a recent survey of the Dublin Foundation[12] shows that from 1999 to 2007 the number of documents produced by social partners had not increased. More precisely, there is no constant trend showing an increase in texts, and studies show that their number may vary greatly from one year to another. The results also differ greatly depending on the sectors.

At cross-sectoral level, the diagnosis is not so different when we consider the number of texts adopted. Over a period of 12 years (1995–2007), only six collective agreements were concluded in accordance with art.139 of the Treaty. It corresponds to an average of one agreement every two years. The result regarding sectoral agreements is no higher, with five agreements between 1998 and 2008. At any rate, there is no increase in the number of texts adopted if we count the documents having a binding effect.

There are some results at company level where different texts have been adopted within the European work councils. The most recent figures count almost 150 texts signed in more than eighty multinational companies.[13] However, the powers of the European Works Councils (EWC) are limited to information and consultation. It is therefore only on a voluntary basis that multinationals agree to transform the EWC into a negotiating body.

In any case, qualitative differences appear when we consider the nature of the texts adopted. A striking element is the huge variety of headings given to those instruments (framework of actions, declarations, agreements, codes of conduct, common opinions etc). Only on the basis of these titles can one notice that documents with a purely recommendatory status predominate over legally binding ones.

In a communication published in 2004,[14] the Commission tried to set up a typology of the results of the European social dialogue.[15] The communication identifies four categories of documents: agreements implemented in accordance with Article 139(2); process-oriented texts; joint opinions and

---

[12]   European Foundation for the Improvement of Living and Working Conditions, *Dynamics of European Sectoral Social Dialogue*, 2009.

[13]   European Commission, 'Mapping of Transnational Texts Negotiated at Corporate Level', EMPL F2 EP/bp 2008.

[14]   Partnership for Change in an Enlarged Europe – Enhancing the Contribution of European Social Dialogue, COM 2004 557 final.

[15]   On this typology, see Mazuyer (2007).

tools; and procedural texts. Each category contains various types of documents. The first category gathers agreements implemented by a Council decision and autonomous agreements implemented by the procedures and practices specific to management and labour and the Member States. The second category encompasses frameworks of action, guidelines and codes of conduct, policy orientations. The third contains joint opinions, declarations and tools, while the content of the fourth is limited to procedural texts.

This typology raises many observations. Firstly, it is sometimes difficult to understand the difference between two types of documents in terms of their content and legal scope. The various formulas blur the frontier between the different instruments. The Commission calls for greater clarity in the European social dialogue and for better consistency and transparency.[16] This is the case when it comes to frameworks of action, declarations or policy orientation. Secondly, the Commission communication of 2004 shows how documents with recommendatory status prevail over the binding ones. Most of the categories relate to documents which are only recommendatory. Thirdly, another distinction may be drawn between texts addressed to the EU institutions and documents addressed to national affiliates of the European social partners. Fourthly, it is worth noticing that the Commission considers some documents as being 'new generation' texts. This is the expression the Commission uses to refer to documents established by social partners independently of the European institutions' agenda. Autonomy has been a permanent preoccupation of the social partners since the Laeken declaration. The development of a bipartite autonomous social dialogue is reflected in the fact that social partners present their own social agenda and take initiatives without consideration of the Commission or Council agenda.[17]

In this respect, social partners prefer implementing their collective agreements through their own procedures and to take charge of their evaluation at national level. In theory, autonomous social dialogue has a wide scope mainly because social partners are not bound by the restrictions of competences established in the Treaty. However, it is strange that for the Commission some issues are excluded from an autonomous social dialogue. In its 2004 communication[18] the Commission rejects autonomous agreements relating to fundamental rights.

---

[16]   Partnership for Change in an Enlarged Europe – Enhancing the Contribution of European Social Dialogue, COM 2004 557 final, p.11.

[17]   Branch (2005, 321–346).

[18]   Partnership for Change in an Enlarged Europe – Enhancing the Contribution of European Social Dialogue, COM 2004 557 final.

On the other hand, new-generation texts refer to documents which emphasize monitoring processes and implementation on a longer term and in particular at national level.

. . . TO COLLECTIVE BARGAINING?

The promotion of social dialogue and its institutionalization in the law making process at European level have not generated significant developments in EU regulation in the field of labour relations. In fact, in terms of legal rules, the results are modest. In addition, some conditions are still missing to establish a collective bargaining system at EU level.

Limited Results

Social dialogue is beginning to lose its regulatory function at European level. It is no longer conceived as an alternative to legislation. This trend is clearly shown by the statistics: less than 2 per cent of the texts adopted at sectoral level are agreements with binding effects.[19] Fewer than 10 per cent are expected to have any impact at national level. Most of the documents elaborated through social dialogue do not have any binding effect. The same conclusion may be drawn at cross-sectoral level.[20]

Furthermore, it seems that social partners face growing difficulties to enter into negotiation or to reach agreement at community level. Resistance may come from the employer and more recently from the trade union. The refusal of the ETUC to enter into negotiation for the revision of the European work councils is a good example,[21] as is the refusal of the employers' organization to negotiate on the risks of exposure to CMR substances. The failure of the negotiations on temporary agency work provides a clear example of the difficulty to reach agreements.

This evolution is likely to continue if we consider the future of European social dialogue in the light of the recent agendas of the European social partners and the one issued for 2009–2010. The previous agendas were considered as rather weak in terms of commitments for regulatory instruments and viewed as a sign of crisis for social dialogue.[22] The work program adopted for 2009–2010 follows the same pattern. This program is

---

[19] European Foundation for the Improvement of Living and Working Conditions, Dynamics of European Sectoral Social Dialogue, 2009.

[20] Pochet (2006).

[21] Michon (2009).

[22] Degryse (2005).

very modest in terms of law making initiatives. It mainly concerns actions already launched by the previous programs. It also confirms the trend towards the promotion of non-binding instruments. The text foresees continuing the negotiations started in October 2008 about an autonomous framework agreement on inclusive labour markets. Social partners also reassert their choice for an autonomous social dialogue. All the other proposals are recommendations or frameworks of actions. Most of the new initiatives regard studies notably concerning the implementation of already adopted framework agreements, framework of actions and recommendations.

The most promising level for collective bargaining seems to be the company one. European work councils have been conceived as mere information and consultation bodies and not as negotiation bodies. However, this structure may become a transnational collective bargaining body on a voluntary basis. Practical experience shows that substantial and innovative transnational agreements have been signed in some European multinational companies.[23] In this respect, an evolution has been observed in the functioning of EWCs, from information and consultation to negotiation processes.[24] The number of joint texts has been growing over the years even if it remains rather marginal compared to the number of EWCs.[25] Moreover, behind a variety of titles not always in concordance with their content (charter, code of conduct, agreement, guidelines, declaration), the texts adopted are mainly of recommendatory nature and lack mechanisms of enforcement.[26] Even if there is a trend towards negotiation, the question remains whether this activity may be considered as a form of European level collective bargaining. It also worth noting that this issue is not addressed by the new directive.

---

[23]   Béthoux (2009a).

[24]   European Foundation for the Improvement of Living and Working Conditions, *European and international framework agreements: practical experiences and strategic approaches*, 2009, p. 20.

[25]   Even if the number of texts and their classification differ from one study to another, the reports show an increase of joint texts concluded. In 2001, a report identified 22 joint texts in nine multinationals for around 700 EWCs (Carley (2001). In 2007 the Commission recorded 147 texts signed in 89 companies for 800 EWCs, the EWCs being the main signatory party for half of the texts (European Commission, Mapping of Transnational Texts Negotiated at Corporate Level, EMPL F2 EP/bp 2008).

[26]   Some studies show that differences exist in particular between codes of conduct and international framework agreements, see *Codes of Conduct and International Framework Agreements: New Forms of Governance at Company Level*, Eurofound, 2008.

At sectoral and cross-sectoral level, social dialogue becomes a consulting body for European institutions. Over the past 10 years the majority of the texts produced have been common positions intended for the European commission.[27] In fact, social partners have returned to lobbying in Brussels. However, their line of action has changed. Formerly, trade unions on the one side and employers on the other used to defend their positions before the Commission. This procedure, informal but also formalized through institutionalized consultations, allowed the Commission to draw up proposals taking into account the different positions of the trade unions and employers' organizations and eventually arbitrate between them.

To some extent this approach is no longer relevant today. Social partners are treated as a single advisory body. The Commission expects the trade unions, more precisely the ETUC and the employers' organizations, BusinessEurope, to reach common positions as social partners. The Commission is no longer an arbitrator between two options or approaches. Besides, the points of view of social partners, considered as joint lobbying, are viewed as only one amongst others (NGO, regions).

Another concern is the effects of the texts adopted at EU level by social partners. To start with, it is difficult to assess the impact of documents having only a recommendatory status. This statement is valid also for texts designed for European institutions and national Member States or members of the European organizations at national level.

Secondly, there is a problem of application with agreements adopted in accordance with art.139 EC and implemented through the procedures and practices specific to management and labour and the Member States. This procedure leaves implementation to the national affiliates of the European signatories' parties. It also depends on the national industrial law systems and the nature of the collective instruments at national levels.[28] Taking those two elements into consideration, the full and *erga omnes* application of these texts raises many doubts.[29]

Such an autonomous way of implementation does not guarantee this full and *erga omnes* effect. This is a direct result of the diversity of national industrial relations. Not all of them provide for collective agreements of binding and *erga omnes* effects. In this sense, subsidiarity would hamper the effective application of the European collective agreements. In 2008,

---

[27] European Foundation for the Improvement of Living and Working Conditions, Dynamics of European Sectoral Social Dialogue, 2009, p. 28; Pochet (2006).

[28] Schiek, D. (2005, 23–56).

[29] Vigneau (2002, 653–683).

a report on the implementation of the agreement on stress at work was presented.[30] The result shows that the European agreement has been transposed through various instruments of very different legal nature and scope. It ranges from collective agreements, statutory legislation to codes of conduct or guidelines. This transposition may be considered as satisfactory[31] because it led many Member States and national social partners to start discussions and negotiations about this issue. In other words, the agreement has put this problem on agendas at national level. However, it is difficult to find a positive result beyond this. This state of play derives from the fact that the agreement does not impose any precise measures to reduce stress at work and therefore leaves much space to its implementation at national level. The enforcement of such an agreement appears even more difficult to assess due to the absence of any precise obligation.

The Commission is aware of this problem and has announced its proper monitoring of these agreements.[32] Notably, the Commission will assess the extent to which the agreements contribute to the achievement of the Community's objectives. If the objectives are not fulfilled, the Commission may consider proposing a legislative act. In other words, the actions and agreements of the European social partners are under the scrutiny of the Commission.

This problem of implementation of European agreements also exists for texts adopted at sectoral level and within European work councils.[33] It has led the Commission to envisage the adoption of an optional framework for transnational collective bargaining.[34] This proposal purported to provide the social partners with an instrument to formalize the nature and results of the social dialogue. This proposal has given rise to great criticism from the employers' organizations and no longer seems to be on the agenda of the Commission.

---

[30] See http://etuc.org/IMG/pdf_Final_Implementation_report.pdfhttp://etuc.org/IMG/pdf_Final_Implementation_report.pdf (accessed December 2010).

[31] Legros (2009); European Foundation for the Improvement of Living and Working Conditions, Dynamics of European Sectoral Social Dialogue, 2009, p. 12.

[32] Partnership for Change in an Enlarged Europe – Enhancing the Contribution of European Social Dialogue, COM 2004 557 final, p.11. On this possible framework, see Laulom (2007), pp. 623–629.

[33] On the applicability of European works council agreements, see Blanke (2005).

[34] Social Agenda 2005-2010, COM (2005) 33 final.

Missing Conditions

Weak activity in terms of collective bargaining despite the current context of dynamic social dialogue may be likely in the light of various elements. Some conditions for the development of an industrial relations system at European level having a regulatory dimension are still missing.

First of all, a major problem is the fact that the employer side, in particular BusinessEurope, still refuses to give a regulatory dimension to social dialogue at European level. This reluctance to assume the role of bargaining agent and law maker at European level impedes the emergence of a real industrial relations system at European level.[35]

In this context, there are few means to incite employers to give a regulatory function to social dialogue at EU level. As summed up by Brian Bercusson in a henceforth famous formula, the 'shadow of the law' may be an incentive to sign collective agreements at EU level. If collective bargaining at European level appears in principle a bipartite process, the positions and orientations of European institutions are essential. In this sense, this incapacity of European social dialogue to set labour regulations could lead the Commission to be more active and provoke a return of the hard law in European social policy.[36]

Collective bargaining may also be imposed by linking negotiation to information and consultation as decided by the ECJ.[37] By creating an obligation to negotiate, the Court creates a framework for collective agreements. At company level, experience shows that the link between information/consultation and negotiation is already in place when specific situations such as a restructuration occur.[38]

Secondly, at EU level, workers and trade unions do not have industrial action which is the traditional means to compel employers to sit down at the negotiation table. Industrial actions at EU level are still difficult to organize at cross-sectoral, sectoral as well as company level.[39] The development of a true bargaining system at EU level requires its protection by the European legal order and by the ECJ in particular, as far as

---

[35]   Keller and Bansbach (2001, 419–434).
[36]   Pochet and Degryse (2009).
[37]   C-188/03, *Junk v. Kühnel*, 27/01/2005.
[38]   Moreau (2006, 308–318). See also Carley (2009); European Foundation for the Improvement of Living and Working Conditions, *European and International Framework Agreements: Practical Experiences and Strategic Approaches*, 2009, pp. 63ff; Béthoux (2009b, 478–498).
[39]   Denis (2006, 671–678).

the right to strike is concerned.[40] In this sense, the recent ECJ *Viking* and *Laval* cases clearly undermine the power of trade unions to settle conflicts through collective bargaining.[41] This case law provides an extra obstacle for trade unions, while at the same time the European Court of Human Rights on the one hand connects the right to collective bargaining and freedom of association, and on the other guarantees the right to strike.[42] It is also worth observing that this link is made by article 28 of the Charter of fundamental rights which treats both collective bargaining and collective action.

Thirdly, some important problems remain to be solved. Amongst these is the determination of the agents entitled to participate in negotiations and conclude collective agreements. If this problem has been partly solved at inter-sectoral and sectoral levels, it remains at company level with the question of the legitimacy of the EWC.[43] In this respect, trade unions ask to be in charge of signing these collective agreements.[44]

In the end it is difficult to predict the future of European social dialogue. Will it remain a framework for formal and informal consultations for the European institutions and a source of recommendations for Member States and national social partners? Or will it reach a further stage and provide a true platform for negotiations recognized by the European legal order, as instruments of legal effect and as part of European law.

REFERENCES

Bercusson, B. (1992), 'Maastricht: A Fundamental Change in European Labour Law', *Industrial Relations Journal*, **23** (3), 177.
Bercusson, B. (2006), 'Négocier dans l'ombre de la Cour', *Europe et société*, 65–66, 103.
Béthoux, E. (2009a), 'Le dialogue social transnational dans l'entreprise: dynamiques européennes', in A. Jobert (ed.), *Les nouveaux cadres du dialogue social*, Brussels: Peter Lang, p. 189.
Béthoux, E. (2009b), 'Vers une representation européenne des salaries. Les comités d'entreprises face aux restructurations', *Sociologie du travail*, **51** (4), 478.
Blanke, T. (2005), 'European Works Council Agreements: Types, Contents and

---

40   Bercusson (2006).
41   Chaumette (2008); Robin-Olivier and Pataut (2008, 80–88); Rodière (2008, 47–66); Vigneau [Q17].
42   Marguénaud and Mouly (2009).
43   Lhernould (2008).
44   European Foundation for the Improvement of Living and Working Conditions, *European and international framework agreements: practical experiences and strategic approaches*, 2009, p. 28.

Functions, Legal Nature', in Comisión Consultiva Nacional de Convenios Colectivos (ed.), *Collective Bargaining in Europe*, Madrid: Ministerio de trabajo y asunto socials, p. 395.

Branch, A. (2005), 'The Evolution of European Social Dialogue Towards Greater Autonomy: Challenges and Potential Benefits', *The International Journal of Comparative Labour Law and Industrial Relations*, **21** (42), 321.

Carley, M. (2001), *Bargaining at European level? Joint texts negotiated by European Works Councils*, European Foundation for the Improvement of Living and Working Conditions, Luxembourg.

Chaumette, P. (2008), 'Les actions collectives syndicales dans le maillage des libertés économiques', *Droit social*, February, p. 210.

Degryse, C. (2005), 'Le dialogue social interprofessionnel en crise', *Bilan social de l'Union européenne*, Brussels, Institut syndical Européen, p. 244.

De la Porte, C. (2003), 'The Open Method of Coordination: A New Supranational Form of Governance?', *European Law Journal*, p. 190.

De la Rosa, S. (2005), ' La stratégie européenne de l'emploi à l'heure des nouvelles directrices intégrées', *Droit social*, **12**, p. 1210.

Denis, J.M. (2006), 'Les mobilisations collectives européennes: de l'impuissance à la nécessité d'alliance', *Droit social*, **6**, p. 671.

Didry, C. and A. Mias (2005), *Le moment Delors – Les syndicats au cœur de l'Europe sociale*, Brussels: Peter Lang, p. 301.

Keller B. and M. Bansbach (2001), 'Social Dialogue: Tranquil Past, Troubled Present and Uncertain Future', *Industrial Relations Journal*, **32** (5), 419.

Langlois, P. (1993), 'Europe sociale et principe de subsidiarité', *Droit social*, February, p. 201.

Laulom, S. (2007), 'Passé, present et future de la négociation collective transnationale', *Droit social*, **5**, p. 623.

Legros, B. (2009), 'La transposition de l'accord-cadre européen du 8 octobre 2004 sur le stress au travail', *Semaine Juridique*, Edition sociale, **26**, p. 19.

Lhernould, J.P. (2008), 'La négociation collective communautaire', *Droit social*, p. 34.

Lyon-Caen, G. (1993), 'Le droit social de la Communauté européenne après le Traité de Maastricht', *Droit social*, Chron.XXXIII, p. 151.

Lyon-Caen, G. (1997), 'Subsidiarité et droit social européen', *Droit social*, April.

Marguénaud, J.P. and J. Mouly (2009), 'La Cour européenne des droits de l'homme à la conquête du droit de grève', *Revue de droit du travail*, **9**, p. 499.

Mazuyer, E. (2007), 'Les instrument juridiques du dialogue social européen: état des lieux et tentative de clarification', *Droit social*, **4**, p. 476.

Michon, F. (2009), 'Intérim et temps de travail: deux directives difficiles à conclure', *Chronique internationale de l'IRES*, **116**, p. 3.

Moreau, M.A. (2006), 'Restructurations et comités d'entreprise européens', *Droit social*, March, p. 308.

Pochet, P. (2006), 'Le dialogue social interprofessionnel, une analyse quantitative', *Chronique international de l'IRES*, **116**, p. 48.

Pochet, P. and C. Degryse (2009), 'Agenda social: le retour de la " hard law"', *Bilan social de l'Union européenne 2008*, European Trade Union Institute, p. 97.

Robin-Olivier, S. and E. Pataut (2008), 'Europe sociale ou Europe économique', *Revue de droit du travail*, February, p. 80.

Rodière, P. (2008), 'Les arrêts Viking et Laval, le droit de grève et le droit de la négociation collective', *Revue Trimestrielle de droit européen*, **1**, p. 47.

Schiek, D. (2005), 'Autonomous Collective Agreements as a Regulatory Device in European Labour Law: How to Read Article 139 EC', *Industrial Law Journal*, **34** (1), 23.

Vigneau, C. (2002), 'Etude sur l'autonomie collective au niveau communautaire', *Revue Trimestrielle de Droit Européen*, **4**, 653.

Vigneau, C. (2008), 'L'encadrement par la Cour de justice de l'action collective au regard du Traité de Rome', *Semaine Juridique*, Edition générale, I, 10060.

18.   Can we rely on a new development of the European social action?

Jean Jacques Paris

Brian Bercusson knew how to share his constantly renewed interest with his students, of which I was part, in the development of European social law that he analysed in a critical and constructive way. He thought this interest was intimately linked with the knowledge he had of the social actors involved and their ability to act to reinforce social rights and solidarity links in Europe.

Indeed, his courses at the European University Institute (EUI) in Florence were not only aimed at acquiring or strengthening knowledge of European labour law but also at familiarising us with the training context and changes in this law, 'the law in context', which must refer to the ways in which those (in particular social partners) involved in its creation or implementation work.

This is how after benefiting from Brian's seminars over several years I had the opportunity to really discuss and exchange ideas with him on the content of his proposed 'posting of workers' directive when I worked at the European Commission and administered the directive in question. He was enthusiastic about the idea of adopting a directive aimed at combating the social dumping aspect of the posting of workers and the specific legal knowledge he gave to European trade unions always made a contribution to progress in the writing of the text of the directive.

We were in the mid-1990s and were moving forward under the beneficial effects of the 'Delors period' which proved to be a catalyst for the development of European social dialogue and the adoption of several social directives. The hope of witnessing the implementation of a European social model and the growth of green shoots of European social citizenship were constantly in our minds and in our debates.

The adoption in 1994 of the European Works Council (EWC) directive as part of the European Commission's action programme on the implementation of the Charter of Workers' Fundamental Rights was following the same path, the aim being to avoid the establishment of the single market that would work against the workers' rights. Brian was often asked by the European Trade Union Confederation (ETUC) to share his expertise in this area. As a result, he was participating in the promotion of transnational social dialogue within companies based in Europe and his comments and analyses of the decisions of the European Court of Justice also contributed largely to the elaboration of the ETUC positions when the EWC Directive was recast.

Whereas the 1990s were marked by this blossoming of new laws, the 2000s started with less inspiring horizons from a social point of view.

Legislative progress gave way to the 'opened coordination method', to identifying indicators linked to the European employment strategy and to collecting best practices. Thus, against a background of the Commission's identified desire to simplify European law along with the promotion of initiatives tending to reduce the obstacles to economic freedoms set out in the European Union treaty.

In 1997, the Commission decided to simplify community legislation and to reduce its cadence of production,[1] whilst introducing new social expressions or new concepts into its documents such as 'adaptability', 'employability' and 'flexibility' which will participate to labour law 'modernisation' and to promote 'flexisecurity'.[2]

In this slowing down context where European social policy is submitted to a 'social makeover', it indeed becomes more difficult for European social partners through 'institutionalised' social dialogue[3] or even 'independent' social dialogue,[4] to introduce legislation especially on an inter-professional level.[5]

Such developments would also affect the European Court of Justice jurisprudence. When the Commission is no longer a 'force of proposals' and does not arouse a real dynamic in social dialogue or when, as guard-

---

[1]   Mainly Green Papers or White Papers, as well as recommendations.

[2]   See Commission communication 'Modernising Labour Law to Meet the Challenges of the 21st Century' [COM (2006)708 final dated 22nd November 2006].

[3]   See articles 138 and 139 Chapter 2 of the EU treaty.

[4]   See 139 Chapter 1 of the EU treaty that says that dialogue between social partners in the Community 'may lead, if the parties agree to conventional relationships, including agreements'. This dialogue is said to be independent as the treaty sets out no legal framework for procedures leading to these agreements, or for their conditions of validity or effects. It is the responsibility of the European social partners themselves to regulate their relationships and the resulting texts.

[5]   As the spectrum of inter-professional social dialogue became more reduced compared to the previous decade (the 1990s), the noughties saw the development of sector-based social dialogue – particularly in the different areas of the transport sector.

ian of the treaties, it wants to reconcile at any price the content of social directives or the fundamental rights of workers with economic freedoms, that are provided by the treaty, we must be aware in the long term that the decisions of European judges do not reflect the trends that are themselves the expression of the regression of the European social policies.

Although the strength of the European convictions of such a man as Brian could not be dented by evolutions that are always liable to change, it nevertheless remains that some of them, when they become more ingrained, are sometimes difficult to take in.

This became clear in a decision of the European Court of Justice in the *Laval* case[6] following a preliminary question raised by the Swedish judge (Arbetsdomstolen) asking the Court if European law on free provision of services was able (in its interpretation) to prevent trade unions (in Sweden) taking corrective action aimed at making a service provider in another Member State agree to a Swedish collective agreement benefiting workers posted temporarily by that service provider in Sweden.

In other words, could the implementation of the free provision of services (a fundamental freedom) overrule the right to strike (a fundamental right, particularly under ILO agreements) with the aim of applying provisions favourable to workers?

The positive response from the Court to this question not only weakens trade union rights in Europe, but also all those fighting against social dumping and arguing for more social justice. Brian was even more affected by the judge's decision because he was convinced that the Court was going to follow the conclusions[7] of the Advocate General Paolo Mengozzi who represented most of his thoughts and contributions in this case. The European trade unions' position found no echo with the European judges.

Decisions taken since the *Laval* case in terms of the free provision of services reinforce the position of the Court that has progressively been comfortably installed in its position. To such a point where some informed commentators (Aliprantis, 2010) were able to describe as 'pompous' the position of the European judge in charge of the Luxembourg case [8] that dealt a final blow to any hopes we still had in the high Court of avoiding the fundamental rights of workers having to bow to the requirements

---

[6]   Decision of the Court (Grand Chamber) dated 18 December 2007 (request for a preliminary decision by the Arbetsdomstolen – Sweden) – Laval un Partneri Ltd/Svenska Byggnadsarbetareförbundet, Svenska Byggnadsarbetareförbundets avd. 1, Byggettan, Svenska Elektrikerförbundet.

[7]   Conclusions of the Advocate General Paolo Mengozzi presented on 23 May 2007.

[8]   Court decision (first chamber) 19 June 2008.

of economic freedoms on the basis of the principle of proportionality. Is it disproportionate to do our best to strengthen the dignity of posted workers offering the most acceptable social standards? 'Solidarity is not built in terms of competitiveness and profitability' (Castel, 2009).

'Brian's death is an enormous loss for the ETUC', wrote the representatives of the Maison Syndicale Européenne (MSE) in Brussels. Brian firmly believed in the social mobilisation of social actors, always ready to open the way for social advances and promising horizons.

> Set off on your own two feet, and till nightfall, press it, recognise it, treat it well, this road that, despite places that are full of hatred, shows the germs of wishes granted and across the land of the birds. (Char 1955)

> (Se mettre en chemin sur ses deux pieds, et jusqu'au soir le presser, le reconnaître, le bien traiter, ce chemin qui, en dépit de ses relais haineux, nous montre les fétus des souhaits exaucés et la terre croisée des oiseaux.)

Two areas currently seem to be providing ways of finding a social dynamic on a European level.

The first is international framework agreements (IFAs) that multiplied themselves in multi-national companies in recent years[9] between a number of players such as international and European federations of Trade Unions in different sectors but also European works Councils, national Trade Union organisations and NGOs for example.

The agreements contain social or environmental[10] standards. They are the expression of new constructions of standards that attempt to meet businesses' internationalisation strategies.[11] Whether they are global (optimum degree of internationalisation) and do not recognise national frameworks where they are located or they form multinationals (a less-developed form of internationalisation) that have to deal with the (social, societal, environmental) characteristics of the places in which they work, these companies escape the single hold of a national legal framework.

---

[9]   There are currently about 100 IVAs in place today. Fewer and fewer of these agreements are being concluded.

[10]   The content of IFAs was originally limited to applying the universal standards of the ILO's agreements, then developed particularly with standards relating to the anticipation of change management and restructuring and the social responsibility of supplies and sub-contractors.

[11]   See the work (2005–2007) carried out as part of the AgirE project run by the Alpha Group and Marie-Ange Moreau as a scientific coordinator of the project, http://www.fse-agire.com / IMG / pdf / INTRODUCTION.AGIRE _ RAPPORT _ FINAL _ FR _ 26052008.pdf (accessed April 2011).

It is therefore in the absence of any current legal framework built for international agreement from international or European institutions that these agreements have developed independently in order to guide the social responsibility of international businesses or groups of businesses.

But as jacks of all trades and masters of none, the weakness of IFAs is the absence of legal constraints that, it is true, can only put into perspective at least for now, the advantages of IFAs and Corporate Social Responsibility (CSR).

They nevertheless show new forms of multi-player mobilisation that may work on different levels to create a base of the laws applicable to all employees in the group but also to protect populations across the world against the risk of pollution or create dispensaries and train doctors in regions where the Group has offices or where certain illnesses may be a curse.

Uncertainties over the legal status of IFAs should lead legal experts to putting in place mechanisms that can guarantee that these agreements are complied with. Some have already developed interesting methods (Daugareilh, 2005; Moreau, 2006; Supiot, 2010). Brian would have certainly been one of these pioneers.

The second area that seems to offer new ways for social partners is Socio-Psychological Risks (SSR), that have been the subject of two European framework agreements: one on stress and the other on harassment and violence.

The European framework agreement on stress signed in 2004 by European social partners[12] aims at making management, workers and their representatives aware of problems relating to stress at work. The agreement provides a framework for action in terms of identification, prevention and management of problems that arise in this area. Harassment and violence are the subject of a European framework agreement signed in 2007 by European social partners that want to deal with this question separately from stress at work.

As these are so-called independent agreements, their effectiveness is largely dependent on the manner in which they are perceived and applied in the member states.

Remarkably, they have helped activate and develop social dialogue in Member States. Particularly, the theme of stress was the subject in 2003

---

[12]   The European Trade Union Confederation, Business Europe, the European Association of Craft, Small and Medium-Sized Enterprises and the European Centre of Enterprises with Public Participation and of Enterprises of General Economic Interest.

of a collective agreement in Belgium, Denmark, Sweden and the United Kingdom. The signature of the European agreement on stress has contributed to a development of collective negotiations or debates on the scene in a majority of member states.

National agreements transposing the European agreement on stress were signed in France (National Interprofessional Agreement signed on 2 July 2008 by businesses and unions), Sweden (2005–2006), Spain (inter-professional agreements 2005, 2006, 2007), Finland (interprofessional agreement 2006), Ireland (interprofessional agreement in 2007), the Czech Republic (recommendation to include stress in the negotiations for a collective agreement in 2008), Cyprus (common declaration in 2008), Belgium (interprofessional agreement already in place since 1999), Iceland (interprofessional agreement 2007), Romania (national agreement 2007–2010) and in Denmark (cooperation agreements 2005–2006). In several other countries, debates and round tables have been organised.

In France, agreements have encouraged the collective appropriation of SSR by players and particularly by Health and Safety at Work and Working Conditions Committee (HSWWC) that have new powers of investigation and consultation in this area. Their restructuring work has been remarkable and constitutes new ways of securing employees' career paths.

The contribution of community action is therefore visible here and comes with a change of culture in terms of health and safety. This involves less covering SSR phenomena through the traditional notion of accident at work and repairing the damage done than creating conditions of well-being at work by making employers more responsible for this.

Ideas for the future exist and Brian would no doubt have played an active part in implementing them. It should nevertheless be noted that these initiatives come increasingly from independent action by social partners and are therefore left to the motivation of the parties.

Do those initiatives show that community action in social matters is henceforth in the hands of the social partners, the community institutions staying away from the work of construction of the social standards?

It is not obvious at all in a context where the European social dialogue is (still today) institutionalised; such initiatives could run out of steam if they are not supported by action from institutions and particularly the European commission that is at the crossroads of all European decision-making. Besides, the economic crisis accentuated new social disparities which cannot be fought by the social partners alone, but need the support of the institutions.

As previously mentioned, the Commission has to remain a driving force and must arouse an authentic social dialogue, as provided by the treaty.

Besides, the implementation of the new treaty of Lisbon which aims in particular at strengthening the role of the European Parliament should also allow developing the capacities of action of the European Union in social areas.

The management of the social consequences of the economic policies of the Union cannot be abandoned to Member States often divided in this field or only to social partners. We are waiting for strong and responsible European institutions that reinforce the social dimension of the internal market.

By introducing new 'horizontal clauses' and new provisions on the services of general interest,[13] the Lisbon treaty should allow the opening new ways of social developments and lead, maybe, to a reversal of the case law of the European Court regarding the free provision of services.

REFERENCES

Aliprantis, N. (2010), 'L'arrêt Commission c. Luxembourg et le rétrécissement arbitraire et péremptoire du pouvoir normatif de l'Etat en matière sociale', Colloque Strasbourg, Institut du Travail, 25–26 March.

Bercusson, B. (2009), *European Labour Law (Law in Context)*, Cambridge: Cambridge University Press.

Castel, R. (1995), *Les métamorphoses de la question sociale. Une chronique du salariat*, Paris: Fayard.

Char, R. (1955), *Recherche de la base au sommet*, Paris: Gallimard.

Daugareilh, I. (2005), *Mondialisation, Travail et Droits fondamentaux*, Paris: Emile Bruylant.

Moreau, M.A. (2006), *Normes sociales, droit du travail et mondialisation, confrontations et mutations*, Paris: Dalloz.

Sciarra, S. (2007), in *Modernization of Labour Law: A Current European Debate*, Genève: ILO Publication.

Supiot, A. (2010), *L'esprit de Philadelphie, la justice sociale face au marché total*, Paris: Seuil.

---

[13]   Article 16 of the treaty on the functioning of the European Union.

19. Conclusion: Europe's awakening

Alain Supiot

Kant explains that it is the reading of Hume which drew him out of his dogmatic sleep.[1] This famous statement suffices to remind us that the most invaluable resources of Europe are not in the vaults of the banks, but in the minds of its citizens, who think in several languages[2] and converse beyond the borders. Brian Bercusson and Iota Kravaritou belonged to those European citizens, whose thoughts were directed at how to take Europe out of the dogmatic sleep into which it is falling again. They both left us in 2008, after years of tireless work devoted to the building of a more humane and more supportive Europe. The year of 2008 was also a year of the unprecedented disruption in the building of the so-called 'social Europe'. In fact, the disruption was double. First, the European Court of Justice withdrew from the promise contained in the Treaty of Rome of improving 'living and working conditions, so as to make possible their harmonization, while the improvement is being maintained',[3] and switched to ultra-liberal ideology dismantling social rights. The second was the ideological and financial failure of this ultra-liberal doctrine.

It is between these two events, on 26 February, that I met Brian Bercusson for the last time. It was in Paris where Brian had come to teach for a few weeks. Our conversation was largely focused on the *Viking* and *Laval* judgments, which the Court of Justice had just delivered. This harsh blow against social Europe put an end to our controversies regarding the draft Treaty establishing a Constitution for Europe we had had a few years before.[4] It seemed to me at that time that despite the undeniable

---

[1]   Kant, E. (1783), *Préface des Prolégomènes à toute métaphysique future qui pourra se présenter comme science*, in *Œuvres philosophiques*, Paris: Gallimard-Pléiade, Vol. 2, p. 17.

[2]   Nies, F. (2005), *Europa denkt mehrsprachig; L'Europe pense en plusieurs langues*, Tübingen: Narr.

[3]   Consolidated Version of the Treaty on the Functioning of the European Union (2010), art. 151 (ex. Art.136 TEC).

[4]   We expressed these controversies in a paper written together with Ulrich Mückenberger. This article was to be published in Germany and England,

intellectual and editorial quality of the European Charter of Fundamental Rights, it would not provide a sufficient counterweight to the provisions of the Treaty enshrining the primacy of economic freedoms and the 'market without obstacles' over social rights.[5] It was also the view of Iota Kravaritou, who was a visiting professor in Nantes in spring 2005. She participated with obvious joy in the lively discussions that the referendum on the Treaty aroused throughout France, especially among our students. Contrary to what critics had written, this referendum gave rise to a unique experience of democratic deliberation on the question: what kind of Europe do we actually want? Distributed to all the voters, the draft treaty was at the centre of discussions in all strata of the society. In this atmosphere Iota found once again the inspiration to combat for lively European citizenship which she cared so much about and which found its reflection in her last published text.[6] On the merits, she herself thought too that only a revision of the Treaty provisions on economic freedoms could guarantee the future of social Europe. Brian Bercusson, on the contrary, at that time believed that the integration of the Charter into the Treaty would give the Court a legal basis which would be strong enough to submit the exercise of economic freedoms to the respect for fundamental social rights in order to protect the rights of trade unions and to ensure the compliance with international labour standards while taking account of social legislation on trade unions.[7]

It was in the winter of 2008 that I saw for the first time that Brian who usually had a strong belief in the social resources of Community law, was by then deeply discouraged. He had fought for years and he had given the best of himself so that the *Laval* case would mark a turning point in the building of a European social model, worthy of its name. Now he was wondering about the causes of his failure. Under the guise of his usual humour one could perceive anxiety. He attributed the change in the attitude of the Court to the nationalism of a number of the judges of new member states who pursue political aims and who are indifferent to the common European good. A few weeks later, when the *Rüffert* judgement

---

however it was published only in France. See Bercusson, B., U. Mückenberger and A. Supiot (2005), 'Trois points de vue sur le Traité établissant une Constitution pour l'Europe', *Semaine sociale Lamy*, **1214**, May.

[5] *Ibid.* See also Supiot, A. (2006), 'The Condition of France', *London Review of Books*, **28** (11), June, 24–26.

[6] Kravaritou, Y. (2008), 'Claude Cahun, une citoyenne européenne', in *Actualidad de la justicia social. Liber amicorum en homenaje a Antonio Marzal*, Barcelone: Bosch, pp. 257–276.

[7] Bercusson et al. (2005), p. 9.

was delivered, I wrote to him asking whether this new judicial episode had not exhausted the reserves of his hermeneutic optimism. On 14 April he replied by email which happened to be the last one I received from him. In his colourful French he wrote the following:

> J'admet que mes reserves diminuent avec chaque sentence de la cour de Luxembourg . . . C'est moins le droit communautaire qu'a l'influence, mais plutot la politique geo-politique d'integrer les nouveaux états membres à tout prix, meme de politique social, mais aussi l'abandon de cohérence doctrinale (remplacer par celui doctrinaire) . . . L'avis équilibré de l'Avocat General Bot dans l'affaire Rüffert, ce n'est pas la même droit communautaire qu'applique la cour...Pour des solutions politiques, voir les propos que j'ai fait à une conférence le 3 avril à Copenhagen . . .[8]

He attached to his letter the text from Copenhagen, which in retrospect stands as a doctrinal testament.[9] Drawing lessons from *Viking*, *Laval* and *Rüffert*, he suggested several radical changes of the provisions that the Treaty of Lisbon took over from the draft Constitutional Treaty. Regarding economic freedoms, he wrote: 'The task is to re-draft the provisions on economic freedoms in such a way as to reduce or eliminate their negative impact on fundamental rights; specifically, on collective action, and so as to protect workers'.[10] Concerning trade union freedoms: 'The Treaty should be revised to clarify that economic freedoms may not be invoked against trade unions taking collective action'.[11] Regarding the right to strike: 'The principle of subsidiarity could be reworked to reflect explicitly the protection of collective action'.[12] Regarding the European

---

[8] 'I admit that my reserves diminish with each sentence of the court of Luxembourg . . . It is not the Community law that is to blame but rather geopolitical policy of integrating the new members at any price, even at the price of social policy, but also the abandonment of doctrinal coherence (substituting it with the doctrinaire one) . . . The balanced opinion of Advocate General Bot in the *Rüffert* case is not the same Community law that the court applies . . . For political solutions, see the remarks I made at a conference in Copenhagen on 3 April . . .'.

[9] Bercusson, B. (2008), 'New Institutional Roads to a Stronger Social Dimension', Working paper for the NFS (*Nordens Fackliga Samorganisation*, Council of Nordic Trade Unions) Conference *A New Start for a Social Dimension*, Copenhagen, 3 April 2008, see § 57ff. This text was published with the same numeration but under the following title 'The Impact of the Case-law of the European Court of Justice upon the Labour Law of the Member States. Scope of Action at the European Level', in *Labour Law and Social Europe. Selected Writings of Brian Bercusson* (2009), Bruxelles: ETUI, p.459 ff.

[10] Bercusson (2008), § 48.

[11] *Ibid.*, § 54.

[12] *Ibid.*, § 56.

institutions, he urged a thorough reform of the Court of Justice,[13] including the creation of a social chamber, the decrease in preliminary rulings regarding collective action, the allocation of the right to take action to trade unions and the alignment of the composition of the Court on the basis of the rules of demographic distribution governing other institutions: 'The latest enlargement means there are 13 judges from the "old" Member States and 12 from the "new" Member States. The political consequences of this failure to reflect democratic legitimacy need to be addressed'.[14] Finally, he recommended the adoption of the adequate provisions to ensure the compliance of the EU with international labour law, including the Social Charter of the Council of Europe and the conventions of the International Labour Organisation.[15]

The above reforms for social Europe were suggested by Brian Bercusson before the financial crisis. However, as most of the contributions collected in the present volume show, their actuality and relevance were not undermined by this crisis. Although it should be said that while the necessity for these reforms is undoubted, it is not certain whether these reforms would be sufficient to keep the social Europe alive, because they do not take account of this crisis, which burst out in September 2008, just a few weeks after Brian's death.

Surprisingly, it was the same year that ultra-liberalism lost all its moral and intellectual credibility to which the Community judge had vigorously adhered. The paradox becomes even more apparent if one recognizes that the enlargement of Europe to post-communist countries by no means meant the extension to the east of the 'social market economy' but rather the birth of a 'communist market economy'.[16] This hybrid system, of which China is an unsurpassable model,[17] combines limitless economic

---

[13] *Ibid.*, § 57–60.

[14] *Ibid.*, § 60.

[15] *Ibid.*, § 61–63.

[16] See Supiot, A. (2008), 'L'Europe gagnée par "l'économie communiste de marché"', *Le Monde*, 25 January. The English version is 'Europe Won over to the "Communist Market Economy"', *Global Labour Institute*, available at www.globallabour.info/en/2008/07/europe_won_over_to_the_communi.html (accessed May 2011).

[17] Article 15 of the Constitution of the People's Republic of China stated: 'The state practises economic planning on the basis of socialist public ownership.' This formula was substituted in 1993 by the following one: 'The State practises socialist market economy. The State strengthens economic legislation, improves macro-regulation and control, and prohibits in accordance with law any organization or individual from disturbing the socio-economic order'. Due to the significance gained by the term 'socialist' on the European political arena and due to the fact

freedom for the ruling class and a dramatic limitation of democracy and rights of employees. The difference is that Chinese leaders do not share the naive faith of Europeans in the spontaneous benefits of freedom of movement of the capital and goods: they have opened their borders just to the extent that it is profitable and they have not enslaved their banking system to the dictatorship of financial markets. The situation in Europe, with its leaders clinched on dogma divorced from reality, reminds rather of Brejnevism, a period of political glaciation, a harbinger of unavoidable debacles.

It is within this context that the Court's 'doctrinaire' turn is taking place. It is important to take full account of it and analyse the resistance it arouses if we want to pull the EU out of the dogmatic sleep into which it plunged due to its switch to ultra-liberalism.

A DOCTRINAIRE WATERSHED

With regard to the lessons to be learnt from the ultra-liberal turn of the Court of Justice, we must begin by acknowledging its radicalism. Totally insensitive to criticisms that have been addressed to it and unable to draw any lesson from the crisis of the ultra-liberal model, the Court of Justice continues deconstructing national social rights and the so-called 'liberation of market forces'. The most recent of these liberative 'blows' is its ruling of 15 July 2010, extending the influence of markets on the management of occupational pension schemes by social partners.[18] Eviscerating its earlier judgements, which put collective bargaining[19] and institutions based on solidarity[20] outside the ambit of competition law, the Court asserts without blinking in that case (§ 52) that 'a fair balance' must be struck 'in the account taken of the respective interests involved', namely those of workers to whom a good level of the retirement pension should be guaranteed, on the one hand, and the interests of the banks and insur-

---

that it is often the source for possible confusions with the ideas of 'mixed economy' (which was used as a doctrine by the western socialist party) it seemed preferable to me to translate *shehuizhuyi shichang jingji* (社会主义市场经济) as 'communist market economy'.

[18]   Case C-271/08, *European Commission v. Federal Republic of Germany*, Judgment of the Court (Grand Chamber) of 15 July 2010.

[19]   CJCE, Case C-67/96 of 21 September 1999, Albany.

[20]   CJCE, Cases C-159 and 160/91 of 17 February 1993, Poucet and Pistre (1993) *Droit Social*, 488, note by Philippe Laigre and observations by Jean-Jacques Dupeyroux.

ance companies, the right of which to operate in the pension market the Commission defends.[21] It seems that the savings of pensioners should be of benefit to the pensioners themselves and be managed in accordance with the decisions of their elected representatives should be 'unfair'! In this guideline of uptaking by the markets of social contributions,[22] the Court states that 'solidarity is not inherently irreconcilable with the application of a procurement procedure' because 'the pooling of risks, upon which any insurance activity is based, can be ensured by a body or undertaking that provides pensions' (§ 58). To use the notion of 'the pooling of risks' is like a conjuring trick worthy of a cabaret act, in which out of a magic hat private insurers appear as white knights of the solidarity. 'Solidarity' which favours the insurers is well summarized by the following argument of one commercial which said: 'Why shall I pay as if I was sick when I'm not?'. [23] From this standpoint one cannot really see what the EU will retain from burning social security on the altar of the markets in the name of the 'fair balance' between the level of care of which the patients should benefit and the profit opportunities which their sicknesses open to insurers.

These confusions and regressions do not come out of the blue if one recalls the fundamental idea that stood behind the *Viking* judgement, which asserted that respect for human dignity must be reconciled with the requirements relating to economic rights protected by the treaty.[24] Strangely, this point did not attract much attention from the commentators, while in fact it is the worst of the extravagant drifts of the Court of Justice. The deep meaning of the principle of dignity, as it was stated when the world was emerging out of the horrors of World War II, is that in no case and under no circumstances is it permissable to treat men like animals or machines. Here we do not talk about one fundamental right, among many others, but rather about a *fundamental prohibition* of a civilized legal system. The Court of Justice takes a different stance: respect for human dignity must, it says, be 'reconciled' with free competition, free movement of goods and capital and free provision of services. The reading of the *Viking* judgement raises one doubt: do community judges still know what they are talking about when they talk about the principle of dignity? Do they understand that by placing it on the level of rules governing business

---

[21]   CJUE, Case C-271/08, § 52.

[22]   J.K. Galbraith (2008) was the first to describe this act of privatisation of the social state in his *The Predator State*, New York: Free Press.

[23]   'Pourquoi payer comme un malade, quand je ne suis pas malade?', advertising campaign of Thelem Assurance, Autumn 2010, see www.thelem-assurances.fr/ (accessed November 2010).

[24]   *Viking*, § 46.

law, they basically cast back one of the achievements for which Europe had paid the highest price indeed? We talk here about the principle which Germany in 1949 placed at the head of its Constitution to seal the tomb of totalitarian madness into which Nazism had plunged.[25]

Half a century later, thanks to the wisdom of generations of community judges, respectful of the fundamental principles of national legal orders, the Court had gradually acquired real legitimacy. This kind of legitimacy is always fragile. It becomes even more fragile in relation to a non-elected institution, to say nothing of a community order, distanced from people and suffering from a strong democratic deficit. Some of its decisions could have been strongly contested, but the Court has always been respected. It is this respect that the Court has been losing since it began intoxicating in its uncontrolled legislative power. The *Viking* and *Laval* judgements are clearly a political revenge of those who were unable to impose their views democratically during the adoption of the services directive[26] and the abandonment of the so-called *Bolkestein* proposal.[27] One remembers that the proposal was abandoned in order to minimize the risk of the electoral rejection of the draft Constitutional Treaty. The text of the finally adopted directive rules out the idea presented in the *Bolkestein* proposal, namely the application of the law of the country of origin of the posted worker, with the sole exception for matters covered by the Posting of Workers Directive. The democratically expressed will of the European legislator therefore clearly indicates that these provisions constitute the minimum, not the maximum rights of the posted worker.[28] By reversing this rule the Court shows how little it cares about the respect for democracy in the elaboration of Community law.[29] This contempt is also visible in the way the Court assumes a power to regulate the right to strike, a power which the treaties explicitly do not grant to Community institutions.

It would be fair to say that the Court of Justice is not the only one to rise above the demands of democracy. The European Union became an accomplished model of what Hayek called the 'limited democracy'. One of the explicit goals of the ultra-liberal program was to 'dethrone poli-

---

[25]   *Grundgesetz für die Bundesrepublik Deutschland*, Article 1, § 1 reads: 'Human dignity shall be inviolable. To respect and protect it shall be the duty of all state authority.'

[26]   Directive 2006/123/CE.

[27]   COM (2004)2, final, art. 17.5.

[28]   See on this rule, Moizard, N. (2002), *Harmonisation communautaire et protection nationale renforcée*, PhD Thesis, University Paris Panthéon-Sorbonne, Presses Universitaires d'Aix-Marseille, Vol. 2, p. 762.

[29]   See Malmberg (Chapter 2) in this volume.

tics'[30] in order to prevent ignorant populations from interfering with the economic laws, which are beyond their understanding. 'To them', wrote Hayek, 'the market economy is largely incomprehensible; they have never practised the rules on which it rests, and its results seem to them irrational and immoral . . .The demand for a just distribution in which organized power is to be used to allocate to each what he deserves, is thus strictly an atavism, based on primordial emotions.'[31] The primary objective of the ultra-liberal revolution was and continues to be 'the spontaneous order' of the market, away from the ballot boxes and managed by means of constitutional provisions, such that 'no one can conclusively determine how well-off particular groups or individuals will be'.[32] The lack of effective voting at the community level has made the European Union a ground for the choice of this policy of the eviction of policy. The resistance of the electorate was clearly expressed in many national referenda. But the leaders of the European Union managed to turn around the rejection of the Maastricht treaty by Danish voters, the Treaty of Nice by the Irish, the Constitutional Treaty by French and Dutch voters and the Treaty of Lisbon by the Irish. The tendency seems to indicate that voting results are required only if they meet the wishes of the leaders who organize them.

Thus, Europe has adopted a Western version of what article I of the Chinese Constitution calls a 'democratic dictatorship'.[33] The difference – obviously very important – is that this dictatorship is exercised by a single party in China and in Europe by financial markets. But this difference does not necessarily eliminate the commonalities, particularly a marked aversion to trade union freedoms and the right to strike, which are the pillars of social democracy, no less susceptible than political democracy of disrupting 'the spontaneous order of market'. For a century, social democracy has been a feature of free countries, which in various forms have completed political democracy based on quantitative and electoral principles by mechanisms of qualitative representation of different groups of professional interests.[34] Instead of enslaving trade unions and prohibiting

---

[30] See Hayek, F.A. (1982), *Law, Legislation and Liberty, a New Statement of the Liberal Principles of Justice and Political Economy, Vol. 3, The Political Order of a Free People*, London: Routledge, Chapter 18.

[31] *Ibid.*, p. 165.

[32] *Ibid.*, p. 151 and passim.

[33] The Constitution of the People's Republic of China in Article 1 states: 'The People's Republic of China is a socialist state under the people's *democratic dictatorship* led by the working class and based on the alliance of workers and peasants' (emphasis added by the author).

[34] On the French case see Supiot, A. (2010), 'La loi Larcher ou les avatars de la démocratie représentative', *Droit Social*, pp. 525 ff.

strikes in order to impose from above a certain conception of justice – which has always been the case of dictatorship regimes – social democracy, in contrast, sees conflict of interest as one of the engines for detecting the right rule appropriate for the given time and under given circumstances. The freedom of trade unions, the right to strike and collective bargaining are all necessary for the conversion of relations based on power into relations based on law. In a political system like the European Union, which almost completely escapes from the electoral control, these three instruments remain the only ones at the disposal of workers to challenge the social effects of 'the spontaneous order' of the single market. The Court of Justice deprives them of that freedom by becoming a judge of the reasons of the 'overriding public interest' without which any strike is banned.[35] In this way the Court pulls together all the possible negative consequences of the absence at the community level of a firm legal framework establishing a real social democracy, not just 'social dialogue' deprived of real means of collective action for trade unions.[36] To say that employees cannot go on strike unless public authorities consider that they have a compelling reason of general interest to do so, or to apply competition law rules in part concerning enterprises to trade unions means to deprive collective freedoms of their content and not to reconcile them with economic freedoms. This results in a system typical of a communist market economy, in which loud proclamation of fundamental rights of workers[37] is accompanied by the prohibition upon them to defend their interests freely and collectively.

This policy is dangerous and irresponsible. In a situation when one can no longer express himself through democratic means in the economic field, the deep sense of social injustice perceived in all European countries can easily be diverted to hating each other and rejecting the foreigner. Originally of socio-economic nature, these conflicts become identity oriented. Systematically putting workers of different nationalities in competition with each other, as the Court does, playing Latvians against the

---

[35]   *Laval*, § 101

[36]   See contributions to this volume by Christophe Vigneau (Chapter 17) and Jean-Jacques Paris (Chapter 18).

[37]   The declarations of the type have a placating effect on some lawyers (see, for example, Sabel, C.F. and O. Gerstenberg (2010), 'Constitutionalising an Overlapping Consensus: the ECJ and the Emergence of a Co-Ordinate Constitutional Order', *European Law Journal,* **16** (5), pp. 511 ff), but not the Committee of Experts of the ILO, who do not hesitate to express straighforwardly their position on what trade union freedom and the right to strike actually mean (see their views further in the chapter).

Swedes and Europeans against immigrants cannot but lead to xenophobia and stigmatization of the foreigner. These are no longer the sad images of extreme right parties, but rather a feature of postures and programmes of many governing parties, notably in France. Practising the policy of competition of workers of all countries can hardly be implemented on the territory of one State without violating the principle of equal treatment guaranteed by the European treaties. This violation is indeed flagrant in the recent case law of the Court. It results in that the rights of two employees or two companies working on the same site shall not be the same depending on their nationality.[38] The European Parliament voiced its concerns against this gross violation of the principle of equality in a resolution adopted in 2008, which stresses that 'in the framework of freedom to provide services or freedom of establishment, the nationality of the employer, or of employees or posted workers cannot justify inequalities concerning working conditions, pay or the exercise of fundamental rights such as the right to strike'.[39] The fact that this resolution, which explicitly criticized the *Laval*, *Viking* and *Rüffert* judgments,[40] has neither had any legal or otherwise influence on the subsequent jurisprudence of the Court, nor on the Commission or the Council, proves that there was the need of such a resolution and that the role assigned to elected representatives in European institutions is reduced to that of a democratic *cache-sexe*.

---

[38] See a strong position on the point taken by Antonio Lo Faro in his contribution to this volume (Chapter 13).

[39] European Parliament resolution of 22 October 2008 on challenges to collective agreements in the EU (2008/2085(INI)) JOCE C15E, Vol. 53, 21 January 2010, § 8.

[40] The Parliament emphasised in § 5 that:

freedom to provide services is not superior to the fundamental rights contained in the Charter of Fundamental Rights of the European Union and in particular the right of trade unions to take industrial action, in particular since this is a constitutional right in several Member States; emphasises therefore that the abovementioned ECJ rulings in *Rüffert*, *Laval* and *Viking* demonstrate that it is necessary to clarify that economic freedoms, as established in the Treaties, should be interpreted in such a way as not to infringe upon the exercise of fundamental social rights as recognised in the Member States and by Community law, including the right to negotiate, conclude and enforce collective agreements and to take collective action, and as not infringing upon the autonomy of social partners when exercising these fundamental rights in pursuit of social interests and the protection of workers.

QUIS CUSTODIAT CURIAM?

We can now understand the urgency of the question raised by Nikitas Aliprantis in his contribution to this volume (Chapter 6). What checks and balances are now available to bring the Community judge back to democratic arguments and respect for fundamental principles and social rights? The community institutions have proved unable to do so either because of their legal (in the case of the Parliament) or political powerlessness (in the case of the Council) or because of their ideological adherence to the doctrine of the Court (in the case of the Commission). The calls to order can only come from national or international institutions.

At the national level, this can be done by the judge or the legislator. For the national legislator, the margin for manoeuvre is narrow, and except for assuming some of the risks of the political crisis within the European institutions, national governments will rather tend to seek compromise solutions which under the guise of their loyalty to the injunctions of the Court will limit the damage to their social model.[41] On the contrary, the national judge, and first of all, the constitutional judge, is the guarantor of the respect for fundamental rights and principles and may decide not to blindly follow the interpretations of the ECJ. Thus, the process of the ratification of the Lisbon Treaty provided an opportunity for the *Bundesverfassungsgericht* to recall the limits imposed upon the Community institutions by their own lack of democratic legitimacy. The scope of the decision in question goes far beyond the issues of German constitutional law.[42] The Constitutional Court begins by recalling that 'the *ultra vires* review as well as the identity review may result in Community law or, in future, Union law being declared inapplicable in Germany' (§ 241). More generally, the court states that:

> if an imbalance between type and extent of the sovereign powers exercised and the degree of democratic legitimation arises in the course of the development of the European integration, it is for the Federal Republic of Germany because of its responsibility for integration, to endeavour to effect a change, and in the worst case, even to refuse further participation in the European Union. (§ 264)

---

[41]   The comparison of the impact of the *Laval* judgement in Denmark and Sweden is done by J. Malmberg in his contribution to this volume (Chapter 2).

[42]   Decision 2 BvE 2/08 of 30 June 2009, available at the website of the court www.bundesverfassungsgericht.de (accessed May 2011) (translations in English and French are available). On this judgement see the contribution of Nikitas Aliprantis (Chapter 6). For the analysis in English, see a special issue of *German Law Journal*, **10** (8), 2009, available at www.germanlawjournal.com (accessed May 2011).

If the German Constitution must remain 'the last instance', it is first of all with regard to 'a right of the people to take constitutive decisions concerning fundamental questions as its own identity'(§ 340).

The reasoning of the Federal Court is not therefore a reflection of a nationalist attitude, but rather a desire to defend the universal value of democracy: 'European integration may neither result in the system of democratic rule in Germany being undermined nor may the supranational public authority as such fail to comply with fundamental democratic requirements'(§ 244). Therefore as long as 'the right to free and equal participation in public authority is enshrined in human dignity' (§ 211), 'the principle of democracy may not be balanced against other legal interests; it is inviolable' (§ 216). But the EU does not satisfy any of the democratic requirements which it imposes on its members.

> In a democracy, the people must be able to determine government and legislation in free and equal elections. This core content may be complemented by plebiscitary voting on factual issues...In a democracy, the decision of the people is the focal point of the formation and retention of political power: Every democratic government knows the fear of losing power by being voted out of office.(§ 270)

Nothing like this exists in the EU: there are no elections or other votes which would allow the emergence of a well-organized opposition which has an opportunity to come into power with a programme of action (§ 213). 'Participative democracy' that it claims to develop 'cannot replace the legitimising connection based on elections and other votes', but at most 'complement the legitimation of European public authority' (§ 272). Generally very welcome,[43] this strong reminder of the demands of democracy extends to social democracy. Advocating for a constitutional review of the violations by the European Union of the principles of a social

---

[43] See among others the analysis of Ulrich Mückenberger in this volume (Chapter 15), according to which the German Court by evoking the argument of the democratic deficit in the EU would prevent that one day this deficit would be. On the contrary, one could think that in order to bring some decency and reason to the Court, it is important to have a say like a child in the fairy tale by Andersen who had the courage to say that the king is naked. Although, we should agree with Ulrich Mückenberger that the surge of pride finally made the king behave as if he had heard nothing: '"But he hasn't got anything on!" the whole town cried out at last. The Emperor shivered, for he suspected they were right. But he thought, "This procession has got to go on." So he walked more proudly than ever, as his noblemen held high the train that wasn't there at all.' (The Emperor's New Clothes, available at www.andersen.sdu.dk/vaerk/hersholt/TheEmperorsNewClothes_e. html (accessed May 2011).

state, the *Bundesverfassungsgericht* oulines the following: 'the Basic Law not only defensively safeguards social tasks for the German state union against supranational demands but aims at committing the European public authority to social responsibility in the spectrum of tasks transferred to it' (§ 258). One could hardly formulate it better. It is now hoped that the path thus traced by the German constitutional judge will be followed by its peers in other member states. In France, the Constitutional Council has followed the same logic and ruled that 'the transposition of a Directive cannot run counter to a rule or principle inherent in the constitutional identity of France unless the Constituent power has agreed to the same'.[44]

Other safeguards to the ultra-liberal exuberance of the Court can be identified at the international level. First and foremost, it is the Council of Europe and its bodies monitoring compliance with human rights. In his contribution to this volume, Filip Dorssemont explores the effectiveness of the latter.[45] The Court in Strasbourg (ECtHR) has adopted a method of interpretation of the European Convention on Human Rights which refers to 'general principles of law recognized by civilized nations' and includes all international and European labour norms, including the ILO standards and the Charter of Fundamental Rights of the European Union.[46] Relying on the principle of the indivisibility of human rights, this method allows the ECtHR to impose the respect of fundamental social rights which the Court of Justice of the European Union (ECJ) uses to devoid them of their meaning. The difference in the interpretation of these two European jurisdictions is now obvious. And it will take a legal turn on the day the European Union, as Article 6 § 2 of the Lisbon Treaty prescribes, will accede to the European Convention on Human Rights and Fundamental Freedoms.

---

[44]   See a recent Decision No. 2010-605 DC of 12 May 2010, § 18. See also Decision No. 2006-540 DC of 27 July 2006, §19; No. 2006-543 DC of 30 November 2006, § 6; No. 2008-564 DC of 19 June 2008, § 44. Compare the position of the court of cassation, which pledged allegiance to the Court of Justice (ECJ, 22 June 2010, C-188/10 *Aziz Melki* and C-189/10 *Sélim Abdeli*) deciding that 'the national judge who is to apply within his competence the provisions of the EU law has an obligation to insure full effect to those provisions. However, if necessary, a judge may choose to leave some of the provisions contrary to national legislation inapplicable, even subsequently, without having to request or await their removal by legislative or another constitutional procedure' (Ass. Plén. 29 June 2010, no.1040001 and 1040002).

[45]   See Filip Dorssemont in this volume (Chapter 14).

[46]   12 November 2008, *Demir et Baykara c. Turquie* (no. 34503/97); and CEDH, 21 April 2009, *Enerji Yapi-Pol Sen c. Turquie* (No. 68959/01) which apply this method with regard to the right to strike.

The other body which may respond to the ideological excesses of the European Union is the International Labour Organisation. In response to the comments made by the British Airline Pilots' Association (BALPA) on the impact of the *Viking* case on the exercise of the right to strike in the United Kingdom, the Committee of Experts:

> observes with *serious concern* the practical limitations on the effective exercise of the right to strike of the BALPA workers in this case. The Committee takes the view that the omnipresent threat of an action for damages that could bankrupt the union, possible now in the light of the *Viking* and *Laval* judgements, creates a situation where the rights under the Convention [no. 87 on freedom of association and protection of trade union rights] cannot be exercised.[47]

In response to the British government's statement that this impact will be limited in practice to cross-border collective conflicts, the ILO responds that

> in the current context of globalization, such cases are likely to be ever more common, particularly with respect to certain sectors of employment, like the airline sector, and thus the impact upon the possibility of the workers in these sectors of being able to meaningfully negotiate with their employers on matters affecting the terms and conditions of employment may indeed be devastating. The Committee thus considers that *the doctrine that is being articulated in these ECJ judgements is likely to have a significant restrictive effect on the exercise of the right to strike in practice in a manner contrary to the Convention.*[48]

Although the Committee of Experts has taken care to specify that its task was not to question the reasons behind the *Laval* and *Viking* judgements under Community law, it is hard to imagine a more radical condemnation of their disposition and normative effect. Several reforms are envisaged. They would give more weight to the ILO in this debate. The first, now under discussion, would be to transform its committee of experts into a real dispute settlement body.[49] The second would demand that the EU adhere at least to those ILO conventions which guarantee the principles and fundamental rights at work covered by the ILO's declarations of 1998 and 2008.[50]

---

[47] International Labour Conference, 99th session, 2010, Report III (1A) of the Committee of Experts on the Application of Conventions and Recommendations, at p. 209. 'Serious concern' is emphasized in the original text.

[48] *Ibid.* The emphasis is added by the author.

[49] See on this point Maupain, F. (2010) 'Une Rolls Royce en mal de révision. L'efficacité du système de supervision de l'OIT à l'approche de son centenaire', *Revue générale de droit international public*, September.

[50] The need for the EU to comply with the ILO conventions has been advocated for years by our colleague, Eliane Vogel-Polsky.

STRIVING FOR ANOTHER EUROPE

The presence of these institutional checks and balances is likely to curb the doctrinaire excesses of the Court of Justice, but it is unlikely to get it out of the trap of what Dieter Grimm eloquently described as the asymmetries of the European integration. The two edges of this trap are, on the one hand, the full capacity of community institutions to dismantle national solidarity and, on the other hand, their total inability to build European solidarity. It would be unfair, however, to criticize the Court of Justice alone, because it has actually employed, although in its extreme form, the political choice which goes back to the very foundation of the European Community: to dismiss the idea that there is no true 'common market' without tax law and common social law. This thesis was defended in the 1956 negotiations of the Treaty of Rome by the French prime minister, Guy Mollet, who finally gave up in exchange for the adoption of a common agricultural policy.[51] It was particularly opposed by Bertil Ohlin, a Swedish economist who chaired the panel that the ILO had convened to decide on the social aspects of the future European community.[52] Two arguments were then advanced to dismiss the idea of European social legislation and fiscal policy, which can both be found in art. 151 TEU (art. 117 of the Treaty of Rome). The first was that the functioning of the internal market would spontaneously lead to the gradual harmonization; the second was that the uniformity of these legislations would hamper the international competitiveness of European enterprises.

The Court of Justice should certainly have delineated a normative scope of improving, as required by the Treaty, 'living and working conditions, so as to make possible their harmonization, while the improvement is being maintained', instead of promoting a downward harmonization of wages conditions since its *Viking, Laval* and *Rüffert* judgements. But this case law is only one of the expressions of the new orientations of the European institutions, which are implementing inside the European borders, the tenet of normative competition to be set up between all the countries (and

---

[51] See Scharpf, F. (2002), 'The European Social Model: Coping with the Challenges of Diversity', *Journal of Common Market Studies*, **40** (4), 645.

[52] *Social Aspects of European Economic Cooperation. Les aspects sociaux de la coopération économique européenne.* Report of a group of experts, ILO. Studies and documents, 1956, pp. 102–106, cited by Dumont, D. (2010), *La responsabilisation des personnes sans emploi*, Thesis, Bruxelles: Facultés Universitaires Saint-Louis, p.81ff. See also Spyropoulos, G. (1966), 'Le rôle de la négociation collective dans l'harmonisation des systèmes sociaux européens', *Revue internationale de droit compare*, **18** (1), 19ff.

human beings) around the world. What has actually gradually disappeared in the last 30 years in Europe (but not in China or India) is the idea of the 'internal market', a market established by the law, which sets its limits which are both functional and geographical. In contrast, the idea which emerged under the aegis of ultra-liberalism, is, that law itself is a product, a 'legislative product', whose value is assessed in terms of its competitiveness on the international market of legal norms. Actively promoted by international economic institutions such as the OECD, the IMF and the World Bank,[53] this normative Darwinism has made financial markets the supreme arbiter of the legitimacy of social, fiscal and environmental rules, giving birth to 'a market without limits' in which the *shopping law* little by little supersedes the rule of law.[54]

Obviously such an order is not sustainable in the long term. The struggle of all against all can only lead to violence and the collapse of the economy. Probably the main lesson which should have been learnt from the 2008 crisis is that the deregulation of financial markets (expected to regulate themselves) led to bankruptcy. Instead, the motto, which is recalling the Maoist *Great Leap Forward*, seems to be that we need to '*shift gears*' to quote the staggering title of the editorial of the report of the situation in the OECD.[55] Reflecting on the lessons to be learned from the crisis, this report explains that the implosion of financial markets should in no way undermine 'longstanding policy prescriptions' of the OECD. On the contrary, more efforts are urged to give greater flexibility to labour markets which 'will require reaping efficiency gains on spending, especially in the areas of education and health, and avoiding large increases in harmful labour'. While commending Brazil, China and India for 'major improvements in [their] human capital' (*sic*), the report points to the need to deepen their financial markets (even though they are still clinging to the idea of their superiority because they were less affected by the crisis).

The same blindness is evident in the European Union. As Haris

---

[53]   See the website of the programme *Doing Business* of the World Bank www. doingbusiness.org/ (accessed May 2011), where one can find a world map representing the world as a territory of competing legislations (*Business Planet Mapping the Business Environment*). The Bank is thereby implementing a methodology developed by the economists from the universities of Harvard and Yale Juan Botero, Simeon Djankov, Rafael La Porta, Florencio Lopez-de-Silanes and Andrei Shleifer (2004), 'The regulation of Labour', *Quarterly Journal of Economics*, November.

[54]   See Supiot, A. (2010), *L'esprit de Philadelphie. La justice sociale face au Marché total,* Paris: Seuil, pp. 64 ff.

[55]   OECD, Economic Policy Reforms: Going for Growth 2010: Editorial; available at http://www.oecd.org/dataoecd/30/55/44661994.pdf (accessed May 2011).

Kountouros has excellently shown in his contribution to this volume,[56] not a single serious lesson was learned from the manifest failure of the Lisbon Strategy adopted in 2000. In its *Europe 2020* agenda,[57] the Commission has put forward three priorities[58] and five key objectives[59] for the EU for the next decade. These are not only an extreme example of Brejnevization of the European political language but they reflect a headlong rush toward the mirage of governance by numbers, which is completely disconnected from democracy as well as social and economic realities. None of the key questions posed by the future of Europe and which should actually inform the political debate has been raised therein: market regulation, frontiers of commerce, social, tax or environmental policies. There is not a single principle formulated in this agenda which would even remotely reflect truly human concerns, those related to justice, solidarity, democracy or quality of life. Only two slogans, empty of any axiological content: efficiency and competitiveness.

Thus it becomes apparent that the crisis of 2008 failed to draw our leaders out of their dogmatic sleep into which they had plunged under the influence of the ultra-liberal doctrine. This finding, however, is neither pessimistic nor completely hopeless. In view of the 'brain death' that seems to have affected our institutions, an immense field is opening up before future generations to rethink and rebuild our common European

---

[56]   See Kountouros (Chapter 4 this volume).

[57]   'Europe 2020: A strategy for Smart, Sustainable and Inclusive Growth', COM (2010) 2020, available at http://eur-lex.europa.eu/LexUriServ/LexUriServ. do?uri=COM:2010:2020:FIN:EN:PDF (accessed May 2011).

[58]   'Three mutually reinforcing priorities' are in reality just one – economic priority:

1.   Smart growth: developing an economy based on knowledge and innovation.
2.   Sustainable growth: promoting a more resource efficient, greener and more competitive economy.
3.   Inclusive growth: fostering a high-employment economy delivering social and territorial cohesion. COM (2010) 2020, p. 3.

[59]   The Commission proposes the following EU headline targets:

- 75 per cent of the population aged 20–64 should be employed.
- 3 per cent of the EU's GDP should be invested in R&D.
- The '20/20/20' climate/energy targets should be met (including an increase to 30 per cent of emissions reduction if the conditions are right).
- The percentage of early school leavers should be under 10 per cent and at least 40 per cent of the younger generation should have a tertiary degree.
- 20 million less people should be at risk of poverty. COM(2010) 2020, p.3.

home. There will and there are already among these generations young Iotas Kravaritou and Brians Bercusson who will carry the torch lit and be valiantly guarded by our departed colleagues. In their turn these young scholars will illuminate the winding paths which lead to another possible Europe, rich in the diversity of its cultures and united by a common aspiration for more humanity and justice in the world.

Index